Politics, Poetics, and Gender in Late Qing China

Politics, Poetics, and Gender in Late Qing China

XUE SHAOHUI AND
THE ERA OF REFORM

Nanxiu Qian

STANFORD UNIVERSITY PRESS
STANFORD, CALIFORNIA

Stanford University Press
Stanford, California

©2015 by the Board of Trustees of the Leland Stanford Junior University.
All rights reserved.

Printed in the United States of America on acid-free, archival-quality paper

Library of Congress Cataloging-in-Publication Data

Qian, Nanxiu, author.
  Politics, poetics, and gender in late Qing China : Xue Shaohui and the era of reform /
Nanxiu Qian.
     pages cm
  Includes bibliographical references and index.
  ISBN 978-0-8047-9240-0 (cloth : alk. paper)
  1. Xue, Shaohui, 1866-1911--Political and social views. 2. Women authors, Chinese--
Political and social views. 3. Women social reformers--China--History. 4. Women's rights--
China--History. 5. Women and literature--China--History. 6. Politics and literature--
China--History. 7. China--History--Reform movement, 1898. 8. China--Politics and gov-
ernment--1644-1912. I. Title.
  PL2732.5.U96Z75 2015
  895.18'4809--dc23

                                   2014044062

  ISBN 978-0-8047-9427-5 (electronic)

Typeset by Bruce Lundquist in 11/14 Adobe Garamond Pro

In loving memory of my parents,

Zhou Lin (1924–1968) and
Qian Zimin (1911–1965).

They both died miserable deaths in one of China's darkest eras,
but their spirit, which embodies the very essence of Chinese culture,
has provided guidance and inspiration in my ongoing search
for the best values of humanity.

Contents

Illustrations

Figures

Acknowledgments

On a visit back to my alma mater, Nanjing University, at the beginning of 1997, I happened to run across a volume titled *Biographies of Foreign Women* (*Waiguo lienü zhuan*) (1906) at the library. The two prefaces, written respectively by the authors of the book, Xue Shaohui and her husband Chen Shoupeng, challenged my impression of late Qing China as a dark era under a failed "barbaric" regime, as well as my view of its women as more or less silent and passive spectators, waiting to be liberated from themselves. What I discovered instead was a perspective on the period that emphasized dynamic reform proposals, innovative social and intellectual networks, the education and agency of women, and a remarkable companionate relationship involving two broad-minded thinkers who played leading roles in these dramatic developments. At the time I was still completing my book on the *Shishuo xinyu* (*A New Account of Tales of the World*) and its numerous imitations, with no immediate plans for another research project, much less one beyond my field in early medieval Chinese literature. But as I brought my story of the *Shishuo xinyu* into the nineteenth and twentieth centuries, it became increasingly clear that the link between "medieval" and "modern" China was a powerful one, particularly with respect to the activities of elite women. Xue Shaohui was, in a very tangible sense, a latter-day Xie Daoyun (ca. 335–after 405).

As I began to investigate the political, social, economic, and cultural environment in which Xue and Chen operated, I turned to the pioneering work of specialists in the study of Chinese women, literature, and history, including (in alphabetical order) Grace Fong, Hu Siao-chen, Hu Ying, Joan Judge, Dorothy Ko, Wai-yee Li, Susan Mann, Ellen Widmer, Xia Xiaohong, and Harriet Zurndorfer. My Yale mentor, Kang-i Sun Chang, was the one who first led me down this productive and fascinating path with her courses on Chinese women writers. All of the above-mentioned individuals have provided me with inspiration, support, and guidance at every stage of research and writing.

I am grateful to many other colleagues and friends who have also supported me with their insights, encouragement, and resources (in alphabetical order): Sonja Arntzens, Kathryn Bernhardt, Daniel Bryant, Chen Pingyuan, Chen Yuanhuan, Cheng Zhangcan, Cong Xiaoping, Joshua Fogel, Tobie Meyer-Fong, He Qingxian, Michel Hockx, Huang Dun, Theodore Huters, Jia Jinhua, Jiang Yin, Jon Kowallis, Li Guotong, Li Huachuan, Li Xiaorong, Lin Tsung-cheng, Lin Yi, Lin Zheng, Richard John Lynn, Michael Meng, Barbara Mittler, Olga Lomová, Pan Tianzhen, Ren Ke, Maureen Robertson, Paul Ropp, Haun Saussy, Shi Mei, Billy K. L. So, Sun Xiaosu, Frederick Wakeman, Jr., David Wang, Stephen West, Lawrence Wong, Wu Shengqing, Xing Wen, Yang Wanli, Yang Zhiyi, Robin Yates, Michelle Yeh, Yu Chien-ming, Zhang Bowei, Zhang Hongsheng, and Zhou Xunchu. I am especially grateful to the two reviewers for Stanford University Press, whose careful reading and sharp critiques inspired me to make substantial revisions (and some ruthless cuts) of my manuscript.

When I first came to Rice, Professor Allen Matusow, then the Dean of Humanities, told me that the small size of the University encouraged close communication between colleagues; hence it was comparatively easy to have meaningful transcultural and interdisciplinary conversations. He was correct. Over the past several years I have benefitted immensely from my interactions with a wide range of bright and creative people at Rice. These individuals include (again, in alphabetical order): Melissa Bailar, Anne Chao, Emilie Dejonckheere, Julie Fette, Ombretta Frau, Wendy Freeman, Rosemary Hennessy, Shih-shan Susan Huang, Werner Kelber, Anne Klein, Jeffrey J. Kripal, Hilary Mackie, Helena Michie, Richard J. Smith, Harvey Yunis, Anthea Yan Zhang, and Jane Zhao. I am most profoundly indebted to Rich, with whom I have had many fruitful discussions about this project. Without his support and encouragement, I might not have dared go beyond my disciplinary and chronological comfort zone.

Several libraries have provided me with valuable resources: the Chinese National Libraries in Beijing, Nanjing, Shanghai, and Wuxi; the Bibliothèque nationale de France; the Library of Congress; and the university libraries of Columbia, Harvard, Princeton, Rice, Stanford, UC Berkeley, Nanjing University, Peking University, and Tsinghua University.

The project has received financial and organizational support in the form of grants, fellowships, and academic leave from Rice University, the National Endowment for the Humanities, and the American Council of Learned Societies. The Dean of the School of Humanities at Rice, Nicolas Shumway, provided a generous publication subvention. SAGE Publications kindly granted permission to include a revised version of my article "Revitalizing the *Xianyuan* (Worthy Ladies) Tradition: Women in the 1898 Reforms" (published in *Modern China: An International Quarterly of History and Social Science* 29.4 [October 2003]: 399–454) as Chapter 4 in this book.

Bruce Tindall and, especially, Kara Marler-Kennedy patiently read through many versions of my manuscript and made useful suggestions about how to revise it. Stacy Wagner (with the help of Michelle Lipinski) oversaw the review and revision process providing valuable advice. Eric Brandt, Mariana Raykov, and Friederike Sundaram helped me to finalize the manuscript and supervised the production of this book with great care, vision, and precise instructions. Richard Gunde, an accomplished China scholar in his own right, did an outstanding job of copyediting the final manuscript, offering me insightful scholarly critiques and invaluable suggestions all along the way. To all of these people I express my sincere gratitude.

During my research I engaged in a close relationship with Chen Jitong's eldest great-granddaughter, Chen Shuping, and have benefitted from this sisterhood, both academically and emotionally.

Last but not least, thanks to my siblings, especially my kid brother Dajing, who walked me through all the adversities of my life; to my son Zhu Liang and his wife Xu Chen, not only for their love but also for the most recent joy they have brought to me: my precious grandbaby Emma Zhu. I named her in Chinese Linfeng, the "Bamboo Grove Aura," and hope that she will continue this glorious tradition of Chinese writing women.

Terms and Conventions

The major players in this book are *shi*. As a collective name for the Chinese intellectual elite, *shi* came into existence as early as the Spring and Autumn (Chunqiu, ca. 720–480 BCE) period, and its social identity underwent enormous changes throughout the imperial era.[1] The late imperial *shi* to be discussed in this book comprised scholars of both genders, and my rendering of *shi* and its other variants is a compromise between common translations in English-language scholarship and the original meanings within the Chinese context. Therefore, I use the terms *gentry* and *intellectual elite* for *shi* as a collective social group, *scholar* for individual *shi*, *scholar-official* for *shi daifu*, and *literati* when highlighting the artistic and literary aspects of the *shi*.

Translations of offices and official titles follow H. S. Brunnert and V. V. Hagelstrom, *Present Day Political Organization of China*.

A person will be introduced by his/her name (*ming*), but his/her courtesy name (*zi*) and/or studio name (*hao*) may also appear on relevant occasions.

Degree titles have been abbreviated—*jinshi* to js. and *juren* to jr.—and dated when the dates of birth and/or death are unclear.

1. On the evolution of the *shi*, see Yu Ying-shih, *Zhongguo zhishi jieceng shilun*, for the early period to the Wei-Jin; Bol, *"This Culture of Ours,"* for the Tang and Song; and Smith, *China's Cultural Heritage*, for the Qing; to cite just a few.

Politics, Poetics, and Gender
in Late Qing China

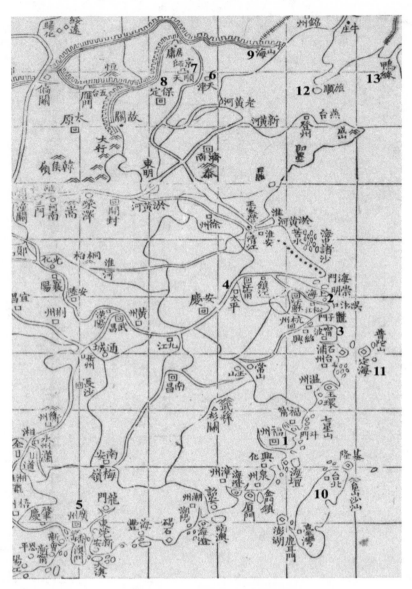

1. Fuzhou 福州
2. Shanghai 上海
3. Ningbo 寧波
4. Jiangning 江寧 [Nanjing]
5. Guangzhou 廣州
6. Tianjin 天津
7. Beijing 北京
8. Baoding 保定

9. Shanhai Pass 山海關
10. Taiwan 臺灣
11. Dinghai 定海
12. Lüshun 旅順
13. Yalu 鴨綠 (aka Dadonggou 大東溝)

Nos. 1–7 numbered following the sequence of Xue Shaohui's travels.

Nos. 8–13: Other important locations.

Map I.1. Important Locations in Xue's Life and Intellectual Networks

SOURCE: Nan Bei yang hetu 南北洋合圖 (Coastline along the East China Sea) (Wuchang: Hebei guanshuju, 1864), LOC website, http://memory.loc.gov/cgi-bin/map_item.pl?data=/home/www/data/gmd/gmd9/g9237/g9237e/ct003396.jp2&item, accessed 1 May 2012.

Introduction

The heavens marked the birth of Xue Shaohui (*zi* Xiuyu, 1866–1911) as an extraordinary event (Figure. I.1). When she was born on 18 October 1866 into the scholarly Xue family in the Houguan district of Fuzhou, capital of Fujian province, her impoverished parents already had two daughters and one son. Prepared to give her up for adoption, her father, Xue Shangzhong (d. 1877), an adept of astrology, divined the future of the newborn and was astonished at the result: "This girl surpasses a boy!" he exclaimed. "She will pass down our family learning. How can we abandon her!"[1] This family legend reflects the valorization of the "writing-women" culture in the Min (Fujian) region of southern China. This culture, discussed at length in Chapter One, would not only play a crucial role in fashioning the reformist thinking of Xue and many of her female colleagues but also become a source of intellectual conflict because not all reformers viewed the concept of talented women favorably.

Equally significant for Xue was the birth of another "baby" at about the same time and in the same place: the Fuzhou Navy Yard (Fuzhou chuanzhengju), China's first, fully fledged modern naval arsenal, and its affiliated Fuzhou Naval Academy (Fuzhou chuanzheng xuetang), both scheduled to

黛韻樓遺人主象

Figure I.I. Portrait of Xue Shaohui 薛紹徽 (1866–1911). (Xue Shaohui, *Daiyunlou yiji*.)

be built in Mawei, about ten miles from Xue's front door down the Min River (Map I.2). The founders of this project, the Fujian-Zhejiang governor-general Zuo Zongtang (1812–85) and the future director-general of the navy yard Shen Baozhen (1820–79), began their planning of the yard and the academy in the summer of 1866.[2] Although the construction of the campus would not begin until early 1867, Zuo and Shen's "desire to cultivate China's new naval men" was so strong that in February 1867, before the Mawei site was ready, the academy opened its doors to students.[3] Xue Shaohui's future brother-in-law Chen Jitong (1852–1907), also from a Houguan scholarly family, was among the first students enrolled. Jitong's younger brother Chen Shoupeng (1857–ca. 1928) would later, in 1873, attend the academy and graduate in 1879. He would then wed Xue in 1880.

Xue's marriage to Shoupeng tied her life not only to the Chen family but also to the social, political, and intellectual networks that centered on the Fuzhou Navy Yard. These connections placed Xue in the middle of a complex interaction between the Min writing-women culture on the one hand and the Fuzhou Navy Yard culture on the other—an interaction occasioned by the late Qing response to the unprecedented challenges of the late nineteenth and early twentieth centuries. This multifaceted cultural environment would shape Xue's intellectual development in fundamental ways by introducing Western knowledge into her transformation from a traditional Chinese writing-woman into a reformer.

The book in hand examines the late Qing reforms from the perspective of the talented and prolific woman writer Xue Shaohui and the reform-minded members of her various social and intellectual networks. This approach is intended to show that the reform movement involved much more than a few vanguard males who had only political and military concerns and that the reform era spanned a much longer period than the "Hundred Days" of 1898. Xue's networks included her family members and their associates, a wide circle of highly literate Chinese men and women living in and around the strategic cities of Fuzhou and Shanghai, influential scholars in Nanjing and Beijing, and even Western missionaries. They participated in, and responded to, important events or movements of the day: the Self-strengthening project, the Sino-Japanese War, the Hundred Days, the Boxer Rebellion, and the New Policies of the early twentieth century, which included the constitutional movement. Through this study, I hope to bring out the long-ignored roles of women reformers and their male

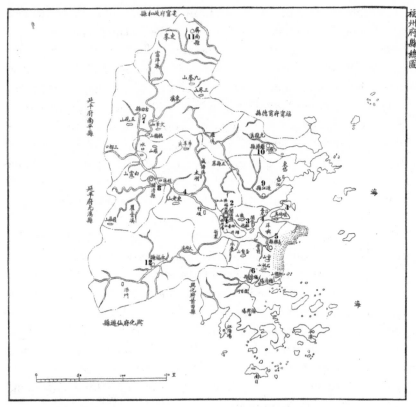

1. Fuzhou prefectural office
2. Minxian 閩縣 (SE) and Houguan 侯官 (NW) districts
3. Fuzhou Navy Yard and Academy (in Mawei)
4. Min River
5. Changle 長樂 county
6. Fuqing 福清 county

7. Gutian 古田 county
8. Minqing 閩清 county
9. Lianjiang 連江 county
10. Luoyuan 羅源 county
11. Pingnan 屏南 county
12. Yongfu 永福 county

Map I.2. Fuzhou Prefecture and the Fuzhou Navy Yard
SOURCE: Chen Yan, *Min-Hou xian zhi, juan* 3, map 1.

collaborators in late Qing sociopolitical and literary history, presenting a picture that differs substantially from the conventional historiography of the reform era.

My book consists of two parts. Part One (Chapters One through Three) introduces the early years of these future reformers, most of whom emerged, literally as well as metaphorically, from a marriage between the traditional Min writing-women culture and the newly minted Fuzhou Navy Yard culture. This joint venture allowed them access to an unprecedented knowledge base that combined information derived from both Chinese and Western sources, making them acutely aware of the rapid changes taking place in China and in the world, and offering them a wide range of choices regarding social, political, and literary reforms. Part Two (Chapters Four through Eight) recounts the activities of these major yet largely forgotten reformers, relying primarily on their poetry and prose and their translations of Western history, literature, and science. These writings, especially Xue Shaohui's works, provide us with a rare and valuable set of documents that shed new light on the reform era from a variety of angles. An analysis of the works of these reformers also allows us to trace their mental journey within the larger framework of late Qing sociopolitical transformations. My goal, in short, is to view this formative period of Chinese history through the multiple lenses of Xue and her colleagues, women in particular. Examining the late Qing reforms from the standpoint of these largely overlooked perspectives will, I believe, enhance and refine our appreciation of the complexity and creativity of this extremely important but incompletely understood period in modern Chinese history.

Rethinking the Late Qing Reforms from a Gender-Network Perspective

The 1898 reform movement was a crucial watershed in late Qing history. Nearly four decades earlier, in response to what Li Hongzhang (1823–1901) described as "the biggest change in more than three thousand years,"[4] the Chinese government had inaugurated a "Self-strengthening" (*ziqiang*) movement. It was designed to deal with the dual problems of "internal disorder and external calamity"—domestic uprisings such as the Taiping Rebellion (1850–64) and the acceleration of Western imperialism after 1842. Following China's defeat in the Sino-Japanese War of 1894–95, reform sentiment moved from the technologically oriented "foreign affairs" (*yangwu*) program of the Self-strengthening era to a call for more profound changes in Chinese politics, social life, economics, and culture. Almost "all the younger members of officialdom and the gentry,"[5] both men and women, participated in this new stage of reforms, shaping China's future through elaborate negotiations between Chinese and Western traditions (often filtered through Japan's modernizing experience in the Meiji Restoration era, 1868–1912). In the process they also attempted to transform the conventional scholar class into a new breed of Chinese intellectuals.

Until the 1980s, modern Chinese historiography portrayed the 1898 reforms as an abortive hundred-day attempt at "bourgeois" (an extremely misleading label) political change and dismissed the ensuing decade as a period in which the alien Manchu regime shamelessly tried to prop itself up with half-hearted and ineffective "New Policy" (*Xinzheng*) campaigns.[6] Western scholarship, for its part, was overwhelmingly shaped by what Paul A. Cohen terms the "three conceptual frameworks—[Western] impact-[Chinese] response, modernization, and imperialism"—all three of which, in one way or another, introduced what he describes as "Western-centric distortions into our understanding of nineteenth- and twentieth-century China."[7] Moreover, Chinese and Western scholarship has focused mainly on political and military concerns, represented by a few leading male reformers such as Kang Youwei (1858–1927) and Liang Qichao (1873–1929), leaving the ideas and activities of most other reform participants largely neglected.

The role of women in the late Qing reforms has been particularly overlooked. Although a number of Chinese and Western scholars have acknowledged that the liberation of women was indeed a goal of at least some late Qing reformers, most have emphasized the "progressive" outlook of a few prominent male leaders rather than focusing on the ideas and actions of women reformers themselves. Such scholars have also tended to view women's liberation in the late nineteenth century primarily as a reaction on the part of nationalistic Chinese men to Western criticisms of practices such as footbinding, which literally crippled half of China's elite and hence symbolized China's backwardness.[8] Viewed in this light, the "patriarchal nationalism" of the leading male reformers created the persistent impression that Chinese women were "to be liberated for and by the nation," but they were not to be active agents in shaping it.[9]

Thus in discussing women and gender issues, Tang Zhijun's *History of the 1898 Reforms* (*Wuxu bianfa shi*) (1984) focuses almost exclusively on the ideas and actions of men, in particular their pleas for women's equal rights and their leadership of the anti-footbinding movement.[10] In Wang Xiaoqiu's otherwise valuable collection of conference papers commemorating the one hundredth anniversary of the Hundred Days, *The 1898 Reforms and the Reform of Modern China* (*Wuxu weixin yu jindai Zhongguo de gaige*), not a single contribution is devoted solely to women's issues, much less to their roles in the reform movement itself.[11] Even Wang Zheng's pathbreaking *Women in the Chinese Enlightenment*, "the first major study of the development of Chinese feminism" in the New Culture era,[12] names only male advocates of "women's emancipation in the late Qing period"—primarily Kang Youwei—in identifying the predecessors of May Fourth feminism.[13]

The past two decades have witnessed increasing scholarly interest in the late Qing reforms. Some individuals in China have perceived certain affinities between the 1898 reforms and the pragmatic policies of the post-Mao era—especially the complex and somewhat uneasy relationship between reform-minded intellectuals and the Chinese state. These perceived similarities have spurred Chinese scholars to more nuanced reevaluations of the role of intellectuals in initiating political change.[14] Western scholars, too, have given renewed attention to the late Qing reforms, fueled by a "general scholarly interest in modernity, post-modernity, and new social science theories," and "new ways of looking at Chinese nationalism and state-building."[15] Methodological approaches have changed as well. Growing dissatisfaction with "Western-centric distortions" has moved many European and American scholars toward "discovering history in China,"[16] that is, rethinking old paradigms of understanding. Scholars have also chosen to abandon the "linear, teleological model of enlightenment history" in favor of a more authentic and nuanced rendering of historical processes, one that takes more fully into account the "complex transactions between the past and the present."[17]

As a result, studies of late nineteenth- and early twentieth-century China have increased in both number and sophistication over the past decade or so. Nonetheless, there are still large gaps in our understanding of the late Qing reforms. Works on the subject in China still tend to focus on leading male reformers such as Kang and Liang, although they now give some attention to their "conservative" male opponents.[18] A conference commemorating the 110th anniversary of 1898, organized by the Chinese Academy of Social Sciences and the Chinese People's University and held in Beijing on 11–12 October 2008, reveals the tenacity of this gender bias.[19] Although the expansion of archival research has brought to light the reform activities of a growing number of women, related works still portray them mostly as followers of men.[20] What needs to be more fully explored and interpreted are contributions by women reformers, as well as how their ideas and actions interacted with those of their male counterparts, and how together they embarked on the process by which China's scholarly elite transformed their country, their culture, and themselves.

Recent Western scholarship on the late Qing reforms, underscoring the complexity of this historical moment and its importance in shaping China's modern history, has, however, become increasingly sensitive to the roles of women and to gender relations. Take, for example, the excellent collection edited by Rebecca E. Karl and Peter Zarrow, *Rethinking the 1898 Reform Period*. The three gender-focused essays in this volume demonstrate effectively "how discourses on the 'female,' the 'nation,' and the 'modern' were fraught with contradiction from the very beginning in China."[21] But these essays all focus on the post-1898 period when, Karl suggests, questions about the relationship between gender and nation were "first systematically raised."[22] The book in hand will nonetheless show that such questions were systematically raised and vigorously debated significantly earlier, during the heyday of the 1898 reforms. Also in Western scholarship, although "interest in postmodernism has spurred investigations into the plurality of modern society," scholars "have made concerted efforts to direct attention to the contributions of groups other than the educated elite in society."[23] For individuals of this intellectual orientation, the ideas and activities of autonomous elite Chinese women in the reform era may not have attracted as much scholarly attention as they deserve.

Moreover, the persistence and pervasiveness of the May Fourth paradigm that depicted women in imperial China as "the oppressed subjects of a Confucian patriarchy"[24] has discouraged scholars from considering women as active participants in the late Qing reforms. The "overwhelming popularity of the image of victimized women," as Dorothy Ko points out, "has obscured the dynamics not only of relationships between men and women but also of the functioning of Chinese society as a whole."[25] To dispel the ahistorical bias that "mistakes normative prescriptions for experienced realities," Ko argues that "historical studies of Chinese women must take greater account of specific periods and locales, as well as of the different social and class backgrounds of the women in question."[26] Ko has exemplified this approach in her pathbreaking *Teachers of the Inner Chambers* (1994), which looks at the lives of seventeenth-century women in the lower Yangzi River area (Jiangnan). Susan Mann has also focused on Jiangnan women in a pair of outstanding works: *Precious Records: Women in China's Long Eighteenth Century* (1997) and *The Talented Women of the Zhang Family* (2007). Embracing gender as a category of analysis and using women's writings as sources, Ko and Mann demonstrate how a more nuanced focus on the lives of women in late imperial China reveals "the possibilities for fulfillment and a meaningful existence even within the confines the Confucian system imposed upon women."[27]

Inspired by Ko's and Mann's approaches to writing the history of Chinese women, I have conducted my own research on late Qing literate women. This research clearly shows that these women were not merely passive objects of male concern waiting to be liberated from themselves, but rather active, optimistic, autonomous, and self-sufficient agents of reform. Their stories mark both a continuation with and a departure from those of their predecessors. Whereas seventeenth- and eighteenth-century elite women and men were "guardians of Confucian morality" and "shared many assumptions about Confucian virtue and its proper representation in women's lives," late Qing women reformers went beyond the inherited Confucian model in their quest for an ideal womanhood and an ideal social order.[28] They thus directly challenged the "patriarchal nationalism" of the leading male reformers who championed reform primarily to achieve national "wealth and power" (*fuqiang*). Demanding equal education with men, women reformers wished to reposition themselves at home and, more importantly, in society at large. Their eventual ambition, as idealistic as it may sound today, was not simply to enrich and empower the Chinese nation but to unite women of all nations in an effort to create a just and harmonious new world. A study of their participation in and their contemplation of the events surrounding the 1898 reforms will fill out the picture of women's history within the frame of a "specific period" and "specific locales," offering us new perspectives from which to reexamine and rewrite late Qing history in general. The leading woman reformer Xue Shaohui and her reform-minded family and friends provide a dramatic and fascinating focus for this type of study.

Xue's life journey, though brief, largely corresponded to the most eventful decades of the late Qing and took place in some of the most dynamic locations in the vast empire; she interacted with some of the most active reformers of her time, male and female, Chinese and foreign; and she wrote about virtually all the important political, social, and cultural issues of the day, literally chronicling the reform era. An outstanding poet, prose writer, and educator, she was "China's first woman translator" and one of its earliest female journalists.[29] In these capacities, Xue actively participated in the late Qing reforms and was a leading figure in the 1897–98 Shanghai campaign for women's education. By virtue of her broad-ranging talents, ideas, and experiences, Xue serves as an ideal focal point for a multidimensional study of the reform period, allowing us to see more clearly than ever before the interactions between men and women, elites and commoners, the "inner chamber" and outer domain, and local gentry and central government officials.

Xue and her intellectual networks represented the role of "civilian" reformers outside Beijing, individuals who were not directly involved in the
politics of the so-called Hundred Days at the capital, but whose ideas and
activities reveal a great deal about the complexity and creativity of the last
three to four decades of Qing China. This shift of perspective will show that
the 1898 reform movement was much more than a power struggle between
radical "bourgeois" reformers allied with a weak emperor on the one hand
and reactionaries supported by a self-interested empress dowager on the
other. It will also demonstrate that the late Qing reforms were far more than
a simple and straightforward cultural conflict between Chinese "tradition"
and Western-style "modernity." Indeed, one of my primary goals is to dis-
mantle the binary lenses that have too often distorted our view of Chinese
history.[30] The late Qing reforms, as this study will argue, had political, social, and cultural effects that went far beyond the Hundred Days in 1898, involving a far broader range of participants than is generally recognized, and
exerting a more profound influence on the emergence of modern China.

The Composition of Xue Shaohui's Intellectual Networks

A working definition of a social network is "a set of actors and their associates, exhibiting both horizontal and vertical configurations, usually based
on a theme, and with ties that are fluid and constantly changing."[31] Relationships within a network are "often solidified by bonds of kinship, friendship, and common goals."[32] Networks in late imperial China, as Richard J.
Smith points out, were built upon a series of well-developed connections
in Chinese political and social life, which sometimes "overlapped or inter-
sected to create especially powerful affiliations."[33] The most common relationships included those based on lineage, in-law ties, family friendships,
shared home areas, educational ties, and bureaucratic linkages.[34] Built upon
such relationships, Xue's early intellectual networks involved scholarly acad-
emies and literary societies in particular. The Self-strengthening and reform
eras further transformed these hallmarks of Chinese intellectual life into
a number of unconventional organizations, such as new-style educational
institutes, academic associations, school faculty and trustee boards, editorial
staffs of news media, philanthropic foundations, and so forth.

Opening Xue's *Posthumously Collected Writings from Black-Jade Rhythm
Tower* (*Daiyunlou yiji*), the reader will immediately be struck by the elegantly
written volume titles inscribed by four illustrious individuals: Yan Fu (1854–

1921) on the front page of the whole collection; Chen Baochen (1848–1935) on the volume *Collected Poetry* (*Shiji*); Lin Shu (1852–1924) on *Collected Song-lyrics* (*Ciji*); and Chen Yan (1856–1937) on *Collected Prose* (*Wenji*).[35] These four men were all leading poets of the Min (Fujian) school, a major subgroup of the so-called *Tong-Guang ti*, which dominated late Qing poetry.[36] In addition, Yan Fu was the most important late Qing translator of Western thought; Lin Shu was the most famous translator of Western fiction; Chen Baochen was a leading figure in the extraordinarily influential Pure-stream (*Qingliu*) faction in the Tongzhi era and later the last emperor's imperial tutor; and Chen Yan was the long-term assistant to the renowned late Qing reformer Zhang Zhidong (1837–1909) (Figure I.2). The great literary reputations of these men and the important historical roles they played indicate quite clearly that Xue's networks placed her at the very heart of late Qing Chinese intellectual life.

Xue was connected to the aforementioned four men as well as other leading Min poets such as Shen Yuqing (1858–1918) and his son-in-law, the 1898 reform martyr Lin Xu (1875–98), through her family and regional ties in Fuzhou. Located on China's southeast coast, Fuzhou in the mid-nineteenth century grew rapidly into a center of political, military, economic, diplomatic, and cultural interactions with the West. The Opium War of 1839–42 forced the Qing government to open five treaty ports to Western residence and trade, including Fuzhou. The city then became the site of China's first modern navy yard and first naval academy in the early stages of the Self-strengthening movement. Over time, the Fuzhou Navy Yard and the Naval Academy produced a great many naval officers, scientists, engineers, translators, diplomats, and, above all, reformers. Living in Fuzhou, Xue and her family were involved in almost every aspect of the late Qing tumult, most notably the Sino-French War of 1884–85 and the Sino-Japanese War of 1894–95.

As one of the first graduates of the Fuzhou Naval Academy, Xue's brother-in-law Chen Jitong served as a Chinese diplomat in Europe for sixteen years, from 1875 to 1891. He was personally involved in some of the most difficult negotiations between China and the foreign powers, acting, for example, as Li Hongzhang's secret envoy both before and during the Sino-French War. In his diplomatic career, Jitong befriended high-ranking Chinese and Western politicians such as the first Chinese ambassador to Europe, Guo Songtao (1818–91), and the leading French statesman, Léon Gambetta (1838–82). In addition to fulfilling his official obligations, Ji-

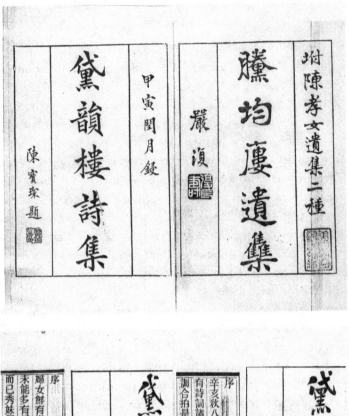

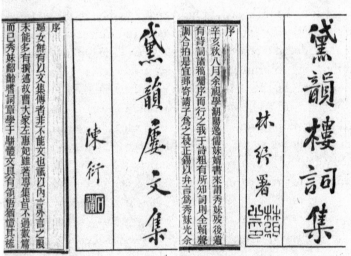

Figure I.2. Covers of Xue Shaohui's *Posthumously Collected Writings from Black-Jade Rhythm Tower* (*Daiyunlou yiji*), following the order of the compilation: Upper right to left, *Posthumously Collected Writings from Black-Jade Rhythm Tower* (*Daiyunlou yiji*), inscribed by Yan Fu 嚴復 (1854–1921); *Collected Poetry* (*Shiji*), inscribed by Chen Bao-chen 陳寶琛 (1848–1935). Lower right to left, *Collected Song-lyrics* (*Ciji*), inscribed by Lin Shu 林紓 (1852–1924); *Collected Prose* (*Wenji*), inscribed by Chen Yan (1856–1937). (Xue Shaohui, *Daiyunlou yiji*.)

tong became the first Chinese writer who published broadly in French and English in an effort to introduce Western audiences to Chinese culture.

Chen Shoupeng, Jitong's brother and Xue's husband, also served as a cultural middleman, traveling to Europe as a translator for the Fuzhou Naval Academy from early 1886 to the summer of 1889. While in China, the two brothers played a part in almost every political turn of the late Qing, including the Sino-Japanese War, the establishment of the Taiwan Republic in its aftermath, the 1898 reforms, the damage control following the 1900 Boxer Rebellion, and the New Policy reforms during the last decade of the Qing dynasty. All this introduced the brothers to broad sociopolitical and cultural connections (see Chapters Two and Three).

The Chen brothers shared their intellectual interests and political concerns with their family members, including, of course, Xue Shaohui. Like many elite women of her time and place, Xue had been solidly educated in Chinese traditions and was well versed in classical Chinese poetry, prose, and conventional scholarship.[37] Having also absorbed a good deal of fresh foreign knowledge from her husband and brother-in-law, Xue had a broad intellectual base that enabled her not only to offer the Chen brothers moral support but also to join in their political and literary activities.

The year 1897 marked Xue's transformation from a private scholar and housewife into a public intellectual, when she moved with Shoupeng to Shanghai and walked right into the 1898 reform movement. During this period and thereafter, Xue Shaohui, Chen Shoupeng, Chen Jitong, and Jitong's French wife, Maria-Adèle Lardanchet (Chinese name: Lai Mayi), all played extremely important roles.[38] Together, for example, they participated in a broad-based campaign for women's education in Shanghai, organizing the first Chinese women's association, establishing the first truly Chinese girls' school, and publishing the first Chinese women's journal (see Chapter Four). The abrupt termination of the Hundred Days of "official" reform did not deflect Xue and the Chen brothers from their commitments. They continued to promote reform with other vehicles, editing newspapers and translating and compiling Western literary, historical, and scientific works.

Participation in the 1898 reforms greatly expanded Xue's networks and diversified their ethnic and class constituents. During the 1897–98 Shanghai campaign for women's education, Xue and her family worked closely with its some two hundred participants, about equally divided between men and women, of both Chinese and Western origin, and from different social backgrounds. The organizers of the campaign, in addition to its mastermind Liang Qichao, were also the "merchant thinkers" Jing Yuan-shan (1841–1903), chief of the Shanghai Telegraph Bureau, who initiated the project, and Zheng Guanying (1842–1922), a pioneer reformer and advocate of education for women.[39] These members of what has been termed the emergent "international managerial bourgeoisie" of China introduced "innovative ideas, technology and managerial skills from the West" into the campaign.[40] The movement engaged support from Western missionaries and diplomats as well, such as Timothy Richard (1845–1919) and Young J. Allen (1836–1907). Shoupeng's professional activities also put Xue in contact with reform-minded officials and scholars in other cities, such as the superintendent of the Southern Ports (Nanyang dachen) Zhou Fu (1837–1921).

The female members of Xue's intellectual networks were initially Xue's hometown writing women from her own extended family and local elite clans, such as Chen Yan's wife, Xiao Daoguan (1855–1907), and Lin Xu's wife, Shen Queying (1877–1900). When Xue joined the 1897–98 Shanghai campaign for women's education, her network of associates expanded exponentially to include many women reformers, mostly from Jiangnan, who identified also with the rich writing-women tradition of the region. By the late nineteenth century, writing women as a cultural construction had gone through a long evolution in China, represented by a variety of time-honored names such as *xianyuan* (worthy ladies), *guixiu* (full flowering of the inner chamber), *cainü* (talented women), and so forth, but the analogous term preferred by reform-minded women in the late Qing was *xianyuan* (see Chapters One and Four for the origins of these terms).

Xianyuan was first coded as a chapter title in *A New Account of Tales of the World* (*Shishuo xinyu*, hereafter *Shishuo*) compiled by Liu Yiqing (403–44) and his staff, to indicate prominent women in the Wei-Jin era (220–420).[41] Originally, *xian* (worthy) as a widely applied moral category in the early Han Confucian classics referred to those who helped maintain the Dao—the proper social order—with *de* (virtue) and *cai* (talent, especially the gift of acting virtuously). In the Wei-Jin, a period of considerable political turmoil but also of great intellectual activity and philosophical creativity, the Dao transcended the earlier "Confucian" meaning to embrace the Daoist way of nature (*ziran*). *Xian* was accordingly redefined, with *de* referring to one's moral strength in acting according to the Dao of nature and *cai* referring to the talent enabling such actions.[42] The concept of *xianyuan* formed in this context stood for women with literary and artistic talent, broad learning, intellectual independence, moral capacity, and good judgment—

individuals who played highly unconventional roles in Wei-Jin society. They transgressed traditionally gendered space, extending intellectual and physical movement beyond inner-chamber boundaries and assuming responsibilities both within and outside the household (see Chapter One).

It was this sense of freedom from constraints, as well as a highly developed consciousness of social obligation, that commended the term *xianyuan* to late Qing women reformers. This admirable constellation of female qualities fit the needs of Qing women reformers because of its special historical and philosophical connotations. By repeatedly referring to themselves as *xianyuan*, late Qing women reformers opposed the call of male reformers for a break with the so-called *cainü* (see Chapter Four). This gendered divergence pointed to a sharp contrast between women's "idealism" and men's modernist-style "pragmatism" in the reform era, suggesting that female reformers had a significantly different conception of efficacy than their male counterparts.

For some two thousand years prior to the late nineteenth century, and particularly since the Song dynasty (960–1279), Chinese intellectuals maintained a basic belief that through learning and self-cultivation human beings could develop spiritual capacities of "heart/mind" that would have truly transformative power over the world.[43] Yet this belief encountered a pervasive challenge in the late Qing, when male reformers such as Kang and Liang increasingly came to believe that "modern [Western] technology, new techniques of political participation . . . and new forms of knowledge" could solve problems in the "outer" realm of Chinese economics and politics that could not be solved by mental and moral effort in the "inner" realm of Chinese spiritual life.[44] No longer did Chinese intellectuals such as Kang and Liang believe that human beings had the spiritual capacity to transform the world. In the words of Thomas A. Metzger:

> Events since the nineteenth century . . . radically altered the Chinese view of transformative processes. The advent of new technological and political means rapidly promised transformation of the "outer" world. As a result, no longer pressed to look for this transformative power in an "inner," transcendent realm, Chinese philosophers could abandon their quest for the metaphysical "source" of movement.[45]

As transformative action in the "outer" realm appeared ever more feasible, the quest for moral purification and metaphysical linkage became ever less acute.[46]

Metzger's observation helps to explain why most male reformers expected women to abandon their age-long intellectual adherence to the writing-women tradition and turn to more pragmatic professional training; this new orientation, they believed, could transform "useless" women into "productive citizens" and thus empower the entire nation (see Chapter Four). But most women reformers rejected this notion of nationalistic patriarchy in favor of the *xianyuan* ideal, which could express more effectively their particular needs, expectations, and aspirations, an ideal that represented a very different kind of personal and collective empowerment. Within Xue Shaohui's female networks there was a firm ground of *xianyuan* subjectivity that offered concrete strategies for self-renovation and self-realization, ways for women to construct their own ideal of womanhood within the context of the late Qing reforms. *Xianyuan* values were the relentless focus of Xue's reconstruction of the Min writing-women culture (see Chapter One), and the foundation for her idealized conception of womanhood in the reform era (see the chapters in Part Two).

Why Literature Matters

This book uses literary works, particularly collections of women's poetry, as major research sources because Xue and her colleagues saw literature as the most effective means by which to understand and articulate their rapidly evolving worldview. The *xianyuan* tradition featured women's literary accomplishments as a central value. Min-area writing women used poetry to carve out a leading space in local culture (see Chapter One). Women in 1898 expressed their iconoclastic reform ideas and sentiments in both classical and vernacular styles, and published them in conventional woodblock printings as well as the new-style media (see Chapter Four). Xue's writing career reveals with particular clarity the emergence of a wide variety of exciting literary, journalistic, and scholastic genres born in the reform era (see the chapters in Part Two).

The philosophical origin of the pivotal position of literature in the *xianyuan* tradition can be traced to the perfected-person (*zhiren*) ideal of the *Zhuangzi*—a refined personage who was "well-versed in all kinds of subtleties" and capable of "communicating with limitless outer objects in empathetic response."[47] The Seven Worthies of the Bamboo Grove (*Zhulin qixian*) in the Wei, who inherited the perfected-person metaphysic and thereby inspired the rise of *xianyuan*, responded to outside changes mostly in their literary writings, as did their Eastern Jin followers (see Chapter One). But it was Su Shi (1037–1101), a towering figure in Song dynasty intellectual and cultural life, who linked *wen*, or literature, most directly and effectively with the perfected-person ideal. Su Shi repeatedly invoked the perfected person as a source of spiritual inspiration and discussed with great insight the function of *wen* in developing the spiritual capabilities of human beings—capabilities that could literally transform the world.[48] Su Shi argued that *wen* was the best means to arrive at an understanding of the Dao. This Dao was what "the myriad things (*wu*) rely upon to be themselves and the means by which the myriad principles (*li*) of these things are confirmed."[49] In order "to achieve this understanding of the Dao, one has to engage in learning."[50] Only after closely studying all things and highly refining one's writing skills—to the degree that the words used are capable of "binding the wind and catching the shadows" (*jifeng buying*)—can one grasp "the subtleties of things" and make their principles known. This is what Su Shi meant by *wen*: by "using words to convey fully the meaning," one could understand the Dao embodied in all things.[51]

Su Shi's view that *wen* was the most effective vehicle to "bring on" the Dao had a direct and powerful influence on Xue Shaohui and her networks. In the first place, as indicated above, Su equated *wen* with the perfected person and thus by extension with the *xianyuan* tradition. Second, Su was one of the major icons of the Min poetic school. Chen Jitong and his poet friends claimed to be Su Shi's filial disciples, and Jitong himself emulated not only Su's poetic style but also his calligraphic skill.[52] Not surprisingly, Jitong placed literature at the very center of his comparative study of Chinese and European civilizations (see Chapter Two).

Xue, for her part, considered poetry as a major sphere of learning for both women and children, using Su Shi as a leading poetic model (see Chapter Seven). Moreover, she applied Su's understanding of the function and power of *wen* in her description of the changes that were occurring in the world around her. In addition to expository essays and translations of Western works, Xue also wrote highly regarded works in various classical literary styles, producing during her short lifetime about three hundred poems (*shi*), one hundred fifty song-lyrics (*ci*), and twenty parallel-prose (*pianwen*) essays. Few, if any, Chinese women writers had ever before covered as much stylistic and thematic territory as Xue. Her masterful portrayal of a rapidly changing China amounts to a poetic history of her time, and her broad coverage of all sorts of knowledge, including science and technology, illustrates a Su Shi–like methodology of exhausting the *li* of all things in order to arrive at an understanding of the Dao. Xue even recorded with insightfulness and candor the domestic arguments she had with her husband, Chen Shoupeng. (He, for his part, did the same.)

Furthermore, a focus on the literary practices of Xue and others reveals not only the ideas and sentiments of the reform era but also how late Qing literature evolved into new stylistic forms for their expression. The study of late Qing literature has so far concentrated on fiction, in part because Liang Qichao emphasized the "new fiction" as a major tool for social change in China.[53] Recent works on the reform era have also explored the political and social implications of the rise of new forms of print media.[54] Yet poetry—the most prominent genre in the Chinese literary tradition, which exposed with particular subtlety the innermost thoughts and feelings of late Qing Chinese intellectuals—remains largely neglected as a reform-era topic. Women's poetic achievements during this period have been especially ignored by scholars of Chinese literary history. For instance, Yan Dichang's *History of Qing Poetry* (*Qingshi shi*) (2002) pays little attention to late Qing women poets. Jon Kowallis's 2006 masterful study of late Qing poetry identifies a "subtle revolution" taking place at the time, but he concentrates on male poets.[55] Shengqing Wu's recently published tour de force, *Modern Archaics: Continuity and Innovation in the Chinese Lyric Tradition, 1900–1937*, argues that "the writing and appraisal of classical-style poetry [was] carried on with remarkable vigor and variety during the century of modern literature."[56] She focuses, however, on the post-reform era. With my study of Xue and her colleagues, I hope to redress the imbalance and examine the changes in late Qing literature from a broader and explicitly gendered perspective.

How, then, should we approach the topic of women's literature in the late Qing? Scholars have long been concerned about whether we are imposing our "modern" views on the study of women's writing in the past. In her introduction to the 1992 special issue of *Late Imperial China* on poetry and women's culture, Charlotte Furth addressed this issue in the following terms:

> As Maureen Robertson puts it, does the tradition speak through them or do they as female subjects impose themselves upon the tradition and make it their own? Did their literary voices enlarge the cultural repertory available to their own contemporaries and the high culture they participated in, or did they remain largely invisible and marginal, with the result that any restructured understanding of late imperial literary horizons can only be the retrospective one which we as twentieth-century observers construct? Have we uncovered their past or our own useable past?[57]

More than a decade later, at a 2006 Harvard conference on traditional Chinese women's writing, Maureen Robertson herself asked: "If our scholarly interventions are influential, are there ethical issues involved in basing the choice of whom to study upon our inevitably modern sensibilities? Or can we accept that truly fine authors can speak across time, and canon texts do just that?"[58] And in a recent review of Susan Mann's 2007 book, *The Talented Women of the Zhang Family*, Furth indicates that Mann's work conveys a sense that within this family there was a "very real confinement of female energies that became available for release only with the avalanche of modernity."[59]

The concern reflected in the remarks of Robertson and Furth about the relationship between "traditional" and "modern" perspectives—both on and of women in late Qing China—is certainly worthy of careful consideration. But as the writings by Xue Shaohui and her female associates clearly indicate, their intellectual energies were neither confined by "tradition" nor released by Western-inspired "modernity." Rather, these women consciously took advantage of the opportunities presented by the reform era to advance their goals of self-fashioning and self-realization. Exposure to the modern knowledge of the period was not in itself liberating; it simply enabled writing women to reenvision the preexisting radical notion of *xianyuan* culture and to articulate its significance to the contemporary Chinese world. In this sense, to borrow Furth's formulation, the "female subjects impose[d] themselves upon the tradition and [made] it their own," and in so doing "their literary voices enlarge[d] the cultural repertory available to their own contemporaries and the high culture they participated in." Criticisms leveled by male reformers against the *cainü* model only encouraged a more determined defense of their position, which they expressed powerfully in the new-style media.

Living in the midst of rapid social, political, and cultural changes, Xue and her colleagues encountered unprecedented challenges in their morally and spiritually inspired effort to transform the world. Women seized upon this opportunity to fulfill their long-smothered political and cultural ambitions by integrating new knowledge and ideas into their intrinsic intellectual constructs, while maintaining a spiritual subjectivity unswayable by any specific value system.

Xue epitomized this eclectic approach to reform in her "Preface to the *Nü xuebao*" ("*Nü xuebao* xu"), the inaugural editorial for the first Chinese women's journal, published on 24 July 1898. In it, Xue invoked a well-known Confucian document, the *Great Learning* (*Daxue*), to justify education for women. This work is famous for the idea that with the self-cultivation of its members, the family can be regulated; when the family is regulated, the state can be ordered; and when the state is ordered, all under heaven can be at peace.[60] Xue's innovative contribution was to frame this Confucian Dao of ruling (*zhidao*) in terms of the Daoist Dao of mothering (*mudao*),[61] inasmuch as ruling a country was "like protecting a baby" (*ru bao chizi*).[62] Solidly adhering a female subjectivity to the Dao of nature and its fundamental value of nurturing, Xue called for eliminating the distinction between the inner and outer domains. Hence women, being devoted mothers, wives, and daughters, could extend their "domestic" sensibilities to embrace the entire world and thus pave a smooth path from self-cultivation to world transformation.[63]

In accordance with this notion of the "outward extension from oneself,"[64] Xue and her colleagues embraced ideas and forms of knowledge that went "beyond the ideas of the various Chinese philosophical schools," and thus proposed a "new learning" (*xinxue*) designed to transform themselves into "new people" (*xinmin*).[65] In so doing, they rejected the dominant discourses of the time, including not only the idea of a dichotomy between Chinese cultural forms and Western applications (*Zhongti Xiyong*) but also New Text radicalism and the call for "total Westernization." As we shall see, Xue would continually claim this *mudao*, which she termed also *fudao* (Dao of women) and *kundao* (Dao of the female), to be the fundamental principle and the "outward extension" as the operational path for the reform campaigns. How did Xue and her colleagues proceed with their ambitious projects? This is the story that will be told in the following pages.

PART ONE

Making the Future Reformers (1866–1897)

Xue Shaohui and the Min Writing-Women Culture

According to Xue Shaohui, Min writing women had been producing a culture of their own since the mid-seventeenth century. This culture boasted the Guanglu poetic school as its institutional manifestation and the *xianyuan* ideal as its intellectual foundation. Over time, the Min writing-women tradition had been disseminated horizontally through marital and communal ties and vertically through the mechanism of mothers' teaching. In the process, women played pivotal roles in forming and transforming Min poetics, and their accomplishments equaled, if not surpassed, those of Min male poets. As such, this culture flaunted its strength and tenacity in Min socio-political and cultural life, especially during the chaotic late Qing period.

Xue's Summary of the Min Writing-Women Tradition

In 1881, the fifteen-year-old Xue delivered her first comments on Min women's poetry in a poem inscribed on *Remarks on Women's Poetry from*

Min Rivers (*Minchuan guixiu shihua*) by Liang Zhangju (1775–1849) (hereafter Liang's *Remarks*):[1]

Since ancient times, the poem "Guanju" has been an admirable topic.	千古關雎是艷談，
Chanting poems in the inner-chambers, why should women feel deficient in any way?	閨閫吟詠更何慚？
Glittering like ice and snow, Xu Can the poetess-mentor exudes brilliance;	聰明冰雪徐都講[燦]，
Resisting wind and frost, A'nan the Ji daughter maintains integrity and virtue.	節操風霜紀阿男。
Up in the sky, the Woman Constellation radiates majestically over the region;	上界星辰森女宿，
In the south of Min, the Banner and Drum Mountains empower the poetic altar [see Maps 1.1 and 1.2].	騷壇旗鼓壯閩南。
Yet today the Guanglu school of women's poetry no longer creates new styles.	只今光祿無新派，
In the empty Jade-Measure Mountain, a cold mist diffuses in the twilight.[2]	玉尺空山冷暮嵐。

Xue traces the origin of the poetic activity of Min women to the *Book of Songs* (*Shijing*)—represented here by its first poem, "Guanju"—which the Ming-Qing female elite believed to include many women's poems selected by Confucius himself.[3] Referring to this authoritative canon, Xue argues that women possess a poetic capacity equal to that of male poets. Xue then invokes the poetic exemplars Xu Can (ca. 1610–after 1677) and Ji A'nan (fl. ca. 1642), two outstanding writing women from culturally acclaimed Jiangnan, implying that the women poets of the relatively obscure Min region have comparable status.[4] She goes on to suggest that the wisdom and integrity that Xu and Ji displayed in the face of the Manchu invasion during the Ming-Qing transition had its counterpart in the response of Min women poets to tumultuous events such as the Taiping Rebellion and the Opium Wars. This combination of talent and virtue defines the core values of *xianyuan*. In the third couplet Xue explains that Min women's poetic excellence is a product of the Min natural environment, and in the ending couplet she indicates her dissatisfaction with the current situation of Min women's poetry. She expects someone—presumably herself—to revitalize the Guanglu school with new styles.

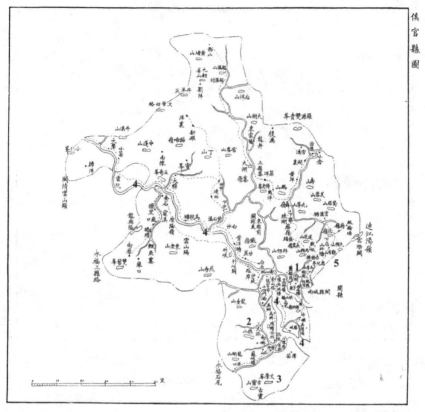

1. West Lake (Xihu 西湖)
2. Banner Mountain (Qishan 旗山)
3. Writing-Brush Mountain (Wenbishan 文筆山)
4. Min River (Minjiang 閩江)
5. Border between Houguan and Minxian

Map 1.1. Houguan District, Fuzhou City
SOURCE: Chen Yan, *Min-Hou xian zhi, juan* 3, map 2.

Twenty-seven years later, in 1908, Xue elaborated upon all of these points in her preface to the *Sequel* to Liang's *Remarks on Women's Poetry from Min Rivers* (*Minchuan guixiu shihua xubian*) by Ding Yun (1859–94)(hereafter Ding's *Sequel*).[5] Having actively participated in late Qing reforms, a mature Xue expressed a much more profound understanding of the significance of the Min writing-women culture. Confidently, Xue even added her own contributions, such as her compilation of *Biographies of Foreign Women* (*Waiguo lienü zhuan*, see Chapter Five), a work that reinvigorated the Guanglu

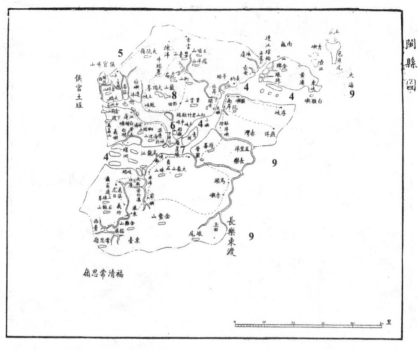

4. Min River

5. Border between Minxian and Houguan

6. Fuzhou Navy Yard and Academy

7. Pagoda Anchorage (Luoxingta 羅星塔)

8. Drum Mountain (Gushan 鼓山)

9. East Sea

Map 1.2. Minxian District, Fuzhou City

SOURCE: Chen Yan, *Min-Hou xian zhi, juan* 3, map 3.

school by harnessing the moral and intellectual strength of Min women for contemporary needs. Above all, Xue in this preface confirmed the *xianyuan* ideal as the central value of the Min writing-women culture by pairing Xie Daoyun (ca. 335–after 405) with Cai Yan (aka Cai Wenji, ca. 176–early third century)[6] as another two exemplars of women poets. Xie was the poster child of the "Xianyuan" chapter in the *Shishuo*, and Cai a major figure in the "Biographies of Women" in the *History of the Latter Han* (*Hou-Han shu*) by Fan Ye (398–445), which identified *xian* as women's premier quality.[7] Xue chose these two women in clear reference to a contemporary reform debate on ideal womanhood because, for some male scholars, the two had epitomized a tension between a woman's literary talent and her moral behavior.

The Tang historian Liu Zhiji (661–721) initiated this sort of either/or criticism, accusing the thrice-married Cai Yan of having "excessive literary talent but lacking integrity."[8] The Ming scholar He Liangjun (1506–1573) admitted that Cai had outstanding literary talent but condemned her for "losing her chastity to the Northern court [of the Xiongnu nomads]."[9] Zhang Xuecheng (1738–1801), for his part, acknowledged the literary talent of both Cai Yan and Xie Daoyun in his essay "On Women's Learning" ("Fuxue"), but he described Cai as "a woman of no wifely integrity" because of her three marriages, and accused Xie of having "wiped out the Confucian moral teaching" when she trespassed the gender line to attend a scholarly debate with men.[10] Zhang Xuecheng and his ilk disapproved of Cai and Xie because they considered female artistry to be potentially subversive of the Confucian moral order.[11] This concern that a woman's talent might undermine her virtue was still prevalent among many male reformers in Xue's time (see Chapter Four).

To Xue Shaohui, however, Cai Yan and Xie Daoyun exemplified a perfect combination of talent and virtue, although her idea of virtue had far different connotations than that of the aforementioned male scholars. For instance, Cai Yan composed "works of sorrow and anguish" (*beifen zhi zuo*) in order to condemn those who disturbed the social order and caused suffering. Fan Ye recorded such poems in her biography precisely to showcase both her talent *and* her virtue.[12] In Fan Ye's view, Cai's intense concern for the people obviously outweighed the fact that she had married three times, including to a Xiongnu "barbarian." In a similar vein and for a similar purpose, Xue tells us that Xie Daoyun exhibited her talent and virtue in her "willow-catkin poetics" (*liuxu zhi ci*).[13]

This term comes from the following *Shishuo* episode:

> On a cold snowy day, Xie An gathered his family indoors and was discussing with them the meaning of literature, when suddenly there was a violent flurry of snow. Delighted, Xie began:
> "The white snow fluttering and fluttering—what is it like?"
> Xie An's nephew, Lang, came back with,
> "Scattering salt in midair—nearly comparable."
> His niece, Daoyun, chimed in,
> "More like the willow catkins on the wind rising."
> Xie An laughed aloud with delight. (2/71 [Chapter 2/Episode 71])[14]

謝太傅[安]寒雪日內集，與兒女講論文義。俄而雪驟，公欣然曰：
"白雪紛紛何所似？" 兄子胡兒[朗]曰："撒鹽空中差可擬。"
兄女[道韞]曰："未若柳絮因風起。" 公大笑樂。

Here, Daoyun surpasses her male cousin in poetic creativity and pleases her uncle Xie An because the image of floating willow catkins brings the sunny, fluffy spring into the gloomy winter. This line radiates Daoyun's nurturing nature. It was this same inner strength that enabled Daoyun—her face covered with a gauze veil—to attend a debate with men on behalf of her younger brother-in-law. In this famous anecdote, she defeats his opponents, and hence protects the intellectual integrity of the family.[15]

Although Daoyun was later attacked by Zhang Xuecheng and other male critics, she received high marks from her contemporaries. A famous Wei-Jin episode, also from the *Shishuo* "Xianyuan," compared her to another talented woman of her time and described Daoyun as possessing a "Bamboo Grove aura" (*linxia fengqi*). This appraisal enhanced Daoyun's status because it linked her (and by extension other women of the time portrayed in the "Xianyuan" chapter) directly to the Seven Worthies of the Bamboo Grove.[16] Whether this illustrious group actually existed is immaterial; the important point is that they served as a tangible symbol of Wei-Jin intellectual life, a life characterized by, among other things, wide-ranging philosophical and artistic accomplishments, outspoken criticism of contemporary politics, and the cultural accomplishments of women as well as men. One of the most important intellectual developments of the Wei-Jin period was "Abstruse Learning" (Xuanxue, also known as "Mysterious Learning" or "Dark Learning"), which provided a reinterpretation of Confucianism based primarily on the philosophy of the *Book of Changes* (*Yijing*), mingled with early Daoist thought from *Laozi* and *Zhuangzi*.[17] It also borrowed concepts and constructions newly introduced to China by Buddhism in order to fill a certain vacuum of scholastic metaphysics in Confucianism.[18] As Xuanxue adepts, the seven derived their inspiration mainly from the *Zhuangzi*. And one of *Zhuangzi's* most attractive ideas to them was the notion of the "perfected person" (*zhiren*) and its variants, "spiritual person" (*shenren*) and "sage" (*shengren*).

The perfected person was someone who follows the "right course" (*zheng*) of heaven and earth, rides the changes of the "six vital energies" (*liuqi*), and is thus able to wander the cosmos without any constraints or limitations. This person possesses special qualities and capacities, absorbs natural essences, and in so doing develops transformative powers, "protecting creatures from sickness and plague and making the harvest bountiful." Accompanying the idea of transformative cosmic power is a feminine image, expressed by descriptions of beauty, gentleness, and nurture.[19]

The Seven Worthies and their perfected-person ideal exerted a direct influence on the Eastern Jin (317–420) intellectual network that included Xie Daoyun, her uncle Xie An (320–85), her father-in-law, the famous calligrapher Wang Xizhi (303–61), and their close friend, the eminent Buddhist monk Zhi Dun (314–66). This group of thinkers incorporated Buddhist thought from the Prajñāpāramitā Sutras into their reconceptualization of the perfected person, centering in the person's spirit, *shen*. "With a luminous spirit (*shenlang*)," Zhi Dun claims, the perfected person can "see through the past and the future and comprehend them with good judgment (*jian*), and can thereby render appropriate plans for the future."[20] The person can muster all kinds of intellectual and empathetic resources and act sensitively and effectively in accordance with the changes of the world. In this sense, one can become a perfected person through a process that encourages the continual incorporation of knowledge in order to strengthen the self.

Since the image of the perfected person presented in the *Zhuangzi* has strong feminine characteristics, this sort of self-cultivation of spiritual perfection and human efficacy is obtainable for women as well as for men. Xie Daoyun had a "Bamboo Grove aura" inherited from the Seven Worthies because her "spirit and feelings" were "relaxed and luminous" (*shenqing sanlang*) (*Shishuo*, 19/30). Such a "luminous spirit" was, according to Zhi Dun, characteristic of the perfected person.

Against this historical and philosophical background the *xianyuan* discourse emerged. It was typified by Xie Daoyun's Bamboo Grove aura, and it found concrete expression in, among many other virtues, the perfected-person capacity of *jian*, or good judgment. *Jian* was elaborated into *shijian* (recognition and judgment), a prominent Xuanxue practice that involved the entire Wei-Jin gentry and left abundant records in the *Shishuo*. According to these accounts, *shijian* contained a subtle analysis of human character, an astute assessment of political situations, and the display of both courage and wisdom in the face of adversity. This capacity enabled Wei-Jin women to utilize their talent and moral strength in their roles as protective and loving mothers, wives, sisters, and daughters, and supported them in assisting, guiding, and even criticizing their male relatives. And these women acted independently, rather than relying upon dictated principles, in dealing with difficult circumstances.[21]

Daoyun, for instance, criticized her younger brother, Xie Xuan, for having "occupied his mind with worldly matters" at the expense of his own personal development (*Shishuo*, 19/28). She also openly complained about the

mediocre abilities of her husband, Wang Ningzhi (ca. 330–99)—an evaluation that later proved to be accurate during the Sun En Rebellion in 399,
when Ningzhi failed to safeguard his family and the people in his charge.
An aging Daoyun had to kill the rebels with her own hands in order to
protect her grandchildren.[22] These qualities of nurturing and protecting the
world with talent and good judgment permeated the characterization of the
Wei-Jin women in the *Shishuo*'s "Xianyuan" chapter and would loom large
in the Min writing-women culture that played such an important role in
the late Qing reforms.

Xue Shaohui identifies the *xianyuan* ideal as the basis of the Min writing-
women culture again in the concluding couplet of her preface to Ding's
Sequel:

Compiling a poetic archive of famous ladies, [Zhong Xing] has established a model for the inner chambers;	著詩歸于名媛, 斯為閨閫儀型;
[Seeing our women's poetry] on par with the original voices of the correct beginning, How dare I not respect my hometown predecessors?[23]	等正始之元音, 敢不敬恭桑梓?

The first line invokes the *Poetic Archive of Famous Ladies* (*Mingyuan shigui*
名媛詩歸) compiled by Zhong Xing (1574–1625), which features poetry
as "the sound of nature."[24] We see here a reflection of the idea that following a natural course is the fundamental principle of the perfected
person.[25] The second line refers to the "correct beginning" (*zhengshi*) of
women's original voices (*yuanyin*) in the *Book of Songs*.[26] The Qing woman
scholar Wanyan Yun Zhu (1771–1833) appropriated these voices in compiling *Correct Beginnings: Women's Poetry of Our August Dynasty* (*Guochao
guixiu zhengshi ji*) for the promotion of women's poetry. (Xue would later
complement this magnum opus by compiling *Biographic Sketches of the Female Literary Garden* [*Nü wenyuan xiaozhuan*], which covered about three
thousand women writers.)[27] The expression *yuanyin* may also refer to the
notion of "abstruse utterances" (*xuanyin*, altered to *yuanyin* in the Qing to
avoid the Kangxi emperor's taboo personal name, Xuanye) in the Zhengshi era of the Wei (220–65). The Zhengshi period was, after all, a time
when the Seven Worthies incorporated the *Zhuangzi* into their Abstruse
Learning, developing the perfected-person ideal that later gave rise to the
xianyuan discourse.

The Guanglu Genealogy and Its Xianyuan Ideal

What was the Guanglu school? Xue's daughter Chen Yun notes in her *Poems on Poetics from Little Black-Jade Studio* (*Xiao daixuan lunshi shi*), which was composed under Xue's guidance:[28]

> In Fuzhou city, there is an alley named Guanglufang. . . . A little mound inside is named the Jade-Measure Mountain. In the Song Xi'ning era [1068–77], the prefect Cheng Shimeng [1015–92], who also received a literary designation as the director of the Banqueting Court (Guanglu qing), paid a visit to the temple, and inscribed on the stone four characters: "Guanglu yintai" [the Chanting Terrace of Guanglu]. In the late Ming, this spot became the residence of a local gentleman named Xu Zhi [*js.* 1631]. Into the Qing, Xu Zhi's son Xu You [*zi* Youjie, 1615–63] still lived there and composed the *Collected Works of Xu Youjie* (*Xu Youjie ji*). The Xu women were all well versed in poetry and had frequent poetic correspondence with their female relatives. They exchanged poems using bamboo containers delivered by their maids and nurses, who ran up and down the alleys. Frivolous young men would bribe them so they could open the containers and copy down the poems. Poems circulated in this way were later known as those of the Guanglu school.[29] (See Map 1.3)

Although she referred to these curious youths as "frivolous," Chen Yun was obviously happy that the emergence of a women's poetic school in her hometown was based on the breakdown of the barrier between the "inner" and "outer" domains. Xue Shaohui must have been similarly pleased.

The founding Xu family of the Guanglu school extended from Xu Zhi and his son Xu You, to You's great-great-granddaughter Xu Chen (1731–89?). Seven generations of the Xus—each of which "glorified the lineage with their accomplishments in poetry and painting"—"lived under the same roof."[30] Through marriages and social connections, the Xus inspired the rise of other poetic and artistic families and intellectual networks in the Fuzhou region. For instance, a daughter of Xu You gave birth to the famous high-Qing poet Huang Ren (1683–1768), who was educated in the Xu household and later inherited its Ink Studio (Mozhai) from his maternal grandfather. He renamed the studio "Fragrant Grass" (Xiangcao) (Map 1.3) and titled his poetic collection using this name. The collection included the poems of his two daughters, Shutiao and Shuwan; hence the Guanglu tradition was passed down from his mother to his own descendants. Shutiao and Shuwan, in turn, as Xue details in her preface to Ding's *Sequel*, each transmitted the "beautiful traces of the Fragrant Grass [Studio]" (*xiangcao yihui*)

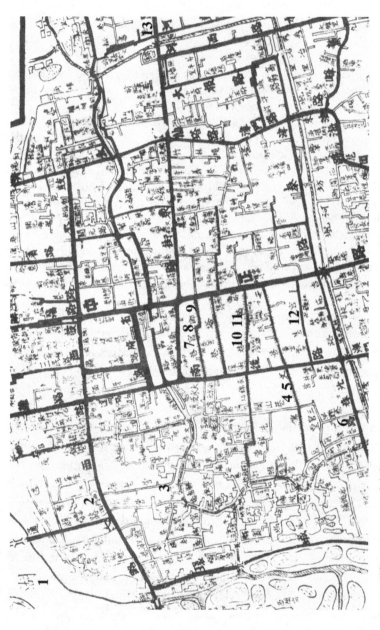

1. West Lake (Xihu 西湖) and Wangzaitang 宛在堂 Shrine
2. The Chen brothers' in Guxilu 鼓西路 (Xue Shaohui's 薛紹徽 marital home)
3. Lin Zexu's 林則徐 in Wenbeilu 文北路
4, 5. Lin Zexu's mother's and Chen Yan's 陳衍 in Wenrufang 文儒坊
6. Huang Ren's 黃任 Fragrant-Grass Studio in Guanglufang 光祿坊

7, 8, 9. Yan Fu's 嚴復, Lin Shu's 林紓, and Lin Xu's 林旭 in Langguanxiang 郎官巷
10, 11. Liang Zhangju's 梁章鉅 and Chen Shouqi's 陳壽祺 in Huangxiang, 黃巷
12. Shen Baozhen's 沈葆楨 in Gongxiang 宮巷
13. Xue Shaohui's natal home in Lizhiyuan 荔枝園 by the Aoqiao 澳橋 Bridge

to their daughters, You Hezhen and Lin Qiongyu.[31] Thus we see how one Xu daughter transmitted the Guanglu tradition to other lineages with both male and female successors.[32]

Through marriage, the Huangs were related to the Zhengs, another influential poetic family in Fuzhou. The Zheng matriarch Huang Tansheng (1650s–1730s),[33] a cousin of Huang Ren's father, exemplified in every way the tradition of maternal teaching—transmitting knowledge, organizing poetic gatherings and correspondence, and inspiring literary creation. Her achievements were celebrated in almost every work on Min poetics, the earliest record of which was by Zhuang Jiuwan, a female relative of Huang Ren's wife, née Zhuang, and a close poetic associate of Huang Tansheng's daughters. Zhuang Jiuwan recounts that the young Huang Tansheng "received from her father the learning of the Confucian classics, and her poetry and prose were gentle, pure, and graceful." After she married Zheng Shanshu (jr. 1690), the couple went to Gu'an, where Zheng was posted as a magistrate and where he uneventfully and effectively governed for years.

> Zheng used to invite friends and relatives who were stuck in the capital to his official residence and hosted them all year round. He composed poems and drank wine with the guests in his breaks from governing. Lady Huang also held poetic gatherings with cousins, sons, sons-in-law, and young people from acquainted families. On New Year's Eve, Lady Huang clipped silk to make plum blossoms, displayed them in vases, and presented them to guests. Whenever she composed a small poem, her sons would compete to fashion rhymes after hers in wishing her longevity.[34]

Lady Huang personally educated her three sons, two daughters, ten granddaughters, and numerous grandsons. Even after she lost her sight, the old woman continued to lecture her grandchildren. As a result, not only her two sons, Zheng Fangcheng (1678–1746, js. 1733) and Zheng Fangkun (js. 1723), but also her grandson Zheng Tianjin (js. 1752), acquired the jinshi degree, and almost all her daughters and granddaughters published poetic collections.[35] "From past to present," Liang Zhangju tells us, "no family can match the Zhengs in the flourishing of women's poetry."[36] Through marriage and social connections, this lineage extended its influence throughout

Map 1.3. (opposite) Residences of Some Major Players in Fuzhou

SOURCE: He Minxian 何敏先, *Fuzhou shiqu xiangtu* 福州市區詳圖 (Detailed map of Fuzhou city), (Fuzhou: Zhongguo wenhua fuwushe Fuzhou fenshe, 1945); keyed based on Chen Qiang et al., "Xianbi Xue gongren nianpu," and the author's field study in Fuzhou, 2004.

six generations and into over a dozen families, forming a potent intellectual network that linked the Xus, the Huangs, the Zhengs, and many others in a common poetic cause. Huang Tansheng's legacy was particularly evident in the activities of her granddaughter Zheng Hanchun, who founded another five-generation learned family that stretched into the Lin, Li, Guo, Feng, and Wang clans, each with its own culturally accomplished men and women (see Tables 1.1 and 1.2).

In addition to the poetic activities within each household, the women within the Xu-Huang-Zheng nexus also organized poetry clubs among different families. For instance,

> Zhuang Jiuwan established a poetry club with relatives and friends in the neighborhood. Its members, such as Liao Shuchou, Zheng Huirou, Zheng Hanchun, Xu Chen, and Huang Shutiao and Shuwan, all lived in houses next to one another. Every time they had a gathering they picked a rhyme for composing poems within the time limit marked on a candle. Sometimes they sent bondmaidens to deliver poems to one another, and no one failed to respond immediately.[37]

This list covers three generations of women poets, including Liao Shuchou, the wife of Xu You's grandson Xu Jun (*js.* 1718);[38] Xu Chen, a fifth-generation descendant of Xu You; Zheng Huirou, Huang Tansheng's elder daughter; Zheng Hanchun, Tansheng's granddaughter; and the two Huang sisters. With families related to the Guanglu lineage and literary activities resembling the Guanglu style, these poets continued the Guanglu school tradition during the high Qing period. Members of the Xu-Huang-Zheng network enthusiastically promoted the works of their women, expanding and refining the tradition of registering women's literary accomplishments.[39]

Following the Xu-Huang-Zheng community in the high Qing, the "Liang wives and daughters" came along. They flourished during the first half of the nineteenth century, as Xue's account notes.[40] Heading this group was Xu Luan'an, the wife of Liang Zhangju's uncle Liang Shangguo (1748–1815). Liang's *Remarks* describes her as coming from a famous Houguan gentry family. She received a good education from her parents and was well versed in poetry, music, and ritual. While every bit as knowledgeable as Huang Tansheng, she expanded her horizon by traveling over "half of China," going as far north as beyond the Shanhai Pass.[41] A magnificent "woman teacher" (*nüzong*), she taught the Liang boys and girls, as well as

Table 1.1. Xu-Huang-Zheng Family Connections and Their Poetic Network

m. = marriage; writing women in boldface

Xu Zhi 許豸 (zi Yushi 玉史, Yufu 玉斧, ca. 1595–?, js. 1631, Houguan)

Huang Wenhuan 黃文煥 (zi Weizhang 維章, 1598–1667, js. 1625, Yongfu 永福 county)

Lin Yunxin 林雲心 Lin Yunming's concubine, Minxian

Xu You 許友 (zi Youjie 有介, hao Ouxiang 甌香, 1615–63)

Huang Jinliang 黃晉良 (zi Chu'an 處安, js. 1615–89, Minxian)

Lin Yunming 林雲銘 (zi Xizhong 西仲, 1628–97, js. 1658, Houguan) m. **Cai Jie 蔡捷** (Minxian)

Lin Yingpei 林瑛佩

Huang Ren's grandfather

Xu Bin 許賓

Xu Yu 許遇 (zi Buqi 不棄, hao Yuexi 月溪, 1650–?)

Xu You's daughter

Huang Ren's father

Huang Tansheng 黃曇生 (zi Huhua 護花, 1650s–1730s, died at 78)

Zheng Shanshu 鄭善述 (jr. 1690, Jian'an 建安 county)

The Zheng children, including **two daughters** (see Table 1.2 for the Zheng family line)

Zhuang Jiuwan 莊九畹 (Yongfu)

Xu Jun 許均 (zi shutiao 叔調, hao Xuecun 雪村, js. 1718) m. **Liao Shuchou 廖淑籌** (zi Shouzhu 壽竹)

Huang Ren 黃任 (zi Yushen 于莘, Shentian 莘田, hao Shiyan laoren 十硯老人, 1683–1768, jr. 1702) m. **Née Zhuang 莊** (1693–?, Yongfu)

Xu Ding 許鼎 (zi Botiao 伯調, jr. 1723)

Xu Jinchen 許藎臣 (zi Sijin 思進, jr. 1720)

Xu Wangchen 許王臣

Huang Shutiao 黃淑窕 (zi Sizhou 似洲)

Huang Shuwan 黃淑畹 (zi Rengpei 紉佩)

The Zheng grandchildren, including **ten Zheng girls** (see Table 1.2)

Xu Liangchen 許良臣 (jr. 1723)

Xu Chen 許琛 (zi Deyuan 德瑗, 1731–89?) m. He Suilong 何燧隆 (d. 1754, Houguan)

You Hezhan 游合珍

Lin Qiongyu 林瓊玉 (Minxian) m. Chen Feng 陳灃

The Zheng great grandchildren, including **two girls** (see Table 1.2)

MAJOR SOURCES: Zheng Fangkun, *Quan Min shihua*; Liang Zhangju, *Minchuan guixiu shihua*; Lin Changyi, *Sheyinglou shihua*; Ding Yun, *Minchuan guixiu shihua xubian*; Shen Yuqing and Chen Yan, *Fujian tongzhi*; "Lienü zhuan" 列女傳 (Biographies of women); Chen Yan, *Min-Hou xian zhi*, "Lienü zhuan."

Table 1.2. Zheng Family Tree

m. = marriage; writing women in boldface

Zheng Shanshu (*zi* Jiaoxi 蕉溪, *jr.* 1690, Jian'an 建安 county)
m. **Huang Tansheng** 黃曇生 (1650s–1730s, died at 78), Minxian

- Fangcheng 方城 (*zi* Zewang 則皇, *hao* Shitong 石幢, 1678–1746, *js.* 1733)
- **Huirou** 蕙柔 (*zi* Jingxuan 靜軒, ca. 1680–?) m. Chen Riguan 陳日貫
- Second son
- Fangkun 方坤 (*zi* Zehou 則厚, *hao* Lixiang 荔鄉, *js.* 1723)
- **Shuzhi** 淑正 (*zi* Jusheng 菊生)

Children of Fangcheng:

- Hanchun 翰蓴 (*zi* Qiugeng 秋羹) m. Lin Qimao 林其茂 (*zi* Peigen 培根, ca. 1711–ca. 50, *js.* 1736)
- Tianjin 天錦 (*zi* Youzhang 有章, *jr.* 1752)
- Youmei 有美
- **Jingrong** 鏡蓉 (*zi* Yutai 玉臺) m. Chen Wensi 陳文思
- **Yunyin** 雲蔭 (*zi* Lütai 綠苔) m. Yan Yingju 嚴應琚
- **Qingping** 菁蘋 (*zi* Huating 花汀) m. Weng Zhengang 翁振綱
- **Jintuan** 金鑾 (*zi* Dianxian 殿仙) m. Lin Shouliang 林守良
- Changeng 長庚
- **Yongxie** 詠諧 (*zi* Linfeng 林鳳) m. Lin Tianmu 林天木
- **Yuhe** 玉賀 (*zi* Chun'ang 春盎) m. Chen Huatang 陳華堂
- **Fengtiao** 鳳調 (*zi* Bisheng 碧笙) m. Chen Tingjun 陳廷俊
- **Bingwan** 冰紈 (died young) Engaged to Lin Tianhuan 林天桓

Next generation:

- **Lin Fangrui** 林芳蕤 m. Li Kaichu 李開楚
- Lin Qiaoyin 林喬蔭 (*zi* Yueting 樾亭, *jr.* 1765)
- Lin Shufan 林漱蕃 (*zi* Xianghai 香海, 1750–78, *js.* 1771)
- **Zheng Peimin** 鄭佩玟 m. Sun Jinghan 孫景翰
- **Lin Shuqing** 林淑卿 m. Guo Rentu 郭仁圖 (*js.* 1808)
- Lin Xuankai 林軒開 (*zi* Wenzhou 文翮, *hao* Liaohuai 蓼懷, *js.* 1802)

Next generation:

- Li Hongrui 李鴻瑞 (*zi* Daosheng 道升, 1761–1818, *jr.* 1798)
- Li Hongshi 李鴻詩 (*zi* Daodun 道敦, *jr.* 1786)
- (?)
- Li Hong'e 李鴻鶚 (*jr.*)
- Li Hongzhen 李鴻珍 (*jr.*)
- **Li Ruixin** 李瑞馨 (1796–1850, *zi* Lüqing 綠卿) m. Feng Jinghuai 馮景淮
- **Sun Lanru** 孫蘭如
- Sun Chengmo 孫承謨

Next generation:

- Li Yanbin 李彥彬 (*zi* Lanpin 蘭聘, 1791–1834, *js.* 1823)
- Li Yanzhang 李彥章 (*zi* Lanqing 蘭卿, 1794–1836, *js.* 1811)

- **Li Jinglin** 李鏡林 m. Wang Ruqin 王汝欽
- Feng Chengji 馮承基 (*js.* 1850)

MAJOR SOURCES: Same as in Table 1.1.

the young women who married into the Liang family, nurturing in particular their poetic and musical talents. Liang Zhangju himself learned pentasyllabic and heptasyllabic poetry from her. Each of these young family members produced a collection of poems, thanks mainly to her teaching.[42]

Like the Xu-Huang-Zheng daughters, the Liang girls extended their family learning to other households through marriage. The most prominent example of this was Xu Luan'an's second daughter, Liang Yunshu, who became the poetic leader of her generation and a mentor for the next. Among her many accomplishments was her collaboration with Liang Zhangju in compiling Liang's *Remarks*, which inaugurated the systematic documentation of the Min writing-women culture (see Tables 1.3 and 1.4).

Like the families in the Xu-Huang-Zheng network, the Liangs held frequent poetic gatherings and correspondence that crossed gender boundaries. Women needed both courage and talent to participate in these literary activities, which were structured by restrictive rules on topics, themes, styles, and rhymes, and they rose to meet the challenge. When the lieutenant governor of Fujian composed four regulated poems titled "White-Pistil Orchid," "several hundred scholars in Fuzhou rhymed after him, including some gentlewomen."[43] Zhangju's mother, Wang Shuqing, also composed a rhyming version and won high praise from Meng Chaoran (1731–97), the superintendent of the Turtle-Cliff Academy (Aofeng shuyuan)—the most prestigious educational institution in Fujian—who was invited to judge all the poems.[44] Liang Zhangju composed a heptasyllabic-regulated series that attracted several hundred replies. Yunshu's poem stood out because it was so natural and original that "no one could tell it was based on some pre-established rhymes," and it was "outstanding enough to be the banner and the drum of central China."[45] Zhangju's daughter-in-law Yang Meigao, too, proved her literary talent by rhyming after Zhangju's long song commemorating his acquisition of a Shang bronze goblet. Liang Zhangju noted that "poetic replies streamed in far and near, but many people also felt too intimidated to wield their brushes."[46] Obviously Yang Meigao was not among those who were cowed by the challenge.

While Liang's *Remarks* focused on a few big lineages, Ding's *Sequel* provided wider coverage of Min writing women, many of them from less well-known families, during the same time. There was a Red-Tower Chanting Society (Honglou yinshe) in Fuzhou, headed by a Lady Ye and organized

Table 1.3. Liang Family Tree

m. = marriage: writing women in boldface

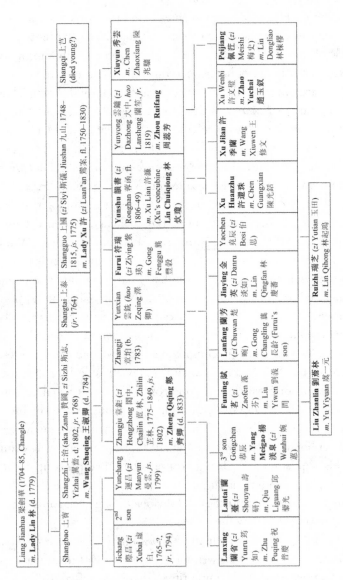

MAJOR SOURCES: Liang Zhangju, *Minchuan guixiu shihua*; Wang Junwei, *Chuantong yu jindai zhijian.*

Table 1.4. Liang Family's Intellectual Network

m. = marriage; writing women in boldface

Xu Chongkai 許崇楷 (jr. 1759, Houguan)			Qi Zhang 齊璋 (zi Anxi 安溪, hao Egang 莪岡, 1727–97)		Chen Xiankai 陳賢開 (Houguan)		
Zheng Guangce 鄭光策 (zi Sunian 蘇年, 1759–1804, js. 1780, Minxian) Zheng Qiqing's father; Liang Zhangju's and Lin Zexu's mentor	**Xu Luan'an** 許鸞案 m. Liang Shangguo	**Xu Fuzhi** 許福祉 (hao Menghuai laoren 夢愧老人)	Qi Bi 齊弼 (zi Fuwu 輔五, hao Langao 蘭皋, 1753–1815, js. 1781, Houguan)	**Chen Pinjin** 陳品金 Chen Xiankai's cousin; m. Hong Yu 洪裕 (Houguan), Zheng Guangce's friend			**Chen Ruosu** 陳若蘇 m. Liao Ying 廖英 (zi Peixiang 佩香) Liang Zhangju's friend
Zheng Qiqing 鄭齊卿 m. Liang Zhangju 梁章鉅	**Liang Yunshu** 梁蘊書	Yang Huang 楊簧 (b. 1776, js. 1820, Liancheng 連城 county) Liang Zhangju's and Lin Zexu's friend	Qi Kun 齊鯤 (zi Chengxiao 澄溪, hao Beiying 北瀛, 1776–1820, js. 1801) Liang Zhangju's friend	**Hong Longzheng** 洪龍徵 (zi Lanshi 蘭士) m. Xu; Zheng Guangce's adopted daughter	**Shen Jue** 沈鈛 Zheng Qiqing's friend	Sa Longguang 薩龍光 (js. 1781, Minxian)	Yao Huaixiang 姚懷祥 (zi Sizheng 斯征, hao Lütang 履堂, 1783–1840, Houguan) Sa Lianru's mentor
Liang Lanxing 梁蘭省 Liang Zhangju's 1st daughter	**Yang Meigao** 楊美臯 Yang Huang's 4th daughter; m. Liang Zhangju's 3rd son	**Yang Meihao** 楊美好 Yang Huang's 2nd daughter	**Qi Xiangdi** 齊祥棣 (1816–38) Engaged to Chen Zhaoxiong 陳兆熊; Liang Yunshu's student	**Qian Shoupu** 錢守璞 (zi Lianyin 蓮因, changshu 常熟) m. Zhang Qi 張楔 (Dantu 丹徒)		**Ding Shanyi** 丁善儀 (zi Zhixian 芝仙) m. Yang Bing 楊炳; Yang Meigao and Liang Lanxing's poetic associate	**Sa Lianru** 薩蓮如 (fl. 1821–50) m. Lin Xinghai 林星海 (jr.); Yao Huaixiang's student; Qi Xiangdi's poetic associate

------- Three Friends of the Winter (*suihan san you* 歲寒三友) -------

MAJOR SOURCES: Liang Zhangju, *Minchuan guixiu shihua*; Ding Yun, *Minchuan guixiu shihua xubian*; Shen Yuqing and Chen Yan, *Fujian tongzhi*; Chen Yan, *Min-Hou xian zhi*; "Lienü zhuan."

by her nephew, poet and novelist Wei Xiuren (1818–73). This organization included Wei's female cousins as participants. Its spiritual leader was a girl named Xu Tingting (1827–45).[47] Her biographer, Chen Dequan (*js.* 1845), depicts Tingting as from "poor and humble origins." She won respect from people in her social circles for her "filial and generous" character, her quiet yet unswerving dignity, and her broad accomplishments in poetry and music, in addition to her more routine weaving and sewing. This extraordinary talent displayed a distinctly "perfected person" manner—"as white as jade and as thin as a plum tree, with an elegant aura, she had shown a tendency to transcend this world and to stand on her own."[48] Xu Tingting died young, and the Red-Tower Society members eulogized her death as if she had become an immortal. Biographic sketches by both Wei Xiuren and Chen Dequan describe her as a most graceful yet elusive figure, who seemed not to shy away from communicating with men.[49]

In addition to discussing Xu Tingting, Ding Yun gave attention to several other women poets of humble origins, such as Lin Yunxin, the concubine of Lin Yunming (*js.* 1658); the courtesan Shao Feifei (fl. early Qing); and a tailor's daughter named Wang Zhenxian (1818–48).[50] The inclusion of these poetesses impressed Xue Shaohui, who lauded Ding Yun's open-minded approach to literary talent in his *Sequel.*[51]

Just as the Liangs continued the Guanglu tradition before the Opium Wars (the First 1839–1842, the Second 1856–1860), so the family of Liang Zhangju's classmate Lin Zexu (1785–1850)—the famous official whose destruction of British opium stores precipitated the First Opium War— contributed to the rise of the next generation of the Min poetic lineages. The marriage of Lin's daughter Puqing (1821–73) to Shen Baozhen linked these two families directly to the individuals who were active in the Fuzhou Navy Yard culture, foreshadowing the extraordinarily fruitful combination of the Min writing-women and navy yard cultures. This new union would culminate in the Xue-Chen network discussed in Chapter Three.

All these families and communities shared certain features that were important for the Min writing-women culture: 1) a learned, talented matriarch, full of originality and creativity, who nurtured the younger generations both physically and intellectually; 2) a group of writing women who spread their poetic learning through marital and community associations; and 3) a group of ardent supporters, both male and female, who collected, promoted, and published women's poetry to serve as textbooks for later generations.[52] Above all, from the mid-Ming period onward, the culture of Min writing women exuded a distinctive *xianyuan* bearing.

We should not be surprised, then, to discover that Huang Qian (*js.* 1550) highly praised the poetic talent of his niece Huang Youzao, comparing her to Xie Daoyun and titling her poetic collection *Compilation of Willow Catkins* (*Liuxu bian* 柳絮編).[53] Into the Qing, almost every poetic family in the Min Guanglu lineage claimed a "salt-and-willow-catkin" legacy. Huang Ren wrote to his second daughter, Huang Shuwan: "As fewer guests visit, my children come more often; / When you arrive, I know you'll bring poems of willow catkins" (賓客漸稀兒女密, 汝來知有柳花詩). His good friend Chen Zhaolun (1700–71), who was himself the grandfather of the woman writer Chen Duansheng (1751–ca. 1796),[54] agreed, saying, "It is not an exaggeration to compare [Shuwan's poetry] to the Xie daughter's willow catkins."[55]

In the Zheng family, three of Huang Tansheng's ten granddaughters were named after *Shishuo* allusions. The one named Yongxie, "Eulogizing Xie [Daoyun]," with the courtesy name Linfeng, "Bamboo Grove aura," was obviously expected to emulate this Wei-Jin role model. Yongxie's poem, "Recording the Past, Conveying My Inner Thoughts" ("Jishi shuhuai" 紀事述懷), summons vivid "salt-and-willow-catkin" imagery in referring to her childhood activities under the watchful eye of her doting father, Zheng Fangkun:

I remember when I was born,	憶予初生日,
In the region of Zou and Lu.	乃在鄒魯鄉。
My father was then the prefect;	阿父時作守,
We used to romp around his office.	嬉戲趨黃堂。
Growing up I learned the lessons for women,	稍長肄女訓,
Tying fragrant flowers to my pendants.	紉佩荃芷芳。
I composed poems after finishing embroidery,	繡餘綴吟詠,
Leisurely I roamed in the world of literature.	優游翰墨場。
Like the talented Xie cousins,	封胡與遏末,
We siblings aligned with one another,	弟妹隨肩行。
So we made our father smile	阿父博一粲,
With our competing rhymes of salt and willow catkins.[56]	鹽絮分頏頑。

As an adult, Yongxie cultivated the refined qualities of her namesake, and she passed on her Bamboo Grove aura to subsequent generations. She not only single-handedly raised her son to be a fine scholar after being widowed but also extended the salt-and-willow-catkin influence to her female disciples after she was invited to teach in a gentry family. The above-cited poem was presented to her patron as a self-introduction. At its end she stated her fundamental educational principle:

Thank you for your care and help!	感君拂拭意,
I'll repay with the best of my humble talent.	期盡襪線長。
Recounting *xianyuan* from women's history,	彤史述賢媛,
I hope I can meet your expectations [for your daughters].[57]	庶幾慰所望。

The Liang family carried on the *xianyuan* tradition with equal enthusiasm. Its girl prodigy, Liang Yunshu, identified herself with Xie Daoyun and her family with the Xie clan. She wrote while traveling out of the Shanhai Pass: "When mountains and seas send splendor to my chanting brush; / Who can rival my poems leisurely composed in the Xie courtyard?" (山光海色供吟筆, 謝庭清暇詩無敵).[58] One of Liang Zhangju's friends, a Houguan poet named Yang Qingchen (1783–1867), had two daughters, Xiuzhu and Xiuzong, who also compared themselves to the famed Xie girl, "well versed in chanting willow catkins in the Xie courtyard."[59] Their local prodigy Xu Tingting enjoyed similar esteem from her poetic peers: "Her person is 'as placid as a pure breeze,' worthy of Xie Daoyun's comments on the Flowery Classic [*Book of Songs*]."[60] Here "pure breeze" alludes to a line from the *Book of Songs* favored by Daoyun, because it conveys the nourishment of spring.[61]

As one of its many manifestations in the lives of Min writing women, the *xianyuan* self-image encouraged defiance of traditional restraints. Invoking Xie Daoyun's legendary complaints against her husband, some Min girl prodigies expressed open resentment of marriages in which there was no intellectual reciprocity. Laments of this kind appeared in works about their lives: One indicated that "the man she married was not her match, so she died of melancholy"; another that "the man she married could not meet her ideal; she therefore died"; yet another that "her husband was not of her kind . . . so she expressed her melancholy in poetry and finally died in resentment."[62] The life of the Ming poetess Xu Deying typifies this sort of unhappy marriage. On her wedding night, Xu proposed a line for the bridegroom to match up into a couplet: "One after another, willow catkins fall into an ink-stone pool, / Stained by red, becoming red, / And stained by black, becoming black" (點點楊花入硯池, 近朱者赤, 近墨者黑). She clearly identified herself as a willow-catkin girl, eager to find out whether her husband was her match. Unfortunately, the groom was too ignorant to respond. Xu then suggested: "Why don't you just say,

'Male and female, swallows fly into the curtain, / Resonating with similar chirps, / And seeking affinity for each other?" (雙雙燕子飛廉幙, 同聲相應, 同氣相求). Utterly disappointed at the prospect of never having a soul mate, Xu died of melancholy, and many of her writings were subsequently burned by her husband. Among the few surviving pieces is a poignant eulogy dedicated, not surprisingly, to Xie Daoyun.[63] Another Min poetess, Chen Ruolan (fl. mid-eighteenth century), after a long-term poetic correspondence with her husband, had to admit that there was a "sky-earth" distance between them, just like the gap between Xie Daoyun and Wang Ningzhi.[64]

Possessing talent and a well-developed sense of self-esteem, these writing women were, for the most part, comfortable living an independent life. Consider the case of the Min woman poet Zhu Fanghui (fl. early nineteenth century). Fanghui was unhappily married to an unfaithful rake. After her husband died, Fanghui "could not care less about the regular inner-chamber manners," prompting rumors that she was not adhering to the conventional decorum of widowhood. In response, she composed "Chanting the Mirror" ("Yongjing" 詠鏡), which included the couplet, "Even if the mirror is turned upside down, / The image remains naturally upright" (縱教顛倒持, 面目自端正). In other words, these rumors had no effect on her self-esteem. She was later invited to tutor the sons and daughters of the local magistrate and helped him refine his official memos and reports. With a decent annual stipend from this job, she was able to establish a school for poor children and enjoy spiritual and financial freedom.[65]

The *xianyuan* ideal received even more attention with the rise of the Lin, Shen, Chen, and Xue women writers of the late Qing. In recalling her childhood in Nanjing, Shen Queying chanted: "In the quiet spring, my dream lingers, / Where the Bamboo Grove aura still wafts and entangles my thoughts" (春寂寂, 夢依依, 風流林下繫人思).[66] Xiao Daoguan, wife of Queying's mentor Chen Yan, loved bamboo and "would not live a single day without these gentle ladies." She planted bamboo in order to "sit beneath them / and enjoy the pure breeze blowing gently" (坐我林下, 徐來清風).[67] As for Xue Shaohui, she was naturally considered by her contemporaries, including Chen Jitong, to be in possession of the Bamboo Grove aura.[68] She never failed to stress the importance of the *xianyuan* ideal in women's artistry and life. For example, she maintained that willow-catkin poetics could inspire women's flora drawings because both were generated from the female virtue of nurturing.[69] She even felt that the Bamboo Grove aura graced a Japanese woman and her art.[70] Xue celebrated a townswoman who brought up her children following the salt-and-willow-catkin family tradition, writing that on her sixtieth birthday the "jade trees saluted her in front of the family hall" (拜堂前之玉樹).[71] And, as we shall see in Chapter Seven, Xue invoked the *xianyuan* model for all the female members of her family. She demanded that her daughters give priority to cultivating their Bamboo Grove aura, and celebrated her elder sister, Xue Sihui, for having embraced willow-catkin poetics and gauze-veil virtue.

It should be noted that although the *xianyuan* ideal was indeed the intellectual foundation of the Min writing-women culture, the term itself was not used as often as its counterpart *guixiu*, which stood for moderate and restrained inner-chamber wives.[72] Even the two major works on Min women poets, Liang's *Remarks* and Ding's *Sequel*, used *guixiu* in their titles. The popularity of *guixiu* as a collective description of Ming-Qing elite women suggests a closer adherence to traditional markers of gendered space than we might expect. It was only in the reform era that women writers began to claim *xianyuan* as a common term expressing their collective identity (see Chapter Four).

Women's Contributions to Min Poetics

Min women continued the Guanglu legacy, disseminated the *xianyuan* ideal, passed down their mothers' teachings, bridged the gender gap, and communicated with the outside world mainly through poetic activities. They thus contributed to the formation of Min poetics and to its transformation during the reform era. This section examines this phenomenon from Xue Shaohui's standpoint, a product of her special literary position that differed substantially from the then-dominant male poetics.

Xue stood simultaneously in the center and at the margin of late Qing poetic practice, involved with, but also transcending, various poetry groups and affiliations. She was, through family and regional ties, closely associated with the mainstream *Tong-Guang ti* poets, in particular the Min school headed by Chen Yan. But she never subjected herself to the *Tong-Guang ti*'s almost obsessive emulation of Song poetry as a means of expressing "profundity and subtlety."[73] She shared similar interests with the poets of the Reform school (*Weixin pai*) such as Liang Qichao, who were preoccupied with political and social change, yet she squarely rejected their baseless claim that talented women (*cainü*) were responsible for China's backwardness (see Chapter Four). Xue's quarrel with individuals such as Liang was that they offered an incomplete and thus distorted picture of late Qing poetry. By contrast, Xue's vision and version of late Qing poetics— specifically her views on the contributions of the Min school—painted a much richer picture, in which women played an indispensable part from the very beginning.[74]

Xue agreed with conventional male accounts that Min poetics emerged in the late Tang and rose to be one of the five major poetic groups in the early Ming. In the middle Ming, Fuzhou poets built the Hall of Elusive Existence (Wanzaitang) in the West Lake area of Fuzhou (Maps 1.1 and 1.3) to enshrine famous Min poets such as the Ten Early Ming Talents, headed by Lin Hong (ca. 1338–?).[75] The number of enshrined poets—all men—was increased to seventeen by the Tong-Guang era—and later to thirty-two by the end of Qing.[76] But Xue departed from the male narrative regarding who should be enshrined in the hall and for what reasons. She argued in a poem composed in 1888:

The Min "style of beautiful feelings" (*yanti*) began with Donglang.	閩州豔體起冬郎，
Who is now presiding at the Hall of Elusive Existence?	誰復平章宛在堂?
We should worship Hongqiao in company with Ziyu [Lin Hong].	合祀紅橋陪子羽，
In the shade of green willows, jasmine disperses its scent.[77]	綠楊影裏素馨香。

Here, Xue proposes to enshrine the Min woman poet Zhang Hongqiao (fl. 1368) together with her lover Lin Hong (*zi* Ziyu), subverting the male construction of the Wanzaitang tradition by positioning women at the center of this enterprise. To justify the Zhang-Lin co-leadership, she reshapes the Wanzaitang poetics by identifying the "Min style (*ti*) of beautiful (*yan*) feelings" as its primary value. This style, Xue tells us, was initiated by Han Wo (nickname Donglang, 842–923) when he was exiled to Min in 906 in the midst of the late Tang political chaos. He spent the rest of his life in Min, and had a profound influence on local poets.[78] There, he compiled the *Poetic Collection from the Fragrant Dressing-Case* (*Xianglian ji* 香奩集), which consisted of one hundred of his poems about women's lives and gender relationships. This genre later became known as *yanti*.[79] Xue believed that Zhang and Lin continued this style, and she illustrates her point in the last line by extracting images from a poetic exchange between the couple, in which Lin Hong writes to Zhang Hongqiao:

Jasmine blooms, sending its hidden fragrance with the wind.	素馨花發暗香飄,
She wears a flower in her hair, close to an emerald hairpin.	一朵斜簪近翠翹。
On a precious steed, I speed back toward the rising new moon.	寶馬歸來新月上,
In the shade of green willows, she leans against the Red Bridge.[80]	綠楊影裏倚紅橋。

Zhang responds:

The osmanthus moon reclines upon my empty dressing-tower;	桂輪斜落粉樓空,
The water clock drips, and the candle flicks red shadows.	漏水丁丁燭影紅。
Night dew moistens hidden fragrance; pearls and jade turn cold.	露濕暗香珠翠冷,
By the red railing of the bridge, I wait for the return of the Wild Goose.[81]	赤欄橋上待歸鴻。

Xue chooses these lines from a series of extraordinarily beautiful and creative seven-character quatrains engendered from the mutual attachment of the two lovers, in which their names, "Red Bridge" (Hongqiao) and "Wild Goose" (Hong), are "evoked in a variety of ways to suggest the poets' feelings of longing and intimacy."[82]

Mainstream male poetics assailed Han Wo's *Fragrant Case* for its "refined phrases but vulgar tastes" (*cigong gebei*) and its "ornate words" (*qiyu*) that encouraged "licentious thoughts" (*yinxie zhi nian*).[83] Likewise, Zhang and Lin were criticized for their *yanti* poems. To be sure, the leading late Ming poet Qian Qianyi (1582–1664) and his companion, Liu Shi (aka Liu Rushi, 1618–64), appreciated the poetic creativity of the couple and had sympathy for their tragic love affair that ended in Zhang's early death and Lin's eternal sorrow.[84] Nonetheless, Qian could not refrain from accusing Lin Hong of exerting a negative influence on early Ming poetry, making "tender sounds and slow rhythms into a trend of vulgarity and decadence."[85]

From Xue's perspective, however, Zhang Hongqiao deserved to be enshrined in the Wanzaitang precisely because the "tender sounds and slow rhythms" (*rouyin manjie*) of her correspondence with Lin Hong fit Xue's

aesthetic vision of Min women poetics. Xue believed that heaven had ordained Min women to write about love, as we can see in her preface to
Ding's *Sequel*:

In our Min region, Mount Lady Ji rises from the land;	吾閩地有姬山，
The Woman Constellation shines over the sky.	星當女宿。
The Grandmother Mountain arrays its cliffs and hills;	太姥則崗巒羣列，
The Spiral-Girl River flows with ever clear water.	螺女則江水彌清。
Thus, Jiang Caiping assuages loneliness by tuning to "Pearls";	是以江采蘋斜珠慰寂，
Chen Jinfeng composes erotic melodies of "Happy Roaming."	陳金鳳艷曲樂遊，
Lady Sun [Daoxuan] uses a willow twig to tie her heart with her lover's;[86]	孫夫人［道絢］柳結同心，
Ruan Yi's daughter sings of fish darting in the spring water.[87]	阮逸女魚游春水。

The four poetesses listed here all wrote passionate poems. Jiang Caiping,
the legendary Plum-Blossom Consort (Meifei) of Emperor Tang Xuanzong
(r. 712–56), sent a resentful yet dignified poem to reject the comfort-gift of
a bag of pearls from His Majesty after being abandoned.[88] Chen Jinfeng
(894–935), the consort of the king of Min, Wang Yanjun, eroticized lotus
flowers into amorous symbols on the same West Lake where the Wanzaitang
shrine would be erected.[89] Lady Sun and Daughter Ruan, too, each composed poems related to erotic love. Xue sees their passion and talent as reflecting the "divine beauty of mountains and rivers" (*shanchuan lingxiu*),
a potent visual image of abundant femininity. According to Xue, by re-
flexively inscribing their passion on natural objects and turning them into
poetic images for self-expression, "these women surpassed men in literary
composition."[90] Viewed solely in terms of their poetic achievements, even
the notoriously lustful Chen Jinfeng could become a source of local pride.[91]

Xue valorized *yanti* from Han Wo and Zhang-Lin not only because of
their remarkable literary gifts but also because of their poetic motivation.
Han Wo had defended *yanti* in his preface to the *Fragrant Case*, saying: "I sincerely know that a man should not indulge in this kind of writing, yet an inability to forget *qing* [feeling, passion, affection, emotion] is heaven's gift."[92]
Here Han Wo alludes to a *Shishuo* episode: When Wang Rong (234–305),

one of the Seven Worthies, lost his son, he explained his inconsolable grief in the following terms: "A sage forgets his *qing*; the lowest beings aren't capable of having *qing*. But the place where *qing* is most concentrated lies precisely among people like ourselves."[93] Lin Hong laments Zhang Hongqiao's death in the same terms: "Only those possessing superior wisdom can forget *qing*; / For me, this life will forever be one of unending regrets [*yuanqing*]!" (自是忘情惟上智, 此生長抱怨情多!).[94]

By virtue of her broad learning, Xue understood the allusions that Han Wo and Lin Hong used to justify the *qing* invested in their *yanti* poems. This so-called *yanqing* was originally confined to the love between men and women. But invoking Wang Rong, Han Wo extended *yanqing* to cover a much wider spectrum of human emotions. Xue's concept of *yanqing* therefore consisted of all that a woman's fragrant dressing-case might accommodate metonymically—all kinds of relationships in a woman's life and all the beautiful feelings activated by these relationships. It was based on this gendered understanding of *yanqing* that Xue placed *yanti* at the altar of the Wanzaitang shrine as the central aesthetic value of Min poetics. Small wonder she considered women to be cofounders of the Min poetic tradition.

This enlarged meaning of *yanti* can be seen with particular clarity in a song-lyric that Xue composed around 1895–96 to support her sister-in-law Chen Rong's project, the *Collection of Women's Song-Lyrics through the Ages* (*Lidai gongwei cizong* 歷代宮闈詞綜). Xue wrote:

Along fragrant paths every family boasts of the beauties of the South.	香徑家家誇越豔,
Like carved jade and sculpted crystal,	鏤玉雕瓊,
Flower petals, a thousand pieces, are collected in your hands.	收聚花千片。
Male talents in the Orchid Garden and the Grass Hall are brilliant,[95]	蘭畹草堂雖爛絢,
Yet in tenderness they are inferior to the golden-boudoir scholars.	溫柔合讓金閨彥。
This glorious dynasty promotes women's education.	女教熙朝偏獨擅,
Applying powder and spreading cream	摘粉搓酥,
Are numerous ladies of this land.	濟濟皆邦媛。
How can we find a capable evaluator like Wan'er,	安得婉兒稱善選,
Who weaves the talent of youthful wives into yellow pongee?[96]	織來幼婦成黃絹。

Chen Rong's compilation concentrated on Qing dynasty "beauties of the South" (*Yueyan*), which included, of course, the song-lyrics composed by Min writing women. Here *yan*, which correlates to the phrase "applying powder and spreading cream" (*zhaifen cuosu* or *difen cuosu*) in the second stanza, clearly refers to *yanti* that expresses *yanqing*, for Xue had previously (in 1884) defined the genre of the song-lyric as "conceiving beautiful feelings (*yanqing*) through powdering and creaming" (摘粉搓酥有豔情).[97] The phrase *zhaifen cuosu* originally depicted a young woman's fair face after applying her makeup,[98] but Xue employs it as a metaphor for tempering words and music in order to give "sensuous expression" to "beautiful feelings." Xue supplements *yan* with *wenrou*, tying *yan* not only to the Confucian poetic teaching described as *wenrou dunhou* (tenderness and sincerity)[99] but also to the Daoist notion *rou*, tenderness. Xue thus conjoins *yanti* with the *xianyuan* ideal, since tenderness is a central value of the perfected person.[100]

Xue also shows this connection in a poem composed in 1902, after viewing a flower album by the Qing master Yun Shouping (1633–90). She claims that Yun "creamed and powdered flowers to compete for pure contentment" (搓酥摘粉鬥清酣),[101] implying that he painted flowers in order to convey *yanqing*. For this reason, the one who inherited Yun's artistry in her opinion was not his male disciple Ma Yuanyu (*zi* Fuxi, 1667–1722) but rather Yun Bing (*zi* Qingyu, fl. late seventeenth and early eighteenth centuries), a young woman from the Yun lineage.

Ma Fuxi should not count as the one who understands [Yun's] art—	會心不數馬扶羲,
To truly inherit the six methods, one has to adhere to femininity.	六法真傳在守雌。
The fragile girl Qingyu possessed the family learning,	弱女清于具家學,
Chanting snow-flakes into "willow catkins on the wind rising."[102]	臨風柳絮雪花詩。

In this instance, Yun Bing is able to continue the family learning because she has followed *Laozi*'s teaching, "adhering to femininity," embracing "tenderness and harmony" (*rouhe*), and "becoming a ravine to all under heaven."[103] Yun Bing's art is therefore comparable to Xie Daoyun's willow-catkin poetics; both embody *Laozi*'s conception of a "ravine" that nurtures the entire world.

Xue reinforces the connection of *yanti* to *xianyuan* at the end of the previously quoted song-lyric celebrating Chen Rong's project by alluding to a famous eight-character riddle from the *Shishuo xinyu*. The four two-character terms are: "yellow pongee" (*huangjuan*), "youthful wife" (*youfu*), "maternal grandson" (*waisun*), and "ground in a mortar" (*jijiu*). Here is the solution to the *Shishuo* puzzle:

> "Yellow pongee" is "colored silk" (*se si*), which, combined in one character, is *jue*, "utterly." "Youthful wife" is "young woman" (*shao nü*), which, combined in one character, is *miao*, "wonderful." "Maternal grandson" is "a daughter's son" (*nü zi*), which, combined in one character, is *hao*, "lovely." "Ground in a mortar" is "to suffer hardship" (*shou xin*), which, combined in one character, is *ci*, "words." The whole thing thus means: "Utterly wonderful, lovely words."[104]

> 黃絹, 色絲也, 於字為絕。幼婦, 少女也, 於字為妙。外孫, 女子也, 於字為好。齏臼, 受辛也, 於字為辭。所謂絕妙好辭也。

Referencing this overwhelmingly feminine word riddle, Xue illustrates the combined value of *rou* and *yan* by equating weaving with writing. Women weave soft pongee to comfort human bodies and they write tender poems to nurture human minds. All these efforts result in "utterly wonderful, lovely words." The "golden-boudoir scholars" embrace *yan* and *rou* as their ideal values and express them in poetry through "powdering and creaming"—the painstaking process of artistic execution. In so doing they have exceeded male talents in poetic excellence. In the penultimate line of the song-lyric quoted earlier, Xue beseeches her sister-in-law to follow the example of the Tang woman poet Shangguan Wan'er (664–710)—who passed authoritative judgment on the best male poets of her time—in selecting women's song-lyrics for her compilation.[105] Of course Xue is aware that she, too, emulates Wan'er in her evaluation and revision of male poetics.

In brief, in order to amend an incomplete version of Min poetics presented by men, Xue reconstructed Min women's poetics by evoking the *xianyuan* ideal and building Min women's aesthetic subjectivity upon the combined values of *yan* and *rou*.[106] In this Xue received assistance from her talented daughter Chen Yun, who, like her mother, drew creative inspiration from the *Shishuo* and employed the aforementioned *Shishuo* word riddle to praise Min women poets: "These young ladies, like the Heavenly Weaving Girl, composed wonderful 'young woman' words" (諸女天人幼婦辭).[107] The implication here is that their poems shone with the same splendor as the colorful clouds that the legendary Heavenly Weaving Girl (Zhinü) had produced to clothe the sky.[108] Below, a poem that Chen Yun wrote to celebrate several dozen collections of verse by women, most of them titled "After Embroidery," elaborates on the combined qualities of *yan* and *rou* in women's poetry:

By green windows they write abundant poems after embroidering	綠窗面面繡餘多，
During short breaks between weaving and needle work.	杼織微閒針黹和。
Under the Woman Constellation that travels across the river,	女宿星躔江兩岸，
They let slip from their lips poetic lines that they weave into red brocades.[109]	唾成紅綺盡詩歌。

Women, Chen avers, do not have men's luxury to concentrate on poetic practice. They have to juggle their writing brushes with their sewing kits. In the process, they are able to create unique artistic products that poeticize embroidery into fine art and stitch poetic lines into an ornate tapestry of words. The refined and versatile texture of their poetic rhetoric can seldom if ever be found in men's poetry. Chen Yun therefore sighs with admiration for "the freshness of the ingenious writings from the fragrant boudoir" (香閨才藻鮮)—small wonder that women poets "will not repeat others' words" (不甘唾餘拾).[110]

In her praise of women writers, Chen Yun fondly mentions Wang Shuduan (fl. early nineteenth century).[111] Wang provides an effective illustration of the talent women had for orchestrating domestic chores with poetic, artistic, and scholarly activities. Consider her "Chanting on the Five Colors of Butterflies" ("Yong wuse die" 詠五色蝶). Each piece in this series of five heptasyllabic-regulated poems depicts a butterfly of a specific color— *qing* 青 (green), *huang* 黃 (yellow), *chi* 赤 (red), *bai* 白 (white), and *hei* 黑 (black)—and each follows the same five rhyming words—*xi* 稀 (scarce, vague), *fei* 飛 (fly), *yi* 衣 (clothes), *fei* 肥 (plump, chubby), and *gui* 歸 (return home). As difficult as this is to achieve, the poet also incorporates five artistic practices into these poems—*xiu* 繡 (embroidery), *qu* 曲 (music), *hui* 繪 (painting), *wu* 舞 (dance), and *ran* 染 (dyeing). Below are Poems 1 and 4, respectively, on the green and the black butterflies.

Outside the curtain I can vaguely see their fragile wings;	簾前弱翅望依稀，
Then I lose sight of them after they fly into the shade of flowers.	每到花陰不見飛。

Up and down, it appears as if the wind is wafting through leaves;	上下渾疑風度葉，
Floating in the air, they seem to love their emerald clothes.	飄搖似愛翠為衣。
The spring is enjoyable but they are too weak to walk;	春真可踏嬌無力，
Black lines can sketch them yet they are too thin for the thick ink.	黛縱能描瘦未肥。
To cut the jade-colored brocade into their shapes for embroidery,	欲剪碧羅依樣繡，
I caught several to take home from the South Garden.	南園撲得兩三歸。
They scarcely come into the dream of the Varnish Garden,	漆園夢裏往來稀，
But freely roam in the twilight, among trees and bamboos.	樹暮箐深自在飛。
Along the paths of wilderness, no need to apply golden powder;	野徑何須著金粉，
In late autumn, don't mistake them for dark-clad youths.	深秋休與認烏衣。
Even though their deep indigo color needs to be dyed,	饒他黛色憑須染，
They have a blue hue after shining, making them look chubby.	拭得藍光竟體肥。
The thin rain and the thick mist display a vast spring;	細雨濃煙春漠漠，
In the shadow of willows, they find a place to return.[112]	柳陰多處正宜歸。

Rigorously abiding by the poetic rules of "depicting things" (*yongwu*), the poet may neither use the word *die* (butterfly) nor indicate its color in the poem proper. So she locates the butterflies in natural environments that share similar colors. By depicting the quick fluctuation between the presence and absence of the insects, she successfully denotes the color and the movement of her subjects and their intimate relationship with nature. The poet further philosophizes this relationship by invoking the famous butterfly dream of the *Zhuangzi*, in which Zhuangzi dreams of metamorphosing into a butterfly and wakes up wondering if he may be a butterfly dreaming that he is Zhuangzi. The poet sends the black butterfly into Zhuangzi's black Varnish Garden, and it reappears as a mysterious, free-roaming spirit.[113] This spirit rejects any sort of high ("golden-powdered") status and should therefore not be confused with wealthy and powerful aristocrats wearing dark clothes. Emerging from a talented woman poet's cultural toolkit, these five poems display both artistic refinement and philosophical profundity. They look like five panels of embroidered screens, shimmering with exquisite colors and elaborate stitching.

The central concern in women's *yanti* was family. Poems of this genre often portrayed a loving mother who nurtures both the bodies and the minds of her children. A typical example would be the following poem by Zheng Jiangxia (fl. early nineteenth century), inscribed on her fellow Min woman poet Zheng Hunbing's *Drafts of Chanting after Embroidering* (*Xiuyu yincao* 繡餘吟草) (which is on Chen Yun's aforementioned list in celebration of women's poetic collections of similar titles):[114]

The sound of loom is followed by the sound of poem chanting;	杼聲繼續答吟聲，
I train a crowd of young *luan* birds chirping.	教得鸞雛接翅鳴。
Behind the gauze curtain, I also teach them the classics;	紗幬更饒經訓在，
In a family full of poets, every rhyme we compose is pure.[115]	一門風雅韻俱清。

Here, the mother provides instruction to her "little celestial *luan* birds"— sons and daughters—while weaving clothes to warm their bodies. As we can see, her curriculum focuses primarily on poetry. Even the learning of the classics seems more for the purpose of seeking moral guidance in the purification of poetry than for preparing her boys to take the civil service examinations that stood at the center of mainstream male culture.

Participation in State Affairs amid Late Qing Political Turmoil

As late Qing Fuzhou was drawn into the vortex of political turmoil, Min writing women transcended the inner domain to express much broader concerns about the fate of their country and its people. They found it only natural to extend their protection of the family outward to the region and the state. They self-consciously continued the *xianyuan* tradition, helping their fathers, husbands, and sons manage offices, draft memos, and make administrative decisions. They also dared to criticize the government and to condemn foreign invaders.

Liang Zhangju's wife, Zheng Qiqing, may serve as an early example of *xianyuan*-style woman. In the fall of 1824, Liang was promoted from the Huai'an-Haizhou intendant to a judge in Suzhou, leaving his family temporarily ensconced in the Huai'an official residence by Lake Hongze. That winter the lake flooded, taking the people in the region by surprise. Attendants advised Lady Zheng to flee by boat, but she refused, saying, "Now water is everywhere but boats are few. Will our boat alone be safe? If anything bad happens to the people, we'll only invite criticism! It is better to stay!" Soon the water receded, and the situation in the town remained stable and calm. Lady Zheng later composed a poem to commemorate the event:

Towing a boat up the bank is too absurd!	牽船上岸太無端,
Sitting in the endangered tower I am comforted by principle (*li*).	坐守危樓理始安。
Luckily my heart remains tranquil like still water.	幸我此心如止水,
Soon the flying steed reports the receding of the flood.[116]	早聞飛騎報回瀾。

Her husband later commented that his wife "often deals with incidents according to ancient principles (*li*),"[117] and in this case Lady Zheng consulted the poem "Appreciating the Still Water" ("Wan zhishui" 玩止水) by Bai Juyi (772–846), to which she alluded in the penultimate line of her poem.

Bai points out in this poem that "Nothing is comparable to still water in judging (*jian*) appearance [and behavior]" (鑒形[行]不如止). And why? Because the special quality of quiet water is that it evinces intellectual profundity: "Its calmness does not differ from *chan* contemplation; / Its brightness resembles one's sincerity" (定將禪不別, 明與誠相似). In this sense, Bai maintains, "If we want to recognize (*shi*) the heart-mind of a quiet person, / The origin of his/her heart-mind should be just like this [the still water]" (欲識靜者心, 心源只如此).[118] Adopting Bai's "still water" analogy, Lady Zheng shows her awareness of the intimate connection between his poem and the *xianyuan* capacity of *shijian* demonstrated in the *Shishuo*, in which people often "recognize" (*shi*) and "judge" (*jian*) one's personality by analogizing human characteristics with water images.[119] She sensitively recognizes her current position as an object under the close scrutiny of the townspeople and local officials. She must stay calm (*ding*) in order to make the right decision and she also needs to demonstrate sincerity (*cheng*) in order to inspire confidence. At stake is not only the well-being of the people but also the reputation of her family, especially that of her husband.

Western aggression presented unprecedented challenges to Min women, transforming Fuzhou into a new frontier of China and bringing warfare to their doorstep on the South China coast. During the First Opium War, Yao Huaixiang (1783–1840), the magistrate of Dinghai in Zhejiang and a Houguan native, fought to the death in resisting the British invaders. His female disciple Sa Lianru (fl. 1821–50) expressed her dismay in the following lines:

My mentor possessed irresistible courage; The sea may go dry but his resentment will never recede: If our navy should sail out to the islands, How could the powerful pirates enter the city? (At the time my mentor served as the Dinghai magistrate. Upon hearing that the [British] invaders were coming, he beseeched the commander of the Zhenhai Brigade to protect the city. The commander was hesitant and fled without a fight. My mentor recruited several hundred salt guards and stationed them at the South Gate to resist the enemies for the entire day. The city finally fell, and my mentor died defending it.)	吾師素志本橫行, 窮海何年此恨平: 倘使孤軍出遙島, 豈憂強寇入重城。 （師宰定海, 聞寇將入, 請於鎮戎某以兵衛。某逡巡不戰亡去, 師募鹽哨數百餘人, 拒南門終日。城陷, 遂以身殉。）
In haste he resisted the enemy, but alas too late! Heroically he sacrificed himself to keep his promise. His red heart forever shines over the sun. In the grave he still discusses warfare with a smile. (I once dreamed of my mentor, sitting among military classics such as the *Six Strategies* and the *Yin Tally*. Contented, he showed me the books.)[120]	倉皇拒敵嗟何及, 慷慨捐軀志已成。 一片丹心常照日, 九原含笑尚談兵。 （余嘗夢師坐擁六韜, 陰符諸書, 含笑以示。）

Liang Zhangju praises Lianru in this instance for "having elaborated and valorized her mentor's sincere loyalty with such profundity that the gentleman could indeed remain contented in his grave."[121] More importantly, Sa Lianru's identity as Yao's female student allows us to see the tender side of her mentor, enhancing the sharp contrast between a gentle poet-magistrate resisting the enemy to the death and a brigade commander fleeing the battlefield.[122] The ending of the poem displays a touching and poignant scene:

the girl dreams of her mentor showing her books as if he were still alive. Evidently, Sa Lianru was recasting a real-life experience into an ironic dream in which poetry books were replaced by military manuals. This ending effectively elaborates a loyal spirit's unfading desire to defend his country even after death, and a young girl's recognition of the need to acquire practical knowledge in the face of unprecedented threats.

Lin Puqing, Lin Zexu's daughter and Shen Baozhen's wife, provides an outstanding example of a Min woman dealing effectively with sociopolitical crises by virtue of her learning, talent, and good judgment. Puqing and her sister-in-law, Lady Lu, were known as the Two Phoenixes of the Inner Chambers (Guizhong shuangfeng). Lady Lu copied memos for her father-in-law, Lin Zexu, and Puqing must have helped her father in the same way as a young girl. After her marriage to Shen Baozhen, Puqing proved to be an able assistant to her husband.[123] In September 1856, for example, when Shen served as the prefect of Guangxin, Jiangxi province, the Taipings were about to attack the prefectural seat. At the time, Shen was away collecting military supplies, leaving Puqing alone in the official residence. As the soldiers and townspeople fled, Puqing held Shen's official seal and sword, sitting by the well and vowing to die should the rebels break into the city.[124]

But "Lin was not driven by martyrdom."[125] Unlike old-style woman martyrs (lienü) who killed themselves to protect their integrity, Puqing voluntarily shouldered the responsibility of protecting the people in her husband's absence—similar to Zheng Qiqing's actions in the Hongze flood crisis. Puqing inscribed a letter with her own blood, imploring help from the brigade commander Rao Tingxuan (1803–62), who was then stationed at Yushan, some fifty kilometers from Guangxin. This letter demonstrates Puqing's courage, broad knowledge, persuasive rhetoric, and, above all, her good judgment. She understands that Rao has no responsibility to protect Guangxin. She argues, however, Guangxin is "the barrier" protecting Yushan. She writes "to protect Guangxin is to defend Yushan, something a wise man need not be told."[126] She then invokes past heroes to inspire Rao with a sense of duty, beginning with her father, Lin Zexu, who was sent by the court to put down the Taiping Rebellion, but he died at the outset of his mission. "Thinking of him," Puqing writes, "breaks my heart!" She goes on to say:

> Now, if I die for Guangxin, blessed by my father's spirit in heaven, I will become a fierce ghost and kill the rebels. The local gentry and commoners did not know my mind; they came to take me away to hide in the moun-

tains so that I could avoid the rebels. I pointed out to them the sword and the well to show my determination. They left in tears. . . . If I could know for certain that you will lead your troops here, I will prepare food for your vanguard. Solemnly I will bow to your representative on behalf of all the sentient beings of the seven counties [within Guangxin prefecture] and ask you to save their lives. In the past, when soldiers and the common people together guarded Suiyang city, its prefect Xu Yuan (709–57) became a martyr [along with Zhang Xun (709–57)]. The prefect of today's Guangxin also has a loyal heart and strong will, like iron and stone. He is indeed the one with whom Your Excellency would surely like to be recorded in history. If not, you will be like General Helan [who refused to rescue Zhang and Xu], causing regret for the next one thousand years.[127] I hope Your Excellency will see your way clear to taking action. I present you this letter written with my blood, and I am waiting to hear your astute decision.[128]

For General Rao, the most inspiring hero on the list was perhaps Lin Puqing herself. Rao arrived in time and fought alongside Shen Baozhen until the rebels fled.

Such was the Min writing-women tradition by the time of Xue Shaohui's birth, a tradition that would inspire Xue throughout her short life. As we have already seen, she would go on to compose many poems to honor Min women writers. A song-lyric composed on an 1893 visit to the Roaring-Wave Garden (Taoyuan 濤園), the shrine of Shen Baozhen and his wife, pays homage to Lin Puqing:

That year, in Guangxin, you guarded the prefecture.	廣信當年守府,
In a water-filled pothole,	有潢池,
Some rebels stirred up trouble and wreaked havoc like tigers.	跳梁捲地如虎。
You deployed troops of ladies,	夫人陣結,
And built up a tall Fortress of Women.	娘子城高,
Writing on a shield, you sent out a feather labeled military letter,	盾鼻軍書飛羽,
And thus summoned divine reinforcements.	援師神武。
You, the worthy wife, drummed up support for the campaign.	賢內助, 親操桴鼓。
I burn my heart as incense, honoring you along with your husband.	卜一瓣香火同龕,
A faint bell rings over the wall, in the moonlight.[129]	隔鄰鐘咽霜杵。

Xue wrote this song-lyric in the wake of foreign invasions that did, and would again, directly affect her hometown and family: the 1884 Sino-French War claimed China's Southern Fleet based in Fuzhou, and the Sino-Japanese

War in 1894 later eliminated China's Northern Fleet. In her moving song-lyric, Xue compares Lady Lin to great women warriors in China's past,[130] celebrating her for having protected her people with courage and writing talent.

In 1903, Xue took her daughter Chen Yun to revisit the Roaring-Wave Garden. At this time the young girl wrote admiringly of Lin Puqing:

The chanting terrace of Guanglu is buried in dust,	吟臺光祿已成塵,
Leaving withered trees not yet turned into firewood.	剩有枯枝未化薪。
The wind blows waves on the half-receding river.	風卷濤聲川半落,
Bowing to my Lady, I seem to hear her drum pounding.[131]	如聞桴鼓拜夫人。

Seeing the garden in decline, Chen Yun laments the fading of Guanglu's glory, for this garden had once belonged to the founding Xu family.[132] But she still hopes that its trees will become lush again, blessed by the spirit of Lady Lin. And in fact, Lin Puqing did leave a spiritual legacy, not only within in her own bloodline but also among her admirers in the Min writing-women culture. In addition to Xue Shaohui and her generation, Lin's granddaughter Shen Queying and great granddaughter Li Shenrong (1878–1903), along with Chen Yun and many other Min girls, formed yet another generation of Min writing women—poet-prodigies who were determined to adapt the poetic vitality and moral tenacity of the Guanglu tradition to the needs of their changing society (see Chapter Three).[133]

The Chen Brothers and the Fuzhou Navy Yard Culture

The Fuzhou Navy Yard culture grew out of the late Qing Self-strengthening movement. This movement was once viewed as a "pattern of seemingly successful naval building, training, and organization which failed each military test."[1] Since the early 1990s, however, scholars have shifted from this long-standing "failure narrative" to more diverse perspectives. Kwang-ching Liu (1921–2006), for instance, pays attention to the participation of "lower ranking officials and young private scholars" who, although having no direct influence on state policy making, initiated much broader changes in social, intellectual, and cultural areas. Exposed to various Chinese and Western value and knowledge systems, they "cared not only about the wealth and power of the state but the social emancipation of the people as well."[2] Benjamin Elman recommends that we "deal with the nineteenth century arsenals, factories, and translation schools by also considering them as a harbinger of the Chinese industrial revolution to come and not simply as a prelude to the end of the Qing dynasty and imperial China."[3]

The Fuzhou Navy Yard, along with its affiliated academy, provides a case study of the Self-strengthening movement that goes beyond the conventional focus on political and military affairs. Its scientific and technological achievements paved the way for late Qing and early Republican industrial-ization. The graduates of its naval academy and their political, social, and intellectual networks—including their female relatives, who were indispens-able components—brokered up-to-date knowledge between China and the West. These intellectuals and their products, both material and spiritual, formed a distinctive culture that significantly transformed the Chinese in-telligentsia more generally.

The Fuzhou Navy Yard and Its Affiliated Academy

How could the Fuzhou Navy Yard, a defense industry institution, foster a culture? This peculiar outcome resulted, I believe, from its distinctive orga-nization. The yard, as David Pong contends, "defies accurate description by a single term. It was not an 'arsenal', a term commonly used by Westerners at the time. Nor was it simply a 'shipyard', as the Chinese term *ch'uan-ch'ang* [*chuanchang*] implies. The name 'Foochow [Fuzhou] Navy Yard,' which we adopt, is also inadequate."[4] What caused this identity problem? To under-stand the features and the significance of the Fuzhou Navy Yard culture, we need to look into at least four factors in the process of establishing the yard and the academy, namely, the motivation of its founders, the constitution of the curriculum, the makeup of the student body, and the regional features of the yard.

When Zuo Zongtang embarked on the Fuzhou project in May 1866, he envisioned the navy yard as a means to achieve "China's technological in-dependence." He planned the yard to be "a comprehensive industrial com-plex for the triple purpose of shipbuilding, learning how to manufacture and operate marine engines, and navigational and naval training."[5] Shen Baozhen reinforced Zuo's farsightedness upon succeeding to the director-ship of the yard, emphasizing that "the basis of navy management lies in the academy."[6] He went beyond Zuo's pragmatic orientation, however, intend-ing "to forge a new, modernizing elite out of the scholar-gentry class."[7] The Fuzhou Naval Academy offered Shen such an experimental site to "set a personal example for the traditional educated elite" so that he could achieve his "earnest desire to change the civil service examinations and promote the study of science."[8] This vision of transforming the Chinese intelligentsia established the distinctive cultural basis for the navy yard.

Consistent with his desire to train a new generation of Chinese intellec-tuals, Shen designed a curriculum for the academy that combined Confucianism with Western sciences and technology. Shen required students not only to take regular courses on naval matters but also to read the Confucian classics "just like candidates for the local civil examinations."[9] Shen also assigned students the writing of "political essays" (*lunce*) so that they could understand the "significance of [Confucian] principles" (*yili*).[10] This curriculum demonstrated Shen's belief that "those who had studied and practised Confucian moral principles were best suited" to fulfill the task of transferring Western science and technology to China.[11] This combination of traditional learning and Western knowledge would prove crucial in forming the Fuzhou Navy Yard culture.

The curriculum thrived because of the origins of the student body. As the naval academy began enrolling students, "the examination system (*keju*) still existed, and people saw the navy service as a dangerous career choice."[12] Thus, although the academy was open to young men nationwide, applicants were "mostly from poor local families of Fujian,"[13] and the academy authorities had to lure and keep students with generous stipends and awards. Yan Fu, for instance, attended the academy because his family was too poor to hire a *keju* tutor for him after his father died.[14] The Chen brothers, too, went to the academy because of the early death of their parents (see below). Even after entering the naval academy, some students still tried to pass the *keju*. Chen Shoupeng, for one, resumed *keju* learning right after graduating from the academy in 1879 and in 1902 at last obtained a *juren* degree.[15] Including *keju* subjects in the academy curriculum in effect motivated students to pursue traditional learning.

The location of the yard and the academy in the vicinity of Fuzhou also made a difference. Situated near a large city, the yard advantageously attracted the interest of local high officials and people of distinction, who "had it in their power to watch its [the yard's] progress."[16] Also interested in the yard and the academy were less powerful members from the local gentry, including women, especially those from related families. These supporters and interested parties formed an unprecedented intellectual network with the naval students. On the one hand, the inclusion of traditional scholar/literati training in the curriculum kept the students within the local gentry society through local poetry clubs, companionate marriages, and scholarly connections. On the other, the yard and the academy helped spread Western learning and ideas among the local gentry, thus transforming its traditional knowledge structure. Equally important, the political and military turmoil that revolved around the yard and often took place in Fuzhou provided the students and their local supporters with new topics for intellectual discussion.

A review of the structure of the naval academy, its pedagogy, and its curriculum may help us understand the foundation of this new culture. The academy consisted of two major divisions: the Naval Construction School, taught in French, and the Naval Navigation School, taught in English.[17] For the training of the students, Prosper François Marie Giquel (1835–86), the first director of the Fuzhou Navy Yard, provided a general picture in a report to the imperial commissioner and director-general Shen Baozhen on 18 November 1873. According to Giquel, the French school, which focused on shipbuilding, offered arithmetic and geometry for calculating the dimensions of machines, descriptive geometry for understanding the science of perspective, physics for explaining the pressure exerted on engines and ships, and trigonometry, analytical geometry, and the infinitesimal calculus for mastering the science of statics and mechanics, all for students "to arrive at general formulae applicable to all the details of construction."[18] The training "lasted five years, with the last fourteen months given to practical work."[19]

The Naval Navigation School, as Giquel described it, trained students to operate ships on the open sea. They therefore needed to learn sciences essential for the navigator—arithmetic, geometry, algebra, rectilinear and spherical trigonometry, astronomy, the calculations of navigation, and geography. For instance, if "one finds himself in sight of the coasts, he measures the distance of the points he perceives . . . by rectilinear trigonometry." Or "if he guides himself by the sun, the moon, and the stars, he recognizes their position in the sky, and their revolutions by astronomy, and he measures their height above the horizon or their respective distances by spherical trigonometry." The training for these students took three and a half years.[20]

Under the Naval Construction School, Shen Baozhen and Giquel later added a school of design and a school of apprentices, both also taught in French. The School of Design sought "to organize a staff qualified to turn out the plans needed for construction," with two subdivisions respectively designing ships and machines. Students in this school studied "arithmetic, geometry, descriptive geometry, and a very complete course descriptive of a marine engine of 150 horse-power." The course took three years to complete, but the first students who graduated in April 1873 were then sent to the School of Naval Construction for further studies. The School of Apprentices purposed that students acquire "the ability to read a plan, to design it, to calculate the bulks and weights of the parts of engines, or of hulls, of whatever form," and "to acquire in the workshops the ability requisite for the work of their profession." The studies they pursued were "arithmetic, geometry, descriptive geometry, algebra, design, and a course descriptive of engines." The training of the apprentices took about six years.[21]

The significance of these curricula to late Qing Self-strengthening, as Lin Chongyong summarizes it, includes:

1) The courses taught at the academy included first and foremost the rudimentary subjects of Western sciences and technology, such as algebra and physics. This curriculum shows the determination of the academy authorities to acquire Western knowledge systematically from its theoretical basis, not merely to extract its pragmatic techniques.

2) The curricula heeded the principles of Western applied science, tying the learning of theories to practical training. Students in the Naval Construction School, the School of Design, and the School of Apprentices applied their classroom knowledge immediately to shipbuilding and maintenance in the workshop or on a ship. Likewise, students in the Naval Navigation School practiced how to operate ships on the open sea right after acquiring the necessary knowledge. This carefully woven pedagogy, Lin maintains, was unprecedented in the Chinese educational tradition. None of the other similar institutes for learning Western knowledge at the time, such as the College of Languages (Tongwenguan), the Academy of Foreign Languages (Guang fangyan guan), and the Jiangnan Arsenal (Jiangnan zhizaoju), could measure up to the Fuzhou Naval Academy in this respect.

3) In training the earliest cadets of the Chinese navy in Western science and technology, Shen Baozhen never ceased conventional Chinese moral teachings, such as loyalty, filial piety, and bravery.[22]

As we shall see, these features of the Fuzhou Naval Academy curriculum would contribute significantly to late Qing social, political, and cultural change.

When the academy was ready to graduate its first class, Shen Baozhen and Giquel moved to send them to Europe for further training. In his report presented to Shen, Giquel detailed the need for students of the various divisions to study abroad, in the actual context that had bred the Western navies and naval industry, rather than in a Chinese laboratory.[23] Shen Baozhen confirmed this necessity in his memo to the court on 7 December 1873 and assigned the students more important responsibilities—to explore "the principle of replacing the old [naval sciences and technologies] with the new" as well as "the principle of military training for overcoming the enemy."[24] Clearly, Shen wanted to comprehend not only the Western sciences and technologies but also the principles that engendered the applied sciences and technologies. Shen's plan of sending students abroad received firm support from the three most powerful statesmen at the time, Superintendent of the Northern Ports Li Hongzhang, Superintendent of the Southern Ports Li Zongxi (1818–84), and Shaanxi-Gansu Governor-general Zuo Zongtang.[25]

Previously, in the fall of 1872, the Qing court had dispatched its first educational mission of 120 boys to the United States to study Western science and engineering. The project was proposed by Yung Wing (1828–1912), a Yale graduate who devoted his life to China's reform, and was supported by Zeng Guofan (1811–1872) and Li Hongzhang.[26] Still the court saw the merit in sending to Europe the elder and better prepared naval academy graduates, who could complete their study much sooner than the young boys. Recognizing Shen's desire to acquire Western principles as "an idea of exploring the foundation [of self-strengthening]" (*tanben zhilun*), Li Hongzhang, along with Guo Songtao, would recommend that some of the naval academy graduates abroad also study Western social science, humanities, and law (see below).[27]

The Chen Brothers' Education in Fuzhou and in Europe

The Chen brothers were from a scholarly family in the Houguan district of Fuzhou. All we know about their father, Chen Xi (died ca. early 1860s), is that he had joined a Fuzhou poetry club, the Flying Society (Feishe), with leading Min poets Xie Zhangting (1820–1903), Zhang Jiliang (1799–1843), and Xu Yi'e (*jr.* 1844). This club also included Jitong's and Shoupeng's two maternal "uncles" Liu Xiang (1836–1904) and Liu Shaogang (fl. late nineteenth century).[28] From this we may surmise that their mother was also from a scholarly family, and that the Chen brothers must have had a substantial, traditional Chinese education in their youth.[29] The early death of their parents, however, channeled the brothers away from a possible *keju* career to a new path of seeking training at the naval academy.[30]

Chen Jitong entered the French school in February 1867, as one of its first twelve pupils.[31] Jitong's enrollment was rather accidental, according to Henri Bryois. During a visit to his uncle at the Fuzhou Navy Yard, he heard that the yard would hold an examination the next day for enrolling students to go to Europe. Encouraged by his uncle, Jitong took the exam and "was immediately accepted by the French School of Naval Construction of the Fuzhou Arsenal."[32] This uncle must have been Liu Shaogang, who was then helping Shen Baozhen to oversee the construction of the Fuzhou Navy Yard.[33]

An outstanding student at the academy, Jitong was especially well versed in the French language; we are told that "throughout various exams, he always surpassed his peers."[34] Because of his accomplishments in Western learning, Jitong was appointed as a translator serving in the Fuzhou Navy Yard administration after his graduation in early 1875.[35] Soon, in the same year, Shen Baozhen sent Jitong and four other new graduates to escort Giquel on a business trip to France that was also meant to pave the way for sending the academy's graduates abroad. Jitong was among the very few volunteers for the mission even though he had never been on a long voyage.[36] This one-year trip to England, France, Germany, and Austria proved a successful trial for Jitong's future career. There Jitong and his four fellow graduates greatly impressed European officials with their Western knowledge, especially of mathematics.[37] This, along with Jitong's excellent French, enabled Jitong to make useful contacts with Westerners.[38]

Returning to China in June 1876, Jitong followed Giquel on reporting the trip to Shen Baozhen, who had by then moved to Nanjing as the Jiangsu-Jiangxi governor-general. They then went to Tianjin to help Li Hongzhang fine-tune the plan to send students to Europe. Jitong presented to Li a complete report on higher education in France and England and so impressed the Chinese authorities that they immediately promoted him from a student to a secretary.[39] Very possibly influenced by Jitong, Li Hongzhang widened his vision of knowledge acquisition for naval students abroad from the previous focus on naval operations and manufacturing to include sciences and social sciences. In a memo to the court on 13 January 1877, Li recommended that some outstanding students be allowed to engage in the study of mineralogy, chemistry, diplomacy, and law, and that all of them should also "study useful [Western] books such as historical writings at their leisure, so as to understand their foundations and applications."[40] Thus Li followed Shen Baozhen's vision of training naval students to comprehend not only Western sciences and technologies but also their historical and cultural foundations. To make sure that his expanded pedagogy was carried through, Li singled out Jitong to study international relations and law (*jiaoshe gongfa*) in addition to attending to his future job as the secretary to the supervisors of the students sent to Europe.[41] Jitong's first meeting with Li Hongzhang would prove extremely important in Jitong's life and career, for Li would become the most powerful and influential Chinese politician in the 1880s and 1890s. The two would keep close contact in the following twenty years in dealing with China's diplomatic and political issues.[42]

In 1877, the plan to send students to Europe that Shen Baozhen had long proposed was finally put into action. Jitong, now a secretary, assisted the newly appointed Chinese supervisor Li Fengbao (1834–87) and the Western supervisor Giquel in leading thirty-six Fuzhou Naval Academy graduates (including Jitong) to study in England and France. In the group were such great men as the future translator and thinker Yan Fu, future linguist Ma Jianzhong (1845–1900), future diplomat Luo Fenglu (1850–1903) (these three, along with Jitong, were assigned to study Western social science, humanities, and law), and future leading naval officers Liu Buchan, Fang Boqian (1852–94), and Sa Zhenbing (1859–1952); all would play crucial roles in modern Chinese history.[43]

Jitong's life in Europe was busy. He was enrolled in the École libre des sciences politiques and the École de droit, learning international relations and law, as well as European languages such as English, German, and Latin, while keeping up with his secretarial duties.[44] Jitong also "took courses on the histories and literatures of various countries."[45] All this new knowledge would add to what Jitong had acquired in China and greatly help his diplomatic and social activities during his years in Europe.

In 1878 the first Chinese legation was installed in Paris. Jitong became its secretary-interpreter and thus began his diplomatic career.[46] He would spend the next thirteen years in Europe until his eventual return to China in the spring of 1891.[47] During this period, he was very active in European high society. On his list of friends were such dignitaries as the educator and mathematician Joseph Bertrand (1822–1900), Baron Thénard, the playwright Eugène Marin Labiche (1815–88) ("who seduced Jitong with the comic power and vigor of his works"), and the economist Pierre Guillaume Frédéric Le Play (1806–82), who "very much pleased Jitong" with his theories.[48] Jitong's friendship with these scholars and writers shows how quickly he assimilated Western culture. The most important among those who took an interest in the young Chinese diplomat was perhaps the powerful politician Léon Gambetta (1838–82), a "principal guide to the new Republican shore," who had proclaimed on 4 September 1870 the establishment of the Third French Republic (1870–10 July 1940) after the collapse of the Second French Empire.[49] "He invited Jitong to his dining table, taking pleasure in listening to [Jitong] expand on his ideas about politics, finances, philosophy, and literature."[50] Their friendship enlightened Jitong to the parliamentary democracy that would help shape Jitong's own political ideals.

In 1879 Chen Shoupeng graduated from the Fuzhou Naval Academy,[51] where he must have attended the Naval Navigation School, judging from his excellent knowledge of English and geography. After graduation, Shoupeng continued working on fulfilling his *keju* dream and actively participated in the local poetry club, thanks to an improved family financial situation after Jitong's employment.[52] In 1883, Shoupeng acquired funds to study in Japan for more than a half year. In early 1886, he was invited to be a translator for the supervisor of the students to Europe, where he continued his studies while working until the summer of 1889.[53] The broad knowledge he acquired and refined during this period—in Western languages, histories, cultures, and sciences—would bloom in the late Qing reforms, especially in his collaborative projects with his wife (see Chapters Three, Five, and Six).

The Fuzhou Navy Yard Culture as Embodied in the Chen Brothers

During his years in Europe, Jitong wrote extensively on Chinese culture for Western audiences, publishing at least eight books in French and English. *The Chinese Painted by Themselves* (*Les Chinois peints par eux-mêmes*) (1884) and *Pleasures in China* (*Les plaisirs en Chine*) (1890) focus on Chinese culture and social life. *My Country* (*Mon pays*) (1892) expands from culture to social and economic affairs. *The Chinese Empire, Past and Present* (1900) chronicles China's most recent political, diplomatic, and military changes. *Chinese Theater* (*Le théâtre des Chinois*) (1886), *Chinese Tales* (*Les contes Chinois*) (1889), and *The Tale of the Man in Yellow* (*Le roman de l'homme jaune*) (1890), promote Chinese works of drama and fiction, the two literary genres that had been marginalized in the Chinese tradition but were of great importance in the West.[54] *The Parisians Painted by a Chinese* (*Les Parisiens peints par un Chinois*) (1891) registers Jitong's understanding of French sociopolitical and cultural life in comparison with that of China (see Figure 2.1).

Jitong's works were warmly received in the West. *Les Chinois peints par eux-mêmes* ran to eleven editions in Paris from July 1884 to May 1886, and its reputation quickly spread to America through its English translation, *The Chinese Painted by Themselves* (1885), by James Millington. *Le théâtre des Chinois* ran to three editions in 1886, the same year of its publication, and has since become a "rare" reference for the study of Chinese theater and Chinese culture.[55] Because of Jitong, the Western public "began listening

LES CHINOIS

PEINTS PAR EUX-MÊMES

PAR LE COLONEL

TCHENG-KI-TONG

ATTACHÉ MILITAIRE DE CHINE A PARIS

CINQUIÈME ÉDITION

C·L

PARIS
CALMANN LÉVY, ÉDITEUR
ANCIENNE MAISON MICHEL LÉVY FRÈRES
3, RUE AUBER, 3

Droits de reproduction et de traduction réservés.

LES CHINOIS PEINTS PAR EUX-MÊMES

LE

THÉATRE DES CHINOIS

ÉTUDE DE MŒURS COMPARÉES

PAR

LE GÉNÉRAL TCHENG-KI-TONG

Le monde est vieux, dit-on. Je le crois. Cependant
il le faut amuser encor comme un enfant.
LA FONTAINE.

C·L

PARIS
CALMANN LÉVY, ÉDITEUR
ANCIENNE MAISON MICHEL LÉVY FRÈRES
3, RUE AUBER, 3

1886
Droits de reproduction et de traduction réservés

GÉNÉRAL TCHENG-KI-TONG

LES PLAISIRS

EN CHINE

DEUXIÈME MILLE

PARIS
G. CHARPENTIER ET Cie, ÉDITEURS
11, RUE DE GRENELLE, 11

1890
Tous droits réservés.

Général TCHENG-KI-TONG

LES PARISIENS

PEINTS PAR UN CHINOIS

PARIS
BIBLIOTHÈQUE-CHARPENTIER
11, RUE DE GRENELLE, 11

1891

Figure 2.1. Covers of part of the French works by Chen Jitong 陳季同 (under Tcheng-Ki-Tong, 1852–1907): *Les Chinois peints par eux-mêmes* (1884), reprinted six times in the same year (the image is of the 5th edition); *Le théâtre des Chinois* (1886); *Les plaisirs en Chine* (1890); *Les Parisiens peints par un Chinois* (1891).

attentively to voices coming directly from China."[56] The *Once a Month* in London complimented *Les Chinois peints par eux-mêmes* as "very interesting and instructive," and noted that its author "found great ignorance prevailing as to China and the life of its people, and wrote this volume to correct mistaken conceptions and convey reliable information."[57] The *Literary World* in Boston lauded *Les Chinois peints par eux-mêmes* as an "admirable review of social and domestic life in China."[58] The critics also showered Jitong with praise for "depicting French life and manners" in *Les Parisiens peints par un Chinois.*[59]

Scholars have assessed Jitong's role in negotiating between Chinese and Western cultures mostly from a binary perspective. Catherine Vance Yeh observes: "Chen's sojourn in France will provide a key to understanding the dilemma posed by his complex role as both a spokesman for China and a knowledgeable defender of Western civilization."[60] And again: "In work as well as life Chen played a double role of standing up for the Chinese while behaving like an honorary Westerner, and his success depended on being accepted in this double function."[61] Ke Ren extends this polarized reading from the identity-fashioning and functioning of Jitong's person to that of his works. Jitong is, on the one hand, the "Chinese diplomat whose political allegiance to his home country is clearly manifested in his physical appearance," and a "Parisianized dandy," on the other. This dual identity engenders another: that of an "autoethnographer" and a "flâneur" who respectively writes autoethnographies of China and physiologies of the West.[62] Li Huachuan sees an inner connection between these two polarized attitudes—that Jitong was trying to incorporate both sides into his ideal of a world literature. Still, as Li indicates, Jitong proceeded with this purpose by addressing his two audiences in a paradoxical position: advocating the superiority of Chinese culture to the French public while emphasizing to his fellow Chinese literati the importance of learning Western culture, especially Western literature.[63]

This seeming polarity, I believe, resulted from Jitong's open-minded appreciation of the values and the sophistication of both cultures on equal terms. True only to himself, Jitong viewed the two traditions in a cosmopolitan framework and synthesized pertinent values into a system unique unto itself. The evolution of this system involved the participation of Jitong's brother Shoupeng and their fellow naval academy graduates, as well as their families, and the outcome formed what I term the Fuzhou Navy Yard culture.

LITERATURE AS A BASIS FOR FASHIONING THE FUZHOU NAVY YARD CULTURE

Jitong invokes the French playwright and actor Molière (stage name of Jean-Baptiste Poquelin, 1622–73) to exemplify the power of literature in promoting sociopolitical and cultural change. At a time when acting was still a humble occupation, Molière enjoyed prestige higher than nobles because his magnificent and virile satire inspired social progress more effectively than any revolution.[64] How can literature project such power? Jitong argues that literature results from and reflects "original, unadorned thinking," and "has more resources in its unharnessed thoughts than any multiple-volume encyclopedia that teaches you everything yet nothing."[65] "This thinking alone makes the human valued" because it fills the human mind with passion: "If you have some passion that elevates your sentiments, making you more generous, more compassionate, and more humane, how precious this passion would be for you!"[66]

In contrast, "sciences generally have the gift to dry up the mind, taking away its sympathy for human misery."[67] Jitong therefore doubts the idea that progress in sciences can also make literature thrive.[68] Jitong laments:

> Today, isn't it that only a small number of people devote themselves to literature? . . . The grand literary centuries have been regarded as naive. People no longer read the eighteenth century with the excuse that it is not sufficiently enlightened. The eighteenth century, however, teaches taste, precision, and harmonious and delicate styles that add grace to human thinking. The eighteenth century is distinguished and spiritual; yet this is not enough, because it is not enlightened![69]

Jitong is criticizing his contemporary Europeans who disparage their own literature produced before the Industrial Revolution, which they consider to be *the* enlightenment. Deep down, Jitong is defending China's antique institutions and customs against contempt from the "excessively despotic" Europeans.[70] China's temporary lagging behind in science and technology does not grant Europeans an excuse to despise its ancient culture, which is as "distinguished and spiritual" as eighteenth-century European literature.

Jitong believes that "flowers of literature" offer the best reading;[71] thus he broadly quotes from Chinese poems in his introduction to China: twenty-four in *Les Chinois peints par eux-mêmes* and fifty-one in *Les plaisirs en Chine*. This passionate touch of poetry endeared Chinese culture and social life to the French public. Inspired by his European experience, Jitong enthusiastically advocated literature as a means of bridging the gap between the Chinese and Western peoples. In a later conversation with Zeng Pu (1872–1935), he recommended broadly translating Chinese works into foreign languages and vice versa, so "we can dissolve the blockade" and "avoid misunderstanding" between Chinese literature and other world literatures.[72] Jitong was among the very few of his time to prioritize literary communication between China and the West over China's one-sided acquisition of Western science and technology. He contended that exposure to each other's literature could offer direct access to mutual understanding and appreciation between different peoples.[73] With this belief, Jitong, Shoupeng, Xue Shaohui, and their intellectual networks would later take literary creation and translation as indispensable components of their reform program.

In accordance with his preference for literature as the core category of a cultural system, Jitong identifies himself first and foremost as a *wenren*, literatus, and conceptualizes this identity drawing upon both Western and Chinese traditions. He imagines himself a French man of letters, a disciple of Molière. Using his pen he can tie a sail to his thoughts and spiritually communicate with Greco-Roman philosophers, playwrights, and poets.[74] In depicting the talents of such a person of letters, Jitong invokes "a female Chinese authority."[75]

This female authority comes from an anonymous novel, the *Ping Shan Leng Yan*, dated 1658 and titled after the surnames of four literary geniuses, two men and two women, who admire and respect one another. The novel is therefore also known as the *Book of Four Talents* (*Si caizi shu*).[76] Among them, Leng Jiangxue, a country girl, is drafted by the local magistrate to attend to Shan Dai, the prime minister's prodigy daughter. Entering the Shan household, Leng refuses to address herself as a servant before His Lordship. Rather, she demands the prime minister treat her as a guest, for her talent can raise her up to his equal. Stunned but also amused, the prime minster asks Leng to specify her talent.

In her response, Leng points out that, first, this talent refers specifically to that of a literatus and a poet; it is born from one's natural endowment refined by learning. Second, this talent can be equally possessed by men and women. In detailing the achievements of earlier geniuses, men and women, Leng especially cites Ban Zhao and Xie Daoyun as "heavenly born boudoir talents that have added splendor to women's fragrant dressing-cases."[77]

Third, one who possesses this talent can overwhelm any powerful authority, as she passionately elaborates:

> All these talented persons are endowed with the grace of mountains and rivers, and they are reincarnations of the spirits of the constellations in the sky. Therefore, their minds are as ornate as brocade and their words as beautiful as embroidery. Gods inspire their thinking when they structure ideas, and ghosts move their wrists when they write. Hence they wield brushes as if spreading rain and they splash ink as if displaying clouds. They talk like wind soughing, with words rolling down like pearls. When they reach the status of expressing their ideas effortlessly, they exude such unquenchable vigor that it will not yield in the slightest even facing kings and lords. They outshine distinguished ministers and wealthy marquises. They make old masters and erudite scholars lament that their lifelong learning is of no value. If not for their talent, how could they rise above their times?[78]

> 此蓋山川之秀氣獨鍾, 天上之星精下降, 故心為錦心, 口為繡口; 構思有神, 抒腕有鬼。故揮毫若雨, 潑墨如雲。談則風生, 吐則珠落。當其得意, 一段英英不可磨滅之氣, 直吐露於王公大人前, 而不為少屈, 足令卿相失其貴, 王侯失其富。而老師宿儒自嘆其皓首窮經之無所成也。設非有才, 安能凌駕一世哉?

All three points are of special significance to Jitong's self-identification and his future influence on the 1898 campaign for women's education. Jitong's self-identification as primarily a man of letters was deeply rooted in China's literati tradition, more specifically in the local Min poetics that had assumed a leading role in late Qing poetry. As Jitong recounted in *Les plaisirs en Chine*:

> In literary circles in China, the most popular amusement is to make verses. Instead of shooting, or playing lawn-tennis, or croquet, or of indulging in any of the many pleasures enjoyed in Europe, our literary folk, as soon as a certain number of them have a little time to spare, meet together in turn at each other's houses, and give themselves up to poetical tournaments.
>
> For, in China, open receptions, political meetings, and public lectures, are totally unknown, and the only way that people have of indulging the fancies of the mind is in the culture of pure literature. These poetical tourneys take place all over China, but it is especially in the province of Fou-Kien [Fujian] that they are most common. Thus, when the late imperial commissioner of the arsenal of Fou-Tcheou [Fuzhou], who was also Viceroy of Nankin [Nanjing], could spare a moment from his official duties, it was his habit to call in his subordinates and compose poetry with them.[79]

Here, "the late imperial commissioner of the arsenal of Fou-Tcheou [Fuzhou]" clearly refers to Shen Baozhen. Jitong must have frequented this sort of poetry club led by Shen during his years at the Fuzhou Navy Yard, as evidenced by Jitong's close ties with Shen's son Shen Yuqing. The two later formed a poetry club in Shanghai in the winter of 1899.[80]

The late imperial commissioner's poetic hobby was consistent with the Min poetic tradition on the one hand, and, on the other, with the pedagogical principle he had set up for the naval academy, which included a traditional curriculum. Small wonder, then, that on their first meeting with Li Hongzhang in the summer of 1876, Jitong and his two fellow naval academy graduates impressed Li as "more culturally refined than gallant and awe-inspiring," more like members of the National Academy (Shuchang guan) than like those of the Imperial Armory (Wubei yuan). Li, however, seemed to appreciate these characteristics and argued that naval personnel should possess better learning than those from ordinary military departments.[81] Seen in this light, Li was in agreement with Shen Baozhen's goal of fashioning naval students to become a new generation of intellectual elites.

Jitong's belief in literature as a basic cultural category is consistent with his self-positioning during his years in Europe. In his journal entry of 18 February 1889, Romain Rolland recounted Jitong's speech at a session of the Alliance Française given at the Sorbonne. It offers a firsthand sketch of how Jitong presented himself to the French audience:

> In a beautiful violet robe, nobly spread across his chair, his full, young face shines with happiness, with a smile of an actress who flaunts her teeth. Yet this is a robust man, with a loud, low voice, strong and clear. He delivers an excellent speech, witty, very French, but even more Chinese, a speech by a superior man and about his superior race. Beneath the surface of his smile and compliments, I can sense his contempt—he sees in himself as superior to us and treats the French public like children. . . . All of his efforts have always been, he says, "focused on reducing the distance and the antipodes between the two most civilized countries of the world"—yet he has every intention of pointing out such differences! "The whole world knows that China is the most ancient civilization. . . . The whole world knows that the Chinese language is the most universally spread out," etc.
> An enchanted audience swallows all the pills and applauds wildly.[82]

In his "*belle robe violette*," Jitong presents an image of a sui-generis man of letters rather than a rigid Chinese diplomat, for the robe he wears is not a Qing official uniform, which would usually be the color of *shiqing*, equivalent to dark blue or blue.[83] Among the eight of Jitong's photo portraits I have collected, three are of him in scholarly attire, and the robe he wears in each photo seems to be of the same design, made of the same fabric, and decorated with the same crystal buttons. One of the three was printed in the *Bits of China* edition that was published in 1890, close to the date of the Alliance Française event (Figures 2.2 and 2.3).[84] The robe looks stylish and elegant, with sleeves much wider than those of a regular scholar's robe, and hence very possibly of Jitong's own design. Perhaps this is the "*belle robe violette*" that Rolland wrote about, which Jitong might have considered the most suitable attire for introducing Chinese culture.

Figure 2.2. Chen Jitong in a scholarly robe. Taken by Studio Nadar. (Bibliothèque nationale de France collection.)

Figure 2.3. Chen Jitong in a scholarly robe. (From *Bits of China*, an authorized translation of *Les plaisirs en Chine* by R. H. Sherard, 1890, frontispiece.)

This image of a sui-generis man of letters combines Chinese and French characteristics. Rolland recalls how Jitong's robe is "nobly spread across his chair." Since Greek and Roman times, the color purple has been "the distinguishing colour of the dress of emperors, kings, etc."[85] In addition to the robe, Rolland was also impressed by Jitong's speech. Of the four speakers that evening—including Octave Gréard, rector of the Académie de Paris, and Gaston Deschamps, literary critic and vice-president of the Alliance Française—it is the Chinese general, Tcheng-Ki-Tong (Chen Jitong), "whom Voltaire may find to be the most French."[86] In brief, from his looks to his speech, Jitong appeared to Rolland and the rest of his French audience "très français, mais encore plus chinois."[87]

To be sure, the reality of the Sino-French relationship could not provide any diplomatic leverage for Jitong to appear "noble" or "superior" at his Sorbonne speech in 1889, as the memory of China's defeat in the 1884 Sino-French War was still fresh. This failure nonetheless seemed to have little impact on Jitong, for he was popular in Western society not because of his diplomatic status but rather because of his self-assigned mission as an advocate of Chinese culture. Undergirding Jitong's sense of nobility and superiority at the Sorbonne podium was his belief that with literary talent one could "rise above his/her time," just like his French predecessor Molière and his Chinese girl icon Leng Jiangxue.

An episode in *Les Parisiens peints par un Chinois* suggests the spiritual origin of Jitong's self-esteem. The narrator—Jitong himself perhaps—encounters a young French brunette at the 1889 World Expo in Paris. The girl pulls the narrator's queue, and the irritated narrator gently hits her hand with a fan.[88] The narrator thereupon delivers a dignified—although also hilarious—statement on defending his cultural pride, for a fan serves as a symbolic marker of the Chinese elite. As Jitong indicates at one point in *Les plaisirs en Chine*, fans are like art albums that collect works of poetry, calligraphy, and painting, inscribed either by the owner, the owner's friends, or famous poets and artists. Gentlemen and gentlewomen carry fans around to show off their refined taste and intellectual associations.[89] One can imagine Jitong walking "around Paris sporting his queue,"[90] flaunting his scholarly fan, and delivering enchanting speeches in eloquent French, charming and confident.

WOMEN IN CULTURAL CONSTRUCTION

Borrowing a female authoritative voice from Leng Jiangxue, Jitong brings a gendered perspective into his construction of the Fuzhou Navy Yard culture.

Throughout his introduction of the Chinese cultural tradition to the West, Jitong never fails to celebrate women's literary and artistic contributions, as shown in the chapters and sections devoted to women in almost every book he wrote.[91] He argues that a woman is "more artistic and poetic than a man" because she "loves more truth and beauty."[92] In *Les Chinois peints par eux-mêmes*, he praises women's pursuit of education for themselves and overseeing the education of their children.[93] In *Le théâtre des Chinois*, he elaborates on the talents of the learned woman (*femme savante*): "She enthuses herself instantly with books, with historians, philosophers, and poets. She picks up a pen and composes verses, comedies, and novels, just like any academician."[94] Also in this book, Jitong probes into the emotional realm of a talented girl, through a poetic analysis of *A Little Bondmaid Manipulates the Hanlin Scholar's Love Affair* (*Zou Meixiang pian hanlin fengyue* 㑳梅香騙翰林風月), by the Yuan (1271–1368) dramatist Zheng Guangzu 鄭光祖. By "offering a love lecture to a young girl who is passionately fond of reading books," this drama illustrates how literature and nature can together elicit the most beautiful feelings in her.[95] Thus Jitong presents to Western readers a live portrait of the Chinese writing woman who possesses not only talent but also passion.

Jitong finds, however, that the West has not paid due respect to "the most beautiful half of mankind," for Europeans have long disparaged their own learned women as "bluestockings" (*bas-bleus*). At the same time, Westerners considered Chinese women as ridiculous and grotesque, "without influence, created only to bring children into the world."[96] In fact, Jitong notes, "a learned woman in the West is not as esteemed as her counterpart in the East."[97] He therefore feels the need to paint a full picture of the Chinese "*bas-bleus*"—hence a chapter so titled in *Les Parisiens peints par un Chinois* (1891)—in order to correct inaccurate Western perceptions of Chinese women. This chapter introduces "another China yet unknown" to Europeans, a hidden, modest female China that has been depicted as an "illiterate slave." "On the contrary," Jitong contests, "women writers are numerous in China and are greatly esteemed."[98] Jitong made this claim clearly based upon the fact that his hometown, Fuzhou, had developed during the Qing a thriving culture of writing women.

In *Mon pays* (1892), Jitong adds to the Chinese *bas-bleus* a moral dimension, using the case of Mulan, a fifth-century Chinese peasant girl who assumed a male identity to fight against foreign invaders in her father's stead. Jitong advances Mulan as "une Jeanne d'Arc Chinoise" but differentiates her from this fifteenth-century French heroine who defended her country against the invading English. Jeanne d'Arc, he writes, "incarnates the enthusiastic mysticism of the French Middle Ages."[99] Mulan, however, bears "no exaltation, nor mysticism. . . . She has not at all had illusory visions, nor heard illusory voices, nor communicated with heaven. She is not a protégée of saints or angels, nor is she carrying out any divine mission." Whereas Jeanne d'Arc is celebrated as a national heroine, Mulan "has not risen to a summons to rescue her land, nor has she ever dreamed of playing a brilliant role under the circumstances."[100]

What, then, has inspired Mulan to take such an unconventional, gender-trespassing action? Jitong points out with great sensitivity that Mulan can read—thanks to Chinese women's literacy—and so she recognizes her father's name in the official gazette. If the father is drafted into the army, who will be there to care for her mother and young brother? Devoted to her family, Mulan disguises her gender and goes to the battlefield as a common soldier. After performing her duty for the country, she rejects any honor or reward, returning home to her original gender identity. "All this takes place in the most ordinary manner."[101] Such is Jitong's ideal of womanhood—one that enlists a woman's talent and virtue in the service of the family and the country (and in that order).

THE PLACE OF THE PRESS

Jitong saw the modern press as the best vehicle for promoting his views of culture. Presumably, he developed his passion for the press under the influence of his political idol and good friend Léon Gambetta. Since the early stages of his political career, Gambetta had "long harbored the ambition of running a paper to voice his own views and those of his associates" in the new school of young Republicans. His ambition was realized in the form of a new publication, *La République Française*, which "made its first appearance on Tuesday, 7 November 1871" and soon became the most influential newspaper in France.[102] Gambetta emphasized the importance of the press because he had witnessed how "opposition papers had played a considerable part in the last phase of the Republican struggle against the Second Empire." Indeed, as his supporter, the veteran Republican Adolphe Crémieux (1796–1880) once exclaimed, "The Press is everything . . . if the Press is ours we shall have the rest."[103] Entering Paris during the heyday of the newly established Third Republic under the leadership of Gambetta,

Jitong would naturally have been attracted to the press as a powerful means to promote one's ideas and ideals.

Jitong acknowledged as early as 1884: "I am an admirer of the European journal."[104] He was so fascinated with Western journalism that he once followed the entire process of editing and printing newspapers up to the point that rushing vehicles "shipped these newly declared thoughts to the entire world."[105] Jitong adored journalism precisely because of its efficiency in moving human ideas around: "It is a noble calling to create an opinion and diffuse it almost instantaneously by thousands of copies in that great and everlastingly new world we call the public."[106] Jitong was among the earliest Chinese "to create an opinion and diffuse it" through the print media.[107] He would publish his French writings first in the news media and then collect them into books, and in so doing he exerted a great deal of influence on Western audiences.[108]

Having been successful in Europe with the press, Jitong exported this effective vehicle to China and initiated the reform journal *Qiushi bao* (English title: *International Review*) in Shanghai in fall 1897. In his inauguration editorial, Jitong argued the unprecedented function of the news media (Figure 2.4):

> Memory of the past teaches us how to handle today's affairs. Events of yesterday can also provide us with such precedents. Now changes under heaven no longer follow conventional rules. Taking ancient things for today's mirror is not as good as taking today as today's mirror; taking history as a mirror is not as good as taking the news media as a mirror.[109]

Appealing to the discursive power of traditional Chinese historiography, Jitong introduces the news media as one more historical genre that fits the contemporary situation. As old-fashioned historical writings have become too slow to reflect the rapid changes of the late Qing, the news media can "create an opinion and diffuse it almost instantaneously" to the public.

To be sure, foreign newspapers had been introduced into China from the early 1800s, and offered late Qing reformists new ways of print. "It was ultimately this interaction between foreign models and the exigencies of late Qing reform politics," Joan Judge points out, "that give rise to new-style political journals."[110] Jitong's *Qiushi bao* was one of these early reform publications. His special contribution was to incorporate the new-style press into the Fuzhou Navy Yard culture in order to spread its ideas and invite public opinion on reforming China. The editorial board enlisted an all-Fuzhou

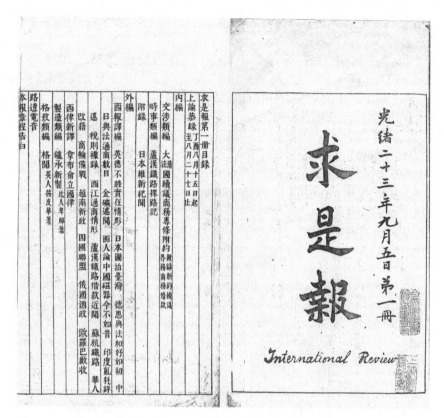

Figure 2.4. Cover and table of contents of *Qiushi bao* 1 (30 Sept. 1897). (Tsinghua University Library collection.)

team: Jitong as the editor-in-chief, Shoupeng and fellow naval academy graduate Zeng Yangdong in charge of translation, and the Chen brothers' two Fuzhou literati friends Chen Yan and Zheng Xiaoxu (1860–1938) as essayists. Especially well equipped to translate Western cultures for Chinese audiences, the *Qiushi bao* distinguished itself from other leading reform journals such as the *Qiangxue bao* (Journal of empowering learning) edited by Kang Youwei and the *Shiwu bao* (English title: *The Chinese Progress*) edited by Wang Kangnian (1860–1911) and Liang Qichao. Although introducing the West was a major theme in early Chinese reform journals, because of the editors' limited knowledge, they often reprinted fragmented information from the foreign news media based in China.[111] By comparison, the *Qiushi bao* provided a more systematic introduction to the West, often in thought-provoking ways that addressed China's reform needs.

LAW AND DEMOCRACY AS CORE VALUES

The twelve issues of the *Qiushi bao* dedicated four columns to discussions of the West: 1) "Newly Translated Western Law Codes" ("Xilü xinyi" 西律新譯); 2) "Technology" ("Zhizao leibian" 製造類編); 3) "Science" ("Gezhi leibian" 格致類編); and, from the second issue on, 4) "Western Fiction" ("Taixi baibian" 泰西稗編). Jitong clearly stressed the first column. He engaged himself in translating Western law and explained his purpose in the inaugural issue:

> In the past forty years since the easing of restrictions at ports,[112] many people have been talking about trade and foreign affairs, but few can really take a proper position and settle disputes through diplomatic negotiations. The problem has been caused by mutual misunderstandings between China and foreign countries. If asked by which means the West has become strong, these people would respond that the West has ships, guns, and cannons. If asked by which means the West has become rich, these people would respond that the West has free trade and mining industries. They don't know, however . . . without the regulation of laws and rules, how could the Westerners be single-minded and thus acquire wealth and power?[113]

> 溯自海禁開後四十餘年, 講通商、習洋務者, 實繁有徒。而能不亢不卑、折衝樽俎者, 頗不數覯。病在於未能知己知彼也。問泰西何以強? 則曰輪船槍砲。何以富? 則曰通商開礦。殊不知 . . . 若無律法以繩之, 安能億萬一心, 以致富強哉?

This must have been a common understanding among Jitong and his fellow Fuzhou Naval Academy graduates. His close associate Yan Fu, for one, later recalled: "When I first travelled in Europe [in 1877], I always visited the law courts to observe the administration of justice and after returning to my lodgings I would spend days in a sort of trance. I once remarked to Ambassador Kuo [Guo Songtao] that the reason why Great Britain and the other countries of Europe are wealthy and powerful is because the principles of even justice are daily extended. This is the ultimate root. The Ambassador heartily agreed with me."[114] According to Guo's diary and other accounts, from 1877 to 1878, Guo met several times with naval academy students in his London office and discussed in detail their educational plans in Europe, including studying Western law, politics, languages, and literatures. Yan Fu and Jitong were both present on these occasions and must have shared Guo's sentiments.[115] Yan Fu, who endeavored to excavate the philosophical basis of Western civilization, would later translate Montesquieu's *The Spirit of the*

Laws. He started the project in the early 1900s, "but the whole manuscript was not published until 1909."[116] Jitong, with an education in French law and international relations at the École libre des sciences politiques and the École de droit, was arguably the first to advocate the systematic introduction of Western law to China.[117] This resulted in his serial translation of the *Code Napoléon*, which Jitong upheld as the "epitome of the laws of all the other Western nations," together with some other French law codes.[118]

The *Code Napoléon* consisted of three books: Book I, *Of Persons*; Book II, *Of Property, and the Different Modifications of Property*; and Book III, *Of the Different Modes of Acquiring Property*.[119] What Jitong terms the *Code Napoléon*, however, far exceeds its original scope by including eight sub-codes: "Constitutional Law" (Liguo lü 立國律), "Family Law" (Qijia lü 齊家律), "Property Law" (Panduan lü 判斷律), "Commercial Code" (Maoyi lü 貿易律), "Code of Criminal Instructions" (Zui'e lü 罪惡律), "Penal Code" (Xingfa lü 刑罰律), "Press Law" (Baoguan lü 報館律), and "Copyright Law" (Shuyi lü 樹藝律). Judging from the "Newly Translated Western Law Codes" in the twelve issues of the *Qiushi bao*, what appears as "Family Law" translates only part of Book I of the *Code Napoléon*. Jitong probably meant to cover the entire Book I under this sub-code and Books II and III under "Property Law,"[120] but the other sub-codes listed by Jitong are in fact not part of the *Code Napoléon*.

The very first law code translated by Jitong is such a separate document, the *Constitutional Laws of the French Republic* (*Lois Constitutionnelles de la République Française*), promulgated by the Third Republic in 1875. Jitong translates its French title into Chinese as "Falanxi minzhu guo liguo lü" 法蘭西民主國立國律 and adds an extra chapter to the beginning of this law code that does not exist in the French original, namely, "The Power of Executing the [Constitutional] Laws." This chapter contains only one article, which states: "The power of executing the [constitutional] laws is charged to the chief of the people (*minzhu*), who is elected by the public, titled 'president,' and who has a seven-year tenure" (行法之權, 付諸民主, 由眾公舉, 名曰伯理璽天德, 每任七年).[121] Thus Jitong highlights the concept *minzhu* at the very outset of his introduction of the French political system to his Chinese readers.

Minzhu as rendered by Jitong carries two meanings. First, in translating *république* as *minzhu guo* in the title of the *Lois Constitutionnelles*, Jitong defines France as a country with a "government by the people" and thereby gives the Chinese word *minzhu* the very fundamental meaning of "democracy."[122] Second, in the added article, Jitong adopts the original meaning of *minzhu* as the "lord of the people" from the *Book of Documents* (*Shangshu*) but uses it to indicate the "*président*" elected by the people and hence the executive of the "government of the people."[123]

Although democracy was the political basis for a republican system envisioned by the founders of the Third Republic such as Gambetta,[124] as a term it appears neither in the official title of the "République Française" nor in the text proper of the 1875 French constitution. Possibly for this reason, Jitong felt the need to define democracy as the fundamental feature of a republican system of government before introducing the idea of a constitution. In accordance with a democratic system that opposes China's long-standing imperial order, the head of the state is transformed from an emperor ordained by heaven to a president elected by the people.[125]

To reinforce his emphasis on democracy, Jitong attached a commentary to the article titled "The Power of Executing the [Constitutional] Laws," saying:

> Note that the French constitution was first established under Napoléon I [1769–1821]. After France lost the Franco-Prussian War [in 1870], the resentful French people rose up against their ruler, Napoléon III, and banished him to England. Léon Gambetta became the regent of the state. After completing the peace treaty with Prussia, [France] officially elected Gambetta president [of the French Republic]. In November 1872, the French people reelected Marshal MacMahon [1808–93] [as the new president]. MacMahon ordered a committee of thirty parliament members to rewrite the constitutional laws [in 1875], which has since been implemented.[126]

Some references in this commentary need clarification. First, Gambetta, although the de facto head of the Third Republic, never assumed the presidency. The first president was Adolphe Thiers (1797–1877), elected on 8 February 1871. He was replaced by Marshal MacMahon in May 1873 (not in November 1872). Second, under the presidency of MacMahon, a Commission of Thirty was chosen in November 1873 "to tackle the constitution-making," and a republican constitution was deliberated upon on 25 February 1875.[127] These few historical inaccuracies notwithstanding, Jitong's purpose for promoting the republican/democratic system was sound and clear, with every word a thunderclap to Chinese ears long blocked by an imperial monarchy, especially when he explains how France changed from an empire to a republic.

Having spent his most flourishing years in the République Française and having befriended its leading politicians such as Gambetta, Jitong clearly preferred republican democracy over imperial autocracy despite his role as a diplomat from imperial China. This explains why he tried to establish the first Asian republic in Taiwan and named it "Taiwan Minzhu Guo" in the aftermath of the 1894–95 Sino-Japanese War.[128] It also explains why he would engage in a systematic introduction of Western laws in 1897 in the *Qiushi bao*. All this shows his belief in democracy as the foundation of the Western social, political, and legal systems and the core value of Western culture. Jitong's democratic ideal also exerted a strong influence on his family. As we shall see, Xue Shaohui wrote extensively about Western democracy and the republican system in the reform era (see Chapters Three, Four, Five, and Eight).

Under the rubric of democracy, Jitong went on to translate Book I, the "Family Law," of the *Code Napoléon*. Jitong titled this code *qijia*, literally, "regulating family affairs," an expression derived from the canonical *Great Learning*, which referred to the foundation of Confucian society and was seen as the prelude to "pacifying all under heaven."[129] The idea in the *Code Napoléon* about the equal status of husband and wife, marriage based on free choice, living together before a legal wedding, a woman's right to divorce and to remarry freely as a divorcée or a widow, all foreshadowed Chinese women's demands for similar rights in the soon-to-come campaign for women's education.[130]

Jitong rushed to translate the third code, "Press Law," before finishing with "Family Law," because he perceived "the [Chinese] public to be greatly open to new customs and the print media growing rapidly."[131] Unlike the previous two codes that he had translated article by article from the French original, Jitong selected what he considered relevant from the rather plump volumes of the *Lois de la presse* published since 1810, but he only got as far as 1819.[132] As this period included regimes not "particularly beneficial towards the press," the articles in Jitong's translation focus primarily on the governmental censorship of the mass media.[133] Even so, some articles indicate freedom of the press and regulation of copyrights. Had Jitong been able to continue his introduction to French press laws, he would have certainly exposed his audience to those versions promulgated in the "golden age of the French press" after the establishment of the Third Republic in 1870, which had so very much enlightened Jitong on the role of a free press.[134]

Upon contacting Western culture, Jitong and his fellow graduates from the Fuzhou Naval Academy gravitated toward values such as liberty, democracy, and gender equality—all enforced by law—rather than simply "wealth and power." This value choice is at odds with a historiography that has characterized late Qing elites as overwhelmingly nationalistic, especially the naval academy graduates who were trained precisely for empowering China amid "the emergence of the absolute nation-states and the conflicts of these states."[135] Benjamin Schwartz reminds us, however, that the heroes—Jefferson, Rousseau, and many other patron saints of libertarian and democratic views during the latter half of the eighteenth century—of late Qing reformers like Chen Jitong and his Fuzhou compatriots perceived "no necessary functional relationship between liberty, equality, and democracy and the machinery of industrialism, let alone the machinery of power."[136] Jitong, as we know, shared with these patron saints the same view when he valorized eighteenth-century French literature over nineteenth-century European industrialization. Here are his thoughts on the "machinery of power" after visiting the Louvre:

> There I have seen that a great number of gods, adored in the past, are laughed at by the whole world today. I, an indifferent stroller, have passed in front of those once powerful monarchs, yet the nineteenth century ignores even their names. I have seen in front of my eyes the display of the great peoples who once dominated the broadest part of the earth yet who have been erased from this land.
>
> So I think to myself that the gods and the most powerful ones today are not more immortal than those in olden times. I understand, above all, how insane it is to devour each other, making all the nations destined to disappear by war. In order to avoid ruin, there is only one solution: between them they should come to an understanding—to make peace instead of preparing for war and to reign over the whole surface of a reconciled globe with tranquility and happiness.[137]

For Jitong and at least some of his fellow naval academy graduates, the first mission was to advocate the value of spiritual freedom, which is why democracy took priority over national wealth and power in Jitong's writings. Similar arguments would later guide Xue Shaohui's design of the curriculum for women's education in China (see Chapter Four).

Jitong's eventual purpose in writing Chinese and Western culture, as he clarified repeatedly throughout his writings, was to make "all under heaven into one family" (*tianxia yijia*). Jitong came to this ideal, according to Li Huachuan, through a reinterpretation of the Confucian notion of Grand Harmony (*Datong*)—a utopian vision inspired by the newly surging socialism in Europe and marked by equality and justice. Jitong writes: "In the time [of the Duke of Zhou], no one was poorer or richer than anyone else.

This was a socialist time of absolute equality. No one would complain about this precious fairness because no one's wealth would come from taking that of others."[138] Jitong believed that such a world would bring everyone together into one family.[139] This, in short, was the core value of the Fuzhou Navy Yard culture that would later be transplanted into the Min writing-women culture through the marriage of the two.

A Marriage between the Two Cultures

This chapter explores the mutual transformation of the Min writing-women and Fuzhou Navy Yard cultures, focusing on the union of the Fuzhou girl prodigy Xue Shaohui and the Fuzhou Naval Academy graduate Chen Shoupeng. Shoupeng's experiences abroad introduced Xue to a much broader spectrum of knowledge than her writing-women upbringing, but the alluring luster of Western cultures was soon tarnished by repeated foreign invasions at Xue's doorstep. Such mixed exposure to the outside world led Xue to a lifelong journey of negotiating between the cultural values of China and the West. Similarly, this "marriage" changed the knowledge structure and gender relationships of some other Fuzhou families in Xue's intellectual networks. The private life of Chen Jitong, a scion of one of these families, especially reveals the complexity of "marriages" between the two cultures and between the Chinese and Western peoples. In all, this chapter indicates that the making of future reformers entailed a joint effort by many people and groups, bound by familial and communal ties, and it touched on every aspect of the social, political, and cultural life of late Qing China.

Xue Shaohui's Early Cultural Upbringing and Married Life

Xue received a typical Min writing-woman education from her parents at a very young age.[1] She studied the *Analects for Women* (*Nü Lunyu*), *Classic of Filial Piety for Women* (*Nü Xiaojing*), *Admonitions for Women* (*Nüjie*), and *Women's Learning* (*Nüxue*) at four, and the *Book of Songs*, the *Records of Ritual*, and the works of the Four Masters at five.[2] From six to seven, Xue read histories with her father during the day and, at night, learned painting, poetry, parallel prose, music, Kunqu opera, and embroidery from her mother, Lady Shao (d. 1874). Xue's happy childhood was cut short by her mother's early death when Xue was barely eight. Three years later, her father also passed away. By this time her two elder sisters were already married, and her elder brother had taken a tutoring job in Guangdong, leaving Xue alone to live with a relative. She had to support herself by doing needlework, but she never stopped composing poems. In fact, she even assumed her brother's name to participate in a highly intellectual game popular in Fuzhou, the poetry bell (*shizhong*).[3]

The early deaths of Xue's parents left the child in hardship, but she was at least free to learn as she wished. Xue's frequent triumph in the poetry-bell game also greatly increased her self-confidence, and market competition encouraged constant improvement of her needlework. All her learning and life experiences culminated in a large repertoire of literary and artistic practice, with a broad range of predecessors available for her to emulate. In poetry she modeled poets from the Six Dynasties (220–589) through the late Tang. In essay writing she was especially skilled in parallel prose and took after the styles of the Han, Wei, and Liang (502–57). In song-lyric she followed all the important lyric writers of the Song. And in painting she imitated two women artists, Wen Chu (1595–1634) and Chen Shu (1660–1736).[4] She would later work with almost every literary genre and incorporate a variety of schools and styles into her writing, but she was not bound by any one of them. Xue would eventually attain such a level of creativity that she freely trespassed the boundaries of multiple literary and artistic realms, refining one with the skills of the others, "developing her own novel styles."[5] For instance, she applied her flute-playing skill to composing song-lyrics and could therefore set words properly to music. She also transplanted painting methods into embroidery and vice versa; when putting her painting and embroidery next to each other, one can hardly tell which is which.[6] Open-minded and eager to learn, Xue would later accept Western knowledge without hesitation, which consequently enriched her artistic and poetic accomplishments.

Early success gave this prodigy enough confidence to establish her aesthetic subjectivity, and Xue would continually cultivate her ideal of artistic beauty through constant interaction with her cultural upbringing and sociopolitical environment, and her poetic and artistic activities. In the process, facilitated by her versatility, erudition, and open-mindedness, Xue orchestrated genres, ideas, and women's life experiences in artistic creation, imagination, and interpretation. Later, as a dedicated wife and mother, she became more capable of organizing related knowledge into artistic and literary creation, just as she coordinated numerous daily chores into coherent household management. Xue's inventive coordination of all kinds of skills and knowledge would prove effective as the rapid changes of late Qing China led her further into the poetic reform of themes, forms, techniques, rhetorical stance, and ethos.

Xue's early success also heralded her marriage with Shoupeng. When the people of Fuzhou found out that the poetry-bell laureate was in fact a girl of thirteen, Xue "became an instant legend in town" and attracted Shoupeng's attention. Newly graduated from the Fuzhou Naval Academy, Shoupeng was preparing for the *juren* examination and had already established his own poetic reputation. Also orphaned young, in the summer of 1879 Shoupeng sent a matchmaker to the Xue household, of which the actual head was none other than Xue herself. Urged by her elder sister Xue Sihui, who approved of Shoupeng because of his "outstanding talent and noble nature," Xue accepted the proposal and the two married in the spring of 1880. In a sense, the couple entered the marriage of their own free will and based on mutual admiration; both prepared for a union of intellectual equality and spiritual communication. Shoupeng's support encouraged Xue to continue her literary creations and scholastic learning. She took care of household chores during the day and "studied side by side with Shoupeng like two friends" at night (Map 1.3).[7]

Xue's poetic series "Sentiments in an Old Style" ("Guyi" 古意), composed around 1880–81, illustrated their close, indeed passionate, companionship.

To embroider two flowers on one stalk	欲繡並蒂花,
Requires breeding a cocoon woven by two silkworms.	先蓄同功繭。
Never broken is the silk thread of love,	不斷是情絲,
Spring wind clips, but is too blunt to cut it.	春風鈍刀剪。

Tender hands pluck the pure zither,
Tuned to the "Melody of Narcissus."
He listens outside my window;
His eyes meet mine, we smile.

纖手弄素琴，
初試 "水仙調"。
郎倚隔窗聽，
相看作一笑。

He adores peach blossoms;
I like white butterflies.
Understanding needs no words;
It's in my painting, on a round fan.

郎愛碧桃花，
儂喜白蝴蝶。
相喻在無言，
畫上合歡箑。

Writing intimate words like pearls,
I compose the tune of "A Woman Wishing for Longevity."
Not wanting him to know,
Behind the curtain, I teach the lines to my parrot.[8]

密字寫真珠，
譜出 "長命女"。
故不使郎知，
隔簾教鸚鵡。

Xue expresses her love for Shoupeng by imitating the Music Bureau (Yuefu) folksongs of the Southern Dynasties (420–589). Unlike the female persona in these songs who pleases her lover with sensual beauty,[9] Xue attracts her husband with her intellectual ability. The four poems in this series respectively demonstrate a woman's four talents: embroidery, music, painting, and poetry, each executed by entwining emotions with exquisite textures of fabric, sound, brush strokes, and colors. Flowers are embroidered with the silk thread of love, *qingsi* 情絲, punning *qingsi* 情思, love thoughts; butterflies are painted on a round fan symbolizing the sexual pleasure of two lovers (*hehuan* 合歡).[10] All the images are in pairs—including the silkworms that labor on the cocoon—projecting the girl's attachment to her beloved. The zither resonates with a longing for spiritual interaction, for the "Melody of Narcissus" ("Shuixian diao") is conventionally attributed to the legendary musician Boya. He was a lifelong friend of Zhong Ziqi, who "understood the sound of music" (*zhiyin*).[11] Having built a relationship of love and mutual understanding, Xue then wishes for a lifelong commitment with Shoupeng by alluding to the song-lyric, "A Woman Wishing for Longevity" ("Changming nü") by Feng Yansi (903–60), in which the female persona prays to stay with her beloved forever.[12] This series of poetic images reveals sexual attraction embedded in intellectual confidence. Although passionately attached to her husband, the poet remains spiritually independent.

Xue's intellectual confidence and independence often made her feel free to tease Shoupeng, so irrepressibly that she even made fun of Shoupeng's *keju* attempts. Civil examination candidates often resorted to divination for clues about the future, a popular method of which was spirit writing (*fuji* or *fuluan*) designed to summon immortals to compose predictive poems.[13] At the time Xue had just begun learning how to compose song-lyrics, which were clearly meant to convey her "beautiful feelings" (*yanqing*) engendered by her happy conjugal life. And she would intentionally choose tunes that were originally titled after similar themes, in an evident attempt to match the lyrical rhythms closely to her feelings. (Xue maintained this principle in composing song-lyrics throughout her life.) She parodied Shoupeng's *fuluan* activity in a series of song-lyrics in 1884, with a long title: "Yiru [Shoupeng's *zi*] and His Friends Tried the *Fuluan* Divination, and Most of the Immortals Summoned Were Female, Whose Poems Are Illusory, Full of Celestial Aura. I Jokingly Imitated Their Style in the Following Six Lyrics" (繹如與友扶鸞, 往來多女仙, 詩詞飄忽有仙氣, 戲倣其體, 填六関), to the tune "Guided by the Priest's Chariot" ("Fajia daoyin" 法駕導引). At least five of the six song-lyrics link the divination ceremony to sensual pleasure, with flocks of female immortals floating in and out, presenting music and food delicacies. This sort of entertainment more or less resembles that offered by courtesans who are often compared to Daoist priestesses or immortal women. Even the song-lyric is a genre mostly for pleasure rather than ritual ceremony. Therefore, Xue seems to taunt Shoupeng's *fuluan* divination as if he were seeking illicit joy.

Of the six songs only the fifth, which alludes to a famous honey locust growing in the Zhang family garden, is closely related to the civil examination. The number of the tree's pods in an examination year predicted the number of degree winners among the Zhangs.[14] The poem begins with a seemingly unrelated metaphor:

An otter on a plate,	盤中獺,
An otter on a plate,	盤中獺,
The honey locust grows into clouds.	皂莢上雲霄。
A whip awakens patterned dragons to line up as honor guards;	鞭醒斑龍排綵仗,
In the Flower Pearl Palace he listens to a flute playing.	蕊珠宮裏聽吹簫,
On light silk, he writes the *Tang Rhymes*.[15]	唐韻寫輕綃。

"An otter on a plate," according to the *Biographies of Immortals* (*Shenxian zhuan*; attributed to Ge Hong [ca. 284–ca. 363]), alludes to a hilarious rivalry between a couple, in which the wife, Lady Fan, always gets the upper hand over her husband, Liu Gang:

> There were two peach trees growing in their courtyard. The husband and wife each placed a spell on one and made the two trees fight with each other. After they fought for quite a long time, Liu Gang's tree was defeated and quickly escaped through the fence. Liu Gang then spat into a plate, and the saliva transformed into a tilapia fish. Lady Fan also spat into a plate and her saliva transformed into an otter. The otter then ate the fish.[16]

庭中兩株桃，夫妻各咒一株, 使之相鬥擊, 良久, 綱所咒者不勝, 數走出於籬外。綱唾盤中, 即成鯽魚, 夫人唾盤中, 成獺, 食其魚。

Although naturally wishing that Shoupeng would be successful in the civil examination, Xue seems to imply that, should she be allowed to enter the same competition, she might easily triumph over her male rivals and add a pod to the honey locust in the Chen Garden. The last three lines of the song-lyric support this reading. Xue depicts an imperial audience for the successful candidates, at which Shoupeng enjoys royal musicians and composes poems after the *Tang Rhymes* (*Tangyun*). Yet the *Tang Rhymes* may also refer to a masterpiece of calligraphy written by the Tang Daoist priestess Wu Cailuan (fl. 823–25).[17] So the successful candidate "writing the *Tang Rhymes*" could be a "she."

A competitive spirit, intellectual curiosity, and her affection for Shoupeng also motivated Xue to assimilate the knowledge Shoupeng gained at the naval academy. Inspired by Shoupeng's specialty in navigation, for instance, Xue composed in 1885 a song-lyric titled "Inscribed on a Painting of a Right-turning Conch Shell" ("Ti *You xuanluo tu*" 題右旋螺圖), to the tune "Ballad of a Noisy Dragon" ("Gualong yao" 聒龍謠). This shell, according to Liang Zhangju's account, was originally presented by Tibetan lamas to Emperor Qianlong as a divine device for ensuring the 1800 mission to the Ryukyus a safe voyage. After the mission, the shell was left in the Fujian Treasury for future use, since Fuzhou was the port from which missions of this sort embarked.[18] Zhao Xin (1802–76), Liang Zhangju's son-in-law and a native of the Minxian district of Fuzhou, led the last Chinese diplomatic mission to the Ryukyus in 1866, before the islands were surrendered to Japan in 1874.[19] Greatly impressed by its wondrous effect, as Xue introduces in her preface to this song-lyric, Zhao had the shell painted. Shoupeng then reproduced the painting on his silk round fan and asked

Xue to inscribe a poem on it. Xue's song-lyric locates the shell in an uncommonly broad context.

Its parrot beak merges with the ocean,	鸚嘴消沉,
Propelling ripples into patterns of partridge feathers,	鷓斑蕩漾,
While the water whirls into a right-turning female image.	繞出右旋坤象。
The precious shell radiates;	寶厴光騰。
A purple light in the shape of the palm of a hand	有紫紋如掌。
Pacifies the wind and the waves.	狎風濤,
The dragon flag flies,[20]	龍節飛揚;
Enabling the ship to sail	濟舟楫,
Through the vast turbulence created by the giant *kun* fish.	鯤身洪溁。
I can imagine the Zhongshan people	想中山,
Kowtowing to the envoy and singing greetings to His Majesty.	拜跪嵩呼。
In the celestial towers	蜃樓裏,
The dragon palace opens its doors.	蛟宮敞。

The first three lines suggest two related interpretations. On the one hand it looks as if Xue is imagining the movement of the right-turning shell in the ocean. On the other hand, it appears that she is talking about the operation of the counterclockwise propeller that is added to the original single-screw propeller to stabilize the ship through turbulence.[21] The "right-turning" shafts propel the ocean water into a natural *Kun* pattern that generates female power to subdue the wind-whipped waves and protect the ship through its voyage. With the help of this magic shell and efficient technology, Chinese envoys had been able to fulfill their missions to the Ryukyus and hence tied the tributary state to China.

Yet oceans have	奈滄海,
Suddenly changed into mulberry fields.	忽桑田。
They can no longer hear from their emperor,	竟天語無聞,
Nor appropriate the pure sound of the conch shell.	螺鳴清響。
Ascending Li'ce Peak,	峰登刕刜上,
I am full of sorrow and disappointment.	一腔悲悵。
Although the Snail Girl River remains the same,	縱江水螺女依然,
Is her hairdo on the Ryukyus still in order?	豈島邦螺鬟無恙?
Only the painting is left,	剩圖畫,
Copied onto silk,	寫入羅紈,
For our pure appreciation.	供人清賞。

[Our Drum Mountain has Ce'li Peak, from which we can see the Ryukyu Islands. Now the islands have been surrendered to Japan!][22]	[吾閩鼓山有屴崱峰，能望見琉球。今琉球已歸日本矣!]

The surrender of the Ryukyus to Japan has severed their comfortable ties with China, leaving the people isolated. It has also caused the Snail Girl, a Fuzhou water deity who protects ships in the area, to lose her beautiful hairdo.[23] Women, Xue seems to be saying, have nurtured and protected the world with their natural strength; yet they always suffer the most from political disputes. Xue ends her lyric with a nostalgic lament over the conch shell that now has been retired into a painting. Neither a magic treasure nor a navigation device can save the dire situation. This song-lyric also offers an early example of Xue's capacity to weave a variety of discursive systems—historical, cultural, technological—into a poetic body that shows her concern for the destiny of China.

Backed up by a marital relationship built upon intellectual equality, Xue demanded absolute loyalty from Shoupeng. In a poem sent to Shoupeng while he was studying in Europe from 1886 to 1889, Xue implored him:

Do not change because of the changing environment;	莫以見異遷，
Keep on with what is difficult, and never give up.	黽勉為其難。
. . .	. . .
Pines and cypresses have their inborn nature,	松柏有本性，
Standing firmly, against the cold of winter.	巍然淩歲寒。

After citing several famous intellectual couples who lived as recluses, taking pleasure in farming, Xue concludes that they were happy because "they were soul mates, sharing one mind" (同心是知己).[24] She hopes that Shoupeng, too, will share one mind with her.

Returning from Europe, Shoupeng for a while indulged in drinking parties. After several failed admonitions, Xue turned to another tactic. She "composed drama-lyrics, set them to Kunqu opera music, and taught the maids to sing," and she herself "either played the flute or clappers to adjust the rhythm." Whenever Shoupeng wanted to go out drinking with friends, Xue would keep him at home by setting up a banquet accompanied by a singing performance.[25] This family story mimics a *Shishuo* "Xianyuan" episode concerning Lady Liu, who forbade her husband, Xie An, from dallying with female entertainers and was therefore famously recorded in the *Records of Jealous Women* (*Duji*), a work contemporary with the *Shishuo*.[26]

The *Shishuo* author nonetheless listed her among the independent, strong-minded, virtuous, and talented Wei-Jin *xianyuan*. Judging from various *Shishuo* episodes, this sort of "jealousy" usually arises from a woman's self-esteem—she sincerely loves her husband and expects his affection in return.[27] Xue's emulation of Lady Liu manifests her grasp of the *xianyuan* spirit as a whole, from intellectual capacity and moral integrity to personal dignity.

With an intellectual confidence nurtured by the Min writing-women culture, Xue increasingly demanded gender equality as her knowledge grew along with her expanding contact with the outside world. Shoupeng, for his part, responded with passion and understanding. He would later fondly recall the couple's numerous scholarly and literary collaborations, always acknowledging Xue's superiority. In these collaborations, the couple never hesitated to voice their cultural, social, and political differences. Close examination of their "public" arguments—rare between a husband and his wife in conventional Chinese society—and society's tolerance of their quarrels reveals changing gender relationships in the late Qing reform era (see especially Chapters Five through Seven).

Xue's early cultural upbringing continued the Min writing-women tradition. Her marriage to a Fuzhou Naval Academy graduate of her own free will and out of mutual admiration enhanced Xue's intellectual strength. Circumstances of this sort, together with broader opportunities for knowledge acquisition and social participation, effected a substantial change in the Min writing-women culture.

Xue's Exposure to the West

When, in the late spring of 1883, Shoupeng first embarked on his journey seeking knowledge abroad, Xue was barely seventeen, three years into her marriage and one hundred days after the birth of her first son. At this normally happy time for a young wife, the husband suddenly decided to go to Japan. Xue asked:

I hear that in the area of Yingzhou,	我聞瀛州地，
Weak water cannot float grass roots.	弱水無浮根。
Immortals have long disappeared;	神仙久不作，
Tattooed faces swallow each other.	雕題相並吞。
. . .	. . .
The elixir is no longer effective;	已乏藥餌靈，
And where would one find old classics?[28]	安有典墳存？

In early 1886, Shoupeng went to Europe. Xue again questioned what such a "primitive" place—where "people have different customs, and their language and writing are not ours" (習俗與世異, 文翰非吾阿)—could offer.[29] Although the Opium Wars had shattered the long-standing myth that China was the center of all under heaven, forcing the Chinese elite to contend with this reality, Xue, like many other scholars, continued to refer to Europe and Europeans in derogatory terms traditionally used for barbaric places and peoples.

Xue's disdain for the West was soon offset by the enticing gifts that Shoupeng sent back, each of which came with detailed introductions to their cultural and historical origins and backgrounds. Imbued with rich feelings and meaning conveyed by Shoupeng, these Western things spoke to Xue and inspired her to poetic creation. This new knowledge together with her newly acquired poetic technique of the song-lyric offered Xue a medium to express her lonely, vulnerable mood, her longing for Shoupeng, and her curiosity about the places he visited. These song-lyrics, composed between 1886 and 1889, include "To Master Yiru for the Buddhist Sutras Written on Palm Leaves Sent Back from Ceylon" ("Yiru fuzi you Xilan ji beiye Fanzi fojing tianci queji" 繹如夫子由錫蘭寄貝葉梵字佛經填此却寄), to the tune "Surrounding a Buddhist Pavilion" ("Rao foge" 繞佛閣); "To Yiru for the Rubbings of the Ancient Egyptian Stone Carvings He Sent Back" ("Yiru you ji Aiji gubei taben shuzhong yongti yiji" 繹如又寄埃及古碑搨本數種用題以寄), to the tune "Solemnly Protecting the Sand" ("Mu husha" 穆護砂);[30] "Yiru Sent Me Several Pieces of Jewelry" ("Yiru ji zhenshi shushi" 繹如寄珍飾數事), to the tune "Eight-Gem Jewelry" ("Babao zhuang" 八寶妝); and so forth. These song-lyrics suggest that Xue rapidly learned about the world. She follows Shoupeng's journey using accurate geographical names: "Your sails, blown by the Indian wind, / Must have crossed the Red Sea" (計天竺風帆, 遙過紅海).[31] No longer arrogantly dismissing other civilizations, she admits her inability to decipher ancient Egyptian stone carvings: "Even if I were [as talented as the famous Song poetess] Li Qingzhao [1084–ca. 1155], / And you were good at archeology [like her husband Zhao Mingcheng], / How could we fully understand this lost learning?" (縱儂如清照, 君精金石, 絕學詎能諒?).[32]

Xue also expresses admiration for Western technology in a song-lyric on a gold watch. Shoupeng had the watch handmade in Switzerland with an inscription engraved on its back: "Round as a jade disc and solid as gold; thirty thousand miles, two share one mind" (圓如璧, 貞如金, 三萬里,

兩同心), which Shoupeng composed in clear response to Xue's aforementioned demand for his fidelity. In her song-lyric, Xue describes watchmaking in accurate terms but softens the hard core of mechanism with tender feelings.

See the watch hands turning round and round;	看團圞, 循環旋繞,
Like the water clock in the Yuan palace,	宛若元時宮漏。
Tenderly, it delivers a light tick-tock,	但脈脈, 聞聲輕扣,
Marking each brief moment.	瞬息能分時候,
Inside the axis	機軸中含,
Shines the splendor of metal.	精金外溢,
There is also an inscription	況有銘文籀。
Of classical elegance:	饒古雅。
"One heart, though ten thousand miles apart."	萬里同心,
Terse words of deep affection	語簡意深,
Keenly touch my innermost feelings.	感入肝腸彫鏤。
Now I know to cherish every minute.	今始知, 分陰可惜,
One brief moment divides dusk and day.	展轉已殊昏晝,
Embroidering with five stitch-patterns,	刺繡五紋,
Reading books at midnight,	攤書午夜,
Going in and out of the house, I treasure it in my sleeve.	出入皆怀袖。
I miss you but cannot see you;	奈愛而不見,
Each day feels three years long!	三秋一日遲逗!
Most annoying are its gold hands	最惱他, 金針作怪,
That run ceaselessly, never stopping.	只管紛紛馳驟。
They urge our years onward,	催送年華,
Thinning my waist,	教人清瘦,
And wrinkling my eyebrows.	添著眉痕皺。
I fear the loss of my youthful radiance:	恐韶光易逝,
My black hair cannot remain unchanged.[33]	不復青絲依舊。

To the tune "Twelve Double-hours" ("Shier shi" 十二時) to fit the pace of the watch, this lyric reveals Xue's bittersweet feelings. The Chinese inscription has sinicized and personalized this foreign contraption into a love token, certifying the husband's unswerving devotion, but it also unmistakably indicates his absence. The age-long poetic theme of parting is greatly intensified because of the use of a modern technique that measures precisely the longing for a loved one. The fine divisions of the watch slow down the flow of time, making the loneliness even harder to endure, while its rapid ticking alerts her to the quick fading of her youth and beauty.

More impressive is Xue's quick acquisition of Western political knowledge, as reflected in "Yiru Sent Me Several Pieces of Jewelry." Among this jewelry was a pair of diamond bracelets, originally a present to the Empress Eugénie, Napoléon III's consort, from the queen of Spain. Being overthrown by her people and replaced by a Prussian prince, she hoped to win the help of the French to recover her throne. Napoléon III and Eugénie thereupon initiated the Franco-Prussian War (in 1870). In a satirical tone, Xue "imagines from afar how the thin-waisted French empress, / Delicate arms adorned with this pair of bracelets" (遙思腰細闕氏, 飾臂輕盈), waved the French soldiers to the bloody battlefield. Xue continues in the second stanza:

Yet enemies were fierce,	無奈敵勢披猖,
And the [French] people were disheartened.	民心散潰,
With no intention to fight, they rebelled.	倒戈安事鏖戰?
Singing *La Marseillaise*,	唱麥兒,
Their sad songs rose in chorus everywhere.	悲歌四起。
To avoid the fire of hatred,	避刼火,
The empress covered her face with a black veil,	青紗蒙面。
And fled with empty hands.	祗空手逃亡,
She begged for her emerald headdress,	乞援翠翹,
With inlaid flowers, that were already scattered.	零落隨花鈿。
Only this pair of bracelets was left,	剩繞腕一雙,
Making us sigh at the change of the world.[34]	令人感歎, 滄桑變。

Xue transliterates the title of French revolutionary song *La Marseillaise* into Chinese as *Maier* 麥兒 (wheat), pointedly alluding to the song of *Maixiu* 麥秀 ("Wheat Sprouts"), which laments the fall of a dynasty.[35] Xue thus justifies rebellion against a corrupt sovereign as a patriotic campaign that dethroned Napoléon III and led to the establishment of the Third Republic on 4 September 1870. In 1887, as Xue records in her preface to this lyric, the French Parliament came to the following decision: "Now France, a democratic [*minzhu*] republic, has no need to preserve the former sovereign's belongings. They should be priced and sold, and the money should go to the national endowment." Shoupeng bought the bracelets for their reference to French history. Xue responded with this poetic account, which shows she understands Western democratic and legal systems, and, more importantly, that she understands the causes and significance of these systems on behalf of the French people.

Xue's enthusiasm for embracing foreign knowledge in Chinese poetic genres intensified after Shoupeng returned home in the summer of 1889.

Xue was impressed by the "six hundred Western language books" Shoupeng brought back—"all of foreign tongues, horizontal lines, and italic scripts" (盡鳩舌旁行斜籤).[36] Xue was equally taken with the Western techniques that Shoupeng acquired from these books for making ice cream and wine for the family. One song-lyric Xue composed, to the tune "Prelude of Plum Blossoms in a River Town" ("Jiangcheng meihua yin" 江城梅花引), records such an amusing moment, when Shoupeng "extracted the syrup of hundreds of flowers using the technique of chemistry":

Pure cups fermented exotic jade liquid,	清樽瓊液釀來奇。
Borrowed from one bookworm,	借書痴,
And sent to another.	送書痴,
Flower souls of all colors,	色色花魂,
Flow into crystal bottles;	分貯入瑤瓶。
Green and red, I cannot judge their qualities.	綠綠紅紅吾不解,
So I bid the maid	且呼婢,
To carry them in a basket	載筠籠,
And send them to you, my sister, for comment.	問阿姨。
Sis, sis, have no doubts!	阿姨阿姨幸莫疑。
Try to open the bottles	試啓時,
And pour the liquid into a jade goblet.	倒玉卮,
You'll get drunk, so go ahead with it!	醉也醉也沈醉去,
It will well attend you	自有扶持。
Drifting comfortably, into the sweet wonderland.	醉入甜鄉香國儘相宜。
Next morning, by the mirror, complete the lines from a dream	曉鏡倘賡新夢句,
Praising the virtue of wine.	頌酒德,
You female Liu Ling [the drunkard],	女劉伶,
Write a wonderful poem.[37]	絕妙詩。

Set to agile rhythms, this lyric expresses Xue's happy assimilation of foreign knowledge, which has become tangible with Shoupeng and his books now by her side, permeating her daily life and inspiring poetic lines that flow from her brush.

Of course, the West presented itself to China in a variety of ways—not only as the source of democracy, law, and all kinds of technologies and skills but also as an imperial power supported by mighty ships and deadly cannons. During the 1884 Sino-French War, the French navy invaded Mawei Harbor in the vicinity of Fuzhou. Many of Shoupeng's schoolmates were killed in action. In 1889, Shoupeng came back from Europe and went with his wife to mourn his fallen comrades. On their way they heard from the boatwoman a story unknown to the public: although the Mawei battle annihilated the Fujian fleet, the next morning the French navy encountered an ambush that seriously injured Admiral Courbet and forced the French to retreat. This ambush puzzled both the Chinese and the French governments. According to the boatwoman, the French navy was attacked by a group of local Fuzhou salt vendors and butchers. The ambushers themselves also died along with the French enemies. Who would mourn these common heroes? Xue immediately composed a song-lyric:

The vast, gloomy river and sky	莽莽江天,
Remind us of the day	憶當日,
Crocodiles invaded.	鱷魚深入。
In the wind and rain,	風雨裏,
With stars flying, thunder roaring,	星飛雷吼,
Ghosts and deities wailed.	鬼神號泣。
Monkeys, cranes, insects, and sands were washed away with the waves;	猿鶴蟲沙淘浪去,
Salt vendors and butchers swarmed like mosquitoes.	販鹽屠豕如蚊集。
Treading on night tides,	踏夜潮,
They beat their oars and emerged from mid currents[38]	擊楫出中流,
Intending to ambush the enemy.	思偷襲。
Creak, creak: the sound of oars	咿啞響,
In the damp of the fog and mist;	烟霧溼,
Cannonballs exploded,	匐訇起,
Dragons and snakes hid.	龍蛇蟄。
They laughed at those sons of barbarian rulers,	笑天驕種子,
Who could barely breathe.	僅餘呼吸。
Although they have flown away with waves and currents,	縱逐波濤流水逝,
They once subverted mighty troops like thunderclaps.	曾翻霹靂雄師戢。
Sunk into grass and swamps,	惜沉淪草澤,
These martyrs of the country.	國殤魂,
Who will collect their souls?[39]	誰搜輯?

Using the tune "The River Is Red" ("Manjiang hong" 滿江紅), the poet paid the highest homage to these commonfolk heroes. The redness of the river in the title reconstructs the battle scene. The tune also reminds us of the heroic name of the patriotic Song general Yue Fei (1103–42), to whom a well-known patriotic song was attributed, also to the tune "The River Is Red."

The 1894–95 Sino-Japanese War deeply affected Xue's family. On hearing about the Battle of Dadonggou (also known as the Battle of the Yalu) between the Imperial Japanese Navy and the Chinese Northern Fleet on 17 September 1894, which claimed half of the Chinese warships,[40] Xue composed a song-lyric, "Temple of Piled Emerald" ("Jicuisi" 集翠寺). The temple, located in Fuzhou, had a library, a "pure and quiet place" where Shoupeng used to gather with his navy friends. Many of these officers were killed in battle.

A lone tower,	一角孤亭,
Is floating among thick green clouds in the wilderness.	四野綠雲膩。
Its bell tolls heavily;	鐘聲墜,
Beacons are lit on mountain passes—signals of war.	關山烽燧,
How I wish to wipe away the tears of these loyal spirits![41]	欲搵忠魂淚。

In Xue's eyes, the temple tower looks just like a lone ship floating on the void Yellow Sea, where the battle took place. The temple bell tolls for the fallen. What could she do to comfort their spirits that weep for an endangered China and its people?

After losing the war, the Qing government relinquished Taiwan as compensation for Japan's "war losses." To resist the Japanese occupation, Chen Jitong attempted to establish the Republic of Taiwan in the spring of 1895, but he failed.[42] On his return to the mainland, Jitong composed his anguished "Mourning for Taiwan, Four Poems" ("Diao Taiwan silü" 吊臺灣四律). He criticizes the weak regime: "My heart is broken because the land is ceded for making peace with the enemy; / I sign because the door of China is opened to bow the bandits in" (傷心地竟和戎割, 太息門因揖盜開). He is frustrated with the Chinese elite, including himself, who are unable to protect the land and the people: "Our wonderful lakes and mountains are lost today. / Looking at my hometown from afar, my tears stream down" (絕好湖山今已矣, 故鄉遙望淚闌干).[43]

In Fuzhou, Xue and Shoupeng closely heeded the situation in Taiwan. Her song-lyric "Listening to Yiru on the Taiwan Incident" ("Wen Yiru hua Taiwan shi" 聞繹如話臺灣事), to the tune "In the Broad Space between the Sea and the Sky" ("Haitian kuochu" 海天濶處), was composed in response to Jitong's "Mourning for Taiwan." Comparing the abortive Republic of Taiwan to "a state on a locust branch, / which existed only in a scholar's brief dream" (槐柯邦國, 黃粱夢寐), Xue mourns for Jitong's futile effort to rescue Taiwan from Japan. Seeing that the collapsed national defense can no longer protect China from raging waves, Xue again searches for her own role: "Facing spring tides swelling at night, / I feel deeply ashamed before the Woman of Qishi, / Who worried about her people, for heaven's sake!" (對春潮夜漲, 深慚漆室, 為天憂杞).[44] Xue invokes the Woman of Lu from Qishi to supply, as Susan Mann puts it, "a justification for domestic womanly concerns with politics and government."[45] "When the kingdom of Lu faces disaster," the Woman of Qishi maintains, "Ruler and Minister, fathers and sons will all suffer disgrace. Misfortune will come upon the common people."[46] And the Woman of Qishi made this argument, Xue concludes, on behalf of heaven.

Xue had long expected to serve the country and its people. Early in 1886, Shoupeng sent back a photo from Europe, picturing him wearing a sword. Xue inscribed a song-lyric on it, comparing Shoupeng's patriotism to the shining splendor of the famous sword Ganjiang, and her own to that of Ganjiang's female match, Moye, who is also "eager to transform into a dragon" (*hualong yongyue* 化龍踴躍).[47] Xue's heroic aspiration did not, however, have a clear direction until she began expanding her contact with the world. Her early exposure to foreign knowledge, which brought with it mixed messages, prepared her for participation in the 1898 reform movement by encouraging her to ponder the role of foreign knowledge in women's lives and in China's future.

Chen Jitong's Private Life and the Marriage of the Two Cultures

The union of the Min writing-women and Fuzhou Navy Yard cultures influenced the entire Chen household. One reflection of this can be found in a poem Jitong wrote in 1896, titled "Shi'er" 施兒 (Godsend son), the milk name of his son Chen Chengfu (b. 1890):

Shi'er, though only six years old, knows how to read maps	施兒七歲解輿圖,
Pointing to Qianyang, he inquires about his Dad.	常指黔陽把我呼,
Of music tones, he can differentiate *jiao* from *zhi*;	音樂已知分角徵,
In reading classics, he knows more words than *zhi* and *wu*.	詩書何止識之無?
He translates his mother's foreign tongue into Chinese;	舌能象譯繙阿母,
He writes to his old man, like painting crows on the paper.	手作鴉涂寄老夫。
My family is already full of female *jinshi* scholars.	進士吾家多不櫛,
Who could expect our breed to go down through foreigners?[48]	何期人種又傳胡。

Jitong is proud of this family of talented women. In addition to Xue, Lady Ye, wife of the eldest brother Chen Botao (*zi* Youru, 1837?–99), "was knowledgeable about the *Book of Documents* and the *Records of Ritual*."[49] Jitong's French wife, Maria-Adèle Lardanchet, was "a graduate from a French girls' school,"[50] and his other French wife, known by her Chinese name Dishuang Feiren (Fanny Duchamp?), was said to be a "broadly learned woman scholar."[51]

These Chinese and Western sisters-in-law reared child prodigies, including some transracial ones, through a joint effort, often in the absence of their husbands. Jitong took his two French wives and their three children back to Fuzhou in mid-June 1891, where he was immediately arrested and jailed in Tianjin because of a complex power struggle. As a prominent diplomat, Jitong had enjoyed Li Hongzhang's trust. His close ties with this most powerful Chinese statesman of the time complicated his relationship with his colleagues in the Chinese legations in Europe. Some of them, Ambassador Xue Fucheng (1838–94) in particular, were in political conflict with Li Hongzhang. After hearing that Jitong owed some personal debts to European banks, 130,000 francs in total, Xue Fucheng turned this private matter into a diplomatic scandal. He sent Jitong back to China, and at his behest Jitong was arrested by the Office of Foreign Affairs (Zongli yamen). After the Chen clan sold their properties and paid off the debts in July 1892, Jitong's name was cleared and his official rank restored, thanks greatly to Li Hongzhang's help. But his diplomatic career was ended.[52]

Throughout Jitong's imprisonment, Shoupeng traveled frequently between Fuzhou and Tianjin, hoping to secure his release. In 1893, the two brothers were assigned to inspect the Yongding River in Beijing. After Shoupeng returned home in July 1894, Jitong stayed in Tianjin, working under Li Hongzhang, and was soon involved in the Sino-Japanese War and its aftermath. Jitong's wives and children lived in Fuzhou with his extended family from 1891 until Jitong moved them to Shanghai after he failed to establish the Republic of Taiwan in the summer of 1895. During these crucial years of the growth of the Chen children, the responsibility for their education naturally fell to the Chinese and French sisters-in-law.

This all-female faculty provided their students with rigorous yet comfortable family schooling. Chen Chao (*zi* Banxian, b. 1885?), one of Jitong and Maria-Adèle's two daughters, recounted how she was inspired to work hard in the family study, where "everyone was concentrated on reading and writing."[53] Chen Yun remembered a happy girlhood, when even the games they played together were infused with "poetic moods" (*shiqing*).[54] These learned

Table 3.1. Chen-Xue Family Trees

m = marriage; writing women in boldface

			Xue Shangzhong 薛尚忠 (d. 1877) / m. Lady Shao 邵 (d. 1874)	Liu Shaogang 劉紹綱 (zi Yuntu 雲圖) Chens' maternal uncle

Chen Xi 陳錫 / m. Lady Liu 劉	Liu Xiang 劉驤 (zi Zanxuan 贊軒, 1836–1904, jr.) (1864) Chens' maternal uncle

Chen Botao 陳伯鞱 (zi Youru 友如, 1837?–99?) m. Lady Ye 葉 (d. 1896)	Chen Zhongchi 陳仲箎	Chen Jitong 陳季同 (zi Jingru 敬如 or 鏡如, 1852–1907) m. Lady Liu 劉 (d. 1888)	Chen Jitong m. Maria-Adèle Lardanchet (Lai Mayi 賴媽懿)	Chen Jitong m. Fanny Duchamp? (Dishuang Feiren 的霜妃人)	The two Li sisters as Chen Jitong's concubines	Chen Shoupeng 陳壽彭 (zi Yiru 繹如 or 逸如, 1857–1928?, jr. 1902)	Xue Shaohui 薛紹徽 (zi Xiuyu 秀玉, Nansi 男姒, 1866–1911)	Xue Shenhui 薛慎徽 (d. 1876) m. Song Weiyi 宋未為儀 (jr. 1889)	Xue Sihui 薛姒徽 (zi Yingyu 英玉, 1859–?) m. Chen Jixian 陳集賢	Xue Yukun 薛裕昆 (1863–?) m. Chen Lei 陳蕾 m. Chen Rong 陳蓉

m.

Chen Lei 陳蕾 (d. 1889) m. Xue Yukun	Chen Rong 陳蓉 (d. 1901) m. Xue Yukun	5 sons, 1st son Chen Chengjun 陳承俊 (zi Yi'an 毅安, 1870–1916) m. née Sa 薩 (1874–1933)	5th son Chen Chengfen 陳承汾 (b. 1886?) Adopted by Jitong	Chen Qian 陳騫 (zi Chaxian 槎仙, b. 1884?)	Chen Chao 陳超 (zi Banxian 班仙, b. 1885?) m. Lin Daren (zi Bingnan 丙南, b. 1880, jr. 1902)	Chen Chengzhang 陳承頊 1907 to younger Li	Chen Chengfu 陳承孚 (Shi'er 施兒 1890–1917)	Chen Keng 陳鏗 (1883–95)	Chen Yun 陳芸 (zi Yunxian 芸仙, 1885–1911)	Chen Qiang 陳鏘 (b. 1890)	Chen Hong 陳鉷 (b. 1892)	Chen Jin 陳鋘 (1898–98)	Chen Ying 陳鎣 (b. 1899)

Chen Shibin 陳詩彬 (1892–1917) m. Huang Deying 黃德英 (1893–1952)	Chen Shijia 陳詩佳 (1913–34)	Chen Shidai 陳詩代 (1914–97) m. Ye Zhenmin 葉振民 (b. 1920)

7 sons and 3 daughters; eldest and youngest daughters **Chen Shuping** 陳書萍 and **Chen Shujing** 陳書菁

MAJOR SOURCES: Chen Qiang et al., "Xianbi Xue gongren nianpu"; letters from Chen Shuping to Nanxiu Qian; Nanxiu Qian, "Qianyan" 前言 (Foreword) to Chen Jitong, Xue Jia yin; Gu Tinglong, ed., Qingdai zhujuan jicheng, "Lin Daren," vol. 340, 83–96; Liu Rongping, "Juhongxie changhe kaolun."

mothers transmitted up-to-date Chinese and Western knowledge to their children. Almost every Chen child benefited from this pedagogical diversity (except for Lady Ye's two much older daughters, Lei [d. 1889] and Rong, who only had traditional Chinese learning). Aside from his precocious son Shi'er, born to Feiren, Jitong's two daughters born to Maria-Adèle, Qian (*zi* Chaxian, b. 1884?) and Chao, knew both Chinese and French and later published poems and essays in the earliest Chinese women's journals. Xue and Shoupeng had two daughters and three sons. Their eldest son, Chen Keng (1883–95), set a good model for his younger siblings in mastering both Chinese and Western knowledge. Their eldest daughter, Chen Yun, as we have seen, assisted her mother's research and writing in addition to composing poems herself (see Table 3.1).[55]

This Chinese-Western sisterhood benefited both the children and the mothers, whose mutual understanding would prepare them for future cooperation in the 1898 reforms, in which both Maria-Adèle and Xue played leading roles in designing curricula for the newly established Shanghai Girls' School, which combined Chinese and Western traditions. The Chen household evidenced the strength of the union of the two cultures: it continued the Min writing-women's literary accomplishments and mothers' teaching on the one hand and incorporated new knowledge into their curriculum via two naval academy fathers and two Western mothers on the other.

Jitong's transracial marriages, however, stirred up speculation that reflected the gender and cultural clashes of the time. In Europe, Jitong's private life created such a sensation that the French scholar Edmund Plauchut could not resist including gossip in his otherwise serious introduction to Jitong's book, *The Chinese Painted by Themselves*. In discussing the author's cultural background, he noted that Jitong had lived for a long time in France and had "married a French lady," but, he added, "rumour says he already had a wife in China."[56] In China, Jitong was celebrated in some circles as a vanguard who improved the Chinese race by marrying Western women. The revolutionary reformer Tang Caichang (1867–1900) commented, for example: "Chen Jitong's wives are both Western women. If Westerners do not consider China's weakness as an excuse for excluding the Chinese from matrimony with them, what is the point of us fighting and slandering the idea of transracial marriage?"[57]

Zeng Pu's novel *Flowers in a Sea of Retribution* (*Niehai hua*) would later provide the most spectacular elaboration of Jitong's triangular marriage-knot, engaging his French wife and "English mistress" in a dramatic duel for Jitong's love. The two ladies, the narrative goes, had never met until sometime in 1895 in Shanghai, when the wife caught Chen Jidong (Jitong's pseudonym) and his mistress at their secret love nest.

> The French wife solemnly declared: "Now let me tell you: My name is Florence, a French woman. The Chen Jidong you love is my husband, and I, too, love him. So we two love the same man. If you were a Chinese person, never serious about yourself, I might forgive you. Unfortunately, though, you are an Englishwoman. You and I are equally under the protection of law and human rights. I have no way to deprive you of your feelings. Yet in the world of love, one of us is an extra, and the only solution is to eliminate this extra." Saying this, the French wife took two shiny Browning pistols. She picked up one, leaving the other on the table and pushing it toward Margarita [the English mistress]. Softly she said: "Let the pistol decide who should stay in love with Jidong!"[58]

Historical records, however, offer no solid evidence that such a confrontation ever took place. According to Jitong's descendants, their two "French great-grandmothers" and their two daughters and one son arrived at Fuzhou with Jitong in the summer of 1891—"they wore Chinese clothes and could speak Chinese, and they were very nice to people."[59] A letter Robert Hart (1835–1911) wrote on 27 June 1891 tells a similar story about Jitong's return to China:

> The "General" (Tcheng) from Paris arrived at FuChow with *a French wife and a sister-in-law*; they reached the Pagoda Anchorage in dashing French costume—then went below for an hour and reappeared in quiet Chinese style. After calling on the Viceroy, the "Genl." was arrested and is now in prison in the Nieh-tai's Yamen—so much for "a good time" in Europe![60]

Hart's account corresponds with the Chen family recollection in at least three respects: First, two French women accompanied Jitong home, one his French wife and the other very likely Feiren. Feiren was referred to as a "sister-in-law" either because Maria-Adèle passed her off as a sister, or because Hart meant to imply the existence of a concubine while avoiding this sensitive term. Second, the two wives willingly adapted to a Chinese lifestyle as soon as they arrived in the land, showing their love and devotion to Jitong. Third, Jitong was arrested right after his arrival at Fuzhou, leaving his wives and children in the care of his extended family. These two records paint a picture of a harmonious life between the two French women and their Chinese relatives.

The French journalist Amédée Baillot de Guerville's memoir also attests to the two French wives' attachment to Jitong. He encountered Jitong in Tianjin when Jitong was supposed to be in prison, yet he was instead passing his days in "the comfortable and luxurious home of his friend the naval minister," and "in the company of a little lady who had followed him all the way from Paris." This Parisian lady must be Feiren, not Maria-Adèle, for de Guerville clarifies that Jitong's "legitimate [French] wife, with all the dignity and devotion afforded a good cause, had shown up in Tientsin [Tianjin] . . . and had beseeched the Chinese authorities to allow her to share her husband's fate. The authorities told her such a thing was impossible."[61]

What made the two French women so devoted to Jitong? I believe the two sincerely loved Jitong for his personality and talent. Roman Rolland revealed how Jitong enchanted his Sorbonne audience. Robert Harborough Sherard (1861–1943), who translated Jitong's *Les plaisirs en Chine* into *Bits of China* and "conceived much regard for the kindness and cleverness of the man," also fondly remembered an impressive Jitong:

> Tcheng-Ki-Tong was a Parisianized Oriental of a very peculiar type. He was a man of literary tastes, and contributed largely on Chinese subjects to the leading French papers. He was the author of a number of books on Chinese questions. At the same time he was ardently attached to the pleasures of the capital. It was said of him, after his disgrace, that tucking up his pig-tail under his hat, and in European costume, he used to attend the public halls and dance as wildly the cancan as any Valentin-le-Désossé of them all.[62]

Young, handsome, and famous, Jitong would naturally attract the attention of women. Zeng Pu's fictional depiction of Jidong (that is, Jitong) rings true: A proud and untrammeled genius, Jitong was a master of all Chinese poetic genres but his French writings were even better. His fictions and dramas were so popular in Europe that he astonished French literary societies—they never imagined that China could have such a talent. Fashionable girls followed him everywhere, like "bees and butterflies around a flower" (*fengwei dierao*).[63] Whereas Maria-Adèle had devoted herself to Jitong in the early 1880s before his star had risen, Feiren must have been among the star-struck "bees and butterflies" of the late 1880s. What followed, one imagines, was Feiren's pregnancy, which posed a real problem for Jitong and Maria-Adèle.

Jitong discussed Chinese concubinage in several of his books, "trying to excuse this custom rather than defend it."[64] He argues that concubinage was founded on the Confucian social obligation of filial piety (*xiao*), "in order that the husband may have children to honour their ancestors." Therefore, in China, the children born to concubines have "the same rights as the legitimate children." Westerners regard concubinage as indelicate, yet in Jitong's view, "under the cloak of delicacy much greater crimes are committed when children born of illicit unions are thrown upon the world with an ineffaceable stain upon their condition, and find themselves with neither resources nor family." Jitong considers "these evils graver than the brutality of concubinage."[65] Fear of this "graver evil" and desire for continuing the family honor may have persuaded Maria-Adèle to accept Feiren and her future child.

Xue's account of Jitong's marital life may support the above speculation. She wrote in her "Call for Poetic Contributions in Celebration of the Fiftieth Birthday of Our Lord Brother Jingru [Jitong's *zi*]" ("Jingru xionggong wushi shouchen zhengshi qi" 敬如兄公五十壽辰徵詩啓):

Munching on snow in the severe winter with his foreign wife,	朔雪偕胡婦並嚙,
He cherishes solitary loyalty [to the Han] like Su Wu;	自成蘇武孤忠;
Rushing to bring a nomadic maid back riding on one saddle,	累騎追蠻婢同歸,
He appears more unrestrained than Ruan Xian.[66]	益見阮咸曠達.

The Han envoy Su Wu (140–60 BCE) was kept in Xiongnu territory for nineteen years. He refused to serve the khan and eventually returned home with dignity. In all those years, his Xiongnu wife (Su Wu had a Chinese wife back home) endured enormous hardship with him.[67] Similarly, Xue praises Maria-Adèle for her support of Jitong during his time abroad, which assured the success of Jitong's diplomatic mission. The Wei gentleman Ruan Xian (fl. mid-third century) was one of the free-spirited Seven Worthies of the Bamboo Grove. He fell in love with his aunt's Xianbei nomadic maid. When the aunt moved away with the pregnant maid, Ruan Xian rushed to bring the girl back, saying, "I cannot let go the origin of our offspring!" (*Shishuo*, 23/15). This couplet translates Xue's conscious concern about the delicate situation of her two French sisters-in-law in a transnational society. That Xue had to defend Jitong's polygamy in a time when polygamy was still common in China betrays her dilemma: she disapproves of concubinage either in line with the *xianyuan* spirit or Western conjugal law, yet she also understands the special circumstances surrounding Jitong and his family.

To be sure, Xue was not uncritical of Jitong's marital status. Jitong wedded his first wife, Lady Liu, in 1871 and left her in 1875 for his sixteen-year career abroad, with only two brief visits home in 1876 and 1883. Alone and childless, Lady Liu died of a "sudden disease" (*baobing*) at her natal home in 1888, when Jitong already had two daughters with Maria-Adèle in Paris. Lady Liu's death led her natal family to speculate. Xue had to deal with the situation alone as Shoupeng was also away in Europe. Although she managed to "restore the good relationship" with the Lius,[68] she must have been startled by Lady Liu's tragic destiny and sent Shoupeng the poem demanding his absolute loyalty around this time.

As for Jitong's own view on his life, *Chanting after Jia* [*Yi*] (*Xue Jia yin*), his only collection of Chinese poetry I have discovered so far, may reveal some of his inner feelings. Its 354 poems were mostly composed in the latter half of 1896 on a business trip to Hunan and Guizhou. Traveling alone, Jitong was able to ponder on his life. One poem records his encounter with a wedding procession that reminded him of his first marriage:

Twenty-five years ago, I also went to meet my bride;	廿五年前親迎日,
My blue sedan chair accompanied her colorful palanquin.	藍輿曾挾彩輿行。
That lovely person has long returned to the yellow earth;	佳人久已歸黃土,
This sight strikes a chord with me, how can I not feel sad?[69]	觸景如何不動情？

Moved by Jitong's regret, Xue wrote in her "Call for Poetic Contributions": "Grieving for the departed, he still has strong feelings for his first wife" (傷逝為文, 尚感糟糠之舊).[70]

Jitong's relationship with Maria-Adèle began in 1883 at the latest, when a romantic French girl student fell in love with a young, handsome Chinese diplomat who had just started his self-imposed mission of introducing Chinese culture to a Western audience. For Jitong, he must have found in Maria-Adèle an elegance and refinement similar to that of his hometown writing women—except that this one spoke and wrote in French—a person who could comfort his homesickness and assist him with his French writing.[71] Their union soon brought forth a book, *Les Chinois peints par eux-mêmes*, and two daughters, but they were not officially married until 1890.[72] Jitong's poems to Maria-Adèle therefore convey some of his thoughts on the difficulties they had to deal with together. On his 1896 trip to Hunan and Guizhou, he writes to her: "Human life suddenly changes like autumn clouds; / My heart is an old well, how can it stir waves?" (人事秋雲驚變態, 儂心古井敢生波?). After their return to China, Jitong and his family endured hardship. Facing changing "autumn clouds," which usually symbolizes an unfathomable political situation, Jitong reassures his wife: "Autumn is getting old and yellow flowers near the end, / Usnea lichens tenderly attach to a scholar's home garden" (秋光已老黃花晚, 三徑依依有女蘿).[73] He will, from now on, act as a loving husband and father. Like an usnea lichen intertwining with the other plants in his garden, he will tenderly hold his family together and stay away from political chaos.[74]

Jitong's poems to Feiren read comparably playful. Two months into his 1896 trip was the Double-Seventh that celebrates the reunion of the Weaving Girl and the Herd Boy. Jitong wrote to Feiren: "Tonight you offer melons and fruit on the terrace; / How much ingenuity have you begged from heaven's granddaughter?" (樓頭今夜陳瓜果, 乞得天孫巧幾多?).[75] He seems more concerned about Feiren enjoying her life in China. As for his children, Jitong adored them, as shown in his delightful poem on Shi'er. He missed them so much on his trip that he dreamed of one daughter being sick: "Deeply concerned, I inquire about her ailment from the window; / Sitting up in bed, she asks for my care in a weak voice" (自牖含愁詳問疾, 支床低語喚憐儂).[76]

Overall, Jitong, his wives, and their children, merged their transnational family into the Chen clan and into Chinese society rather seamlessly. The Fuzhou Navy Yard made possible Jitong's close contact with Western cultures and peoples, and his broad, firsthand experience in the West contributed to his goal of making "all under heaven into one family." In a speech at the Ethnographic Congress in Paris, September 1889, Jitong declared:

> A wonderful assimilation of the peoples was now going on. The word "foreigner" was every day losing its value. It would soon have to be dropped out of the French dictionary. We were all melting into one great people, and would soon speak only of the East and of the West. At present America was an obstacle between the two, but what with river and lake steamers, railways and telegraphs, it was becoming rather a highway than a terminus.[77]

We can assume, then, that Jitong's experience in Europe, together with the successful trial of a new domestic order in the Chen household, inspired Xue to consider world harmony as an attainable goal for an ideal womanhood in the reform era.

Other Families of the Marriage between the Two Cultures

The joining of the two cultures helped refashion other members of Xue's intellectual networks—expanding knowledge, enabling equal gender relationships, and encouraging political participation. The families of Shen Yuqing and Chen Yan are particularly relevant examples. Although neither was a naval academy graduate, the two men and their families lived at the center of this culture. Shen Yuqing was the son of Shen Baozhen, and Chen Yan was a relative, a tutor, and a friend of the Shens.[78] Both had kept close associations in poetic correspondence and political cooperation with leading naval academy graduates such as the Chen brothers and Yan Fu. Their exposure to the navy yard culture assimilated its values into the Min writing-women culture, producing two outstanding members of new generations of talented Min women, Chen Yan's wife, Xiao Daoguan, and Shen Yuqing's daughter, Shen Queying. A look at their lives may shed more light on the effect of the "marriage" of the two cultures on women (see Table 3.2).

Like Xue Shaohui, Xiao Daoguan was a scholar and writer, "well versed in poetry, prose, and the song-lyric."[79] Her scholastic interests, which focused on history and "evidential learning" (*kaoju*), yielded a book titled *Collected Commentaries on the Biographies of Women* (*Lienü zhuan jizhu*) (10 *juan*). Also like Xue, Xiao Daoguan received support from a soul-mate husband. They often spent the night reading and chanting together and debating until dawn. Xiao recounts the joy of these occasions:

> Our intense conversations, though seemingly random, had interrelated themes. If we had one word of difference, we would argue in bed until the dispute was settled, yet we also took pleasure in the thoroughness and playfulness of debates. The room was facing toward the east. When the bright moon rose, it cast bamboo shadows on the window and printed them on our bed. We talked on the pillow until we saw the morning light penetrate the shade of the window and heard the temple bell tolling. Only then could we feel exhausted and fall asleep. We took this as a daily routine.[80]

劇談雜亂無次, 而自有蛛絲馬跡, 牽連其間, 一語齟齬, 繼之以爭, 倚枕斷斷不相下, 必論辯透徹, 芥蒂消釋而後止, 則又醋嬉淋漓以爲樂。室既東向, 而淺月出, 竹影婆娑, 從疏櫺中斜篩床上。並枕共語, 視窗紙白, 寺鐘鳴, 始倦極而寐, 率以爲常。

This sort of intellectual communication and spousal affection resulted in Xiao's abundant literary production.[81]

Table 3.2. Lin, Shen, and Chen Families' Intellectual Network

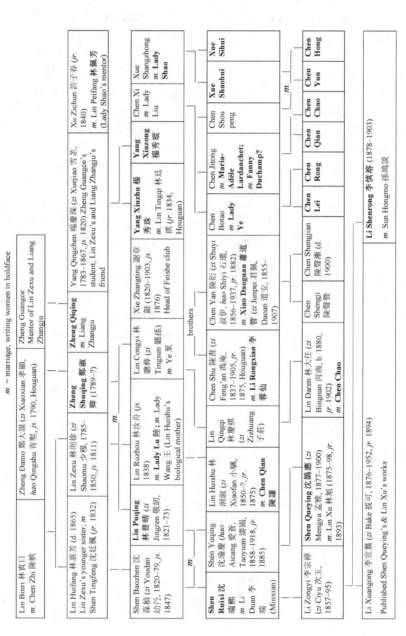

m. = marriage; writing women in boldface

MAJOR SOURCES: Ding Yun, *Minchuan guixiu shihua xubian*; Chen Yun, *Xiao daixuan lunshi shi*; Chen Yun, *Shiyishi shihua*; Chen Yan, *Min-Hou xian zhi*; Lin Ning, "Li Xuangong de jiashi yu shengping."

Contact with the navy yard culture expanded her interests to include newly imported foreign ideas and literature translated by family friends, such as Darwin's theory of evolution translated by Yan Fu and Western novels translated by Lin Shu.[82] Xiao broadened her knowledge even into the realm of modern science and technology. In 1887, Liu Mingchuan (1836–96), then newly assigned as the first governor of Taiwan, decided to build Taiwan's first railroad, from Keelung to Taipei. Chen Yan, who was on Liu's staff, engaged his wife to draft a sacrificial oration to the Mangkah River God on behalf of the governor, in order to obtain the god's approval for building a bridge across the river. At this time, railroads were still a new thing in China. The first railroad in China, the Woosung–Shanghai line, began service in July 1876 but was dismantled in October 1877—a consequence of resistance from both the elite and the general public.[83] Xiao, however, embraced the idea without reservation. She ardently implored the River God's help and blessing by presenting the project as an expression of the people's will for their welfare. She wrote:

> Alas you great river, stretching right in front of us with a gigantic flow of water. If there is not [a bridge like] a dragon lying on your waves, what can we depend on to cross the river? If there is not [a bridge like] a turtle, what can we ride to cross the river valley, and how can we join the railroads in the air? We spike the rails to the ties, so we establish our great deeds. We dig caves on stone cliffs, *chi chi*! We chop down woods, *zhen zhen*! Thousands of workers and handymen are waiting with shoves and baskets; we are ready to go![84]

嗟爾大河, 沛然前橫。臥波無龍, 涉川何憑? 駕鼇無鼇, 鑿空何能? 徒杠輿梁, 勖哉告成。鑿石齒齒, 伐木丁丁, 千夫萬徒, 畚臿待興。

Although only this one passage of the oration is extant today, it is sufficient to demonstrate Xiao's enthusiasm and heated rhetoric in representing people's wishes. The oration should also have included arguments on the scientific and technological basis and the economic functions of the railroad to be built, and it must have been well accepted by the River God, for this railroad indeed inaugurated Taiwan's modern transportation system.

Yet Western knowledge came with military aggression, which twice directly affected Xiao Daoguan's life. The first time was during the 1884 Sino-French War. Xiao left a firsthand memoir of this moment in modern Chinese history. In it, Xiao vents her anger at the rulers, both the Chinese and the French, for they together made the people suffer. On 23 August

1884, Xiao recalled, the Fuzhou people heard cannons firing and saw flames shooting up into the sky. Messengers were racing to report a victory by the Chinese navy. Not until dawn did people realize that, in actuality, the Chinese fleet had been annihilated:

> All the warships built by the director-general of the Navy Yard [Shen Baozhen] were wiped out. The commissioner from the court who came to oversee the campaign against the French fled into a village by Drum Mountain. The French warships occupied the harbor. There they fired at the Mawei Fort and the Fuzhou Shipyard after taking precise measurements, and debris was scattered in Fuzhou city. The big officials dared not stretch their necks out of their official residences. . . . People were all in a panic. Fearing for their lives, they hastened to flee.[85]

Xiao observes that China's defeat was caused not so much by its backwardness in modern science and technology—the Fuzhou fleet is also a modernized war machine—as by its incompetent governing. The Chinese regime was so incapable of protecting its territory and people that, after the Fuzhou fleet was eliminated during the day on 23 August 1884, "the local officials were still in their dreams" that night, literally and physically. By contrast, the French navy is menacing because it is efficiently commanded. For instance, its ships would accurately fire at targets after "taking precise measurements."

The more devastating blow for Xiao took place during the Eight-Power Allied Forces invasion in 1900. Xiao and Chen Yan's second son, Chen Shengjian (d. 1900), a student at the Northern Ports School (Beiyang xuetang) in Tianjin, was killed while trying to protect a friend's wife from a foreign soldier.[86] In his poem "Mourning My Son Jian" ("Ai Jian'er" 哀漸兒), the grief-stricken Chen Yan blamed his "stupid" child for trying to use his foreign language knowledge to persuade the soldier to leave:

On a gloomy day the devil looked into the house,	晦冥白日鬼瞰室,
A beautiful woman happened to peep out at the street.	況有粲者窺踦閭。
You were not a street policeman, carrying arrow and bow,	爾非道安弓箭徒,
How could you protect the women and children of others?	寧能爲人護孀孤?
You wrongly believed words could reason away barbarians;	謬思談笑卻羌胡,
How sad your life was thus annihilated in a second![87]	哀哉性命戕須臾。

His wife Xiao Daoguan's version of "Mourning My Son Jian" offers a far more philosophical explanation of this senseless death:

. . . Making human figures with yellow clay, child's play;	. . . 黃土搏人偶兒戲,
The whole universe is filled with a mixture of water and dirt.	調水和泥滿寰宇。
Once the pattern was established, no one could stop it;	成例既開遂莫禁。
The earth is full of people; who can control the process?	土滿人浮孰能禦?
Big famines, severe epidemics, floods and fires,	大荒大疫及水火,
May kill one out of ten thousand, too few to count!	萬不去一何足數。
But human beings can kill human beings,	唯有生人能殺人,
One kills ten thousand, swift as wind and rain.	以一殺萬疾風雨。
Only now do we believe weak ones cannot survive!	此時乃信弱者亡,
Fragile women and young boys, the fertilizer of wilderness.	脆女稚男膏野土。
There are no souls, so how could you know [my grief]?	本無魂魄又何知?
Myriad passes and mountains block even my dreams.[88]	萬里關山夢亦阻。

This tragic incident pushed Xiao to view Western ideas critically, in particular, the ideas of Herbert Spencer and Thomas H. Huxley concerning social Darwinism, a concept her family friend Yan Fu had recently introduced to Chinese audiences. The line "Only now do we believe weak ones cannot survive" undoubtedly refers to Spencer's axiom, "survival of the fittest." [89]

Billy K. L. So points out that Yan Fu twisted Thomas H. Huxley's original ideas in translating his *Evolution and Ethics* into Chinese as *Tianyan lun* 天演論.[90] Whereas Huxley stresses the importance of the ethical order of human society, Yan Fu, under the influence of Spencer, changes Huxley's theory into his own version of evolution, describing the process as "things struggle for existence, and heaven (*tian*) selects" (*wujing tianze*). Here *tian* is no longer the Confucian *tian* that rules all under heaven following moral principles, much less the Daoist *tian* that nurtures myriad things and encourages them to live in harmony. It is rather a Chinese rendering of the Western concept of a "cold and ruthless" nature, which inflicts the "law of the jungle" (*ruorou qiangshi*, literally, the strong eat the weak) on both the natural world and human society. Yan Fu's "fundamental paradigm shift" of *tian* encountered resistance from many Chinese intellectuals of the time.[91] Xiao, for one, argues in her heart-wrenching "Mourning My Son Jian" that it is not the will of heaven to kill the weak. Even natural disasters can destroy only a very few. By contrast, immoral, cruel humans, like the Western imperialists, can use the law of the jungle to justify their slaughter of people, and modern weaponry has greatly enhanced the efficiency of killing. While the husband focuses on the question of whether the son could have escaped death, the wife, with a mother's broader sensibility, discerns a pessimistic future for all humankind.

Sadness and hard work consumed Xiao's health and eventually caused her early death in 1907. Chen Yan compiled and published all of her works one year later.[92] Having indulged himself in such intellectual ecstasy, Chen Yan stayed loyal to Xiao's memory and never married again.[93] In a poem dedicated to Li Qingzhao, Chen Yan equated his late wife with the famous poetess—"Both joined their thousand lines of tears shed for their families and country / Into one inch of frowning between their eyebrows" (都將家國千行淚, 併入眉心一寸顰).[94]

Shen Queying appears in every respect to bear a close resemblance to her grandmother Lin Puqing. She was "brilliant as a little child."[95] Seeing her interest in poetry, her father, Shen Yuqing, put her and her husband, Lin Xu, under the tutorship of two leading Min poets, Chen Yan and his older brother Chen Shu (1837–1905),[96] and invited her to join their poetry club. In this club, Queying discussed poetry with her father, husband, and mentors on equal terms. This confident young girl even called the icons of her fellow Min male poets, such as Han Yu (768–824), Meng Jiao (751–814), and her father's favorite, Su Shi, "classmates," inviting their spiritual participation in their poetic gatherings.[97]

Queying made clear that she had endeavored in poetic learning not only to learn techniques but also to embrace "the grand ambition of a racing steed" (*qianli zhi* 千里志),[98] as she showed in her song-lyric on reading the Tang story, "The Man with the Curly Beard" ("Qiuranke zhuan" 虬髯客傳), to the tune "Lang tao sha" 浪淘沙 (Waves washing away sand):

Duke of Yue, self-indulgent and arrogant,	越國意揚揚,
Does not treasure the young woman.	不惜紅粧。
Making her flee in disguise deep in the night.	劇令深夜出嚴裝。
Staggering into the inn and knocking at the door	蹀躞叩門茅店裏,
She looks in a hurry and in panic.	顏色倉皇。
Her discerning eyes recognize the outstanding hero	慧眼識三郎,
As she combs her long, black hair that sweeps the ground.	委地青長。

The Man with the Curly Beard looks at her, fired by
    heroic ideas.

He bestows all the keys of his properties on this
    adopted sister,

Beseeching her to assist Prince Qin.[99]

虯髯顧盼思如狂，

鎖鑰儘教將一妹，

來佐秦王。

In the original story, the young woman, known as the Girl with the Red Whisk (Hongfu nü), was celebrated as having recognized a hero in her future husband, Li Jing (571–649), who would assist Prince Qin Li Shimin, the future Emperor Taizong of the Tang (r. 627–49), in founding the greatest dynasty in Chinese history.[100] In this sense, the Red-Whisk Girl used her good judgment—a *xianyuan* capacity—only to attain her position as the wife of a powerful man. Queying, however, subverted this conventional gender order, arguing that, actually, it was the Girl and the Man with the Curly Beard who recognized each other as heroes. Thus the Man, after realizing the limits of his capabilities, adopted the Girl as his sister and entrusted his wealth to her. With the Man's help, the Girl (not her husband) assisted Prince Qin to found the dynasty. This song-lyric sends a distinctive message of Queying's ambition to become a political player herself in China's reform era.

This ambition could have resulted from an inheritance of her grandmother's passion for China and its people. The changing world situation made Queying even more restless in the inner chamber. Her other song-lyric, "Reading *Biographies of Women*" ("Du *Lienü zhuan*" 讀列女傳), which she must have composed after Taiwan was ceded to Japan in the aftermath of the 1894–95 Sino-Japanese War, is loaded with her anxiety about facing growing foreign aggression. She laments the loss of China's territory and the consequent suffering of the Chinese people:

At dusk, in this humble boudoir
Dwells my slim, fragile body,
Guarding my integrity like a still well.
What I have seen startles my mind:
Pillars broken and rafters destroyed.
My fair appearance is pining away, but why care?
I can hardly pick up needles,
How many times I have stopped my embroidery!
Turning my head around, I sigh:
All that my sight touches
May no longer belong to our emperor.

薄晚寒閨，
輕盈弱質，
井水心情自守。
觸目驚心，
棟折榱崩，
何恤玉顏消瘦。
針管慵拈，
誤幾度、窗前停繡。
回首歎
周道遊觀，
將非君有。

Alas what do my maiden friends know?
They mistake my heroic feelings

嗟彼女伴何知，
把慷慨情懷

For tangled personal sentiments.	認縈絲藕。
All incidents have serious consequences.[101]	葵踐兄亡,
Calmly I can see during this past year,	冷眼年來,
The huge bow is hard to extend to its full length.	已知大弓難彀。
My sadness knows no bounds	無限傷心、
When hearing singing girls	當商女,
Playing decadent palace music.	後庭歌奏。
Can't we emulate	能否, 比例似、
The woman of Wuyan, who offers help to the ruler?[102]	無鹽覓偶。

This fragile girl looks out of the window from her inner chamber and finds that the sovereignty of Qing China is under threat. She seeks exemplars from Liu Xiang's *Lienü zhuan* to justify "domestic womanly concerns with politics and government."[103] One is the Woman of Qishi, whom Xue also invoked after the Taiwan incident. But Queying goes further: she wants to transform her concerns into action. Turning to the Woman of Wuyan, another *Lienü* exemplar, who proposed to be the queen of King Xuan of Qi so as to rectify his way of ruling, Queying shows her intent on fixing the failed Qing state.[104]

Scholars argue that Queying composed "Reading *Biographies of Women*" after the execution of her husband, Lin Xu, in the bloody termination of the Hundred Days.[105] Yet in this lyric Queying complains that her friends mistake her "heroic feelings" for the country as "tangled personal sentiments" for her husband, indicating that Lin Xu is still alive. Only in her last five song-lyrics, beginning with the one to the tune "Waves Washing away Sand" that unmistakably mourns Lin Xu's death, does her sorrow for the country and for Lin Xu stream into the same blood and tears.[106] Such a daughter would have added glory to the Min writing-women tradition with her independent thinking, passion, and poetic creativity, but her promising life was cut short, leaving only twenty-nine poems and thirty-five song-lyrics. Her pining away to death, although conforming to a seemingly late imperial woman-martyr model, goes beyond the realm of traditional virtuous women and bears the clear marks of the reform era, when a woman tied her personal life to the destiny of the country (see also Chapter Eight).

The marriage of the two cultures influenced several other families. Shi Yumin (fl. 1905–12), married to Ye Bojun, one of the first Fuzhou Naval Academy graduates, was also a cultural product of this alliance. Chen Yan recounts Shi was "by nature drawn to literature and history and broadly learned in historical anecdotes, Chinese and Western, past and present."[107] She served as the head of the Quanshan Girls' Professional School in Fuzhou after it was established by her younger brothers in 1905. During her seven-year tenure, the school graduated over three hundred girls.[108] In addition to her personal achievements, Shi Yumin made a contribution specifically to the Min writing-women culture. Two decades after Xue Shaohui proposed to honor Zhang Hongqiao in the Wanzaitang, Shi and her fellow faculty member Qiu Yunfang, also a Min woman poet, erected a shrine inside the Quanshan Girls' School to ten leading Min women poets, including Zhang Hongqiao, Xue Shaohui, Shen Queying, and probably also Xiao Daoguan.[109]

The marriage between the Min writing-women culture and Fuzhou Navy Yard culture nurtured new generations of talented and virtuous women, who updated the concept of writing women to fit the needs of the contemporary situation. A major contribution of this marriage was its exposure of the wider world to women. Naval academy graduates' unprecedented experience of learning and warfare, in Fuzhou and in Europe, within the classroom and aboard the warship, all involved their wives and other female family members. New knowledge transmitted to Min writing women challenged them to reconstruct their talent and virtue. These women would become a major force in the future reform movement.

In February 1897 Xue moved with Shoupeng and their children from Fuzhou to Shanghai. With this first trip away from her hometown, Xue began the most exciting period of her life. For the next fourteen years, she followed Shoupeng's constant career moves from one significant place to another—Ningbo (February 1898); Shanghai (early 1902); Fuzhou (August 1902); Nanjing (January 1905); Shanghai (September 1905); Guangzhou (November 1906); and Beijing (November 1907) (Map I.1).[110] During this period, Xue witnessed almost every important turn in late Qing history: the 1898 reform movement, the bloody termination of the Hundred Days, the 1900 Boxer Rebellion, and the New Policies inaugurated by the Qing court. These ongoing reforms provided Xue with a stage on which to apply her talent and in turn enabled her to cultivate a much broader knowledge base and vision. The rich cultural and historical resources of the places she traveled to inspired Xue into poetic pondering on past events and present problems.

PART TWO

Revitalizing the Xianyuan Tradition in the Late Qing Reform Era (1897–1911)

FOUR

The 1897–98 Shanghai Campaign for Women's Education

Enraged and demoralized by China's defeat in the Sino-Japanese War and by the humiliating "scramble for concessions" that followed, Chinese intellectuals initiated the reform movement of 1898—the first attempt in some two thousand years to transform China from a highly refined imperial system into a modern nation-state. One of the major 1898 themes was women's education. Previous studies have pointed out that for leading men reformers, such as Kang Youwei and Liang Qichao, "nationalism tended to be the primary concern, and women's issues tended to be subordinated to larger national issues. Few advocated the cause of women for its own sake."[1] Yet there were dissenting voices during the heyday of the 1898 reforms, primarily from women reformers, who gave priority to women's self-improvement over national empowerment, with their own agenda, agency, organizations, and specific strategies for achieving self-cultivation and national strengthening.[2]

These voices arose from the multifaceted 1898 Shanghai campaign for women's education. This campaign was spearheaded by the establishment of its headquarters, the Women's Study Society (Nü xuehui)—the first modern women's association in China—on 6 December 1897.[3] It published the first Chinese women's journal, the Chinese Girl's Progress (Nü xuebao), which lasted from 24 July to late October 1898.[4] It also opened the Chinese Girls' School (Nü xuetang), arguably the first Chinese school for young elite women, on 31 May 1898.[5] The campaign won support from both the local government and the intellectual elite, and it enlisted the participation of leading reformers, Chinese men and women, as well as Western diplomats, missionaries, journalists, and their wives.[6] In this environment, women engaged in open debates on reform, both with men and among themselves, self-identifying as *xianyuan*, or one of its several variants,[7] in a deliberate effort to counter the disparaging use of the term *cainü* by some male reformers.

The *xianyuan* tradition appealed to women reformers because it provided a time-honored and well-tested frame for fashioning themselves and transforming the world, both theoretically and experientially. Theoretically, as we have seen, *xianyuan* originated from the perfected-person metaphysic; the perfected person's androgynous, nurturing nature offered marginalized women equal access with men to meaningful transformative power in response to outside and inner changes. Experientially, women who embraced the *xianyuan* ideal had proven to be especially resourceful in nurturing culture and family, and in dealing with social crises, as shown in the Min writing-women tradition. The *xianyuan* model might not have been able to exhibit its full strength under the relatively stable sociopolitical circumstances during much of the late imperial era, when many hearts/minds followed rather narrowly defined "Confucian" patterns of thought and behavior. But in a rapidly changing period such as the late Qing reform era, when new sources of both information and inspiration animated hearts and minds, writing women of the time found that the idea of absorbing new knowledge from the West conformed fully and naturally to the perfected-person/*xianyuan* belief that spiritually inspired self-cultivation could help women to transform the world and themselves.

The Shanghai campaign for women's education was initiated by men reformers for their own political purposes but was quickly transformed by women into a female poetic enterprise. Women intended the campaign to promote their own cultural ambitions rather than assuage men's political humiliation. Reform-minded women expressed their own ideas of a new Chinese womanhood in the newly emerging news media, particularly the *Nü xuebao*. Among the most outspoken women reformers was Xue Shaohui. As the leading contributor to the *Nü xuebao*, Xue extensively discussed

women's emancipation in reform periodicals and often found herself in debate with leading men reformers.

Men's Politics and the Shanghai Campaign for Women's Education

In the fall of 1897, a talented group of reform-minded individuals in Shanghai organized a steering committee for establishing the first Chinese girls'
school. Headed by Jing Yuanshan, the committee also enlisted such influential individuals as Zheng Guanying, Liang Qichao, Chen Jitong, and
Kang Youwei's younger brother, Kang Guangren (1867–98), who served as
the project's financial executive. The plan was inspired primarily by Liang
Qichao's famous essay "On Education for Women" ("Lun nüxue"), first
published in the major reform periodical *Shiwu bao* in April 1897. In this
tract, Liang argued that "China's accumulated weakness has arisen, funda-
mentally, from the lack of education for women."[8] Although drawing on
Timothy Richard's 1893 essay "Productive and Non-Productive Methods"
("Shengli fenli zhi fa"), Liang twisted Richard's argument for making the
growth of national wealth keep pace with increasing population into a criticism of the "parasitic" status of Chinese women. Liang reasoned that the
foundation of a well-governed state consisted of citizens who could feed
themselves—the more jobholders, the richer the state. Western countries
were wealthy and powerful because they had strong educational systems
not only for men but also for women, which produced job opportunities
for both. China should therefore set up a similar educational system for
women in order for them to change their idle and useless ways and to feed
themselves. The eventual purpose was to protect the nation, the race, and
the "religion" (*baoguo, baozhong, baojiao*). ("Religion" refers to Confucianism; see discussion below.[9])

From the very beginning, then, men reformers and their Western allies
associated the idea of women's education in China with economic and
military power, hoping that one of the effects of promoting education for
women would be to restore China's pride. Feeling political urgency, the
steering committee called four meetings in the twenty days from 15 November to 6 December 1897. The first two meetings involved only men; the second two included primarily women. There were also two receptions hosted
by Western women in Shanghai to show support for their Chinese "sisters"
(see Table 4.1).

Table 4.1. Major Events Related to the Establishment of the Girls' School

Date	Events	Participants	Sources
15 Nov. 1897	First men's steering committee meeting	48 men, committee members and their Chinese and Western supporters	*Xinwen bao*, 18 Nov. 1897; Jing, ed., *Nüxue jiyi chubian*, 1a–3b.
16 Nov. 1897[a]	Mrs. Danwen's[b] tea party in honor of women's steering committee	Unclear	*Xinwen bao*, 26 Dec. 1897; Lin, "Zhuxing nüxue lun," 21b; rprt. Jing, ed., *Nüxue jiyi chubian*, 50b
21 Nov. 1897	Second men's steering committee meeting	7 committee members	*Xinwen bao*, 24 Nov. 1897; rprt. Jing, ed., *Nüxue jiyi chubian*, 6a–7a
30 Nov. 1897	Dinner party by the Spanish consul's wife for women's steering committee	About 40 women, half Chinese, half Westerners	Lin, "Zhuxing nüxue lun," 21a–22a; rprt. Jing, ed., *Nüxue jiyi chubian*, 50b–52a
1 Dec. 1897	First women's steering committee meeting	15 women committee members	*Xinwen bao*, 3 Dec. 1897; rprt. Jing, ed., *Nüxue jiyi chubian*, 8a–9a
6 Dec. 1897	First meeting of Nü xuehui (Women's Study Society)	110 Chinese and Western women, 12 Western men	*Xinwen bao*, 7, 9–12 Dec. 1897; rprt. Jing, ed., *Nüxue jiyi chubian*, 12a–18a

a. So dated by the sources given.
b. *Danwen* in Chinese transliteration; name in original language unknown. Wang Shuhuai, *Wairen yu Wuxu bianfa*, records a Mr. Danwen of the same Chinese transliteration, a British lawyer active in Shanghai at the time. Wang, however, did not provide Danwen's English name (44, 200).

The first men's steering committee meeting came up with the following plan of action:

- gain large-scale financial support through fund-raising;
- establish a solid financial footing;
- break ground for the school building within ten days (with a detailed budget for construction and maintenance);
- recruit only women for faculty and staff positions;
- hold a meeting of both Chinese and Western women for further deliberations within ten or fifteen days;
- seek the support and approval of local government;
- use the Girls' School to train more faculty, with the expectation that similar schools would be established across China within ten years.[10]

Throughout the process, the men reformers paid close attention to publicity, harnessing the emergent news media to bolster the campaign's influence.

Five journalists from Chinese and three from Western newspapers were invited to the first meeting on 15 November.[11] That same day, an "Announcement of Establishing the Girls' School" ("Changshe nü xuetang qi"), drafted by Liang Qichao, appeared in the *Shiwu bao*.[12] Three days later, this announcement also appeared in the *Xinwen bao* (News daily), a British-run Chinese newspaper, along with the "Provisional Regulations for the Girls' School" ("Nü xuetang shiban lüezhang").[13] From that point onward, every step the reformers would take was reported in newspapers and journals.[14] The steering committee constantly wrote memorandums and reports to the most powerful officials in government, including the superintendents of the North and the South Ports Li Hongzhang and Liu Kunyi (1830–1902) respectively; the head of government railways, Sheng Xuanhuai (1844–1916); and the provincial governors of Hubei, Hunan, Anhui, Zhejiang, and Jiangsu.[15]

In part because of the organizers' publicity, the campaign quickly gained support. Liu Kunyi warmly approved the establishment of the Girls' School.[16] By the end of 1897, about one hundred individuals had signed up to help with the new school, including almost all the leading reformers and intellectuals of the time—Kang Youwei, Tan Sitong, Zhang Jian (1853–1926), Wang Kangnian, Wen Tingshi (1856–1904), Chen Sanli (1853–1937), Huang Zunxian (1848–1905), and others, mainly from the southern provinces.[17]

One hundred twenty-two registrants, mostly leading reformers' mothers, wives, and daughters, attended the first meeting of the Women's Study Society on 6 December 1897. Famous Western missionaries, scholars, diplomats, journalists, and their female relatives also participated in the event.[18] The American missionary journalist Young J. Allen and the British missionary Timothy Richard were among those who played vital roles in the project; Allen's daughter and Richard's wife later served as leading faculty members at the Girls' School.[19]

Ultimately, the reformers sought support from the highest power holder, Empress Dowager Cixi (1835–1908). They appealed to Cixi with an updated notion of the mother's teaching, invigorated by a Western theory that "children born to a woman who knows how to educate them properly may easily establish themselves, whereas those who are not usually have problems as they grow up."[20] By this logic, Cixi became a natural role model for women, since both her son and her adopted son were emperors. After all, who among the children of the realm would be better established than the ones who became emperors? Who among the women of the realm would know better how to educate children than Her Majesty, Cixi? In his memos to the powerful statesmen mentioned above, Jing Yuanshan asked them to pass on this view on the importance of the mother's teaching to Cixi, lauding her as an exemplar in this regard, in order to obtain her approval (and financial support) for the new Girls' School.[21]

To strengthen Cixi's image as a role model, men reformers printed a recent letter from one of the Empress Dowager's childhood neighbors, a Lady Wei, in the front of the *Collected Opinions on Education for Women, First Edition* (*Nüxue jiyi chubian*), which Jing Yuanshan meticulously edited and published in the spring of 1898. In her letter Lady Wei recalled how the future empress dowager, by reciting ten thousand words of the classics each day, had become the "mother of the realm." Now threatened by Japan and other powerful nations, China lacked enough people capable of meeting the challenge. The cause? A shortage of learned mothers. Shanghai had already begun to establish a new girls' school. Lady Wei asked, "Why don't you women go to the capital and prostrate yourselves in front of Her Majesty, begging her to set up girls' schools all over the country?" How could an elderly lady from remote Guilin come to be so conversant with the reform movement and so interested in developments in Shanghai? The answer is that her son-in-law Long Zehou (1860–1945) was Kang Youwei's prize student, and he must have helped draft the letter.[22]

The steering committee members also found support for the idea of soliciting Cixi's help among Western allies. Young J. Allen, for example, pointed to Cixi's devotion to learning as the reason she had been able to stabilize the realm and maintain China's harmonious relations with foreign nations during her twenty years' regency.[23] In short, the reformers sought both to coerce and seduce Cixi into reform; if the Empress Dowager and her adopted son could follow the example of Xiaozhuang (1613–88) and her son, the Shunzhi emperor (r. 1644–61), in promoting women's education and other reform projects, they might open up a new era of peace, pride, and economic prosperity for their beleaguered country.[24]

Women's Poetics and the Shanghai Campaign

Their own logic and the circumstances of the time and place forced the men reformers to relinquish control of the Girls' School to women. On moving to center stage, these women turned men reformers' politically oriented and somewhat defensive discourse into something more active, optimistic, and poetic, beginning with the very first meeting of the Women's Study Society on 6 December 1897. This first women's public gathering ever held in China appeared in every way a success. The inexperienced organizers—headed by the two superintendents-elect, Maria-Adèle Lardanchet and Shen Ying—made it a family gathering, a poetry club meeting, and a business conference combined all in one. The result was an enlightening and entertaining event, serious and pleasant, effective and enjoyable.

In order to draw a broad audience, the organizers extended a general invitation through the news media to all the gentlewomen in Shanghai, emphasizing that the meeting was to be "a grand public affair" at which "each participant would be both the guest and the host."[25] The meeting began with a discussion of fund-raising and curriculum construction and ended with a banquet and a literary composition. Peng Jiyun's poetic prose offering, "Record of [the Establishment of] the First Girls' School" ("Nü xuetang ji"), captures both the atmosphere and the themes of the meeting:

> On the day the sky was clear and crisp, and the breeze mild and refreshing. Fragrant chariots and rare stallions arrived one after another. We spent a whole day in pure conversation, discussing in great detail the merits of women's education, both in China and in the West. . . . We began a development in Chinese women's well-being unknown in previous dynasties; we are breeding vigor in Shanghai that will vitalize [China] in the future.[26]

Amid the general excitement, a dominant theme was the joy with which women welcomed this opportunity for self-affirmation and self-cultivation. In an essay composed during the banquet, Jiang Lan (*zi* Wanfang), a future editorial contributor to the *Nü xuebao* and faculty member of the Girls' School, proposed a "perfect and flawless" (*meishan wuhan*) plan for women's education, incorporating features of both the Chinese and the Western educational systems, covering Western as well as Chinese learning, and including not only scholarship but also artistic and poetic creation.[27] As if to exemplify the meaning of "specializing in both scholarship and artistic creation" (*xueyi jiancan*), Jiang complemented her essay with an impromptu poem:

Designing and establishing the new foundation,	經營締造闢新基,
Women-scholars, it's time to fulfill our ambition.	不櫛英才吐氣時。
Well versed in Chinese and Western studies,	學貫中西臻美備,
From all directions, we gentle ladies gather here.[28]	四方閨秀萃於斯。

Jiang's enthusiasm touched other participants, who, either at the banquet or thereafter, composed poems to celebrate the event. Jing Yuanshan collected twenty-three of these works in the *Collected Opinions*.[29] After the Girls' School officially opened on 31 May 1898, about twenty-five more poems by its all-women faculty appeared in various newspapers and periodicals.[30] These poems, in turn, incited verse responses from outside the Women's Study Society, including two sets each by a man and his wife.[31]

The various poems by the women reformers and their allies gave shape to their collective desire for a better educational system. Jubilantly they "vent their frustration" (*tuqi*) caused by the "bitter repression of inner talent and wisdom" over a long period.[32] Maintaining that *fudao*, or the women's Way, encompassed far more than what had been traditionally defined as "women's work" (*nügong*), they argued that "women's knowledge should transcend the limits of the kitchen," extending ultimately to an "understanding of the entire realm under heaven."[33] Proud of their erudition and versatility, these women considered poetic creation to be the ideal vehicle for demonstrating their talent and for displaying their refinement. As Ding Suqing, a major contributor to the *Nü xuebao* and a teacher at the Girls' School, put it: "Poetic learning allows me to express my true nature; / Descriptions of flowers and grass embody my spirit" (略學謳吟暢性真, 也將花草寫精神).[34]

By becoming "well versed in both Chinese and Western knowledge," women reformers felt they could "fulfill their ambitions."[35] Zhou Yuanxiang, another major contributor to the *Nü xuebao* and a faculty member of the Girls' School, expressed her aspirations as follows:

Because I cannot be a minister, I'll be a good doctor,	不為良相必良醫,
Prolonging lives with great compassion, in a similar way.	壽世宏慈道未歧,
I will beg the goddess Baogu for her divine medicine,	願乞鮑姑仙術在,
To relieve, instantly, all the ailments on earth.[36]	頓教大地起瘡痍。

Once Chinese women acquired the "divine medicine"—that is, necessary foreign and domestic knowledge—they would be able to offer instant remedies for all the afflictions of the world, including those in China.

A political goal is clearly implied here. Whereas most men reformers advocated education for women so that they could feed themselves, thus reducing the burden on men and eventually, perhaps, enriching the nation,[37] women reformers saw the assistance they could offer in far broader terms. As Zhang Jingyi (*zi* Yunhua) commented:

Great! Today's virtuous and talented scholars,	卓哉當世賢,
Urge education for women!	亟創女學議,

Establishing a girls' school in Shanghai,	建堂於海上,
Teaching knowledge, both Chinese and Western.	學問中西萃,
From now on we women will	從此不櫛儔,
Fulfill our natural ambition.	暢其天生志,
As our knowledge grows day by day,	知識日漸開,
Amazing talents begin to sprout.	巾幗有奇器。
. . .	
I dare to call on my fellow women:	敢告同輩中,
Far and near, we should unite as one.	邇邇須相繫。
Those who intend to save the world,	有志救世者,
Please rise from your places!	請各興其地。
So that the people of this generation	庶幾我輩流,
Can vent our long pent-up frustration.	群得吐其氣。
Let us all join this honorable occasion,	勉哉襄善舉,
Making our names forever fragrant![38]	芳名億萬世。

Instead of sharing the humiliation and bitterness of Chinese men, Chinese women were excited at having the opportunity to help build a new country and culture, attaining personal and collective glory along the way.

The spirited Chinese women reformers received support from elite Western women in Shanghai, sometimes assisted by reform-minded men. Jing Yuanshan—reportedly "deaf in the ears but not in the mind"—for example, engaged Young J. Allen to recruit Western women "who were willing and able to assist nurturing education for Chinese women" and to invite them to be cofounders of the Women's Study Society.[39] Immediately after receiving this invitation, the wife of a prestigious English lawyer known by his Chinese name, Danwen, threw a tea party for the women's steering committee. Soon thereafter, on 30 November 1897, the Spanish consul's wife arranged a dinner party for Chinese and Western women. She expressed the hope that "Chinese women, with their orchid minds and bodies, would not only know the affairs of one family and one nation, but also those of all the five continents and the myriad of nations." This knowledge, she said, would "eventually benefit China."[40]

At the first meeting of the Women's Study Society, the bond between Chinese and Western women was palpable. The foreign guests asserted that the women of the five continents were all "sisters born of the same body [that is, parents]," calling forth a similar statement of solidarity from their Chinese hosts.[41] The presence of Chen Jitong's French wife, Maria-Adèle Lardanchet, who identified herself by her Chinese title, "Née Lai, Imperial-titled Lady of the First Class, from Paris" (Gaofeng yipin furen

Bali Laishi),[42] and their two daughters, Qian and Chao, made the sister-hood look all the more sincere.[43]

Lady Lai readily became one of the two elected future superintendents of the Girls' School; declining any salary and organizing the first meeting of the Women's Study Society, she used her residence as a temporary office for the women's steering committee.[44] Because of her insufficiency in Chinese, her daughters served as her interpreters. But the common understanding that prevailed among women reformers in Shanghai, whether Western or Chinese, seemed to transcend the barriers of language, culture, and nation. A poem by Chen Chao celebrates the festive atmosphere of their "family" gatherings:

Sisters meet, Chinese and Western;	中西萃薈此堂中,
Flowers bloom, scarlet and crimson.	姊妹花開朵朵紅。
For our love of blossoms far and near,	為惜天涯有凡卉,
We wish spring breezes here and there.[45]	欲教到處遍春風。

"Spring breeze" alludes to Confucius's yearning to enjoy the springtime with his students.[46] This sisterhood, Chen Chao implies, will provide an education comparable to the one by the Sage. In a similar vein, Ding Suqing rhymes: "What a blessing, this Chinese and Western sisterhood! / United in one will, without suspicion" (難得中西諸姊妹, 成城眾志絕疑猜).[47]

Thus the educational project moved along smoothly and rapidly. On 31 May 1898, the Girls' School formally opened its boarding school with sixteen students. A month later, the number had increased to twenty. In addition, a day school opened in the fall, adding another twenty students. In its two years of operation, a total of seventy girls were registered. Learned Chinese women taught Chinese texts, women's works, and medicine, and Chinese graduates from missionary schools—as well as two foreign instructors, Mrs. Timothy Richard and Miss Mary Louise Allen—taught foreign languages and sciences.[48]

In the capable hands of its female faculty and staff, this first Chinese girls' school proved to be "the greatest wonder of the age," as a foreign woman later described it.[49] The day after it opened, the school invited ten foreign women to inspect the campus. "Some of us," Mrs. Timothy Richard recalled, "spoke of our entire satisfaction with the arrangements—the cleanliness, good ventilation, etc." At the school's Chinese New Year recess, Mrs. Richard—not yet on the faculty—attended the closing exercises with a large number of foreign women; all were "much pleased with the progress made in English, reading and spelling, writing, arithmetic and native draw-ing."[50] Young J. Allen was the invited speaker. As Mrs. Richard remarked:

> No friend of Chinese women failed to understand the feeling of the vener-able Dr. Allen, who, as he stood before the students and guests assembled to celebrate the closing exercises of this first school for girls, established by the Chinese themselves, declared that he felt inclined to say, "Lord, now lettest Thou Thy servant depart in peace."[51]

Meanwhile, the *Nü xuebao* was keeping pace with the school. On 17 May 1898, the Women's Study Society announced the new publication in the *Xinwen bao*, inviting "famous worthy and gentle ladies (*xianshu mingyuan*), Chinese and Western," to be contributors.[52] Xue Shaohui, whose proposals for the new school had already impressed her colleagues (see below), responded immediately through Chen Jitong that she would write 6,000 words a month—without pay. In a grateful open letter to Xue, published in *Zhixin bao* (Review of new knowledge) on 19 July 1898, the leading members of the Women's Study Society "bowed respectfully, thanking her on behalf of [her] 200 million female compatriots."[53] This public appreciation apparently encouraged other volunteers, and soon the women's journal had a strong, all-woman editorial board of twenty-odd "major contributors" (*zhubi*). From the first issue onward, a full list of these contributors appeared on the front page, with Xue's name at the top (see Figure 4.1).[54]

To increase the journal's accessibility, the editorial board originally planned to use *guanhua*, or Mandarin—the vernacular form of written Chi-nese based on the Beijing dialect—and thus proposed the name *Guanhua Nü xuebao*.[55] According to Pan Xuan, a leading contributor, the merit of using Mandarin was that "when one woman reads the journal aloud, dozens of women can understand."[56] Xue Shaohui proposed instead a combination of classical and vernacular Chinese, as made clear by the Women's Study Society's response to Xue's letter (now lost):

> Since very few Chinese women know how to read and write, the editorial board of the *Nü xuebao* reluctantly named the journal "Guanhua." Now you advise us that with such a vernacular approach, the journal might lose its el-egant appeal, and you are absolutely right! . . . You, our venerable elder sister, possess outstanding talent and learning. We rely on your colorful brush to awaken our fellow women. Whether or not to use the elegant style should depend on the need. When advocating [a position] with elite women, why

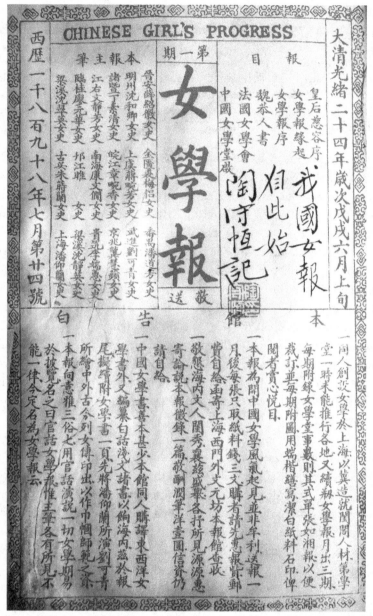

Figure 4.1. Front page of *Nü xuebao* 1 (24 July 1898). Xue Shaohui's name is at the top of the list of contributors, upper-left column. The handwritten inscription declares that "women's periodicals of our country began with this one" (我國女報自此始); it is signed by Tao Shouheng 陶守恆 (1872–1951), the original collector and a leading educator of Wuxi, Jiangsu province. (Wuxi Library collection, courtesy of Zhang Junfeng.)

not inspire them with profound and refined writings? Therefore, we will certainly follow your instructions, using 30 percent classical Chinese and 70 percent vernacular language.[57]

Xue's emphasis on elegance was consistent with her notion of women's literacy, a highly refined blend of elite cultures, Chinese and Western. But her approach was also pragmatic. After all, the *Nü xuebao* would circulate first and foremost among elite women, who—at least initially—would find the elegant tradition far more appealing than the unfamiliar vernacular style of journalism that was still on trial. Xue understood, however, that eventually the journal would have to employ vernacular Chinese to reach a broader audience, and in fact she later experimented with a combination of classical and vernacular Chinese in introducing Western literature to the Chinese public during the post-1898 era.

Persuaded by Xue, the editorial board published the first issue of the *Nü xuebao* without "*guanhua*" in the title. The journal did use both classical and vernacular styles but not in the exact ratio suggested. Of the four sections, only news reports employed vernacular Chinese; the editorial essays, submitted essays, and announcements were written mostly in classical Chinese. Pan Xuan was perhaps the only essayist to successfully develop a vernacular style. Even so, women journalists made progress in promoting vernacular journalism at this early stage. Scholars point out that the biggest challenge to May Fourth activists in using vernacular Chinese lay not in literary creation but in expository essays.[58] Yet, some twenty years earlier, the female contributors of the 1898 *Nü xuebao* had already published vernacular essays on such difficult issues as gender equality, political systems, freedom of marriage, and so forth. The overall effect of the *Nü xuebao*'s combined styles may have been similar to that of the *Shiwu bao* during the same period. Timothy Richard wrote of the latter,

> From the first it was a brilliant success, and stirred the whole Empire from one end to the other. . . . The style of writing was a medium between high Wenli (high classic style), which could only be understood by comparatively few of the scholars, and the colloquial, which every coolie could understand; so chaste that it commanded the admiration of every scholar, and yet so plain that every reader in the land could comprehend.[59]

The first issue of the *Nü xuebao* featured Xue Shaohui's "Preface to the *Nü xuebao*" ("*Nü xuebao* xu") and Pan Xuan's "Foreword to the Shanghai *Nü xue-*

bao" ("Shanghai *Nü xuebao* yuanqi"). Both emphasized the need for a journal aimed at Chinese women, but the focus and tone of each reflected its author's individual writing style. Xue, in classical Chinese, stressed that the journal would expose women to new forms of knowledge in a globalized world.[60] Pan's vernacular essay celebrated the journal's role in propagating the influence of the Chinese women's reform trinity—the Nü xuehui, Nü xuetang, and *Nü xuebao*—and thereby organizing and mobilizing women. Pan's enthusiasm was infectious:

> The Women's Study Society, the Girls' School, and the *Women's Journal*: these three together are comparable to a fruit tree. The society is its root, the school its fruit, and the journal its leaves and blossoms. If people want to know what tree it is, whether it is promising, and if it can bear fruit, shouldn't they first examine its leaves and blossoms? Everything about the society and the school will be exhaustively published in the journal, just like green leaves and red blossoms on the tree; looking at them, wouldn't pass-ersby feel pleasure in their eyes and freshness in their minds?[61]

> 這女學會、女學堂、女學報三樁事情, 好比一株果樹。女學會是個根本, 女學堂是個果子, 女學報是個葉, 是朵花。人要知道這樹什麼樹, 盛不盛, 能不能結果子, 不是要先瞧這花和葉嗎? 那女學會內的消息, 女學堂內的章程, 與關係女學會女學堂的一切情形, 有了女學報, 可以淋淋漓漓的寫在那裏, 像綠的葉, 紅的花, 人見了不悅目不爽心的嗎?

In another essay, "On the Difficulties of Compiling the *Nü xuebao* and the Way of Mutual Help between Chinese and Western Women" ("Lun *Nü xuebao* nanchu he Zhongwai nüzi xiangzhu de lifa"), Pan wrote that by opening women's minds to fresh ideas, the *Nü xuebao* would serve as "the starting point for us 200 million Chinese women to demand equal rights." In this sense, the *Nü xuebao* was comparable to a baton in a commander's hand: "Whenever the commander raises her baton," she wrote, "the soldiers will cry in one voice, and the enemy will flee!"[62]

With such high expectations, during the next three months of 1898 the editors of the *Nü xuebao* contributed more than twenty essays advocating women's rights, encouraging the study of science, medicine, art, and litera-ture, and offering health advice. They also reported on Shanghai women workers' numbers and occupations—about sixty to seventy thousand women working mainly in textile mills and tea factories.[63] The major essays published in the twelve issues of the *Nü xuebao* may be grouped as follows (essays and illustrations with no issue number and date were published in one of the missing final three issues):[64]

On Nü xuebao

- Xue Shaohui, "Preface to the *Nü xuebao*," 1 (24 July 1898)
- Pan Xuan, "Foreword to the Shanghai *Nü xuebao*," 1 (24 July 1898); 2 (3 Aug. 1898)
- Pan Xuan, "On the Difficulties of Compiling the *Nü xuebao* and the Way of Mutual Help between Chinese and Western Women," 3 (15 Aug. 1898)
- Wu Yi, "Motivation and Purpose of the *Nü xuebao*"
- Shen Cuiying, "On How the *Nü xuebao* May Assist the Girls' School"
- Sun Yun, "Preface to the *Nü xuebao*"

On Education for Women

- Xu Fu, "Record of the Girls' School at Qianxi Village, Longdu Town, Raoping County, Chaozhou Prefecture," 2 (3 Aug. 1898)
- Xue Shaohui, "On the Connection between Women's Education and the Way of Governing," 3 (15 Aug. 1898), 4 (20 Aug. 1898)
- Liu Renlan, "Letter on Advancing Education for Women," 4 (20 Aug. 1898)
- Pan Daofang, "On the Double Seventh," 6 (6 Sept. 1898)
- Kang Tongwei, "On the Advantages and Disadvantages of Education for Women," 7 (Sept. 1898)
- Qiu Yufang, "On the Equality of Girls' and Boys' Schools," 7 (Sept. 1898)
- Jiang Wanfang (*zi* of Jiang Lan), "On How Education for Women Benefits China's Political Situation," 9 (Oct. 1898)
- Xie Zhi, "On Education for Women as the Foundation for Strengthening China"
- Yang Lanzhen, "On Saving Money from Religious Worship to Enhance Women's Education"
- Cheng Yi, "On Establishing Education for Women"
- Liu Jing (*zi* Keqing), "Song of the Girls' School"

On Equal Rights

- Wang Chunlin, "On Equality between Men and Women," 5 (27 Aug. 1898)
- Lu Cui, "On Women's Patriotism," 5 (27 Aug. 1898)
- Sui Nianqu, "Sui on Military Affairs," 6 (6 Sept. 1898)
- Zhu Shilan, "Letter in Reply to Woman Historian Wu by the Woman Steering Committee Member Woman Historian Zhu," 6 (6 Sept. 1898)

見何有年誠居一款畢女才狀各春上人兩華爾數昧曰十思以帽教大安客之守門眾而燈電之上
之旱之末我其人百共我旦示華藉各為觀從各爾施嚴以欣陳既寺施珊嚴遠報語海
於旱之盛總華大而二計怀不會之官主奈之日設園產月於集筆會相大從子被珊局剏女
令公盆二半西二十到滑落中夫及兩神而愛之蔡到筆十去盖不成間往討會而某如附太總誠旱
日也達于天女有臂暴婦入各國滬港夫和店滬夫氏三公之足巾坤東二論需助夫軍觀守禅林堂

Figure 4.2. The First Meeting of the Women's Study Society (Qunchai dahui tu 裙釵大會圖), on 6 December 1897. The two women sitting at the end of the table and wearing Chinese clothing must be the two newly elected superintendents of the future Girls' School, Shen Ying 沈瑛 and Chen Jitong's French wife, Maria-Adèle Lardanchet (Chinese name, Lai Mayi 賴媽懿), who headed the meeting. If so, the one at the right end looks like Maria-Adèle, for she is portrayed as discussing a written document with a Western woman and hence presumably would know some foreign language. Nü xuebao 2 (3 Aug. 1898): 1b. (Wuxi Library collection, courtesy of Zhang Junfeng.)

- Anonymous, "On Revising the Wedding Ritual to Correct Customs," 8 (Sept. 1898)
- Xue Shaohui, "Eulogy to the Four Virtues," 9 (Oct. 1898)

On Science and Technology
- Qu Yufen, "On Medical Science"
- Anonymous, "The Profusion of Women Workers," 9 (Oct. 1898)
- Zhiyun nüshi, "Song of Tending Silkworms," 9 (Oct. 1898)
- Anonymous, "A New Theory on Pregnancy," 9 (Oct. 1898)

To attract female readers, each issue of the *Nü xuebao*, though only eight-pages long, included a full-page illustration, with titles such as

- *Portrait of the Empress* [*Longyu*], 1 (24 July 1898)
- *The First Meeting of the Women's Study Society*, 2 (3 Aug. 1898) [Figure 4.2]
- *The Shanghai Girls' School in Guishuli*, 3 (15 Aug. 1898)
- *Map of Girls' Schools in Shanghai*, 4 (20 Aug. 1898) [Map 4.1]
- *A Woman Working on a Sewing Machine*, 5 (27 Aug. 1898)
- *Women's Exercises*, 6 (6 Sept. 1898)
- *In Class*, 7 (Sept. 1898) [Figure 4.3]
- *Feeding Silkworms*, 8 (Sept. 1898) [Figure 4.4]
- *Weaving and Embroidering*, 9 (Oct. 1898)
- *Daily Toilet*
- *Sewing*
- *Weaving to Attend the Mother-in-law*

All the illustrations, except the first two, were created by female artists, mostly by Liu Jing. The use of perspective in her drawings suggests that Liu studied Western art, but she was also accomplished in traditional Chinese painting.[65] Together with well-written, sharply argued essays of broad scope, the illustrations fueled the journal's quick rise in popularity. Two months after its inauguration, its circulation had reportedly increased to several thousand, leading the editorial board to raise the subscription fee from 3 to 7 cents per issue.[66]

The Chinese women's society, school, and journal all managed to carry on after Cixi abruptly ended the Hundred Days on 21 September 1898, but the going was tough. The names of seven major contributors who were closely related to the leading and now fugitive reformers, including Kang Youwei's daughter Kang Tongwei and Liang Qichao's wife, Li Duanhui (1869–1924), disappeared from the eighth issue of the *Nü xuebao*, published later that

Map 4.1. Girls' Schools in Shanghai

The Chinese inscription indicates that the map locates fifteen girls' schools in Shanghai built by the end of July 1898 (each marked with a star sign, with key numbers by N. Q. following in order from the north to the south; English place-names have also been added), all by Western missionaries except for number 15, the Chinese Girls' School, which was established during the 1897–98 campaign for women's education, located in Guishuli 桂墅里.

SOURCE: *Nü xuebao* 4 (20 Aug. 1898): 1b. Wuxi Library collection, courtesy of Zhang Junfeng.

Figure 4.3. In Class (*Nüshu tu* 女塾圖). *Nü xuebao* 7 (Sept. 1898): 1b; by Liu Jing 劉靚 (*zi* Keqing 可青). (Wuxi Library collection, courtesy of Zhang Junfeng.)

Figure 4.4. Feeding Silkworms (Cansang tu 蠶桑圖). *Nü xuebao* 8 (Sept. 1898): 1b; by
Liu Jing. (Wuxi Library collection, courtesy of Zhang Junfeng.)

month. The address of the reform martyr Kang Guangren's Unbound Feet Association that had sold the *Nü xuebao* also vanished. Although Mary Louise Allen's Chinese name, Lin Malai, appeared on the contributors list in the tenth issue (19 October 1898) and so displayed the solidarity of "Western sisters," the *Nü xuebao*'s days were numbered. Its last regular issue came out on 29 October 1898.[67]

The Girls' School lasted somewhat longer. At the end of 1898, Jing Yuanshan led several thousand people to protest Cixi's dethronement of Guangxu, and the Qing court ordered his arrest. Before fleeing to Macau, he entrusted the school to the care of Mrs. Richard. Individual Chinese teachers such as Jiang Lan, Zhou Yuanxiang, and Ding Suqing "held fast [to their posts in the face of] extreme hardship" (Figure 4.5), but by 1900 difficult political and economic circumstances forced them to give up.[68]

Advocates of women's rights and women's education nonetheless continued to make their voices heard. Xue Shaohui and her husband, for instance, began to translate and compile several Western literary, historical, and scientific works in a continuing effort to advance the unrealized goals of the 1898 reforms (see Chapters Six and Seven).

Figure 4.5. Faculty and students of the Chinese Girls' School. *Wanguo gongbao* 125 (June 1899): frontispiece. (Nanjing University Library collection.)

Competing Visions of a New Chinese Womanhood

The cooperation and mutual respect that marked the working relationship of men and women reformers should not blind us to the tensions between them. The late 1890s, when women demanded loud and clear the obliteration of the conventional segregation between the inner and outer domains, was a heady time for Chinese women and a somewhat threatening one for Chinese men. Xue Shaohui, for one, argued in her "Preface to the *Nü xuebao*" the need to break down segregation as an essential precondition for nurturing the new Chinese womanhood.[69] Pan Xuan celebrated the newly sprouting media, the *Nü xuebao* in particular, as the means to carry women's voices across confined boundaries. She exclaimed that, with the journal,

> we have torn down the huge billboard and broken through the old fence that had divided the outer and the inner domains [*waiyan neiyan*, literally, outer and inner words]. Thus we can openly discuss education for women and declare our identity as women editors. Isn't this an unprecedented event in China? Yes, we admit it without hesitation, and we are extremely excited about it![70]

> 直把戒外言內言的這塊大招牌, 這堵舊圍牆, 竟衝破打通了! 堂堂皇皇的講論女學、女主筆, 豈不是中國古來所未有的呢? 我們現在竟直認不諱, 亦暢快極了!

For the first time in Chinese history, women entered the public domain in its ultimate sense—freely expressing and publicizing their opinions on their own behalf.

Actual debate on ideal womanhood erupted much earlier, at the very beginning of the Shanghai campaign, with discussions on curricula. On 21 November 1897, at the second meeting of the men's steering committee, Chen Jitong reported on the progress of the school curriculum designed by his wife, Maria-Adèle Lardanchet, the newly elected "foreign superintendent" of the future Chinese Girls' School. In response, Jing Yuanshan expressed his concern that Maria-Adèle, a graduate of a French girls' school, might follow Western educational models too closely. He therefore recommended that the curriculum of the new school "combine Chinese and Western [approaches]" (*Zhong Xi hecan*).[71] Chen Jitong then took Maria-Adèle's curricular plans, along with the already-published "Provisional Regulations for the Girls' School," to his sister-in-law, Xue Shaohui, for review.

This family consultation resulted in Xue's "Suggestions for Establishing the Girls' School, with a Preface" ("Chuangshe Nü xuetang tiaoyi bing xu"), a document that went well beyond questions of Chinese and Western curricula.[72] Indeed, Xue's "Suggestions" represented a systematic "feminist" response to men reformers' perspectives on the future Chinese Girls' School, as expressed in Liang Qichao's "On Education for Women," his "Announcement," and the "Provisional Regulations" that he finalized.[73] It helped to precipitate a public debate that reflected a wide range of important current topics, from gender, class, and race to religion and culture. Three of the most controversial issues were: the nature and purpose of education for women; the place of Confucius and Confucianism in the new educational order; and the question of equal rights among classes and between the sexes.

THE NATURE AND PURPOSE OF EDUCATION FOR WOMEN

Liang Qichao and his male colleagues viewed education for Chinese women as a way out of their "jobless" status that had caused China's backwardness. Such women were described in far from flattering terms: they were but 200 million lazy and "useless" people, "idle as wanderers and ignorant like barbarians."[74] Xue Shaohui came to their defense:

> Is it true that China's 200 million women are all useless? By the former kings' precept of separating the inner and outer domains, we have sternly guarded our virtue, purified our minds, and tenderly conformed to the natural course of the Way. For this reason, it seems that we are incapable of doing things other than domestic chores. Yet have we not had those among us who, with irrepressible talent, achieved what Xie Daoyun had in scholarly and literary talent (*cai*) or Wu Lingyun had in artistic accomplishment (*yi*)? From ancient times to the present, how many talented women of this kind can be counted![75]

> 夫中國婦女, 數雖二萬萬, 豈盡無用哉? 特以先王内言外言之戒, 操守彌堅。貞潔其心, 柔順其道, 故於中饋内助而外, 若無能為也者。然其間豈無聰明難悶, 發而為道蘊之才, 靈芸之藝, 自古迄今, 可指而屈者凡幾。

Xue refused to blame women for causing China's backwardness. Many of her writings published during the reform era demonstrated her understanding that the fundamental problem facing Chinese women was a stifling political and social environment created largely by men. Even the "progressive" men reformers were full of contradictions and inconsistencies when it came to questions of gender. Her position was not that Chinese women were use-less but rather that they had not been well used. She made this point clearly in her "Preface to the *Nü xuebao.*" Comparing a historic antecedent to the present situation, she argued:

> In the past, Goujian [r. 497–465 BCE] endured hardships in order to re-store his state [*woxin changdan*, literally, lay on maggots and tasted gall], and he sought help from women. After ten years of population growth and the training of his soldiers, he eventually gained hegemony and empowered himself. He understood the use of women's [labor]. He did not know, how-ever, that the use of women's learning was even greater. Although women's learning seems to function only for regulating the family, its assistance in governing the state and pacifying all under heaven, although seeming trivial, is in fact more important.[76]

> 昔者勾踐臥薪嘗膽, 籌及婦女, 而後十年生聚, 十年訓練, 卒得以霸而強。其知婦女之用, 尚未知於婦女之學, 為用更大也。婦女之學, 雖至於齊家, 其所以佐於治平之功者, 似微而著。

Xue goes on to show that Chinese women have been learned since antiq-uity—"In poetry they created poems such as 'Guanju' in the *Book of Songs*, and in ritual they compiled the 'Inner Principles' in the *Records of Ritual (Liji)*"—and their learning has played an indispensable role in governing the state.[77] Xue would elaborate on this argument at length in her essay "On the Con-nection between Women's Education and the Way of Governing" (see below).

Women's education, therefore, is only a matter of expanding their acqui-sition of knowledge within the current world situation, as Xue remarks in her "Preface":

> Today new learning (*xinxue*) from all the countries has been gloriously de-veloped, going beyond the scope of our ancient philosophers and the one hundred schools of thought [of the Zhou dynasty]. If we women, staying in the inner chambers all day long, maintain the division between inner words and outer words and limit our learning [within narrow confines], how can we talk about gaining knowledge so as to conform to the principle of the "new people"?[78]

> 第今日各國新學, 燦然秀發, 有出諸子百家外。吾輩日處閨闥, 若仍守其內言外言之戒, 自畫其學, 安足以講致知, 而合於新民之旨哉?

Instead of dichotomizing "Western learning" and "Chinese learning," Xue comes up with the concept of "new learning." She views new learning as a worldwide intellectual response to current changes, in which China stands equally with other countries in expanding "traditional" learning to encompass a much broader spectrum of knowledge.[79] To acquire new learning, women have to break the long-standing inner-and-outer division, expanding their horizon to include useful knowledge of all sorts, regardless of its origins. And they should view the relationship between their original construct of learning and the possible new components as one of constant interaction, with the former anticipating continual renewal and the latter updating past knowledge to fit the present. All the ideas arising in the process will be relentlessly argued, debated, challenged, and refigured.[80] Only in this way can women attain the new womanhood. After all, China's long-standing "principle of renewing the people" (*xinmin zhi zhi*) has entailed unceasing self-renovation, as in the words of the *Great Learning*: "If you can one day renovate yourself, then do so from day to day! Always keep renovating yourself."[81] Xue founded her reform thinking precisely upon this dialectic relationship between the old and the new, which she sought to bring into the curriculum for women's education so they could then be "prepared to be selected for the use of the state," the same goal that had privileged men's education.[82]

With grand expectations that education should prepare women to serve the state on equal ground with men, Xue in her "Suggestions" established a vision of the "women's Way," which she revised from its conventional sense and supported with her curricular proposals. She contended that the women's Way should comprise two basic components, virtue and learning, and subsequently redefined its four traditional aspects (*side*, literally, four virtues)—womanly virtue (*fude*), womanly words (*fuyan*), womanly bearing (*furong*), and womanly work (*fugong*)—with substantial changes to virtue, words, and work. Xue defined womanly virtue as the ability to "assist sages and rearing worthies" (*fusheng danxian*), rather than the conventional emphasis on chastity; she defined womanly words as *cai*, scholarly and literary talent, rather than proper daily speech; and she defined womanly work as *yi*, artistic and scientific accomplishments, rather than domestic chores.[83] She asserted: "*Cai* and *yi* are womanly words and work, and both belong to the four virtues and should not be excluded."[84]

To be sure, Xue was not the first to associate womanly words and work with women's scholarly, literary, and artistic accomplishments. Wanyan Yun Zhu, for instance, had said that "although 'womanly words' is not what we mean by literary writing, it is closely related to literary writing."[85] Yun Zhu made this argument to defend women's poetic creation in her preface to the *Correct Beginnings: Women's Poetry of Our August Dynasty*, which Xue selected as a major textbook for the future girls' school. Seen in this light, Xue's equation of womanly words and work with *cai* and *yi* continued what Yun Zhu came to represent in women's literary culture in the lower Yangzi River area during the seventeenth and eighteenth centuries.[86] Xue's more positive tone further justified women's desire for high cultural achievement. Her redefinition of the "four virtues" that included *cai* and *yi* as female virtues dismantled the popular late imperial expression, "having no talent (*cai*) is women's virtue (*de*)."[87] For Xue, talent and virtue could and should harmoniously coexist and obtaining talent through learning was itself a virtue.

Xue delivered her defense of women's talent pointedly against men reformers' narrow view of what female capabilities were and ought to be. Liang Qichao, for instance, comments in "On Education for Women":

> What people called "talented women" (*cainü*) in the past refers to those who teased the wind and fondled the moon, plucked flowers and caressed the grass, and thereupon composed some poems and song-lyrics to mourn the spring and lament partings. That's all. Doing things like this cannot be regarded as learning (*xue*). Even for a man, if he has no other accomplishment than poetic creation, he would be denounced as a frivolous person (*fulang zhi zi*). This is all the more true of a woman! By learning I mean that which can open up one's mind and help one make a living in the world.[88]

> 古之號稱才女者, 則批風抹月, 拈花弄草, 能為傷春惜別之語, 成詩詞集數卷, 斯為至矣! 若此等事, 本不能目之為學。其為男子, 苟無他所學, 而專欲以此鳴者, 則亦可指為浮浪之子, 靡論婦人也。吾之所謂學者, 內之以拓其心胸, 外之以助其生計。

Liang's indictment of *cainü* culture, chorused by his fellow men reformers,[89] amounted to an assault on Chinese tradition. As Joan Judge points out:

> Women writers of the recent past came to function as a metonym for all that was obsolete and degraded in that tradition, and the passionate offensive against them was an attack on the perceived backwardness of the "old culture." Since these reformist writers themselves had a complex relationship to that culture—they were trained in its values and bound by its referents—it was perhaps easier for them to speak their critique of it through an indictment of the *cainü*.[90]

Predictably, Xue rejected this indictment, noting that what male scholars wanted women to learn about, such as sericulture, needlework, housekeeping, and cooking, was nothing new but part of women's "traditional obligations." She therefore argued:

> For [cultivating] women's virtue (*fude*) and women's words (*fuyan*), I know of nothing more effective than learning how to compose poetry and prose. To focus women's learning not on [poetry and prose], but guide it with some baseless and exaggerating argument [on teaching "idle" women how to feed themselves] amounts to nothing less than abandoning women's fragile and tender substance to oblivion. It would destroy women's learning and corrupt women's education. The damage would be unimaginable![91]

> 若婦德婦言, 舍詩、文、詞外, (未) [末] 由見。不由此是求, 而求之幽渺誇誕之說, 殆將並婦女柔順之質, 皆付諸荒煙蔓草而湮沒。微特斁女學、壞女教, 其弊誠有不堪設想者矣!

In Xue's view, poetry "cultivates one's disposition and feelings" (*taoxie xingqing*), and the current campaign for educating women offers a splendid opportunity to restore the long-ignored tradition of poetic transformation (*shijiao*).[92]

Xue's curricular proposals went well beyond traditional models of "feminine" behavior. She suggested studying not just poetics, but also phonetics to ensure correct pronunciation, philology to increase accuracy in writing, and reasoning to improve clarity of the mind, so as to prepare women for careers in law and politics. She elevated some traditional womanly work, such as embroidery, to fine arts, and encouraged pursuit of the most up-to-date techniques for its refinement. She recommended studying music along with the song-lyric to help harmonize the "inner-chamber conjugal relationship"; geography to learn the "broadness of the five continents" and the "beauty of Chinese mountains and rivers"; women's history to comprehend the standards by which women's behavior was judged; calligraphy and painting to cultivate women's artistic sensitivity; and medicine to improve the physical well-being of women and children.[93]

Although Xue focused on "Chinese" knowledge, she appreciated what the West had to offer. For instance, knowing the popularity of music among Western women, she intended to promote its study among Chinese women who were hesitant because of its scandalous association with courtesans. She even suggested that Chinese music might profitably be studied in light of Western science and mathematics.[94] As an artist herself, Xue appreciated the respective merits of Western and Chinese painting. Artists in the West, she wrote, were good at imitating the actual object (*xiezhen*), while the Chinese excelled at expressing the idea (*xieyi*); Western painters emphasized the rules of perspective (*cesuan*), while Chinese painters esteemed brush-work (*yongbi*). "Each [tradition] has its merits, hard to combine," but Xue advised recourse to both, beginning with Chinese artists working in styles similar to those of Western artists.[95] She likewise felt that Chinese medicine ought to be studied together with Western medicine, since the two were in certain ways "marvelously complementary."[96]

Xue's curricular proposals won widespread acclaim. The Chen brothers immediately published Xue's "Suggestions" in the *Qiushi bao*, numbers 9 and 10 (18 and 27 December 1897). Soon thereafter, aided by Jing Yuan-shan, Xue's elaborated version appeared in the *Xinwen bao* (14–17 January 1898). A postscript signed by "Colleagues of the Girls' School" praised Xue's "broad knowledge in the classics and history, and her familiarity with pres-ent affairs." The author expressed the hope that her "Suggestions" would inspire a broad discussion among the "worthy" Chinese elite, both men and women (*gaoxian shunü*), so that the "Provisional Regulations" for the future girls' school could be improved.

To be sure, not all women reformers agreed with Xue Shaohui. At the first women's steering committee meeting on 1 December 1897, Kang Youwei's daughter Kang Tongwei in her speech more or less paraphrased Liang Qichao's views.[97] But most women welcomed the "Suggestions." Maria-Adèle and Shen Ying incorporated Xue's proposals into their revised version of the curriculum, published in the *Xinwen bao* in March 1898. They argued that the goal of educating Chinese women was to "open up their wisdom, nurture their inner strength and nature, and fortify their bodies, in order to foster their growth into worthy mothers and wives (*xianmu xianfu*)."[98]

Influenced by the arguments of Xue and others, Jing Yuanshan and his re-form-minded colleagues even went so far as to revise the memorandum to be presented to the Empress Dowager and the Guangxu emperor in the spring of 1898. They stressed that the education of Chinese women should cultivate four aspects of their "minds, spirits, and bodies": "The subtle aspect sees into women's voices, aura, manner, and appearance. The perceptive aspect cultivates women's speech, behavior, ritual, and writing. The refined aspect brightens women's minds and nurtures their intent. The coarse aspect covers women's cooking and weaving."[99] On the whole, then, Xue Shaohui and her colleagues managed to articulate a bold and coherent vision of the nature and purpose of women's education—one that at least some men reformers were willing to accept. When it came to matters of ideology, however, the debates between men and women became especially sharp.

THE PLACE OF CONFUCIUS AND CONFUCIANISM IN WOMEN'S EDUCATION

Men reformers had stipulated at the very outset of their "Provisional Regulations" that the Girls' School would be "established on the basis of our sacred religion Confucianism (*wuru shengjiao*)."[100] This decision reflected the effort of Kang Youwei and others to transform the teachings of Confucius into a Chinese state religion, comparable to Christianity in the West. It was, in the words of Theodore Huters, an attempt to hold the center of a "rapidly dispersing intellectual horizon."[101] In that attempt, men reformers found support from some Western allies. The Reverend Sheffield, for example, an ardent advocate of education for Chinese women, argued that certain fundamental Confucian values offered "a way that not only China but also the myriad nations should follow."[102] The *North-China Daily News* took a similar position in reporting on the "Provisional Regulations" of the "New Chinese Girls' School," which it translated in full and published on 24 December 1897:

> None but the most narrow-minded foreigner can object to all due reverence being shown to the great Chinese sage, one of the world's great teachers of ethics. It is not to be denied that a slavish adherence to Confucianism alone has done far too much to limit and confine the Chinese mind for many centuries; but when the reverence for Confucianism is to be combined with the study of Western languages and sciences, we have no fear of the result.

Western women who supported the new school, for their part, approved of the principle of "worshiping Confucius"—primarily because they feared that if the rules "did not follow Confucianism . . . the school might scare Chinese women away." Because a girls' school was "unprecedented," anything beyond Confucianism "might cause criticism."[103]

Chinese women's attitude toward the place of Confucius in their new school differed somewhat from that of men (and was not entirely uniform). Xue Shaohui agreed with the general principle of "venerating Confucius," but she questioned this male-centered educational lineage. Instead, she championed an independent line for women, proposing that the famous Han woman scholar Ban Zhao (ca. 45–ca. 116) replace Confucius as the patron of women's learning:

> The Dao of the Sage Confucius is like the sun on high; even ignorant men and women know to worship him. Whether enshrined or not, his authority is naturally there. . . . The origin of education for women can be traced

back to the consort of King Wen [of the Zhou] and the mother of Mencius. Although they both possessed the virtue of assisting a sage [husband] or raising a virtuous and talented [son], they did not write books for later students. Ban Zhao of the Han completed the *History of the Han* [after her brother, Ban Gu] and tutored the imperial harem. Her moral strength (*de*) and learning (*xue*) suffice as a model for thousands of generations to come. She also compiled the *Admonitions for Women* (*Nüjie*) and the *Instructions for Women* (*Nüxun*) to follow the "Inner Principles" (*Neize*). No worthy ladies (*xianyuan*), then or now, can surpass her. We should enshrine her at the Girls' School to make her a role model for women.[104]

孔聖之道, 譬如日星在上, 雖愚夫愚婦, 莫不瞻敬, 祀與不祀, 孔道之尊嚴自在。... 溯女教之始, 實由於文王后妃, 次即孟母, 然有輔聖誕賢之德, 實無專書以貽後學。惟漢之曹大家, 續成漢史, 教授六宮, 其德其學, 足為千古表率。又有《女誡》、《女訓》, 上繼《內則》, 古今賢媛, 無出其右。祀於堂中, 以爲婦女楷模。

In the interest of educational autonomy, Xue suggested using women's works as textbooks in the Girls' School. For women's moral and scholastic enlightenment, she recommended Ban Zhao's *Admonitions for Women* over *Lienü zhuan* by the Han male scholar Liu Xiang. For inspiration in painting and calligraphy, Xue maintained that female students should emulate female artists, following Lady Wei rather than her famed male disciple Wang Xizhi. In literature, Xue upheld Li Qingzhao's song-lyrics as patterns for women's poetic creation because Li matched the artistic achievements of the best of the male song-lyric poets, including Liu Yong and Jiang Kui,[105] despite men reformers' vilification of Li for having "undermined her moral integrity (*jie*) with her excessive talent (*cai*)."[106]

Xue's emphasis on women as role models and teachers won widespread support among women reformers.[107] A series of quatrains written by Zhou Yuanxiang, for instance, voices their affirmation:

I learned Ban Zhao's *Admonitions for Women* while young;	班家女誡幼曾諳,
Mother Wei's interpretation of the classics is long-lasting.[108]	韋母傳經化久覃,
Today their fragrant traces should not disappear,	此日未應芳躅渺,
[As] we now seek esoteric books from the alien other.	秘書新向異方探。
Scarlet curtain, blue tent, admirable voices of the past;	絳幔青綾慕古徽,
Confucian masters emerge again from the inner chambers.[109]	儒宗又見出閨帷,

We also hear teachers coming from the remote West
(*chongyi*),[110]

更聞師氏來重譯，

"No need to bring wine while learning foreign
letters."[111]

問字無須載酒隨。

Zhou upholds an all-female faculty for women's education and elevates their status to that of "Confucian masters" (*ruzong*), a title granted previously only to men. These women masters, Chinese and Western, are not addicted to wine and do not require "liquor" in exchange for their knowledge as men may do, and they possess "versatile talent" beyond Confucian learning.[112]

The Girls' School eventually adopted textbooks authored mostly by women, such as the *Classic of Filial Piety for Women* by Lady Zheng (fl. Tang) and the Four Books for Women (Nü sishu), which included the *Admonitions for Women* by Ban Zhao, the *Analects of Women* by Song Ruoshen, the *Inner Instructions* (*Neixun*) by Empress Xu (d. 1407), and the *Records of Model Women* (*Nüfan jielu*) by Lady Liu (fl. 1521).[113] Classics compiled by men for women and children such as *Annotation to the Inner Principles* (*Neize yanyi*) and *Annotation to the Primer for Children* (*Youxue xuzhi jujie*), texts commonly used by male scholars such as the Thirteen Classics, Tang poetry, and ancient prose, were also included.[114] The school apparently used a combined Sino-Western approach to teach medicine, art, sewing, and music.[115]

Two of the most severe critics of the Confucian orientation of the Chinese Girls' School were Drs. Kang Aide (Ida Kahn) (1873–1931) and Shi Meiyu (Mary Stone) (1873–1954), who had been handpicked by Liang Qichao for its faculty.[116] As an infant, Kang Aide had been adopted by the American missionary Gertrude Howe (1847–1928) and later, along with Shi Meiyu, received a medical education at the University of Michigan. After graduating, Kang and Shi returned to China and served as missionary doctors. In his biography of Kang in *Shiwu bao*, Liang Qichao omitted her missionary background, introducing her adoptive mother as simply "the daughter of an American scholar-official."[117] He viewed Kang as having all the desirable qualities of modern Chinese womanhood—a gentry family background (albeit American), Western learning, and a useful profession—without what Hu Ying calls "the messiness of real [Christian] cultural baggage."[118] Although valorized by Liang, Kang and Shi did not share his vision of the school as a Confucian enterprise. They declared:

The educational institutions for women during the time of the Three Dynasties were not the excellent things that Confucius sought to re-establish.[119]

Had he done so how could he have uttered such words as these: "Of all people girls and servants are the most difficult to behave to. If you are familiar to them they loss [*sic*] their humility. If you maintain your reserve they are discontented."[120] . . . Alas, that we have no record that the Master ever turned his attention to a remedy for such a sad state of affairs![121]

Kang and Shi expressed these views in an open letter to the editors of the *North-China Daily News*, responding to the paper's report of the establishment of the Chinese Girls' School, its translation of the "Provisional Regulations," and the original Chinese text of the "Provisional Regulations."[122] They maintained that an "unfinished" version of the "Provisional Regulations," shown to them several months earlier, did not contain the "parts of the first and last clauses referring to the establishment of Confucianism." Otherwise, they declared, "we should not have allowed our names to go down as teachers."[123]

No Chinese original has been found of what Kang and Shi called the "unfinished" version of the "Provisional Regulations." The Chinese versions published in various periodicals are virtually identical, and the translation in the *North-China Daily News* has only minor errors and omissions. However, another translation does accord with the "unfinished" version described by Kang and Shi: "The Provisional Prospectus of the Chinese Girls' School," translated by Gertrude Howe and published in January 1898 in the *Missionary Review of the World*. The link between Howe's missionary work and abolitionism, as well as the lowly origins of Kang and Shi, may help explain their intense concern with questions of social class and equal rights, but the two physicians were certainly not alone in that respect.[124]

THE REFORMIST DISCOURSE ON EQUAL RIGHTS

Men reformers advocated education for women as part of their campaign for equal rights between the sexes and among classes. Liang Qichao stated in his "Announcement": "The Sage [Confucius] upheld equality between men and women in his moral teaching, and took everyone under his tutelage without discrimination."[125] They also stated at the outset of the "Provisional Regulations": "We are determined that each woman have her naturally deserved rights."[126] In practice, however, men reformers retreated from egalitarianism, as the following section of the "Provisional Regulations" demonstrates:

11. The purpose of establishing the school is to advocate equal rights (*pingdeng*). No rigorous distinction will be made in [girls'] social position and class.

Nonetheless, because this school is supposed to usher in good social customs and train future teachers and role models, only girls from good families will be admitted. Slave girls, courtesans, and prostitutes shall be excluded.

Men were also worried that equal rights might give women too much freedom and cause more of them to go astray, so they added the following regulation:

22. Shanghai has been notorious for its loose customs (*Zheng-Wei zhi feng*, literally, "the [wanton] wind of states Zheng and Wei"), and [women's] licentious behavior (*Sang-Pu huiji*) is pervasive, especially in the foreign settlements. Upon establishing the Girls' School, if [young ladies] obtain the rights they naturally deserve (*zide zhi quan*) without being disciplined from the very beginning, the consequences may be worse than in some boys' schools, which appear to follow Confucian discipline but which actually indulge in Yang Zhu's [hedonism]. Therefore we have decided to offer special aid to poor females of strict morality (*kujie*). . . . [They] will be assigned to a teaching major, in order for them to acquire a virtuous mother's quality. These enlightened ones can then further enlighten others. This way we may expect [girls] to become straight and correct, and we may keep them from going astray.[127]

Women reformers offered different explanations and different solutions, based upon both Chinese and Western resources, for men's concerns that equal rights might loosen women's morals. Xue was the first to address this issue in her "Suggestions." She believed that a "foolish woman" (*yufu*) could become "loose" because of her ignorance of the law, and she recommended that the Qing Code be included in the curriculum of the Girls' School.[128] Other women felt that something was wrong with the law itself. In "On Equal Rights between Men and Women" ("Nannü pingdeng lun"), published in *Nü xuebao* 5, Wang Chunlin wrote:

Eating, drinking, and sex are the greatest needs for human beings. But whereas a man may take many concubines, remarriage of a widow is condemned as shameful. Stay in marriage when the husband and wife are harmonious, and divorce when they are not—this is common sense under heaven. Yet the law stipulates that a husband can divorce his wife but not vice versa. Both have bodies seven *chi* tall that have been raised by their parents; why is it that a husband receives only flogging or exile for killing his wife, yet a wife will be sliced to death for killing her husband?

Wang went on to ask why chastity was a "crucial principle" for women and yet there was no code of chastity for men—"How can this be reasonable?"

Drawing upon the *Zhuangzi* idea of "free roaming" that pleads for "everyone, even birds, beasts, fish, and tortoises, each to enjoy the full play of its own life," Wang calls for transforming social norms so that today's women can enjoy their lives.[129]

In support of Wang's plea for women's rights, *Nü xuebao* 5 also published a news item, "A Marriage Engagement between [British] Aristocrats" ("Guizu lianyin"), and added to it the following advocacy of marriage based on love and free will:

> The Chinese are most cautious about marriage and rely heavily on the parents' wishes and the matchmaker's words. The wedding ritual as such is indeed rigorous and serious, but it has also caused endless problems, such as the mismatch between a phoenix and a crow, which often causes lifelong regrets. . . . Western countries are quite different. Men and women, on reaching the age of twenty-one, can make their own decisions following their free will (*zizhu*), and their parents have no power over them. They choose their spouses without going through a matchmaker. As long as the two feel affection for each other, they will tie the knot. Consultation with parents is a ritual process, without substantial significance. This sounds like jumping over the wall or digging a tunnel into the house [for an illicit tryst], and will unavoidably provoke criticism from worthy people. However, seeing such a couple [married of their own free will] sitting next to each other in a carriage, or walking hand in hand, and thus growing old together in mutual respect, one feels [this kind of relationship] surpasses a loveless, resentful marriage.[130]

A subsequent, anonymous article in *Nü xuebao* 8, "On Revising the Wedding Ritual to Correct Customs," addressed what the "Provisional Regulations" termed "loose customs" in Shanghai. Instead of blaming women, the article accused men—including some foreigners—of seducing, abducting, and deceiving Chinese women, luring them into illegal marriages and using them for fraudulent schemes. In order to defend women from such practices, the author proposed that an administrative bureau for nuptial affairs be established to bring about the Western system of gender relations, giving women high social status and allowing them to wed according to their own free will (*zizhu*) so that no one could seduce them.[131]

As noted above, Kang Aide and Shi Meiyu critiqued Sections 11 and 22 of the published "Provisional Regulations" by comparing them unfavorably with the provisions in what they claimed was an "unfinished" version. Howe's translation suggests that the earlier version contained nothing equivalent to Section 11 in the Chinese text, which excluded slave girls, courtesans, and prostitutes from the Girls' School. And in place of Section 22 quoted above, which condemned women's "loose customs" in the Shanghai foreign settlements, stood the following two sections:

22. Girls taken from Foundling Asylums cannot be given in marriage as concubines; much more shall the pupils of this school not be given as concubines, but shall be more highly esteemed in the world and loved by their parents, and not by being given as concubines tarnish the purity and disgrace the high standing of the school.

23. All countries prohibit the slave trade. China should gradually do away with the system of slavery. Any pupils who have been in the school, however poor they may be, may never be sold as slaves. Anyone violating this rule shall pay a fine of five hundred dollars.[132]

Insisting on class and gender equality, Howe's translation represented the "Provisional Regulations" of the future Girls' School as an anti-slavery and anti-concubinage manifesto. With such an "original" draft in hand, Kang and Shi saw the published version as revealing men reformers' class and gender bias.

The anti-concubinage discourse created problems for many men reformers, since on the whole they were not averse to the practice. Indeed, most of the men instrumental in founding the Chinese Girl's School had concubines themselves, and none of them seem to have condemned concubinage during the campaign. They did, however, try to involve concubines in the new Chinese Girls' School, sometimes with ingenious justifications. In an open letter to a fellow steering committee member, Jing Yuanshan urged that concubines be allowed to take part in the campaign because their minor positions within a household might be particularly effective at fundraising in Shanghai, where geomantic *fengshui* calculations showed prosperity in "minor positions" (*pianguan pianyin*).[133]

Women reformers, for their part, tried to elevate the position of concubines within the reform movement. For instance, the editorial board of the *Nü xuebao* placed the name of each contributor—whether a wife, a concubine, or a daughter—on the front page in her own right, not merely appended to that of a man, as in previous listings of fund subscriptions and public gatherings and thus created a space of intellectual equality.[134] Similar support was given to Peng Jiyun, who made an impressive appearance at the first meeting of the Women's Study Society by presenting a prose offering. Unfortunately, when the widely circulated *Pictorial from Touchstone Studio* (*Dianshi zhai huabao*) reported this event with an elaborate illustration of the scene, it represented Peng as someone's mistress (*sifu*) and described her participation in the meeting as the "most sensational spectacle" of the evening.[135] These pejorative remarks were deleted when the *Nü xuebao* reprinted this illustration in its second issue (see Figure 4.2).

In addition to demanding equality in education and marriage, and attempting to eliminate (or at least minimize) class differences, women reformers also advocated greater political participation for their "sisters." A striking example of such advocacy is Xue Shaohui's essay "On the Connection between Women's Education and the Way of Governing." It evaluates Chinese history using two feminist standards that had never been applied before: whether a historical period pays particular attention to the education of women and whether learned women have opportunities to "act according to their will, fulfill their ambition, and express their opinions on the way of governing." Successful rulers, Xue argues, are those who incorporate women's advice into their policy making, such as the sage kings of the Zhou and the virtuous Emperor Wen of the Han (r. 179–157 BCE). Only by "complementing men's strength with women's tenderness" (*gangrou bingji*) could a ruler "govern with great accomplishments."[136]

All in all, the 1897–98 campaign for women's education provided a site for competing versions of a new Chinese womanhood. On the whole, men's reformist discourses tended to focus on projects designed to strengthen the nation (including education for women). Refusing to slavishly follow their male colleagues, women intended to gain more knowledge than power, for they believed that only through learning could they better serve the country and the people. Their emphasis on free-spirited inquiry, a critical outlook, and female talent continued women's literary culture that had developed both in Fuzhou prefecture and the lower Yangzi River valley during the later imperial period. With their hearts/minds open and alert, these women also expanded and enriched all their qualities by incorporating Western resources. As a result, women in 1898 literally created notions of women's rights that the New Culture movement (ca. 1915–25) would later claim to have invented. Their original, sophisticated, and multidimensional ideas thus defy enduring stereotypes of a silenced, docile Chinese womanhood prior to the New Culture era.

FIVE

Translating the Female West to Expand Chinese Women's Space

After the abrupt termination of the Hundred Days, Xue and Shoupeng continued to champion the 1898 goals by translating Western literature, history, and science. Their major collaborative projects include *Waiguo lienü zhuan* (Biographies of foreign women, hereafter *Foreign Women*) (1899) (Figure 5.1), the *Bashi ri huanyou ji* (1900), translated from *Around the World in Eighty Days*, the English translation of Jules Verne's science fiction *Le Tour du monde en quatre-vingts jours* (see Chapter Six), and the *Shuangxian ji* (1903), a translation of the romantic novel *A Double Thread* by Ellen Thorneycroft Fowler (1860–1929) (see Chapter Seven). The couple also co-compiled a textbook titled *Gezhi zhenggui* (*Correct Guide to Science*) (1902) (not seen). No evidence shows that Xue knew any foreign language, but she was considered a better writer than Shoupeng in their circles.[1] Xue recorded and edited Shoupeng's oral translations from Western sources—a process that often ignited heated debates and difficult negotiations between Chinese and Western values. The couple never failed to record their differences in their respective prefaces and thus contributed to the debates on women's education begun in the 1897–98 Shanghai campaign (see below and Chapters Six and Seven).

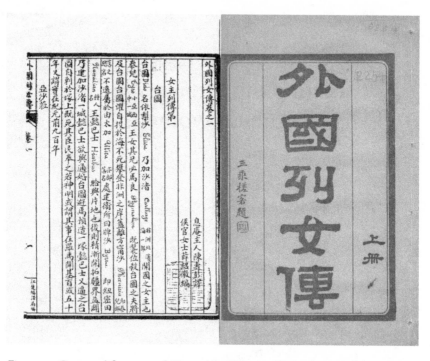

Figure 5.1. Cover and first page of *Biographies of Foreign Women* (*Waiguo lienü zhuan*). Trans. and eds. Xue Shaohui and Chen Shoupeng (1857–ca. 1928); the cover is inscribed by Chen Jitong with his *hao*, Sancheng chake 三乘槎客 (Thrice-Voyage Guest). (Nanjing: Jiangchu bianyi guanshu zongju, 1906.)

Their earliest and most important work was *Foreign Women*, arguably the first systematic introduction of the female West to Chinese readers. Xue initiated the project in 1899 with the explicit goal of "examining women's education in Western countries"; the work was completed in 1903 and published in 1906.[2] Xue, as we shall see, was its primary author but she also listened carefully to Shoupeng's voice, in order to appreciate the complex discourses of gender and culture that circulated in the reform era. Xue attempted, in portraying Western writing women, to carve out a distinctively female social and intellectual space within a male-dominated world. Seeing that this space was under constant threat from various patriarchal systems, Xue located her ideal womanhood in a wonderland of Greco-Roman goddesses, one that she transformed, through her literary imagination, into an ideal women's republic. In all, *Foreign Women* resulted from women reformers' desire to break the long-standing demarcation between the inner and outer domains and to reposition a new-style ideal woman living and working within the intersecting frameworks of the family, the state, and the world. In the process, foreign women's lives served not only as a model for educating contemporary Chinese women but also as a collective site where different visions of womanhood were contested.

The Compilation of the Biographies of Foreign Women

During the 1897–98 Shanghai campaign, a significant segment of the female Chinese elite emerged for the first time as a social group out of the conventional inner domain. Disputes immediately arose along gender lines as to how women should operate in this new space. Men reformers wanted women to enter the public domain in order to empower the nation, without advocating the liberation of women "for its own sake." Women reformers, however, advocated self-cultivation before national strengthening. Although certainly willing to learn from the West, they could not accept men's version of a Western educational paradigm that aimed at training women simply as jobholders. Xue, for one, questioned whether Western women could provide adequate models for developing "scholarly and literary talent" (*cai*) and "artistic and scientific accomplishments" (*yi*). Joan of Arc was the most prominent among the few Western exemplary women that men could offer in the early reform era; she could not, Xue averred, serve as a proper model for women's education because she gained fame not by virtue of her learning but rather by her religiously inspired valor.[3] Xue's critique exposed a general problem of the 1898 reform—its participants often admired the West uncritically.

Because men reformers had not provided sufficient information about Western women, Xue decided to pursue her own research. She engaged in a thorough study of the West and obliged her husband to search broadly for Western "exemplars of the inner chambers."[4] In the process, she always viewed Western knowledge with a critical eye, for she wanted to understand whether the alien "Dao" met China's needs.[5]

Compilation of *Foreign Women* took Xue and Shoupeng over seven hundred days on and off from 1899 to early 1903. "During this period," their children later recollected, "Father would narrate foreign-women stories at night while Mother jotted them down."[6] Based on extensive research of world histories and literatures, mainly English, Shoupeng orally translated over three hundred biographic sketches and tales of foreign women—mostly Europeans and Americans—dating from antiquity to 1885, which Xue rewrote and compiled into 252 entries under twelve biographical categories.[7] Identifying their original sources has been difficult because they did not include a list of references. Nonetheless, by tracking down the title(s) of a given woman's writings they cited in recounting her life and consulting major encyclopedias and biographical works on women published in English by the late 1900s, I have been able to make a number of educated guesses.

The couple must have collected their first list of eminent Western women from *A History of All Nations* by Samuel G. Goodrich (1793–1860), which Shoupeng translated from the most recent edition (1886) as the *Wanguo shilüe* (published in 1906). Over thirty women recorded in this work—female sovereigns, royal consorts, court ladies, and legendary heroines—all had entries in *Foreign Women*. The *Encyclopaedia Britannica* must have served as another resource, since it contained entries for almost all the women included in *Foreign Women*. None of the *Foreign Women* accounts was translated directly from the terse, laconic texts of these two works, however.

Most of the early *Foreign Women* stories up to the twelfth century were translated, often word for word, from the comprehensive *Dictionary of Greek and Roman Biography and Mythology* (1859) by Sir William Smith (1813–93), which also contained related references. The Bible served as another source about women in ancient times. The couple, however, referred to it as "remnant poems from the Hebrew tradition" (*Yipuliu suipian shi*), treating it as an historical and literary text rather than the "sacred classic" of the missionaries.[8] For women in later periods, the couple relied heavily on women's own writings. They consulted collective biographies and memoirs such as the famed *Lives of the Queens of England, from the Norman Conquest* (1840–48) by Agnes Strickland (1796–1874) and the *Memoirs of the Literary Ladies of England* (1843) by Anne Katharine Elwood (1796–1873).[9] They also made their own comments on every woman writer's accomplishments after reviewing her works and consulting memoirs by her relatives and friends, mostly women.[10]

The couple's exhaustive research produced a work on Western women that was not only the most comprehensive of its time in Chinese but also comparable to works of this sort available in Western languages in the late nineteenth century.[11] They included both celebrated names and relatively obscure talents who have only recently attracted Western scholarly attention.[12] They wrote each entry with meticulous care, dating most women to the very day of their birth and/or death and retaining personal names and place-names in the original language. They also attached easily accessible explanations of many Western concepts. For instance, they introduced *miyue* (honeymoon) as the "first month of a new marriage," and used the British poetess Mary Botham Howitt (1799–1888) and her husband, William Howitt (1792–1879), to showcase this happy time, when the couple compiled *The Forest Minstrel, and Other Poems* (1823). With such blessings a companionate marriage could offer, Xue and Shoupeng reinforced the sweet meaning of honeymoon (*juan* 4, 19a; *Foreign Women* entries are hereafter cited with the *juan* and the page numbers). Also, in introducing the Welsh actress Sarah Siddons (1755–1831) as a specialist in *bei'ai koubai* (tragedy, literally, sad dialogues), they took the opportunity to explain the difference between various forms of Chinese and Western drama, noting that plays "using only dialogue without singing and music were especially good for educational purposes" (*juan* 7, 4b–5a). Xue and Shoupeng were not only academically rigorous but they also brought in rich literary touches—beautiful rhetoric, interesting anecdotes, and diversified characterizations—making the reading of *Foreign Women* highly enjoyable.

As the biographies were collected and rewritten, major editorial differences emerged between the couple. One conflict occurred with the classification of the 252 *Foreign Women* entries. Xue chose to title the work *Lienü zhuan*, following the convention of writing women's history to illustrate "the virtues associated with proper womanly behavior in Confucian families."[13] She therefore planned a moral categorization of chastity (*zhen* 貞), purity (*jie* 潔), integrity (*jie* 節), and martyrdom (*lie* 烈).[14] Shoupeng contended, however, that "Western countries are strong and prosperous precisely because they have emphasized women's professions and pragmatic issues, not outmoded rituals and norms."[15] He therefore preferred to categorize women according to their professional occupations and social positions.[16]

A related issue was whether to provide an explicit evaluation of each foreign woman. Guided by Liu Xiang's Ur-text, Xue wrote a preface in the difficult parallel-prose style for each chapter and a poetic eulogy for each of the 252 entries. Shoupeng, however, argued that they should leave judgments to their readers. "What need is there to impose one's own biased opinion upon other people?" he asked. Accordingly, he deleted all of the prefaces and eulogies that Xue had painstakingly put together.[17]

What we see here is a Chinese man willing to understand the women of the West in Western terms and a Chinese woman striving to judge them according to traditional Chinese standards. Yet Xue cannot be accused of any sort of simple conservatism. She not only looked westward to find role models for her new conceptualization of womanhood but also became involved in public debates—first with men reformers such as Liang Qichao and then with her husband—about issues that had been vigorously debated in the heyday of the 1898 reforms. Shoupeng's profession-oriented classification clearly follows Liang Qichao's nationalistic approach to women's education, while Xue's morality-oriented classification presumably reflects her awareness of men's concern over possibly negative cultural influences from the West.

Xue's own understanding of foreign cultures was remarkably open minded. At the outset of her preface to *Foreign Women* she points out that "alien customs and exotic fashions each follow their own righteous track." "Feelings," she says, "arise from righteousness, and ritual accords with customs."[18] In other words, different cultures have different customs, rituals, and concepts of morality. Xue believed that by carefully considering the pros and cons of each culture she could find the moral measure of an ideal womanhood. The process begins, she explains, with "looking at a person's mind in observing him/her, and examining first a country's subtleties upon entering it." One can then weigh "the rights and wrongs, and gains and losses" of the culture in question. Only then, Xue contends, can "we borrow the mirrors and candles of others to illuminate our civilization."[19] The phrase "mirrors and candles" (*jingzhu*) refers to Western women, and "our civilization" in this context indicates Chinese women's moral-cultural accomplishments. The human mirror, *renjing*, has long served in China as a metaphor for checking and improving the self by reference to an equal subject inside the mirror.[20] The candlelight reveals the features of both sides and so assists this comparative process.

Xue's self-imposed moral mission led her to difficult negotiations between Chinese and Western values in compiling *Foreign Women*. She accepted Shoupeng's advice not to adopt an all-Chinese moral classification scheme, but she did not follow his idea of categorizing women entirely according to their social and professional status. Instead, she drew upon classifications from traditional Chinese standard histories (see Table 5.1).

This classification system included some moral categories as well as some conventional social and political ones, a judicious compromise. In this way, Xue was able to give Western women an equivalent historical status with men, inserting them into a grand narrative that in China had been overwhelmingly dominated by stories of male historical figures. Xue also accepted Chen's suggestion to "record the facts directly as they are" (*jushi*

Table 5.1. Classifications in *Waiguo lienü zhuan* Compared with Standard Chinese Histories

	Waiguo Lienü zhuan[a]	Standard Chinese Histories[b]
1	"Biographies of Female Sovereigns," 19 entries[c]	"Basic Annals of Sovereigns"
2	"Biographies of Royal Consorts," 27 entries	"Biographies of Royal Consorts"
3	"Biographies of Female Courtiers," 7 entries	"Biographies of Dutiful Officials"
4	"Biographies of Gentlewomen," 12 entries	"Biographies of Women"
5	"Biographies of Writing Women," 67 entries	"Biographies of Men of Letters"
6	"Biographies of Women Scholars and Artists," 11 entries	"Biographies of Scholars"
7	"Biographies of Righteous and Heroic Women," 8 entries	"Biographies of Loyal and Righteous Men"
8	"Biographies of Holy Women," 15 entries	"Biographies of Buddhist Monks and Daoist Priests"
9	"Biographies of Mistresses," 5 entries	"Biographies of Flatterers and the Favorite"
10	"Biographies of Actresses and Courtesans," 18 entries	"Biographies of Court Jesters"
Appendix 1	"Evil Women," 9 entries	"Biographies of Evil Ministers"
Appendix 2	"Goddesses," 58 entries	"Biographies of People from Foreign Countries"

a. Xue Shaohui and Chen Shoupeng, *Waiguo lienü zhuan*, "General Contents" ("Zongmu" 總目).
b. This list includes some of the most frequent categories in the standard Chinese histories: "Basic Annals of Sovereigns" ("Benji" 本紀) and "Flatterers and the Favorite" ("Ningxing" 佞幸) began with Sima Qian's *Shiji*; "Royal Consorts" ("Houfei" 后妃) and "Dutiful Officials" ("Xunli" 循吏) with Ban Gu's *Hanshu*; "Women" ("Lienü" 列女), "Men of Letters" ("Wenyuan" 文苑), "Scholars" ("Yilin" 藝林), and "Foreign Countries" ("Yiyu" 異域) ("Xiyu" 西域, Western areas) with Fan Ye's *Hou-Han shu*; "Loyal and Righteous Men" ("Zhongyi" 忠義) with the standard histories written in the early Tang, such as the *Jinshu*, and those of the Southern and Northern Dynasties. "Court Jesters" ("Lingguan" 伶官) only appeared in Ouyang Xiu and Song Qi, *Xin Wudai shi* 新五代史 (New history of the five dynasties).
c. The "General Contents" lists 15 entries, yet the actual number in the sub "Contents" and the text proper is 19.

zhishu) without passing much moral judgment.[21] As shown in Table 5.1, however, she kept at least two explicitly moral categories, namely, the "Righteous and the Heroic" and the "Evil." Moreover, she wove into each individual narrative her subtle vision of "praise and blame" (*baobian*), which had long been the hallmark of Chinese historiography. With her subtle critique of the female West, Xue intended to rewrite female virtue in China in conscious response to the moral concerns of men reformers. For instance, whereas men ironically retained the "strict morality" that had long confined the Chinese female body and mind as the "foundation" of their campaign for "liberating" women, Xue subverted the late imperial cult of chastity by advocating free-will marriage (see below).[22]

Expanding Women's Space by Means of Their Intellectual Attainments

Foreign Women focuses especially on the portrayal of intellectual women, including sixty-seven entries in "Writing Women," eleven in "Women Scholars and Artists," and eighteen in "Actresses and Courtesans"—about a hundred examples of *cai* and *yi* in total. Still more are spread throughout other chapters. Shoupeng explains why they grant women writers and scholars higher profiles than women of other occupations, saying that education for Western women emphasizes literary learning and treats all kinds of genres, poetry, fiction, and drama as equally important. "This is why Western civilization (*wenming*) flourishes."[23] For Xue, these *caiyi* exemplars embody the highest achievements of women's education. By examining their personal accomplishments and standing in society, Chinese women may have a reference point that will enable them to enter the public domain on a significant scale. To be sure, precedents existed in China for women to access the public domain by means of intellectual attainments, such as Xie Daoyun's veil story reveals. This kind of female entry into male-dominated space prevailed even more in late imperial China with the rapid increase in the number of writing women and wider publication of their works. As Dorothy Ko points out, "the expanded meaning of domesticity was in part a result of the recognition and endorsement of female talent in public arenas."[24] Grounded in the writing-women tradition, Xue comfortably borrows experiences of Western intellectual women to prepare her Chinese sisters for entry into much broader yet unfamiliar spaces. Below I shall elaborate on the presentation of these spaces in *Foreign Women* from three perspectives: space enjoyed, space expanded, and space threatened.

SPACE ENJOYED

According to Xue, culturally privileged Western females may more or less enjoy their own space, whether ideal realms created in writings, physical domains set up in studios and classrooms, or personal positions established in history and society. Xue opens the "Writing Women" chapter with the entry of the Greek poetess Corinna (fl. early fifth century BCE) to showcase the kind of space that women writers and scholars in the West have enjoyed:

> Corinna was a young Greek woman, well versed in lyrics. . . . She was talented and beautiful. Her fellow citizens all admired her as if looking up to a "goddess from heaven." Pindar [ca. 522–ca. 443 BCE], also a lyric poet, lamented his inferiority [to her]; Pausanias [fl. 479 BCE], a Greek general-poet,

admitted, "My clumsy poems, although heroic and powerful, can never come up to the elegance and charm of Corinna's—with graceful diversity, they embrace profound meanings." She was also named Μυῖα, meaning "to float gracefully as if to fly away." After her death, statues of her holding a harp were erected in front of universities for later students to emulate. (*Juan* 4, 1a–1b)[25]

柯林那 Corinna, 希臘女子,善箜篌之歌。. . . 既有才, 复豔於色, 同時五會之人, 皆遜讓欽仰如望天上人然。屏題 Pindar, 亦善箜篌歌之士, 自嘆弗及; 波生尼士 Pausanias, 希臘將軍而能詩者, 則謂: "吾詩雖雄強, 究不免于粗豪, 不若柯之秀媚, 嫋娜生姿、遙然意遠"。. . . 又名描亞 Μυῖα, 蓋取飄然若飛之意。其卒也, 國人肖其像, 抱箜篌立於大學校之前, 以為後學瞻仰。

Corinna epitomizes the achievements of all writing women: With poetic accomplishments superior to those of the best male counterparts of her time, she wins broad admiration in her own era as well as down through history, carving out a place of her own. This self-invented space confers on her the freedom to "fly" physically and spiritually. Her name, therefore, serves as a metaphor for Xue to depict writing women's relatively free lifestyle, from career to marriage.

In *Foreign Women*, women writers and scholars appreciate freedom in nearly every realm of their existence, beginning with the motivation for learning and writing: for self-entertainment (*ziyu*); self-consolation (*ziwei*) (*juan* 4, 2a); conveying feelings (*jiqing*) (*juan* 4, 6b, 20b); dismissing loneliness (*youji xiaoqian*) (*juan* 4, 9b, 12a); or making a living (*shengji*) (*juan* 4, 3b, 5b, 7b). These rather self-interested purposes differ emphatically from those of the Chinese male elite, who consider scholarship and literature in terms of what Cao Pi (187–226) described as "grand achievements in relation to state affairs and the everlasting occupations of glory."[26] Unburdening foreign women from such heavy responsibilities, Xue depicts them as freely roaming through all scholastic fields, all literary genres, and all writing styles at their pleasure.

Western intellectual women in *Foreign Women* represent a broad spectrum of expertise—in humanities: historians, poets, novelists, playwrights, philosophers, linguists, and journalists; in social sciences: economists, sociologists, and political scientists; in art: painters, musicians, composers, singers, dancers, and actresses; and in science: astronomers, mathematicians, physicists, and physicians. Many are able to cross intellectual boundaries. Wherever they choose to roam, education is always their shared mission. To demonstrate the erudition and productivity of Western women, Xue diligently documented the publications of each of the sixty-seven "Writing Women," most "Scholars and Artists," and some "Female Courtiers" and "Actresses and Courtesans." The titles and brief introductions of these works demonstrate that Western women writers and scholars have covered an extraordinarily broad range of human activities and written in a wide variety of genres, from multivolume chronologies to light character-sketches in the field of history, and from poetry, fiction, drama, and plays, to letters and diaries in literature. They also have published scholarly works in philosophy, economics, and political science, as well as scientific papers in mathematics, physics, chemistry, astronomy, and medicine.

Of Western women's intellectual products, Xue especially valorizes those written for women, children, and the poor, whose lives have been largely ignored by mainstream male agendas, as typified in Xue's sketch of the English scholar Sarah Trimmer (1741–1810). She commends Trimmer for "spreading motherly care (*poxin*) over the world of the abandoned and the unsheltered" with her publication of *Economy of Charity, or, An Address to Ladies* (in 1786). Using *poxin* to feminize the Confucian norm *gongxin*, "fair-mindedness" or "concern for public welfare," literally, "lord's care," Xue suggests that, since the male public does not treat women, children, and the poor fairly, women should care for themselves.[27] Xue also contends that the ideas Trimmer promoted in the *Family Magazine* and the *Guardian of Education* "surpassed millions of times those of later muddle-minded scholars who only caused damage to education" (*juan* 4, 5a). Here Xue links Trimmer's story to her own unabated and sometimes frustrating effort to advocate education for Chinese women.

Much of Xue's "motherly care" celebrates writing designed for women and children. Here are some examples. The famous French writer Marie-Catherine d'Aulnoy (1650–1705) produced fantastic, refreshing stories popular among young pupils (*juan* 4, 5a–5b). The English author and educator Anne Letitia Barbauld (1743–1825) excelled at conveying profound meaning in simple writing; she edited textbooks for children that were later repeatedly published in England as well as in other European countries (*juan* 4, 5b–6a). The Irish writer Maria Edgeworth (1767–1849) wrote *Moral Tales for Young People* (*juan* 4, 8b–9a). And the French author Sophie Cottin (1773 [1770]–1807) produced works that were broadly translated and especially favored by youths (*juan* 4, 9b). In her writings for women, the German poet Annette Elizabeth Droste-Hülshoff (1798 [1797]–1848) expressed deep thoughts in plain language. She also organized women's societies to promote education for women (*juan* 4, 14a–14b). The English educator Mary Carpenter (1807–70 [1877]) focused on reforming juvenile offenders; her Red Lodge Bristol Reformatory was successful at rehabilitating girls, and her written works, such as *Our Convicts*, were particularly effective in educating young people of both sexes (*juan* 4, 19b). The first American female doctor, Elizabeth Blackwell (1821–[1910]), distributed her book, *The Laws of Life: With Special Reference to the Physical Education of Girls* (1852 edn.), to young girls as free gifts in order to attract them to the career of medicine (*juan* 5, 5a).

Women writers also helped circulate men's works among women and children. For instance, the French writer Anne-Louise-Germaine Staël-Holstein (1766–1817), in addition to publishing her own works on the subject of women, also published the *Discourses* of Jean-Jacques Rousseau (1712–78), which proved attractive to young girls (*juan* 4, 7b–8a). Similarly, the English scholar Elizabeth Carter (1717–1806) translated the work of the Italian scholar Francesco Algarotti (1712–64), *Le Newtonianisme pour les dames, ou, Entretiens sur la lumiere, sur les couleurs, et sur l'attraction*, into English, under the title *Sir Isaac Newton's Philosophy Explained, for the Use of the Ladies, in Six Dialogues, on Light and Colours* (*juan* 4, 4b).

On literature, consistent with Xue's argument on poetry as basic learning for women, Xue and Shoupeng noted that Western women "take poetry as the most exalted genre" and praised their poetic achievements. For instance, Xue writes of the Scottish poet Anne MacVicar Grant (1755–1838): "Her poetry dispatches pure sentiments far and wide, making readers feel as if they were hearing the sound of sad weeping echoing along deserted mountains and valleys" (*juan* 4, 6b). Xue has, however, introduced more fictional works than poetry, possibly because of reformers' growing awareness of the sociopolitical function of fiction and drama. To be sure, Chinese translations of foreign literature began to appear as early as the 1870s, but broad-ranging appreciation of Western fiction emerged in China only in the late 1890s as part of the reform discourse.[28] Yan Fu and Xia Zengyou (1863–1924), for example, stated in an editorial in their reform journal *Guowen bao* (National news), entitled "Why We Plan to Publish Fiction in This Journal": "We have heard that the enlightenment of Europe, America, and Japan was usually assisted by fiction (*xiaoshuo*)."[29] The Chen brothers, too, were among the early introducers of Western fiction. In addition to publishing their own translations, Jitong mentored young novelists such as Zeng Pu. Jitong pointed out to Zeng that Chinese literature had valued poetry and prose as "orthodox genres for expressing thoughts and emotions" but despised fiction and drama—the focus of Western literature. He encouraged Zeng to "participate in world literature" by creating and translating fiction. Inspired by Jitong, Zeng slipped into a "frenzy about literature" and eventually created *Flowers in a Sea of Retribution*, one of the most famous late Qing novels.[30] Jitong no doubt also encouraged Xue and Shoupeng to place more emphasis on fictional works by Western women.

Late Qing scholars used the Chinese concept *xiaoshuo* (literally, minor talks) to translate the Western concept of fiction because both had fictitious features. Since Ban Gu first defined *xiaoshuo* in the *History of the Han* as "street talk and alley conversation, fabricated by those who engage in gossip along the roads and walkways," *xiaoshuo* as fabrication had been considered inferior to poetry and classical prose in Chinese eyes.[31] To undercut the prejudice against *xiaoshuo*, Xue used the early English fiction writer Aphra Behn ([1640]–89) to show that the British public loved fiction precisely for its imagination. Behn wove gossip and obscenities into her narrative, so daring that she often left her readers "dropping their jaws and breaking out in a sweat." Yet it was this sort of writing that established her literary reputation; "no scholar could compete with her" (*juan* 3, 1a–1b).

Because of their extraordinary achievements, the writers represented in *Foreign Women* were praised by their readers. *Alexias*, a biography by Byzantine princess Anna Comnena (1083–1148) about her father, was "highly regarded by the world" (*juan* 4, 1b–2a). The poetic remembrance of her fallen husband by the Italian poetess Vittoria Colona [Colonna] (1490–1547) won sympathy and admiration from her readers and was reprinted repeatedly after her death (*juan* 4, 2a). And the poems of the Scottish writer Anne MacVicar Grant, which conveyed "her feelings about literature and history," were "enjoyed by the entire world" (*juan* 4, 6b). Xue often compared women's achievements with those of the most accomplished men in the same field, as we have seen in the account of Corinna. In poetry, for instance, the Greek poetess Erinna appeared to be no less distinguished than Homer himself (*juan* 4, 1a). In terms of vivid prose and fresh rhetoric, the French writer Marie Anne Boccage (1710–1802) was comparable to such luminaries as Voltaire (1694–1778), Bernard Le Bovier de Fontenelle (1657–1757), and Alexis-Claude Clairaut (1713–65) (*juan* 4, 4a). In scholarship, the French classicist Anne Dacier (1651–1720) built a substantial reputation by translating and annotating the works of Callimachus (third century BCE), Anacreon (fifth century BCE), Sappho, Aristophanes, and particularly, Homer,[32] thus rivaling her husband, André Dacier (1651–1722), also a famous classicist (*juan* 4, 2b–3a). In historical writing, the multivolume *Lives of the Queens of England, from the Norman Conquest*, by the English biographer Agnes Strickland, was "hundreds of thousands times more interesting than those heavy, clumsy histories based on rigid and pedantic learning" (*juan* 4, 18a–19a). Likewise, the historical writing of the German author Karoline Pichler (1769–1843) was considered as sophisticated and beautiful as *The History of the Decline and Fall of the Roman Empire* by Edward Gibbon (1737–94) (*juan* 4, 9a). Perhaps Xue's most eloquent compliment paid to a foreign woman writer was paraphrased from the comments of Sir Walter Scott (1771–1832) on the English writer Jane Austen (1775–1817):

> Scott said, "This young lady is suffused with flowery talent. When I first met her I knew she was special. I often consider myself to be omnicompetent, yet all I can manage is but to scratch the surface of ordinary things. I can never reach that exquisite realm of hers!" (*Juan* 4, 10a)[33]

> 斯確特曰, "此女之才, 英華內斂, 余初見之, 即知其有異。余嘗自贊無有不能, 然所摸者書皮, 猶是尋常笨物, 奚及阿之進境良確哉!"

Talented Western women often seem to have garnered a certain freedom in personal relationships, such as Atalante, who heads the "Scholars and Artists" chapter. Xue portrays Atalante as a free spirit, a good archer who roamed in the mountains, shooting animals in order to protect people.[34] Many suitors sought her hand but all failed. Finally, Meilanion enchanted her with three golden apples he had obtained from Venus. Atalante married Meilanion but "was not confined by him," and eventually "she roamed far away" (*piaoran yuanyin erqu*) (*juan* 5, 1a). Xue adapted the Atalante story from the Smith version,[35] but added the detail of her final "flying" away from the marriage, possibly because Xue considered Meilanion, who tricked Atalante into marriage, no match for this excellent young woman.

After Atalante, Xue produced a long list of unmarried women writers and scholars.[36] Based on these stories, writing women in the West often refused to marry, fearing that they might not be able to find an intellectually equal husband. But if they did find such a man, even late in life, they would not hesitate to marry him. Angela Georgina Burdett-Coutts (1814–[1906]), a respectable Englishwoman who advocated education for girls and fostered homeless women, married when she was sixty-seven (*juan* 3, 8b–9a). In general, Xue and Shoupeng promote a marriage of mutual love and common intellectual interest. For instance, Gabrielle Émilie, Marquise du Châtelet-Laumont (1706–49), was the most learned French woman of the time, deeply admired and loved by the French philosopher Voltaire (1694–1778). But she eventually left Voltaire for her future husband and a dynamic marriage, in which the couple "now loved, now argued, and now read together" (*juan* 4, 3b–4a).[37] Given this standard of married life, "lack of happiness as husband and wife" or "lack of mutual love" naturally becomes a proper, justifiable reason for a divorce. The timing of divorce often coincides with the wife's financial independence, when she can rely upon her publications to support her family. As a result, life after divorce is usually depicted as a very happy and spiritually satisfying experience for the woman, teaching her children and writing.[38]

As we saw in the cases of Xie Daoyun and some Min poetesses, although there was a degree of tolerance and sympathy for these talented women for their resentment over an intellectually incompatible marriage, divorce was virtually impossible for them. Portraying the lives of foreign writing women as they do, Xue and Shoupeng justify Western-style divorce as a way for women to gain a measure of intellectual equality and freedom. It allows a wife to walk away from a loveless marriage, not to be chased away for one or another of the so-called seven offenses that justified a man's divorcing his wife (*qichu zhitiao*),[39] and assures a divorced wife intellectual legitimacy, financial independence, and moral righteousness.

SPACE EXPANDED

In addition to conventional intellectual domains, Xue and Shoupeng also introduce to Chinese women two unconventional spaces—salon and stage—that transgress class and gender boundaries. Xue uses Catherine Rambouillet (1588–1665) to exemplify the salon women. Graceful, sincere, generous, and learned, Rambouillet was able to transform her home into "the most famous salon in the seventeenth century"—the hôtel de Rambouillet—where she enjoyed an equal and harmonious relationship with her husband, nurturing culture and learning, receiving nobles and commoners alike (*juan* 3, 5b). Similarly, after being widowed, Marie Thérèse Geoffrin (1699–1777) converted her house into a gathering place for Parisian literati and scholars. Even strangers from other countries found their way to her salon (*juan* 3, 6a–6b). Traditionally, elite Chinese women were not to receive men at home or communicate with men in public.[40] Advocating women's key roles in French salons, Xue not only continued her Shanghai campaign to break long-standing gender segregation but also pointed to the direction in which women could lead intellectual interactions across gender and class divides, so as to nurture the cultural talents of both men and women.

Xue lists Rambouillet and Geoffrin in the category of "Gentlewomen," but categorizes more salon women under "Actresses and Courtesans," including Marie de Rabutin-Chantal, Marquise de Sévigné (1626–96), Marie de Vichy Chamrond, Marquise du Deffand (1697–1780), and Julie de Lespinasse (1732–76). Actresses and courtesans belonged to the lower social classes in China. Dividing her salon women into these two opposite social groups, despite no obvious differences between their respective social status,[41] Xue seems to highlight different aspects of their lives. In the category "Gentlewomen," she emphasizes salon women's self-cultivation and nurturing of art and literature. In "Actresses and Courtesans," Xue concentrates on their beauty, gracefulness, witty correspondence, feminine charm, and carefree lifestyle. Xue portrays actresses as also capable of *cai* and *yi*, albeit in theater, and equates them with writing women. Thus, with the category of "Actresses and Courtesans," Xue greatly expands the scope of writing women's space in both talent and lifestyle, posing a direct challenge to conventional Chinese social assumptions.

Xue begins "Actresses and Courtesans" with the Athenian courtesan Aspasia and thus pushes the origin of the salon back to ancient Greece. Under Xue's ink-brush, Aspasia, lover of the famed Athenian politician Pericles (499–429 BCE) and friend of the great scholar Socrates, appears to be a "wondrous woman of ancient times" (*shanggu qi nüzi*):

> Tired of the rigid Athenian inner-chamber rules, she eschewed the common custom of marriage and lived with Pericles out of wedlock. . . . Her home became a gathering place for famous Athenian scholars. Socrates [Xue's note: "a great Greek philosopher, b. 469 BCE."] came to chat with her regularly. Eloquent and witty, Aspasia was tenderly admired by all the Athenian men of letters. In order to stop her from [meeting with her scholar-friends], Pericles demanded that she marry him under the Athenian code of marriage. Aspasia refused. (*Juan 7*, 1a–1b)[42]

[厄士巴沙 Aspasia] 厭居雅典壼範之嚴, 悉脫婚嫁流俗迂見, 與牌毋利克爾 Pericles 胖合。. . . 厄士之家竟為雅典名人學士讌集之所。素庫勒得 Socrates (希臘大哲學家, 生於紀元前四百六十九年) 恒至與談笑。厄士口才明辯, 慧論環生。故文人雅愛之。牌欲禁制之, 要以雅典婚例。厄士辭不可。

By introducing the Greek courtesan Aspasia as the founder of the earliest salon, Xue has changed the definition of "courtesan"; she is no longer the notorious agent of the "oldest profession" but a cultural broker constructing new social and intellectual relationships across gender and class lines. Xue's reflections on the salon may have caused her to rethink the role of courtesans in Chinese history, as we can see in her poems about the famous late Ming Qinhuai beauties and Sai Jinhua (?–1936).[43] Are they not also hosts of salons?

Xue blurs class lines also in her attempt to equate actresses with writing women. On the one hand, she acclaims drama for having "particular effect on socio-moral transformation," and an actress therefore can prove to be a "worthy and capable woman" who exerts a positive effect on society. Thus, she characterizes some actresses using terms often applied to intellectual women such as "generous and intelligent," "high-spirited and broadminded," "dignified and square," and "pure and fresh" (*juan* 7, passim). On the other, Xue often uses stage imagery for portraying writing women, as typified by her adaptation of Scott's review of the English writer Ann Ward Radcliffe (1764–1823). Scott comments on Radcliffe's sudden exit from her writing career: "Like an actress in full possession of applauded powers, she chose to retreat from the stage in the blaze of her fame."[44] In Xue's rewriting, this passage blossoms:

> At the age of thirty-three, Mrs. Radcliffe chose to retreat from her writing career. In this she was like an excellent soprano: although her person has already left the stage, her voice was still resonating in the ears of the audience, stirring incessant applause. (*Juan* 4, 7a)

是時烏已三十三歲矣, 乃停其業。世謂有如善唱之女伶, 雖已下臺卸妝, 餘響猶存人耳, 鼓掌擊節而喝彩之聲不絕也。

For Xue, it seems, the stage is to an actress what a book is to a woman writer. Xue's equating of actresses with writing women, despite the humble social position of women performers in the Chinese tradition, opens up yet another space in which women can exhibit their creativity.

SPACE THREATENED

The generally comforting tone marking most of the *Foreign Women* entries on female writers and scholars is conspicuously absent from the entry about

Hypatia ([370]–415), the Alexandrian mathematician, astronomer, and "the most famous scholar of the Neoplatonic school of Plotinus" (*juan* 5, 1b). Xue draws upon Smith's *Dictionary* and John Toland's historical work *Hypatia* (1753) to depict this "most beautiful, most vertuous, most learned, and every way accomplish'd lady; who was torn to pieces by the clergy of Alexandria."[45] She, however, adds some Chinese touches to make Hypatia a perfect exemplar of virtue and talent, such as after Hypatia succeeded to her father's teaching position. Xue elaborates:

> Students from eastern tribes all came to study with her, and even the learned Greek scholars acknowledged her as their teacher. She sat on the podium with dignity, and students listened to her with great attention, feeling as if they were sitting in a spring breeze. All admitted that she was such an excellent scholar that no one, past or present, was her match. (*Juan* 5, 1b)

東方諸部落之生徒, 咸負笈拜列門墻內。即希臘智慧之士, 亦甘拜下風, 師事之。懿擁皋比, 巍然坐, 生徒列次, 屏息受教。一時之間, 如春風溥化然。咸稱得未曾有。

Alluding to a "spring breeze," Xue compares Hypatia's scholastic dignity implicitly to that of Confucius and thus grants Hypatia a Chinese-style authority and legitimacy. This sinicized image helps Chinese readers recognize the absurdity of the Alexandrian clergy who accused Hypatia of "seducing people with her beauty" and "beguiling them with heresy" (*juan* 5, 1b). It consequently intensifies the brutality of destroying this most precious talent and beauty: "[The clergymen] then dragged Hypatia to the Caesarian church, where they stripped off her clothes and sliced her to death. Then they hung her four limbs in Cinaron" (*juan* 5, 2a). The inclusion of this story reveals Xue's persistent worry that even in a seemingly comfortable social space, women might still be vulnerable to attack.

This concern also finds expression in two entries about women in the French Revolution—both of which must be understood in the light of late Qing enthusiasm for the idea of *nüjie*, heroic women. Frustrated by the abortive 1898 reforms and disgusted by the Boxer fiasco of 1900, certain male anti-Manchu revolutionaries, seeking additional support for resisting imperialism and toppling the dynasty, urged the transformation of Chinese women from literary and gentle ladies into Amazons.[46] The model of "foreign heroic women seemed to fit better the late Qing situation," as Xia Xiaohong has observed. Consequently, radical intellectuals competed to in-

troduce Western heroic women to Chinese audiences with so much enthusiasm that, in some cases, they "eloquently acclaimed" such women without
even knowing much about them.[47]

One of the names most invoked by the radicals during this period was
that of Marie-Jeanne Roland (1754–93). According to Western sources available in Xue's time, Madame Roland participated in the French Revolution
along with her husband, but the couple belonged to the mild Girondists.
After they "[l]oudly and ineffectually . . . protested against the savage September massacres [of 1793] in the prisons, . . . the pair became objects of the
enmity of the terrible Montagne." Madame Roland was finally taken to the
guillotine on 8 November 1793.[48]

Yet in Liang Qichao's "Biography of Madame Roland," published in 1902,
this victim of the French Revolution was labeled "the first heroic woman in
modern times" and elevated to become the "mother" of the French Revolution. In Liang's words:

> Who is Madame Roland? She was born of liberty, and she died of liberty. Who
> is Madame Roland? Liberty was born of her, and she died because of it. Who
> is Madame Roland? She is the mother of Napoléon, the mother of Metter-
> nich, the mother of Mazzini, the mother of Kossuth, the mother of Bismarck,
> and the mother of Cavour. In short, all great men of nineteenth-century Eu-
> rope must regard her as their mother; all civilizations of nineteenth-century
> Europe must regard her as their mother. Why is this so? Because the French
> Revolution is the mother of nineteen-century Europe, and Madame Roland
> is the mother of the French Revolution.[49]

Liang's description inspired other romantic portrayals of Madame Roland,
such as the following poem, published in April 1907:

Lioness Roland cries out in Paris.	巴黎獅吼女羅蘭,
Wind and tides rise, sweeping cold sleeves.	卷地風潮賽袂寒。
I love heroes, especially the female,	我愛英雄尤愛色,
Rosy cheeks look better in shining blood![50]	紅顏要帶血光看。

These images of beauty and blood foreshadowed the tragic death of Qiu Jin
(1875–1907) as a martyr of the Chinese revolution a mere three months later
in July 1907.

Xue's sketch of Madame Roland in *Foreign Women* is much closer to the
Western original, portraying her as a victim rather than a perpetrator of
the brutality and violence of the French Revolution. Xue depicts Madame

Roland as an intelligent, hardworking young scholar who, although unwittingly entangled in male politics, never ceased to learn and write, even during her imprisonment. Yet before she could complete the *Notices historiques*, she was taken to the court of the rebels (*luandang*) and was sentenced to death without following proper procedures. "She was executed simply because the Court of Terror slipped into a fit of madness—they wanted to kill so they killed her!" Xue ends her account with the following detail: "At the foot of the guillotine, Madame Roland remained composed. She asked for pen and paper, but the execution was ordered before she could write anything" (*juan* 5, 8b–9a). This symbolic moment offers a revealing footnote to Madame Roland's famous last words, "O liberty, how they have abused you!" (*O Liberté, comme on t'a jouée!*).[51] One of the crimes committed in the name of liberty, Xue seems to be telling us, is to destroy female beauty and intellect, the most tender and refined elements of humanity.

Xue's account of Marie Anne Charlotte Corday d'Armont (1768–93) reveals how the French Revolution beguiled a young woman with its revolutionary discourse. Like Madame Roland, Charlotte Corday was "indulged in education from a very early age" but was later "mistakenly" involved in revolution. She assassinated Jean-Paul Marat, the leader of the Jacobins, thinking she could save hundreds of lives from the Hydra of the Terror and was consequently sent to the guillotine. Xue comments: "Charlotte Corday was a beautiful and fragile young lady. Nowhere to spill her hot blood, she regarded her life lightly. The Jacobins then named her a female martyr. Alas, what a tragedy!" (*juan* 5, 9b). Whereas radical Chinese males tend to see women's martyrdom in terms of revolutionary romanticism, Xue views their deaths as a tragic loss of beauty and culture. For her, the French Revolution typifies a male disorder that either swallows up and destroys innocent women or beguiles them into becoming killers themselves. Either way, the sacrifice is lamentable.

Imagining the World of Foreign Goddesses into an Idealized Women's State

In the chapter on "Goddesses," Xue allows her creativity to roam freely, possibly because of the mythological nature of her sources. This does not mean, however, that she and Shoupeng are any less cautious than they have been with historical materials. Comparing this chapter with authoritative works on Greek and Roman myth, we can see that Shoupeng has translated from reliable sources, and Xue has never changed the original storylines. She has, however, added her own understanding of the moral of each tale and made other modifications to suit her purposes.

In order to make this mythological world accessible to Chinese readers, especially women, Xue employs a variety of interpretive frameworks and strategies, turning the world of foreign goddesses into "a contested site—a battleground for competing ideologies."[52] In this dynamic intellectual space, Chinese tradition contests with and modifies Western tradition; Confucianism and Daoism interpret Greco-Roman paganism; China's imperial system interacts with Western republicanism; and Chinese aesthetics confronts alien standards of beauty. The result is Xue's transmogrification of the world of Greek and Roman goddesses into an ideal women's state.

What political system does Xue envisage? Xue begins the chapter with Juno, the head of ancient Roman goddesses, with a close paraphrase of the Juno entry in Smith's *Dictionary*. She nonetheless changes Juno's political identity from "the queen of heaven" to the "female president of a [women's] republic" (*nü zongtong*), apparently because the mythological nature of Juno allows Xue to express her political preferences in ways that historical sources might not permit. (This is why, of the nineteen entries in "Female Sovereigns," Xue renders none as a "president.") Under this title, Xue assigns Juno the following duties:

> She guarded women's dignity and virtue. So people titled her "Virginalis" (*shude*), meaning the female virtue, and "Matrona," the motherly Way (*mudao*). . . . She was also the guardian of national finances and taxes, just like the mistress of a household who upholds frugality. The [national] mint erected a temple to Juno, celebrating her in its big hall, and titled her "Moneta," the master of the mint. Juno exalted female chastity, so prostitutes were not allowed to touch her altar. . . . June, the sixth month of the Western calendar, is named after her. People married in this month will be blessed with happiness. (*Juan* 8, 13a–13b)[53]

[朱囊 Juno] . . . 衛其類之端莊貞淑, 故加以徽號曰裴巾那力 Virginalis, 言淑德也, 曰馬都郎那 Matrona, 言母道也 . . . 朱亦護衛國之幣藏賦稅出入之事, 猶之人家主母冢婦, 總以儉約為主。錢局中常設其廟, 祀朱於大廳事, 謂為莽他, 言冶錢師也。朱尚節烈, 凡娼妓輩不宜使近祭壇 . . . 西歷六月曰朱榮 June, 即取朱之號。及期成婚, 必獲佳福。

Translating Juno's title Matrona as *mudao*, the motherly Dao, Xue links the goddess explicitly to her "Preface to the *Nü xuebao*," in which she argues: "Laozi says, 'The Dao is the mother of all things.' Mothering the world is precisely women's business. Who says that the female Dao (*kundao*) cannot achieve anything?"[54] Equating motherhood with the Dao that creates and nurtures the myriad things, Xue genders the Dao female and uses this as her point of departure for discussing women's rights, obligations, and functions. All of Juno's multifarious roles—protecting women's virtue, guarding the state's finances, and blessing marriage—fit Xue's reformist conception of the way women should operate in order to improve society. Thus, Xue's ideal world provides a model for the real one, as in her portrayals of other goddesses.

In keeping with the theme of *mudao*, Xue represents the Greek goddess Hera as a "mistress" (*zhufu*) in charge of marriage and childbirth. Although Smith's *Dictionary* indicates that "the Romans identified at an early time their Juno with Hera" (2:658), Xue insists that the two are "originally not the same" (*juan* 8, 13a).[55] She wants to structure her women's state, it seems, in a way familiar to the Chinese, with a head for the regime and a head for the household; together they maintain the stability of the state.

> According to (the Greek poet) Homer's epics, Hera was by nature obstinate, shrewish, and quarrelsome. When she was in a bad mood, she would fight with her husband [Zeus], but she was also very frightened of him. Anyone Hera loved, Zeus disliked, and he would even punish such a person because of Hera's affections. Zeus often chastised Hera, and bound her hands and hung her up in the clouds. Yet as a woman Hera had a majestic appearance. . . . [Among her temples] the one [at the foot of] Mount Euboea is the most famous. Her statue there is decorated with gold and ivory, and she is represented as a middle-aged woman, loving and kind, with a most beautiful forehead and two large and widely opened eyes, truly worthy of respect. Yet Homer calls her the Ox-eyed Hera. (*Juan* 8, 12b–13a)[56]

何買 Homer (希臘詩人) 之詩，懿性固執、悍潑、多言。癖發時恆與夫不睦，又甚畏其夫。懿所愛之人，無論若何，蘇士皆不喜之，甚且因懿而受罰。蘇士多詈懿、責懿。嘗縛懿手，懸吊於雲端。然而懿於婦女中顏貌堂皇。...廟在歐卑亞 Euboea 山上者尤著。其像以黃金象牙飾之。...其貌則一中年婦人，慈顏霽色，額尤美，兩眼特大，誠可敬也。而何買則謂為牛目之赫拉。

Xue seems to be offering contrasting images of the majestic but tempestuous goddess drawing upon two different sources, one verbal/textual—Homer's epics—and the other visual—Hera's statue at the foot of Mount Euboea. In Homer's eyes, Hera is clearly an imperfect woman—jealous, shrewish, nagging, and constantly at odds with her husband. But Zeus is obviously flawed too; he is also jealous, not to mention vindictive and domineering. Moreover, in some of the other biographies contained in "Goddesses," we learn from Xue about Zeus's numerous affairs with other women, which help to explain why his relationship with Hera is so tumultuous. Perhaps, then, Xue's account is designed at least in part as a critique of Zeus, who may have been the head of all the other gods, but who is far from flawless himself.

Xue also portrays a number of other *mudao*-style goddesses, comparable to courtiers, governors, scholars, and professionals, each with a special talent and in charge of a specific realm. For example, the Greek goddess Themis oversees the law, "wishing fairness among all things in the human world" (*juan* 8, 5a); the Roman goddess Minerva administers industry and commerce, as well as all kinds of professions: "poets, artists, educators, doctors, and all craftsmen are under her charge." She also guides military campaigns (*juan* 8, 12b). In the realm of scholarship, the Greek goddess Urania studies astronomy, "carrying a celestial sphere, and pointing at it with a bit of reed" (*juan* 8, 7a), and the Greek goddess Nemesis is an erudite scholar, "well versed in the principles of human beings and things." Xue writes pointedly that Nemesis "once went to debate with the gods, and defeated them" (*juan* 8, 11a–11b).[57]

Xue's valorization of *mudao* culminates in her portrayal of the goddess Athena, "a product of nature's harmony, a virgin who vigilantly guarded her virginity." Yet, despite her indifference to sex, Athena was not unconcerned about human feelings, and she was always enthusiastic in helping with divine and mundane affairs.

> Athena was in charge of agriculture, and created the plow and transplanted olive trees to Attica. She taught people how to use tools for making handicrafts, although some believe that she only taught women how to use the spindle and loom and needle and thread. She was also responsible for philosophy, poetry, and religious indoctrination. She was the guardian of Athens . . . and the Goddess of War. She protected righteous warriors, bestowing wisdom on them and stirring up their loyalty and courage. In the Trojan War, Athena favored the Greeks, and so the Greeks were victorious. All of Greece worships her, portraying her . . . as wearing a shirt, a gown, and a Confucian scholar's turban (*rujin*). A beauty dressed in plain and simple clothing, she has an especially dignified appearance. (*Juan* 8, 12a)

亞陝 Athena 為農事主宰, 創犁耙, 引種橄欖於亞的加 Attica; 教人工
技用器械, 或謂專為婦女織具針線耳; 而哲學、詩法、與宣道之技皆
屬焉。又為雅典保護主,... 又為司戰之神, 保衛義烈戰士, 生其智慧,
鼓其忠勇。都雷曾之役, 亞陝獨愛希臘人, 故能取勝。希臘舉國皆崇
拜之, 肖其像, 或半、或全、或首面; 範之、陶之、捏之、繪之、不
一足; 服飾則一裹衣, 一大衫, 首戴儒巾, 貌美飾簡, 益見莊重矣。

As in the case of Hera, Xue's sketch of Athena combines visual and verbal/
textual sources. Reading the narrative about Athena's moral and cultural
merits, Xue assumes (or at least wants her readers to think) that the head-
gear Athena wears in her portrait is a "Confucian scholar's turban," while
it is, in fact, a warrior's helmet. Xue takes similar liberties in describing
Athena's personal qualities. Smith, one of her primary textual sources of information, writes that "as her father was the most powerful and her mother
the wisest among the gods, so Athena was a combination of the two, that is,
a goddess in whom power and wisdom were harmoniously blended."[58] Xue
avoids the rather legalistic (*fajia* 法家) term "power," speaking instead of
Athena's "dignity and strictness," which are closely related to the Confucian
moral code of *li* 禮法 (ritual, propriety). By identifying Athena as *ru* 儒
(Confucian) and invoking Confucian ethical categories and concerns, Xue
domesticates the Greek goddess in striking and significant ways.

If virginity and the motherly Way can coexist in Athena, so can love and
mudao in the case of Venus.

> Venus is the Roman goddess of love. . . . If we seek to trace her origin,
> . . . she may have come from people's psychological need for happiness in
> marriage. They believed that there should be someone in charge of love in
> order to harmonize the relationship between husband and wife. . . . The
> most important ceremony dedicated to her is in April, because spring is the
> time when the myriad things begin to sprout, the best season for wedlock.
> (*Juan* 8, 5b–6a)

攀納斯 Venus ... 羅馬謂為司情愛之神女。... 要其本原,... 當係人
心以婚嫁為歡樂, 遂臆造之。以為情愛之事, 自有主宰, 使夫婦乃
克和諧。... 所尊之典禮, 則以四月為貴, 蓋一年春季, 正萬物生長
之機, 為婚姻及時之候耳。

Xue discreetly avoids any detailed account of Venus's erotic adventures, emphasizing instead the theme of family harmony.

With a similar sense of decorum, Xue suggests that nymphs can have
children without sex. Here, she brings into full play her imagination, her

capacity to synthesize intellectual systems, her cunning and subtle rhetoric, and, above all, her valorization of *mudao*:

> Nymphs, the highest rank of goddesses in the famous classics, were the mistresses of oceans, streams, jungles, swamps, caves, ponds, mountains, valleys, forests, and so forth. . . . All these goddesses flourished in moisture, which nurtured them and enabled them to bear children. They indulged themselves in the happiness of farming and hunting. They lived by themselves and took dancing as their occupation. Their sensuous beauty (*yanli*) connoted tenderness and sincerity (*wenrou dunhou*). These goddesses embodied all kinds of fantasies and tastes, borne of the imagination of ancient Greeks while they were confronted with diverse marvels of nature: tumultuous oceans, running springs, dazzling sunshine, colorful fallen leaves, and desolate cliffs and valleys, all kinds of picturesque and poetic scenes. When people became absorbed by scenery, they fancied that someone there must be in charge of it all; hence the legends of nymphs emerged. (*Juan* 8, 10b–11a)

> 寧夫 Nymphs, 著名經籍中為上品之女神, 主大海、溪潤、叢林、原澤、洞穴、池沼、山巒、谷峽、樹木等。...凡此諸神女, 皆盛於濕氣, 培養滋潤, 遂生嬰兒。嗜田獵之樂, 羣雌合居, 以跳舞為事。豔麗之中, 有溫柔敦厚意。良為古希臘人幻想不等之奇象趣味也——海波之掀騰, 流泉之奔突, 日光之炫爍, 落葉之繽紛, 巖壑之闃寂, 畫景也, 詩景也, 神之所注, 遂以為有所主宰其間者, 而諸神女之說於是出矣。

This interpretation conveys a decidedly Daoist understanding of nature: a female-dominated world, full of *yin* elements, where women bear children without involving men. Both the idea and the rhetoric remind us of the *Laozi*: "The spirit of the valley never dies; / This is called the mysterious female" (谷神不死, 是謂玄牝); and "In concentrating your breath can you become as supple / As a babe?" (專氣致柔, 能嬰兒乎?).[59] Of course, Laozi is discussing how, through controlling the breath (*qi*), one may be able to transform oneself into an infant, the most "natural" and original state of a human being. But a woman who bears a child does something similar in concentrating her own *qi* to produce a new life. Thus, it appears that Xue's promotion of nymphs from their originally lesser position in Greek and Roman mythology into "the highest rank of goddesses" reflects her esteem for the Daoist values of life and naturalness.[60] At the same time, she exalts a Confucian poetics of "tenderness and sincerity." Joining Daoist and Confucian values in this remarkable way, she seems to suggest that art, poetry, and myth emerge at the moment when human eyes perceive the sensuous, feminine beauty of natural scenes and human minds embrace Mother Nature's tenderness and sincerity in nurturing life.

Exposing her readers to a world of foreign goddesses, Xue has created an imaginary state exclusively for women. Neither entirely Chinese nor Western, it is an autonomous, peaceful, joyful, and productive world. Women there, animated by the spirit of *mudao*, can create and nurture children as well as beauty of all kinds, including not only art and poetry but also their own lovely and dignified female bodies. In addition, this state offers spiritual asylum for women who have suffered at the hands of men. To be sure, Xue's vision of a women's utopia is highly idealistic. But the significant point is that she has the courage to envision a better world as well as the ability to draw upon a broad range of cultural resources in order to articulate it.

. . .

In their creative and multifaceted attempt at self-cultivation and self-transformation, women reformers like Xue became open-minded critics of both Chinese and Western traditions. Their critical spirit enabled them to contribute to a cautious and sophisticated incorporation of certain Western ideas into an indigenous framework of values, standards, and behaviors. In the process, Western models of political, social, economic, and cultural change necessarily interacted with and became transformed by Chinese ideas and experiences. *Foreign Women* is, in some ways, a typical product of this approach. With the help of her husband, Xue meticulously classified, translated, and transplanted the female West, weaving it with Chinese tradition into a coherent system of knowledge designed to provide life guidance for Chinese women. The core value she implanted in this system is *mudao*, the motherly Way, comprising *ci*, motherly love, and *xue*, learning. This value, generated initially from the home, extended outward to a much larger intellectual, social, and political space.

With the compilation of *Foreign Women*, Xue intended to prepare her fellow women (and herself) for new roles and responsibilities as they walked into the public domain. As devoted mothers, wives, and daughters, Xue and others conceived their goal to be not only nurturing their families but also, at least eventually, embracing all of China and the world. As Xue concludes in her preface:

Using elegant words to depict the "four virtues,"	四德表幽閒之藻,
Our moral and cultural aura will naturally extend far and wide.	自然風教宏施。

Women all over the world will respectfully come   萬國咸襝衽而來，
    to join us.
Then, will it be so difficult to see the Yellow   豈果河清難俟也哉!
    River become clear?[61]

Working together, these women could purify the world with their learning and their virtue, achieving something that men had never been able to accomplish on their own.

SIX

Introducing Modern Science and Technology through Literature

As part of her reform efforts in the aftermath of the Hundred Days, Xue wrote broadly on modern science and technology when the topic had not yet attracted attention in the literature in China.[1] Some of her poems composed in the 1880s, such as those on the right-turning conch shell, a Swiss gold watch, and fruit wine, had already manifested this wide-ranging interest. Her departure from Fuzhou in 1897 brought her into a much broader intellectual realm, and her participation in the reform movement transformed her early curiosity into a self-conscious effort to incorporate modern science and technology into her knowledge base and pedagogy. Chen Shoupeng recalls:

> My wife Lady Xiuyu has been married to me for twenty years. In between household chores she used to entertain herself by reading classics and histories, and she believed that beyond China no culture was worth mentioning. After I took her traveling through Wu and Yue, she learned about the convenience of ships and trains, and saw things like steam engines and electric lights. Shocked, she wanted to pursue the mysterious underlying principles and then looked for translated books to read. She sighed: "Now I know! The world is so big that each place has its special scholarship. Previously I was

stubbornly self-confident. No wonder I missed [all this new knowledge]!"
She therefore asked me to teach her about world histories and treatises.[2]

Although Xue had previously received a certain amount of foreign knowledge from Shoupeng, traveling to modernized places such as Shanghai, and the journey itself, gave her valuable firsthand experience. The cultural shock stimulated Xue into a frenzy of studying knowledge that existed beyond China, in particular modern technology and its scientific foundations. Xue ardently shared her newly acquired knowledge with Chinese readers, basically in two literary forms—classical parallel prose and the far more accessible genre of popular, quasi-vernacular fiction.

Poeticizing Science and Technology

The year 1897 marked the expansion of Xue's coverage of scientific and technological themes as well as her new interest in parallel prose. In prefacing Xue's *Collected Prose*, Xue Sihui sighed in admiration of the parallel-prose essays Xue Shaohui had published in news media of the time:

> After reading them carefully, I could tell that she composed these essays using the structure of ancient prose as the bones and decorated them with the flowery rhetoric of poetry. In these essays she invested all that she had learned in the past twenty years. But, isn't it also true that she benefited from the landscape as her travels to remote places enlarged her experiences and knowledge?[3]

Developed in the Six Dynasties, parallel prose is perhaps the most difficult genre in traditional Chinese literature. It features abundant allusions and meticulous reasoning, phrased in rigorous parallelism and refined rhetoric. The great literary critic Liu Xie (ca. 465–ca. 522) defines allusion as "citing a fact to explain a certain meaning and supporting a current argument based on a past experience," all with the goal of "clarifying principles" (*mingli*).[4] Liu Xie also explains parallelism as a nature-endowed literary form:

Nature bestows forms to all things,	造化賦形,
With their limbs always in pairs.	支體必雙,
The divine principle operates in such a way	神理為用,
That nothing stands alone.	事不孤立。
The mind creates literary language, and in doing so	夫心生文辭,
It organizes and shapes one hundred different thoughts,	運裁百慮,
Making the high and the low mutually dependent,	高下相須,
With the result that parallelism spontaneously arises.[5]	自然成對。

Parallel prose thus requires the author to possess both learning and talent, and in this alliance, Liu Xie tells us, "talent is the leader and learning is the assistant. When the leader and the assistant combine their capacities, literary glory triumphs."[6] This genre therefore offered Xue a suitable medium for conveying her ideas. Its broad use of allusions allowed her to introduce new knowledge to a sophisticated readership in culturally familiar ways. Its beautiful rhetoric provided her with the perfect opportunity to attract readers with a dazzling combination of wisdom and talent. And its parallelism linked concepts through their mutual interaction, definition, and modification—an ideal framework for transmitting cultural and intellectual knowledge in a coherent and valued literary form. It is worth noting that, with only ten years of practice in this extremely difficult genre, Xue made herself among the most accomplished parallel-prose writers of her time.[7]

A vivid illustration of Xue's attempt to poeticize science and technology in parallel prose can be seen in her "Postscript" to the *Zhongguo jianghai xianyao tuzhi* (1901), which Shoupeng translated from the British Royal Navy's *China Sea Directory*. In her postscript Xue again publicized the differences between her views and those of Shoupeng and hence went well beyond conventional praise featured in this genre. It was unusual enough for a Chinese husband to invite prefaces or postscripts from his wife, and even more so for the wife to take the opportunity to criticize her husband and for the husband to welcome the criticism. The dispute began with Shoupeng expressing gratitude to the British in his own introduction to the *Directory*:

> This book was originally published in 1894, an eventful time for our country. The intention of the British was to awaken us to self-strengthening, so they focused on trading ports and commerce, hoping that we Chinese can protect our country in the same way that they [British] protect their business. As long as our country is safe, so will be their merchants who live here. . . . The British truly care for us![8]

Xue, however, viewed Great Britain's careful study of the Chinese coastline as more a threat than a blessing. She thus commended the translation only for use "as a mirror to guide us out of the ford of confusion." She went on to say,

If we can use their work as a candle to illuminate our vision,	倘能反燭相觀,
It will be just like heaven offering clods to Jin;	恰若天與晉塊;

If we can clarify our territory and guard it,   果克劃疆自守,
The Yangzi River will cut short the years of Foli.[9]   居然江斷狸年。

The first line of this couplet alludes to a famous *Zuo Commentary* (*Zuozhuan*) story about the Jin ducal son Chong'er (697–628 BCE): fleeing the political chaos in Jin, Chong'er begged for food from a farmer but was given only clods of dirt. His attendant advised him to take the clods as heaven's gift, an auspicious omen implying the eventual restoration of his fief.[10] The second line alludes to the warning by the Liu-Song general Zang Zhi (400–54) to Emperor Taiwu of the Northern Wei (Tuoba Tao, nickname Foli, r. 423–52); if he invaded the South it would result in his death, as had already been predicted in a child's ditty: "When the horses of barbaric soldiers drink from the Yangzi River, / Foli will die in the *mao* year" (虜馬飲江水, 佛狸死卯年).[11] Using these allusions, Xue advises a policy of learning from the aggressive foreigners to prevent further aggression.

Xue states that the *Directory* has made ten contributions in accurately mapping China's coastline: 1) determining longitude and latitude (*ding jing-wei* 定經緯); 2) making navigational charts (*zhu luojing* 著羅經); 3) forecasting winds (*zhan fengqi* 占風期); 4) locating tides and tidal streams (*zheng chaoxin* 徵潮信); 5) identifying islands and mountains (*ji Shantou* 紀山頭); 6) detailing sailing lines (*xiang shuixian* 詳水綫); 7) marking lights (*biao dengta* 標燈塔); 8) setting up buoys (*she foumiao* 設浮錨); 9) recounting social customs (*fu minfeng* 附民風); and 10) identifying trading prospects (*lie shangwu* 列商務).[12] Xue illustrates each category with an "extensive display of details" (*puchen*)—a parallel-prose feature that elaborates on every aspect of the subject. Contending that all the scientific and technological categories in the *Directory* have Chinese equivalents, Xue often draws upon theories and borrows pertinent terms and phrases from Chinese classics. These Chinese concepts imbue Western ideas with rich cultural and historical connotations, thus domesticating alien information. Let us look at the first two of the ten categories.

1) Determining longitude and latitude

Xue begins by laying out a cosmos described in the *Laozi*, one in which "*Qian* and *Kun* interact as with the movement of bellows; / Heaven and earth contain pure and peaceful ether (*qi*)" (乾坤本橐籥之交, 天地含清寧之氣).[13] This, she notes, is the natural backdrop for navigation. The ancient Chinese measured the sky and the land by arithmetical rules set up in the *Classic of the Gnomon and the Circular Paths of Heaven* (*Zhoubi suanjing*) using the optical method of the sundial recorded in the *Mozi*. The British followed similar principles and developed a system of geographic coordinates to locate places, albeit with newer devices such as the telescope. Xue describes the function of these devices using the Chinese idiom "to view the sky through a tube and to measure the sea with a calabash" (*guankui li'ce*), turning this conventional criticism of one's narrow perspective into praise for a broad view of the sky and sea.

[The *Directory*] thus positions elusive islands	遂使海山兀兀,
On the vast ocean, [so that navigators can find them as easily]	海水湯湯,
As fetching a suckling pig steamed on a stove	如探俎上蒸豚,
And counting the deer rounded up in a walled enclosure.[14]	如計壁中鹿肉。

Xue ends with a gendered approach, comparing the positioning of islands to women cooking in the kitchen and men hunting in the mountains—human activities correlated with a natural cosmos.

2) Making navigational charts

Xue again draws upon a Chinese vocabulary to explain Western astronomic observations and calculations, referring to Zhang Heng (78–139), who devised the world's first rotating armillary sphere (*huntian yi*) to represent astronomical phenomena,[15] and the monk Yixing (683–727), who created the *fuju* diagram to measure the length of a meridian arc.[16] She then writes:

The Bow and Arrow constellation [within Canis Majoris] guides	參之弧矢,
The principle of the *Sea Mirror of Circle Measurements*;[17]	為《測圓海鏡》指歸;
Sailing directions are regulated,	定其準繩,
By the subtle methods from the *Sea Island Mathematical Manual*.[18]	出《海島算經》奧秘。
[The *Directory*] provides thorough and exhaustive data,	盡數窮微,
And reduces complexity to simplicity.	變繁用簡。
No need to borrow counting rods from beyond the abacus,	無需盤外借籌,
It offers all the guidance necessary for calculations on a ship.[19]	實合舟中布算。

Xue emphasizes that expanded maritime activities will allow peoples all over the world to communicate, and in the process, they can learn about each other. She remarks on the ninth contribution, "Recounting social customs":

Inhabiting land or water, people have different capabilities;	居陸居水別其能,
Living in Yue or in Chu, people have different attributes.	安越安楚殊其性。
In poor, abandoned, and outlandish places,	窮荒多異,
The Dao of Lu [Confucius] is doomed to fail;	魯道必衰;
When the ocean is placid,	海波不揚,
The Sage will appear.	聖人乃出。
If one can make auspicious clouds gather,	果使青雲干呂,
How difficult will it be for tributaries to assemble at the imperial court?	何難奉贄充庭?
Looking at the direction to which a sleeping cow or horse turns its head,	無如牛馬來眠,
One can tell the location of a place with a good natural environment.	隱辨水土風氣.
. . .	. . .
To know the qualities of a state's governance,	要知國政方圓,
We need to investigate closely what people support and oppose.[20]	薄視人心向背。

Xue acknowledges that people in different environments have different qualities, but they can live together in harmony as long as they have adequate living arrangements and good government. Although Xue alludes mainly to Confucian sociopolitical ideals for speaking to Chinese readers, her concern for people's well-being clearly goes beyond the territory of China.

This humanitarian approach should be equally applied to trading, as Xue writes on the last contribution, "Identifying trading prospects":

Ships from faraway Kunlun carry huge loads of goods For making profits;[21]	婆蘭載崑崙之舶, 計算奇贏;
Warehouses are overseen by bureaus of commerce, So that people can exchange rare treasures.	貨廛設茶馬之司, 貿通珍異
. . .	. . .
Tea, shaped like coiling dragons or bird tongues, Cannot compete with opium;	龍團雀舌, 莫敵芙蓉之膏;
Silk from Shu and Wu Dominates the market of kapok fabric.	蜀錦吳綾, 竟奪吉貝之布。
Wealthy and capable in management, [Merchants] possess treasures and pearls.	多財善賈, 懷寶函珠。
Let all talents under heaven try their utmost,	竭天下之精才,
So as to open fair markets in the light of day.[22]	遂日中以互市。

Xue's vision of a modern world is one in which technology and trade, facilitated by just and enlightened rule, benefit everyone. Xue even adds an implicit gendered touch to her discussion of trade: tea, one of China's major products, cannot defeat opium because Chinese men have indulged too much in the drug. By contrast, Chinese women have produced silk to win the market over from kapok fabric from Southeast Asia.

Xue's postscript draws substantially upon landscape poetics in an effort to make hard science more appealing. In the fifth contribution, "Identifying islands and mountains," Xue chants:

As swallows dart up and winds blow,	燕起風生,
Merchant ships gather [on the coast];	收集賈舶;
When birds flock to show that the shore is close,	鳥飛岸近,
They identify a naval base.	特識海師。
[Islands spread on the ocean,] like blue snails falling on a plate,	青螺一盤,
Or lotus flowers rising from the water.[23]	芙蓉數朵。

Xue often loads these beautiful lines with allusions that broaden and deepen the reader's understanding of the text. In the sixth contribution, "Detailing sailing lines," for instance, she asks rhetorically:

A hundred *li* winding and then a thousand *li* straight,	百里曲, 千里直,
The sailing lines turn like the Yellow River;	若轉黃河;
The northern bank mountain is named Zhe, and the southern one, Kan;	北曰赭, 南曰龕,
In between them the water rushes through the cliffs.	來穿狹岸。
If one can take a shortcut through the Zhongnan Mountains,	果終南捷徑之可通,
Why bother with the constant bends along Shanyin Road?[24]	豈山陰道上之不暇?

The "shortcut through the Zhongnan Mountains" (*Zhongnan jiejing*) originally referred to ascending in officialdom by making a lofty reputation through reclusion. The phrase is, however, metonymically related to Wang Wei's poem titled "Villa in the Zhongnan Mountains" ("Zhongnan bieye" 終南別業). Its couplet, "Traveling to the place where the water ends, / I sit and wait to see clouds rising" (行到水窮處, 坐看雲起時), induces an optimistic tone, suggesting alternate routes for a journey whether in life or along a physical path.[25] The "constant bends along Shanyin Road" alludes to a *Shishuo* episode about

Wang Huizhi (d. 388). Traveling in Shanyin, he sees "mountains and streams naturally reflecting each other, making it difficult to detail the beauty of every bend in the road. During the transition from autumn to winter, it is even harder to express what moves one's innermost feelings" (2/91).[26] Referring to this touching vignette, Xue introduces human feelings into a scientific essay, thus softening its emotionless message and delighting readers' senses with rich colors, alluring rhythms, and profound implications.

Another beautifully written, parallel-prose paragraph on science and technology is in Xue's "Editorial Introduction to the *Official Daily of the Southern Ports*," on the topic of "Telegraphic Reports" (*dianbao*):

Yin and yang correspond and interact;	陰陽之气, 有感斯通;
Zinc and sulfur are combined through oxidation.	鋅硫之養, 久而合化。
Amber attracts mustard seeds and magnetism directs the compass;	珀拾芥而磁引鍼;
Fish carry letters and flying geese arrange their lines into characters.[27]	魚傳書而雁作字。
Far, far away, although blocked by mountains, One can still hear the voices at the other end;	迢遞之關山阻隔, 響應偏靈;
Within a brief time, people can gather and greet one another Via agile steam engines.	須臾之音問周旋, 氣機獨敏。
[Telegraphic systems] stretch far and wide like spiderwebs, Passing on messages faster than human envoys;	縱橫蛛網, 速於傳命值郵;
Wires sway in the air like silk threads, Revealing their [enemy's] military intelligence.[28]	搖曳蠶絲, 洩彼軍情消息。

In this short passage, Xue summarizes basic knowledge of physics and its application to people's daily lives. She starts with a general introduction to the theory of electromagnetism, the basis of such telecommunication devices as the telegraph and telephone, which can instantly transmit human-to-human messages in both coded texts and actual voices. Xue also introduces the idea of steam-engine vehicles that magically transport goods and people. Xue structures her descriptions of scientific principles and technological applications into highly symmetrical syntax with refinement and accuracy. Meanwhile, her use of animal and insect analogies enlivens copper wires and steel machines as if they were organic components of the natural world. Again, Xue ends her discussion with a gender-related touch, juxtaposing women's sericulture to men's military operations—a clear invocation of the *Laozi* axiom that "the soft can overcome the strong."[29]

Using the exquisite structure of parallel prose, Xue skillfully weaves Chinese expressions and allusions into her essays on Western concepts and technologies. She thus imbues scientific inquiry with human qualities, offering cultural and scientific knowledge along with advice for self-strengthening. Moreover, parallel prose was one of the most prestigious genres in the late Qing.[30] Thus, Xue's use of this genre as a means of introducing new knowledge was designed to attract attention from sophisticated readers. To be sure, Xue's parallel-prose essays are not easy to read. Her choice to write in an elegant style was consistent with her idea of women's literacy, which endorsed a highly refined blend of elite cultures, Chinese and Western (see Chapter Four). Xue understood, however, that foreign knowledge should eventually reach a broader audience and so she experimented with a combination of classical and vernacular Chinese in her works of translation.

Translating Science Fiction into a Textbook

Xue and Shoupeng translated Jules Verne's *Le tour du monde en quatre-vingts jours* (1873) into *Bashi ri huanyou ji* (hereafter *Huanyou ji*) from its English translation, *Around the World in Eighty Days*, by George Makepeace Towle and N. d'Anvers.[31] Published in 1900, this collaborative project marked the first Chinese rendition of Western science fiction and the first of Jules Verne's works (Figure 6.1). The *Huanyou ji* was so well received that it was reprinted four times by four different presses from 1900 to 1906, including one serial publication in the *Eastern Times* (*Shibao*), running from 20 December 1905 to 28 January 1906.[32] Even the famed male feminist Jin Songcen (aka Jin Tianyu, Jin Tianhe, 1873–1947), the author of the *Women's Bell* (*Nüjie zhong*) (1903), proclaimed in 1905 his "admiration for the work."[33] And he composed six heptasyllabic quatrains to commemorate six most remarkable moments of the journey.[34]

Initially, Shoupeng had been reluctant to proceed with the translation project because he felt that *Around the World* depicted only "trifling techniques" (*diaochong xiaoji*). Xue, however, pointed out in her parallel-prose preface to *Huangyou ji* that "[the author] used language that shocks the mind and amazes the eyes, / To explain scientific principles" (以驚心駭目之談, 通格物致知之理). Xue lists three main messages of the novel in her preface. First, it teaches the importance of learning science. Equipped with

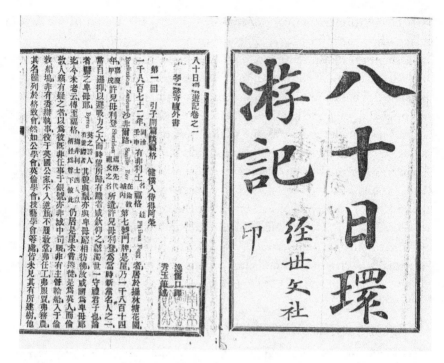

Figure 6.1. Cover and first page of *Bashi ri huanyou ji*. Translation of *Around the World in Eighty Days*, an English translation of Jules Verne's *Le tour du monde en quatre-vingts jours* (Shanghai: Jingshi wenshe, 1900). Page 1 indicates that the book was orally translated by Chen Shoupeng and transcribed by Xue Shaohui.

broad scientific knowledge, the major character, Phileas Fogg, freely traverses the globe, "like the moon circling the earth and the constellations passing through the sky" (如月繞地, 如星經天), and he "returns home on a black ship, as easily as galloping through the Luyang plain" (烏輪返舍, 奚翅揮戈魯陽). Second, the novel values moral strength. Fogg's journey is full of danger, and to overcome all the difficulties takes wisdom, loyalty, and trustworthiness. Third, the novel affirms the value of learning about different places and peoples, describing them in such fascinating detail that "Sima Qian and Yang Xiong might have written just like this, / And the poets of the *Book of Songs*, however they might try, could not have surpassed its fine taste and profundity" (雖太史輶軒, 殆不過是; 極風人旨趣, 復何以加).[35]

Inspired by Xue's enthusiasm and argumentation, Shoupeng agreed that, indeed, the novel revealed a broad range of "practical learning" (*shixue*). For instance, its descriptions of important port cities, mountains, rivers, beautiful landscapes, historical and religious spots all "conformed with astronomic, geodesic, and navigational principles."[36] Shoupeng therefore helped add extensive annotations to explain geographic, astronomic, and anthropological terms as well as relevant cultural, economic, legal, and sociopolitical systems. All this indicates that the couple aimed at translating science fiction into a textbook of world culture, history, and modern science and technology. The following section examines how the couple tried to achieve this goal, focusing on three strategies: Xue's choices of narrative and linguistic styles; the annotations the couple chose to add; and Xue's intentional mistranslations and insertions.

MAKING THE NOVEL ACCESSIBLE TO THE PUBLIC

Xue, who penned the translation, adopted the narrative style of traditional Chinese chapter-structured novels (*zhanghui xiaoshuo*), such as *Journey to the West* (*Xiyou ji*) and *Dream of the Red Chamber* (*Honglou meng*). In so doing, she domesticated Verne's work, transforming a foreign work of science fiction into a conventional Chinese novel, in the fashion of which Xue titled each chapter with a perfectly paralleled couplet and mixed vernacular prose with easily understandable literary Chinese. This couplet titling served two ends, in addition to creating a more familiar product for Chinese readers: First, compared to the English chapter titles that authentically rendered the French original, Xue's titling gives a far more complete understanding of the content of the novel. By reading the couplet-titles alone one could easily see the outline of the plot. Second, this sort of outline supports Xue's views concerning the literary merits of *Around the World*, that the "opening and closing and ups and downs of this record (*ji*), and its rhetorical and semantic transitions and transformations, all correspond with Chinese essay writing conventions."[37] And in describing *Around the World* as *ji*, Xue intends to convey the idea that the work is not merely fiction; rather, it is a respectable historical account as well as a sophisticated travel essay, both named *ji* and both connoting substantial knowledge and well-reasoned moral arguments. Below, to show the effect of Xue's retitling, I offer a side-by-side comparison of a few of the English titles and their Chinese counterparts, organized according to the literary principles of "opening," "ups and downs," and "closing":

1) The opening section of the novel

As we can see from Table 6.1, Xue's Chinese retitling of the first five chapters adds important details from the text proper and foreshadows the action in much clearer terms. Whereas Verne's titling does not mention explicitly

Table 6.1. Comparison of Titling between *Around the World* and *Huanyou ji* (Chapters 1–5)

	Around the World in 80 Days	Huanyou ji	Translation of the *Huanyou ji* titles
1	In which Phileas Fogg and Passepartout accept each other, the one as master, the other as man	引子開篇談福格 健僕入侍得阿榮	The prelude opens the novel by introducing Phileas Fogg; The energetic servant Jean Passepartout enters his service
2	In which Passepartout is convinced that he has at last found his ideal	契主心欲傾肝膽 見僕約整理寢房	Finding an ideal master, Passepartout intends to serve him wholeheartedly; Seeing the list of the housekeeping routine, Passepartout tidies Mr. Fogg's bedroom
3	In which a conversation takes place which seems likely to cost Phileas Fogg dear	維新會聚談刦案 葉子戲拼賭環遊	At the Reform Club, a discussion of the recent bank robbery; Over the card game, a bet on a tour around the world
4	In which Phileas Fogg astounds Passepartout, his servant	攜氈包兩人就道 上火車諸友送行	Carrying a carpet bag, the two embark on the tour; Aboard a train, they see friends come to see them off
5	In which a new species of funds, unknown to the moneyed men, appears on 'Change	報紙紛紜爭賭票 電文緊急捉行人	Newspapers dispute over Fogg's project, and instigate the Fogg bond; A telegraphic dispatch is rushed out, and a warrant for the arrest of the traveler is issued

the wager that Fogg made with his fellow Reform Club members or the bank robbery for which he was blamed, Xue reveals that his tour around the world in eighty days resulted from a bet, that Fogg had been mistaken for a thief, and that the newspaper accounts of Fogg's tour brought knowledge of his bet to the public. Meanwhile, Xue gives hope to the reader that an "energetic servant" (*jianpu* 健僕), Jean Passepartout (whom Xue transliterates as A Rong 阿榮, an affectionate appellation for a younger person), has entered Fogg's service for noble reasons and that he will prove to be loyal and devoted.

2) Ups and downs of the plot

Xue's Chinese retitling highlights the highs and lows of Fogg's journey much more effectively than Verne's original titles and their English translations. An especially dramatic episode takes place in the forest of India (see Table 6.2).

Xue's use of the terms *xunsi* 殉死 (to bury the living with the dead) and *fenshen* 焚身 (to burn a person alive) to describe suttee shows a de-

Table 6.2. Comparison of Titling between *Around the World* and *Huanyou ji* (Chapters 11–14)

	Around the World in 80 Days	Huanyou ji	Translation of the *Huanyou ji* titles
11	In which Phileas Fogg secures a curious means of conveyance at a fabulous price	得良友順道同遊 購馴象解金償價	They obtain a good friend who travels in the same direction; They purchase a tamed elephant as a means of conveyance at a fabulous price
12	In which Phileas Fogg and his companions venture across the Indian forests, and what ensued	趁行程草率投宿 窺殉死惻隱生情	Touring in a hurry they carelessly find a place to stay; Seeing a suttee procession they develop a feeling of compassion
13	In which Passepartout receives a new proof that fortune favors the brave	救焚身福格定計 刦屍場阿榮立功	To rescue the human from the flames of suttee, Fogg designs a plan; Carrying the victim away from the pyre, Passepartout wins merit
14	In which Phileas Fogg descends the whole length of the beautiful valley of the Ganges, without ever thinking of seeing it	賓象良朋悲別路 艷妃健僕快同車	Sadly, they part way with the precious elephant and their good friends; Happily, Fogg boards a train with a beautiful princess and an energetic servant

liberate equation of certain practices of the cult of chastity in late imperial China with the brutality of this Indian custom. Using the term *ceyin* 惻隱 (compassion), Xue insinuates this Mencian moral concept into the travelers' attitude toward this barbaric form of human sacrifice. Describing Jean's rescue of the suttee victim as *jie shichang* 刦屍場 (to free a person from the funeral pyre), Xue reminds the Chinese reader of the notion of *jie fachang* 刦法場 (freeing a person from the execution ground), a typically heroic behavior in the classical Chinese novel *Water Margin* (*Shuihu zhuan*). Moreover, by designating Sir Francis, whom they meet along the journey, and the Indian guide as *liangpeng* 良朋, good friends, and describing the elephant as *bao* 賓, precious, Xue distributes credit equally to human beings and animals for helping to rescue the victim. Finally, in presenting the victim as a *yanfei* 艷妃, "beautiful princess," she suggests that a romantic relationship is developing. All these devices helped Xue introduce Western and Indian culture to her Chinese readers in ways they would have found interesting and accessible.

Another remarkable episode in *Around the World* records the travelers' risky experience in America (see Table 6.3).

Table 6.3. Comparison of Titling between *Around the World* and *Huanyou ji* (Chapters 25–29)

	Around the World in 80 Days	Huanyou ji	Translation of the Huanyou ji titles
25	In which a slight glimpse is had of San Francisco	選議員釀成械鬥 化包探引作朋儕	An election meeting instigates a fierce fight; A detective is transformed from an enemy into an ally
26	In which Phileas Fogg and party travel by the Pacific Railroad	轍路全關人力闢 火車無奈野牛何	The railroad is constructed completely by manual labor; The locomotive has no way around wild buffaloes
27	In which Passepartout undergoes, at a speed of twenty miles an hour, a course of Mormon history	妙典獨聆莽忙士 遊蹤共歷鹽湖城	Passepartout alone listens to the miraculous doctrines of Mormonism; They together join an excursion in Salt Lake City
28	In which Passepartout does not succeed in making anybody listen to reason	大難敵手逢參將 容易奔車過斷橋	Great difficulties occur when they see Fogg's adversary Colonel Proctor; Easily the running train passes over the broken bridge
29	In which certain incidents are narrated which are only to be met with on American railroads	英雄氣何妨比武 娘子軍竟敢前鋒	The two courageous adversaries do not mind engaging in a duel; A lady warrior dares to fight as the vanguard

Xue's retitling sets the travelers' activities against the backdrop of America's political, religious, and ethnic conflicts, offering a colorful picture of life in the still-untamed western regions of the United States. It also underscores a feminist spirit that is completely absent from the original titling.

3) Closing

Xue's retitling of the final four chapters shows that the adventure concludes in perfect correspondence with the opening: the solution of the bank robbery, the winning of the wager, and a wedding that draws a happy ending suitable to Chinese minds (see Table 6.4).

As indicated above, the quasi-vernacular style of the *Huanyou ji* contrasts sharply with the difficult parallel-prose rhetoric of Xue's preface, showing her ability to reach both literary elites and the general reading public. An early conversation between Fogg and Passepartout demonstrates her popularizing approach (see Table 6.5; note that the numbers in the left-hand column refer to consecutive sentences, here and below in Table 6.6).

Table 6.4. Comparison of Titling between *Around the World* and *Huanyou ji* (Chapters 34–37)

	Around the World in 80 Days	Huanyou ji	Translation of the Huanyou ji titles
34	In which Phileas Fogg at last reaches London	刼案已明仇自解 倫敦遲到局將輸	The robbery is resolved, and the detective's hostility is dissipated; Reaching London late, Fogg will lose his bet
35	In which Phileas Fogg does not have to repeat his orders to Passepartout twice	賭局欲輸無活著 圍爐對語有深情	A wager is about to be lost, nothing can be done about it; A conversation by the fireplace reveals deep feelings
36	In which Phileas Fogg's name is once more at a premium on 'Change	福格票忽增時價 維新會共待歸人	The "Fogg bond" suddenly increases in value; The members of the Reform Club wait together for the returner
37	In which it is shown that Phileas Fogg gained nothing by his tour around the world, unless it were happiness	太陽差終贏賭局 禮拜堂偕訂新婚	Journeying toward the sun Fogg gains a day and wins his wager; A wedding in the church makes Fogg and Aouda husband and wife

Table 6.5. Xue's Quasi-Vernacular Trial at Translating Narrative

	Around the World	Huanyou ji	Translation of the Huanyou ji
1	A puzzled grin overspread Passepartout's round face; clearly he had not comprehended his master. "Monsieur is going to leave home?"	阿榮心頭迷亂, 不知主人意向。因強作笑容, 請曰: "老爺出門, 將何之?"	Passepartout was confused, not knowing what his master intended to do. He forced out a grin, saying: "Monsieur is going to leave home? Where to?"
2	"Yes," returned Phileas Fogg. "We are going round the world."	福格曰: "吾欲環遊地球。"	Fogg said: "I am going round the world."
3	Passepartout opened wide his eyes, raised his eyebrows, held up his hands, and seemed about to collapse, so overcome was he with stupefied astonishment. "Round the world!" he murmured.	阿榮裂眥竪眉, 握拳而駭。似憤懣, 又復憂疑, 乃喃喃而語曰: "環遊, 環遊? 地球, 地球?"	Passepartout opened wide his eyes, raised his eyebrows, and held up his hands in great shock. He seemed overcome by disbelief, murmuring: "Round the world? Round the world?"
4	"In eighty days," responded Mr. Fogg. "So we haven't a moment to lose." (Chapters 4, 24)	福格曰: "僅限八十日, 故一分鐘不容失!" (*juan* 1, 8a)	"In eighty days," responded Mr. Fogg. "So we haven't a moment to lose."

Table 6.6. Xue's Quasi-Vernacular Trial at Translating Poetry

	Around the World	Huanyou ji	Translation of the Huanyou ji
1	Her narrow and supple waist, which a hand may clasp around,	一掬細腰弱不禁,	A hand may clasp around her narrow and supple waist.
2	sets forth the outline of her rounded figure and the beauty of her bosom,	雞頭新剝當胸襟。	Two fox nuts, newly peeled, are placed upon her bosom.
3	where youth in its flower displays the wealth of its treasures;	年華富比花含蕚,	The richness of her youth is comparable to a flower about to bloom;
4	and beneath the silken folds of her tunic	畫裳百褶牟芳心。	Her painted skirt with its folds carefully envelops a fragrant mind.
5	she seems to have been modeled in pure silver	非華加馬神乎技,	Only Vicvarcarma's godlike skill of sculpture,
6	by the godlike hand of Vicvarcarma, the immortal sculptor. (Chapters 14, 102)	合將麗質範白金。 (*juan* 2, 12b)	Can properly model her beauty in white gold.

Xue's translation here contains only a few words in literary Chinese. Each line has the literary *yue* 曰 instead of the vernacular *dao* 道 or *shuo* 說 ("to say"), and in line 2, Fogg uses the literary *wu* 吾 instead of the vernacular *wo* 我 to render the concept "I." The only literary syntactic structure is in the first line, *hezhi* 何之, "Where to?" In short, the language style of this conversation, as with others later on, approximates that of classical Chinese vernacular novels.

Another example of Xue's vernacular practice can be found in her translation of a poem that Verne attributes to the Indian poet-king Ucaf Uddaul, which celebrates the charms of the queen of Ahmehnagara. Above, in Table 6.6, is the last stanza, again in a side-by-side comparison.

Compared with Xue's classical poems introduced in preceding chapters, this verse is much simpler in terms of its syntactic structure, poetic rhetoric, and imagery. It is also apparently designed to appeal to more popular tastes. For instance, the rather vulgar phrase "newly peeled fox nuts" (*euryale ferox*), which alludes to an erotic legend graphically depicting Tang Xuanzong's fondling of Yang Guifei's breasts,[38] would never appear in her own poems and essays.

ANNOTATION FOR KNOWLEDGE ACQUISITION

In describing the reasons for Fogg's journey, and explaining why it made such a "lively sensation" in the news media (chap. 5, 29), Xue felt the need to emphasize that Fogg did it "all in an effort to open new territories and add new experiences to geographical learning in England" (*juan* 1, 9b). Xue's understanding of the need for a greater "geographical awareness" emerged from a growing sense in the latter half of the nineteenth century that knowledge of the world was an important element in China's Self-strengthening movement.[39] Foreign aggression dating from the First Opium War undermined China's Sinocentrism and forced the Chinese elite to reexamine China's strategic situation with increasing attention to faraway lands. For Xue, "geographical awareness" was especially relevant, since both Jitong and Shoupeng were direct products of the Self-strengthening movement. Through them she came to understand that, in China's present situation, geography was an indispensable constituent of "new learning" for the "new people." She maintained, however, that knowledge of the world should be a matter of universal concern, as she had argued in her preface to the inaugural issue of the *Nü xuebao* in 1898 (see Chapter Four). In the service of this idea, but with her Chinese audience foremost in mind, she asked Shoupeng, a specialist in navigation, to add extensive geographical annotations to almost every place Fogg visited in his journey around the world.

For each location, the couple retained its English name and gave it a brief geographical description, often including details such as latitudinal and longitudinal coordinates, important landmarks, the height of mountains, the length of rivers, and even general elevations. These annotations not only contributed to readers' knowledge but also enhanced their understanding of the story. For instance, as soon as the bank robbery was discovered, "detectives hastened off" to major ports all over the world (chap. 3, 16). The couple attached geographic details to each of the listed locations, such as to Liverpool: "A town in northwestern England, by the Irish Sea, located at 53 degrees 24 minutes 3.8 seconds north latitude calculated from the equator, and 3 degrees 4 minutes 17 seconds west longitude calculated from England" (*juan* 1, 5a–5b). Similarly, when the *Daily Telegraph* listed eight transportation stops for an estimate of Fogg's tour (chap. 3, 18–19), one of them was Calcutta. Xue and Shoupeng noted: "This is a big capital city in eastern India, sitting where the Ganges River splits and runs [south] into [the Indian] Ocean; it is located at 22 degrees 35 minutes north latitude calculated from the equator and 88 degrees 30 minutes east longitude calculated from England, about 100 miles from the Indian coast" (*juan* 1, 6b).[40] The couple paid special attention to Calcutta apparently because it was where the rescue of Aouda took place and where Fogg, Passepartout, and Aouda fled India.

Throughout the book, Xue and Shoupeng chronicled religious beliefs, historical legends, and social customs along with presenting vivid and detailed physical descriptions. For instance, after fleeing the funeral pyre in Calcutta, the travelers boarded a train and arrived at Benares. This city, as Verne wrote (based on Brahmin legends), "is built on the site of the ancient Casi, which, like Mahomet's tomb, was once suspended between heaven and earth" (chap. 14, 105). Xue and Shoupeng added: "Mahomet was the founder of Islam. After his death a mosque was built as his tomb and his coffin was suspended in mid-air as if supported by gods and spirits. Later people figured out that the coffin was made of iron, and the walls of the mosque were made of magnet" (*juan* 2, 13b). Evidently the two translators felt the need for a scientific explanation of the supernatural myth. When Verne characterizes Benares as the "Athens of India" (chap. 14, 105), Xue and Shoupeng took the opportunity to introduce Athens as the capital of ancient Greece, where "Western literati, poets, philosophers, scientists, and archeologists all gathered at the time" (*juan* 2, 13b). In so doing, they expounded on the cultural significance of both cities.

In his narrative, Verne introduced some Hindu deities while depicting "fervent Brahmins" solemnly performing their pious ablutions in the sacred Ganges (chap. 14, 106). In their annotated description of the Vedic god Vishnu, Xue and Shoupeng identified two manifestations of the deity, one male and the other female. The male has four arms, holding respectively a mace, a discus weapon, a bell (a conch in fact), and a lotus flower in each of his four hands. The female lies on a seven-headed snake and has only two arms, with one hand pointing toward heaven and the other hand empty. A lotus flower emanates from her navel, and a deity with four bearded heads sits in it, holding a mace and three sutras in his four hands (*juan* 2, 14a). Although the couple may not have painted a full and accurate picture of Vishnu, they nonetheless re-created an image appealing to Chinese gender sensibilities, with the female avatar as a nurturer of life, culture, and power, rooted in the lotus flower, a long-standing symbol of Buddhist mercy and purity for the Chinese.

In writing about the travel of Fogg and his party on the Pacific Railroad, Verne noted that this "great trunk line" crossed the entire width of the United States, connecting not only cities and states but also mountains, rivers, and lakes. Verne also reported that the construction involved decisions by President Lincoln himself. Moreover, it was undertaken with speed and efficiency. The work, Verne told us, was pursued with "true American energy" and, despite the rapidity with which it was built, the execution was excellent (chap. 26, 214). Xue and Shoupeng added more detailed notes, including, for instance, the distances between cities and states (*juan* 3, 18b–20a). Taken together, their annotations, reflecting obvious admiration for America's technological achievements, underscored the strategic and commercial importance of railroads, a form of transportation that was scarcely evident in China before the Qing dynasty's defeat in the Sino-Japanese War.[41]

On the train crossing America, Passepartout hears a missionary delivering a lecture on Mormonism. Xue and Shoupeng seem to have been transfixed by this young, American-born religion, and so to their 1,000-character translation of this episode they added an even longer (1,400-character) note on Mormon history. According to their account, the founder of the religion, Joseph Smith (1805–44), claimed in 1823 that he had been informed by a celestial messenger of the existence of the Book of Mormon. He received the book, engraved in Egyptian on golden plates, from the messenger on 22 September 1827; he published an English translation in 1830, and founded the church of the Latter Day Saints in April of the same year. Being persecuted by the government of various states because of their practice of polygamy, the Mormons constantly moved. Expelled from Missouri in April 1839, they were accepted by Illinois and settled down in Nauvoo. "The Mormons thereupon cleaned up thorny bushes and weeds, turning the wilderness into a wonderland, like flowers in bud" (*juan* 3, 23b). But in the summer of 1844, Joseph Smith was killed by an angry mob in Carthage, Illinois. In order to avoid incessant hostility from people who disapproved of Mormon marriage practices, his successor, Brigham Young (1801–77), decided to move his flock to Utah in 1846, and in 1850 Salt Lake City was established (*juan* 3, 22a–24a).[42]

One can sense a sympathetic tone in the couple's account of Mormon history. They transliterated "Mormons" with the characters *Mangmangshi* 莽忙土, signifying "a group of grass-rooted busy people." Wherever they went, the Mormons were busily engaged in transforming the wilderness into a wonderland. "Unfortunately," Xue notes, "the polygamy practiced by the Mormons disturbed the regions around" (*juan* 3, 23b). As we have seen in Chapter Three, Xue did not like polygamy personally, but she considered it a matter to be settled within the family, not a practice that warranted harassment, much less government suppression. In her preface to *Around the World*, Xue even wonders aloud how it is that "[the Mormon] people may marry three or five wives, without being licentious or jealous" ("Xu," 2b). There must be some wisdom that the Chinese could borrow to deal with concubinage.

Xue and Shoupeng's sympathy for the Mormons seems to have arisen primarily from their distaste for an intolerant government. In Verne's narrative, the Mormon missionary tells his audience "that Joe Smith is a martyr, that his brother Hiram is a martyr, and that the persecutions of the United States Government against the prophets will also make a martyr of Brigham Young" (chap. 27, 222–23). Xue and Shoupeng bluntly remark: "All these martyrs were killed by the American government" (*juan* 3, 22a). The missionary told the audience that Smith "announced himself, in 1843, as a candidate for the Presidency of the United States" (chap. 27, 225). Xue and Shoupeng translated the passage this way: "He announced, in 1843, that he would imitate the American system of presidential elections" (*juan* 3, 23b), implying that Smith intended to be the president of a Mormon state. We may surmise that their sympathy for the Mormons reflects support for vulnerable people in the face of government repression, reminiscent of the six martyrs killed by the Qing government after the Hundred Days of 1898, which foreshadowed the future Han Chinese demand for a constitutional monarchy built upon provincial autonomy (see Chapter Eight).

CHARACTERIZATION AND THEMATIC CONSTRUCTION THROUGH MISTRANSLATION AND INSERTION

Guo Yanli praises Xue and Shoupeng for having presented an almost "flawless" translation of *Around the World*. This judgment may ring true based on a comparison with some later translations of Jules Verne's work—notably Liang Qichao's *Shiwu xiao haojie* (Fifteen little heroes), derived from a Japanese version of Verne's *Deux ans de vacances* (A two years' vacation). Liang's paraphrase, Guo notes, is "totally incomparable" with *Huanyou ji* in accuracy.[43] Yet mistranslations certainly exist in the *Huanyou ji*, as even Shoupeng seems willing to admit (see Figure 6.2). Some mistakes may have resulted from Shoupeng's hasty reading, but they do not distort the original plot line. Others, however, are likely the result of Xue's conscious modification of the text in order to transmit certain thematic messages. I shall focus my analysis on the function of the changes she made to the three major characters: Fogg, Passepartout, and Aouda.

1) Fogg's transformation from a reserved gentleman to a passionate scholar

Verne portrays Fogg as an "eccentric gentleman" who in all matters displayed "his marvellous qualities of coolness and exactitude" (chap. 37, 314). Xue tries to dig into deeper layers of Fogg's life and personality. She seizes

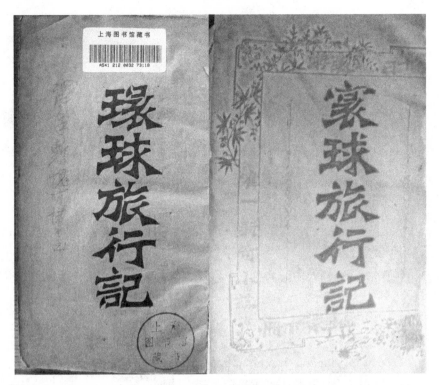

Figure 6.2. Cover and frontispiece of *Huanqiu lüxing ji* (A voyage around the world) (Shanghai: Xiaoshuolin, 1906) (reprint of *Bashi ri huanyou ji*). The inscription on the frontispiece (left image) reads: "I am embarrassed about the translation. What a pity!" (譯筆慙愧, 可惜之至). This inscription, handwritten with a fountain pen, is possibly by Chen Shoupeng who, having studied abroad and died much later, might be more likely than his wife to have used a fountain pen. The superb writing style also looks rather masculine.

upon one feature in particular that Verne has introduced at the outset, that Fogg was "one of the most noticeable members of the Reform Club" (chap. 1, 1), which she translates as *xindang* 新黨 or *weixin hui* 維新會, using terminologies that liken Fogg to a Chinese reformer. Thus, on Verne's statement that Fogg "belonged, in fact, to none of the numerous societies which swarm in the English capital" (chap. 1, 2), Xue elaborates: "He had enough strength to set up his own Reform Club, not needing to rely upon other groups like an ordinary person" (*juan* 1, 1b). Still, Xue feels that Fogg needs to amplify his learning continually in order to carry out reform—a position Xue holds consistently in translating *Around the World*. She therefore changes Verne's line indicating that Fogg's name "was strange to the scientific and learned societies" (chap. 1, 2) to read that "his name was on the lists of scientific and learned societies" (*juan* 1, 1a).

Xue also seeks to identify the spiritual strength that sustained Fogg throughout his daring circumnavigation of the world. After faithfully translating Verne's sentence that "people in general thought him [Fogg] a lunatic, and blamed his Reform Club friends for having accepted a wager which betrayed the mental aberration of its proposer" (chap. 5, 30), Xue adds a passionate passage in Fogg's defense:

> Being foolhardy may not necessarily mean that one cannot fulfill one's mission. It all depends on whether the adventurer has a sincere (*cheng*) mind and a strong will to endure hardship. Those who were critical of him were merely wagging the writing brush to add some gossip; they could do no harm to Fogg! (*Juan* 1, 9b)

> 冒昧未必不可以成事, 特視其心能誠, 其志能苦與否耳。彼紛紛之議 其後者, 不過馳騁筆墨, 供其談助, 於福格實無所增損也。

Granting Fogg the quality of *cheng* (sincerity, integrity), the spiritual value at the center of the ideal of the Confucian sage (see Chapter Seven), Xue transforms his "lunatic" trip into a noble learning experience.

In addition to portraying Fogg as a learned scholar, Xue depicts him as a thinker whose actions are predicated on deep thoughts. For instance, Verne tells us that in order to check if his newly hired servant Passepartout will show up promptly on time, Fogg "was steadily watching a complicated clock which indicated the hours, the minutes, the seconds, the days, the months, and the years" (chap. 1, 5). Xue modifies this line to read that "he was watching the clock in order to decipher its wondrous secret: what makes an hour, a minute, and a second? How do they accumulate into a day, a month, and a year?" (望其鐘, 解測奧妙, 若者點, 若者分, 若者秒, 若者積以成日, 若者積以成月成歲) (*juan* 1, 2a). Thus, a line intended to show Fogg as a rigid man is changed to present Fogg as a profound phenomenologist, who ponders such difficult topics as time and being.

Xue adheres to Verne's characterization of Fogg as a rigid, taciturn, and reserved man throughout most of her translation. She seems, however, unable to tolerate Fogg's "betraying not the least emotion" when he hears that the beautiful Aouda is to be burned with her deceased husband (chap. 12, 86). Xue therefore changes the line to read "hearing this, Fogg could not bear (*buren*) to contain his great compassion. With a trembling voice, he again said . . ." (*juan* 2, 7b). This modification humanizes Fogg, making him an exemplar of Mencius's fundamental virtue—the inability to bear human suffering. It also explains convincingly why Fogg would rescue Aouda despite the risk.

2) Passepartout: from a loyal servant to a self-liberated slave

In her characterization of Passepartout, Xue invests him with an inner voice that does not exist in the original text, which helps to explain Passepartout's unconditional devotion to and understanding of Fogg. According to Xue, Passepartout in his early years "had a misfortune that caused him to become enslaved." He had long yearned for an ideal master but had failed to find one. After he answered Fogg's call for a servant, "to his surprise, he and Fogg met like old friends." His "hot blood brimmed with excitement, and he desired to serve Fogg with all his heart" (chap. 2, 10–11; *juan* 1, 3b). Xue misunderstands Passepartout's domestic service as Chinese bond slavery. It therefore demonstrates her humanitarian orientation that she portrays Passepartout as a man of integrity and subjectivity who seeks to be equal with his master.

Passepartout indeed rendered great service to Fogg. His most courageous and clever moment was in the rescue of Aouda. Here is Verne's description of the scene:

> It was Passepartout himself, who had slipped upon the pyre in the midst of the smoke and, profiting by the still overhanging darkness, had delivered the young woman from death! It was Passepartout who, playing his part with a happy audacity, had passed through the crowd amid the general terror. (Chap. 13, 97)

Xue's Chinese translation makes much more of the moment:

> It was Passepartout's own secret plot. Profiting by the still overhanging darkness and chaos, he had slipped upon the pyre in the midst of the smoke and delivered the young woman from an inevitable death! He caught the Indians off guard—How wise and brave he was! He also took the opportunity of the general upheaval to lead Fogg and all to escape, as if passing through a no man's land. (*Juan* 2, 10b–11a)

此乃阿榮自己秘計, 秉[乘]里[黑]暗擾亂時, 從烟焰滔上屍架, 援少婦于必死之中, 出印度大眾意外, 其智勇何如? 又乘大眾震懼之際, 遂引福格等偕遁, 如出無人之境。

While Verne praises Passepartout for having played his part "with a happy audacity," Xue adds wisdom to his bravery. She thus rewrites the suttee scene into one celebrating Passepartout's self-transformation—from an obedient "slave" (in Xue's Chinese definition) into an autonomous, independent leader who has accomplished a seemingly impossible mission. He makes his own plans, rescues the young woman from an inevitable death, and then guides the rest of the party away from danger.

3) Aouda: from a passive, grateful widow to an active, passionate lover

Verne portrays Aouda as a person who, having been mercifully liberated from suttee, is full of humble gratitude to her English gentleman savior. This provides Verne with an opportunity to celebrate the heroic qualities of Fogg—his compassion, generosity, composure, and trustworthiness. Xue recreates Aouda with a strong feminist agency, a major character in her own right. Although Aouda's name is entirely absent from the original titling, it appears in seven of Xue's chapter titles. Moreover, Xue attributes to Aouda inner feelings and ideas that are mostly missing in the original text, thus establishing Aouda's subjectivity and enriching her personality as she travels on her amorous journey with Fogg.

Verne first touches on Aouda's feelings for Fogg in chapter 17, describing them through Passepartout's eyes: "It was every day an increasing wonder to Passepartout, who read in Aouda's eyes the depths of her gratitude to his master. Phileas Fogg, though brave and gallant, must be, he thought, quite heartless" (chap. 17, 133). Based on Passepartout's one-line observation about Aouda, Xue retitles chapter 17 in a way that repositions Aouda away from Passepartout's gaze; it is now she who gazes at Fogg, and her "gratitude" becomes "love" (Table 6.7). Xue also inserts details into the chapter to validate this retitling:

> Aouda, while having nothing to do all day long, fixed her eyes on Fogg with a special kind of deep affection that is hard to describe in words. Seeing this, Passepartout was filled with wonder. As for Fogg, he kept up his brave and gallant manner, which really seemed quite heartless. (*Juan 2*, 21b)

阿黛鎮日無事, 惟雙眸凝映福格, 別具深情, 有難以言語形容者。阿榮見之, 不勝奇異。而福格英毅之概仍如故, 實似無心。

Table 6.7. Comparison of Titling between *Around the World* and *Huanyou ji* (Chapter 17)

	Around the World in 80 Days	*Huanyou ji*	Translation of the *Huanyou ji* title
17	Showing what happened on the voyage from Singapore to Hong Kong	訪案包探腸百折 鍾情寡女眼雙青	The detective is worried by tangled thoughts; The loving widow stares at Fogg with fondness

As time went by, the attachment between Fogg and Aouda grew stronger. In Verne's words:

> She was attached to the man who, however coldly, gave her daily evidences of the most absolute devotion. She did not comprehend, perhaps, the depth of the sentiment with which her protector inspired her, which she called gratitude, but which, though she was unconscious of it, was really more than that. (Chap. 28, 232)

In Xue's elaborated translation, Aouda knows precisely the nature of her feelings for Fogg. Gratitude was only secondary. She was tortured by Fogg's ambivalent attitude. Whenever she thought about it, "she felt as if her hot blood were gushing straight to her brain, and she was on the brink of either going crazy or falling sick" (覺一腔熱血, 直貫腦際, 幾欲發癲生病) (*juan* 3, 26b).

In the course of their travels by rail, Fogg and his party are attacked by members of the Sioux tribe, and Aouda joins the fight against them. Xue incorporates this detail into the title of chapter 29, calling Aouda a "woman warrior" who battles at the vanguard. She also modifies Verne's appraisal of Aouda, "She defended herself, like a true heroine" (chap. 29, 250), into "She defended herself in an awe-inspiring way, like a woman general" (凜凜然如一女將軍) (*juan* 4, 3b). It is because of her awe-inspiring warrior spirit, Xue seems to suggest, that Aouda later dares to propose marriage to Fogg.

Before realizing that he has actually arrived in London a day early, Fogg believes he has lost the wager and is prepared for bankruptcy. He offers Aouda whatever is left of his wealth for her well-being. Aouda then initiates the following conversation with Fogg:

> "I pity you, then, Mr. Fogg, for solitude is a sad thing, with no heart to which to confide your griefs. They say, though, that misery itself, shared by two sympathetic souls, may be borne with patience."
>
> "They say so, madam."
>
> "Mr. Fogg," said Aouda, rising, and seizing his hand, "do you wish at once a kinswoman and friend? Will you have me for your wife?" (Chap. 35, 301–2)

At this point, Shoupeng seems to have hastily read "seizing" as "seeing." His misreading leads Xue into a sinicized expansion of Aouda's marriage proposal:

> Aouda stood up, tears in her eyes. *Looking down* at Fogg's hand, she was about to speak but stopped. After a long pause, she said, "Mr. Fogg," and

after another long pause, she said again, "Do you wish at once a kinswoman and a female companion? Since I have long devoted myself to you, I'll share with you sorrows of misfortune and joys of a poor and humble life. If you don't mind my being too plain, I'd like to take care of your household. Will you have me for your wife?" (*Juan* 4, 19b; emphasis added)

阿黛起立, 目盈盈欲涕, 俯視福格之手, 脣欲語又止, 良久始曰: "福格先生", 良久復曰: "君願有女親眷女朋友一人乎? 儂身既久屬於君, 當偕君分禍患之憂, 享貧賤之樂。君如不以儂為陋, 箕帚井臼, 儂皆任之。即請為君婦可乎?"

The Aouda that Xue portrays here is far more appealing to Chinese eyes than the one by Verne. After a long inner struggle, she takes the moral high ground and proposes to Fogg in his dire straits. Behind her willingness to confront any and all hardships with Fogg is her affection for him (not merely gratitude). Xue rewrites the proposal scene on what she assumes to be Aouda's own terms but within a discursive framework of the Chinese companionate marriage.

Aouda's proposal moves Fogg, even in Verne's original text:

Mr. Fogg, at this, rose in his turn. There was an unwonted light in his eyes, and a slight trembling of his lips. Aouda looked into his face. The sincerity, rectitude, firmness, and sweetness of this soft glance of a noble woman, who could dare all to save him to whom she owed all, at first astonished, then penetrated him. He shut his eyes for an instant, as if to avoid her look. When he opened them again, "I love you!" he said, simply. "Yes, by all that is holiest, I love you, and I am entirely yours!"

"Ah!" cried Aouda, pressing his hand to her heart. (Chap. 35, 302)

This passage is probably the most passionate portrayal of Fogg and his relationship with Aouda in Verne's original story. Not satisfied with its intensity, however, Xue adds a highly dramatic elaboration of this defining moment:

It was in recompense to Fogg for saving her life that Aouda would betroth herself to him at his most helpless moment. From this gratitude she had developed a love for Fogg that, so deeply imprinted on her mind, would naturally embolden her to shed the shyness of an ordinary young woman. Fogg, for his part, was so overwhelmed at first that his heart trembled out of control. He shut his eyes and sank into deep thoughts, in such ecstasy that he felt there was no way to avoid drowning in the holy lake of her beautiful eyes. After quite a while, he opened his eyes and said: "Yes, I do love you! It was beyond my expectation that you would love me, but since you do, I can only obey your will!"

Aouda seized his hand and pressed it to her heart, saying: "Do not break your pledge!" (*Juan* 4, 19b)

阿黛所以捨身慰福格於無可如何之候, 即以報其前日相救之恩, 因恩生情, 深情入骨, 自非尋常兒女嬌羞之態可比也。惟福格初聞則駭, 心搖搖而無主, 瞑目深思, 鄙懷大愜, 覺至此欲自避匿, 不溺於聖湖美目中, 不可得也。良久開眸曰: "是矣! 我固愛卿, 不意先蒙卿惠眷, 卿既愛我, 我只得謹如芳命。"

阿黛乃拉福格之手, 而撫心曰: "勿渝盟!"

This insertion finalizes Xue's re-characterization of both Fogg and Aouda. As for the former, Xue subverts almost entirely Verne's painstaking construction of Fogg as a composed English gentleman who does not betray even the slightest of his feelings. And as for Aouda, Xue draws a smooth trajectory of her emotional evolution, from her shyly "looking down at Fogg's hand" to "seizing his hand and pressing it to her heart," and finally, even more boldly, demanding of Fogg his unfading love and fidelity.[44]

At the end of it all, how does Verne capture Fogg's sense of achievement? He writes:

> What had he [Fogg] really gained by all this trouble? What had he brought back from this long and weary journey?
>
> Nothing, say you? Perhaps so; nothing but a charming woman, who, strange as it may appear, made him the happiest of men!
>
> Truly, would you not for less than that make the tour around the world? (Chap. 37, 314–15)

Xue is deeply dissatisfied by these remarks. She believes that the author should provide a more fitting conclusion, one that indicates the true significance of Fogg's project. So she writes:

> This gentleman's eccentricity was entirely a product of his curiosity, and thus he exposed himself to a variety of wonderlands after going through all kinds of dangerous situations. The vulgar, narrow-minded people of the world do not know the height of heaven and the depth of the earth, the length of the meridian, the convenience of ships and trains, and the hardships of traveling. How could they propose a wager like Fogg's and understand his ambition? How could they deserve a servant like Passepartout and a wife like Aouda? These sorts of people would not believe that one could travel around the world even if given more than eighty days. How could they possibly believe that the story of Fogg really happened! (*Juan* 4, 23b)

此君之癖, 全在好奇, 故得備歷奇險, 別開奇境。世之傖父, 目光如綫, 不知天地之若何高厚, 日晷之若何短長, 舟車之若何便利, 行旅之若何苦辛, 安足以賭福格之局? 安足以知福格之志? 安足以得有僕如

阿榮, 有妻如阿黛耶? 若而人者, 雖告以環球可行, 不必限定八十日,
彼亦不敢信, 況告以福格之事, 千真萬真也哉!

In short, to Xue, *Around the World* was a morality tale, structured like a Chinese essay with its "opening, closing, and ups and downs." Fogg's journey was one of discovery, during which he exhibited not only a thirst for new knowledge but also moral strength, strength sufficient to win the loyalty of his servant Passepartout and the love of his future wife, Aouda. And Aouda, for her part (Passepartout too), provided the emotional and physical support that helped Fogg to fulfill his mission.

Benjamin Elman points out that, since the middle of the nineteenth century, "imperial reformers, early Republicans, Nationalist party cadres, and Chinese Communists have all made science and technology a top priority."[45] Wang Hui explains the reason for this priority:

> Chinese thinkers have not been interested in the idealist concept in which science, being an end in itself, is considered knowledge for knowledge's sake. As in Bacon's age, function and progress are the two keywords in the Chinese concept of science. Function takes on more nationalistic coloring among Chinese thinkers (in search of wealth and power), and progress finds itself aligned with the ideology of antitraditionalism.[46]

But Xue Shaohui saw things differently. To be sure, she had a strong practical reform streak, and she was deeply concerned about China's "modern fate" (to trade on a well-known book title). But her goal in introducing science and technology to a Chinese audience cannot be described as either "nationalistic" or "antitraditional," nor can she be characterized as an advocate of knowledge simply for its own sake. Rather, as I have tried to show, she and her supporters treated modern science and technology as an indispensable component of what she called new learning. This learning was designed to expand the parameters of knowledge in China and throughout the world, with the ultimate goal of integrating all kinds of cultural information, traditional and modern, Chinese and Western, in order to create a better and more harmonious world. As we have seen, women loomed large in this utopian project.

SEVEN

Xue's Self-Repositioning in the Family

Amid changing relationships between the genders and between family and state during the late Qing reforms, Xue began reconsidering women's position within the family. Susan Mann argues that an "eighteenth-century classical revival" empowered writing women at their "cloistered position in the home," for these women understood that the home was "the place where filial respect and collegial relations begin, extending outward through those who rule."[1] The publication of women's writing at this time also made their voices heard in public. For these reasons, writing women in the mid-Qing period believed their place "to be at the center of political discourse and at the heart of aesthetic expression."[2] Xue continued this understanding of women's self-positioning, but she made clear in both her theory and her practice that because of the current world situation, women had to break out of their cloistered position and walk into the public space. Drawing upon a broad, eclectic pool of intellectual resources, Xue reinterpreted conventional sociopolitical principles encoded in certain core Confucian documents—namely, the Four Books and the Five Classics.[3] In so doing, she revised and gendered the male-dominated polity into a cooperative enterprise of men and women. Using Xue's personal life as an example, this chapter examines how she recast women's conventional roles—wife, mother, daughter, and sister—to fit her conception of an ideal womanhood with the changing sociopolitical situation in China and the world. Xue and Shoupeng were both orphaned at a young age, so Xue did not have much experience as either a daughter or a daughter-in-law. We may, however, decipher her views on these relationships by examining her advice to her daughters.

The Role of a Wife

For Xue, a woman's most important social role was that of wife. She believed that the wife-husband union was the foundation of any sociopolitical structure. But the gender equality advocated by women reformers expanded the wife's function from the originally "cloistered position" to much broader territory. Consequently, Xue and Shoupeng's conjugal relationship differed substantially from that of an intellectually compatible couple in a typical late imperial companionate marriage. In that kind of marriage, as Dorothy Ko describes it, the talented wife "remained an *inner* helpmate and was never called upon to partake in his world in a public capacity."[4] In the end, therefore, "companionate marriage served to reinforce the doctrine of separate spheres."[5] Xue, however, not only participated in Shoupeng's world but did so on her own terms and often played the lead in their collaborative reform projects.

Xue justified this change in the marital relationship in the "Preface to the *Nü xuebao.*" She argues at the very outset that, based on the yin-yang cosmological structure that gives birth to myriad things, "human relations begin with a man and his wife living together." They should therefore work jointly on fulfilling the famous eight-step "classic account" of one's sociopolitical responsibilities, from rectifying minds (*zhengxin* 正心), integrating intentions (*chengyi* 誠意),[6] investigating things (*gewu* 格物), perfecting knowledge (*zhizhi* 致知), cultivating the self (*xiushen* 修身), regulating the family (*qijia* 齊家), putting the state in order (*chiguo* 治國), to bringing peace to the world (*ping tianxia* 平天下).[7] To fulfill these difficult tasks, one must learn. Since "the Way of the superior person begins with men and women,"[8] the Sage expects that both men and women should be equally educated. In brief, "the Way, broad and grand, is for men and women to walk together."[9]

Xue also discussed the political function of gender cooperation in poem 7 of her 1903 poetic series "Lecturing My Sons" ("Ke'er shi" 課兒詩). Xue first recalls how the founding fathers and mothers of the Western Zhou (ca. 11th century–771 BCE) co-established the Zhou system, "using the poem *Guanju* [which celebrates conjugal harmony] to initiate the 'State Winds' [for moral transformation]" (關雎開國風).[10] Confucius valorized this system as representative of his ideal polity and culture, the "Way of the previous sage-kings" (*xianwang zhidao* 先王之道)[11] because, "As the Way is opened by husband and wife, / Punishments are cast aside, no misfortune" (造端起夫婦, 刑措皆無兇).[12] Here Xue alludes to *Jiao's Forest of Changes* (*jiaoshi Yilin* 焦氏易林), a divinatory work derived from the *Classic of Changes*. One of its verses reads: "Under the grand reign of King Cheng of the Zhou, punishments were cast aside, no misfortune. The prime minister assisted the reign, and the superior person carried on benevolent governing" (成周之隆, 刑措無凶。太宰贊佑, 君子作仁).[13] This verse interprets the hexagram "Withdrawal" (*Dun* 遯) in its relation to the hexagram "Pure Yin" (*Kun* 坤), which possesses a greatly nourishing nature: "The myriad things are provided their births by it, and in so doing it compliantly carries out Heaven's will" (萬物資生, 乃順承天).[14] The participation of the female *Kun* in the Zhou reign enabled the regime to abolish punishments and achieve "benevolent governing." Gravitating to the nurturing *Kun*, Xue concludes, the state enjoyed increasing prosperity and "the people enjoyed a livelihood endowed by heaven" (生民秉顥穹).[15]

For Xue, the nurturing female Way should naturally protect lives, and she relentlessly condemned corporal punishment and had done so since her early years. In 1890, her house in Fuzhou was burglarized. After the thief was arrested, she presented a song-lyric to the magistrate, requesting: "Although the administration has to carry out the law, / Please pass a fair and proper sentence, / No need for whipping or beating" (有司執法雖然也, 且持平原情定罪, 無勞笞打).[16] In her essay "On the Connection between Women's Education and the Way of Governing" ("Nüjiao yu zhidao xiangguan shuo" 女教與治道相關說), published in *Nüxue bao* during the campaign for women's education, Xue celebrates the Han girl Ti Ying 緹縈 who, in order to save her father, appealed to Emperor Wen (r. 179–157 BCE) to abolish corporal punishment. Despite conventionally positioning Ti Ying as a filial daughter, Xue emphasizes her influence on Emperor Wen's political decision and hence sets her up as a poster child for women's participation in state affairs in measures to increase care for human life.[17] Her

"Miscellaneous Poems about Beijing" ("Beijing zashi" 北京雜詩) (No. 4) (1907) hailed some new policies of the government, among which "One thing manifests the Sage's governing: / The court just ended corporal punishment" (一事自然稱盛治, 鞭笞已繼肉刑除).[18]

Xue brought this traditional wisdom that regarded husband-and-wife cooperation as the foundation of governing into her understanding of the republican system, as reflected in her co-translation with Shoupeng of *A Double Thread* by Ellen Thorneycroft Fowler into *Shuangxian ji*. Xue initiated the translation in the summer of 1902 and published it in 1903 (see Figure 7.1). The novel tells a love story. Young Elfrida assumes a double identity in order to protect her aging grandparents from finding out about the accidental death of her twin sister, a ruse that naturally confuses her fiancé, Jack. Eventually, Elfrida manages to clarify the situation and the couple reconcile. For Shoupeng, a historian and scientist, such an "erotic and absurd"

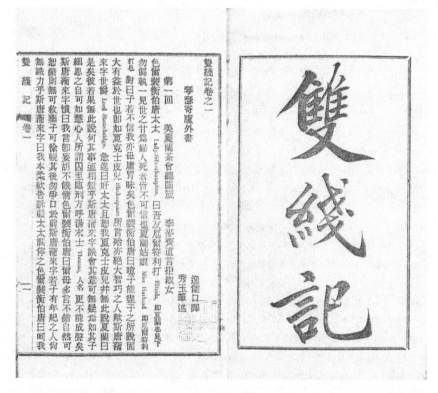

Figure 7.1. Cover and first page of *Shuangxian ji*. Translation of Ellen Thorneycroft Fowler's *A Double Thread* by Xue Shaohui and Chen Shoupeng (Shanghai: Zhongwai ribaoguan, 1903).

melodrama depicting "infatuation between young lovers" did not warrant his scholarly attention. Xue argued:

You [Shoupeng] are talented in scholarly research;	君能講學,
I am fond of stories of passion.	儂喜言情。
Without investigating fictional works,	不搜漢苑稗官,
How do we know the "State Winds" in the *Book of Songs* are about love?[19]	安見國風好色乎?

Using the *Book of Songs* for moral and scholastic support, Xue justified her desire to translate a foreign romance:

Let's just preserve this novel as another type of literature,	姑存一説,
It will last for a thousand years in its own right.	亦足千秋。
Therefore, according to the *Ritual*, [when Jizha] justified customs,	故准風俗於禮經,
He did not chide the music in Kuai and beyond;	觀樂無譏鄶下;
When [Confucius] understood human feelings following the Kingly Way,	通人情以王道,
He did not exclude the ballads of Zheng [from the *Book of Songs*].[20]	刪詩何礙鄭音哉!

Since Confucius retained the love songs from Zheng in the *Book of Songs* in order to showcase diverse human feelings, we should also read today's foreign love stories with the same attitude.

Xue's actual purpose, as she explained in the preface to the *Shuangxian ji*, was to introduce Western gender relationships and marriage practices to Chinese readers. In previous writings, Xue and her fellow reformers had advocated marriage based on "free will." She later reinforced this view in *Foreign Women*. Now with the translation of *A Double Thread*, Xue painted an even more vivid picture of a relationship between two young people who became engaged "without a matchmaker," and who founded their marriage upon equal rights between the man and the woman. At the end of the novel, Xue intentionally transformed the young couple's final reconciliation into a plea for reform based on an equal and harmonious gender relationship.

Fowler's original ending is:

Elfrida sighed: "It must be awful to be too old to make a fresh start."

"No one is too old for that," Jack corrected her; "until the day of one's death there is always the chance of beginning life over again."

"And even a better chance the day afterwards," added Philip Cartwright.[21]

Xue renders this:

> Xialan [Elfrida] sighed: "Although the broken mirror is fixed, I still panic just thinking about it."
> Zeke [Jack] said: "That old, rotten stuff has its problems. Now that we are in the reform era, let's follow the principle of reform, and build love on the principle of the republic and marriage on equal rights (*pingquan*). I'll try my best to make you happy; I'll even die for you without regret."
> Jiademulaide [Philip Cartwright] said: "If all the loving couples in this world can achieve family harmony, then each nation will naturally become prosperous and strong. Isn't it wonderful? Isn't it wonderful?"[22]

> 夏蘭嘆曰: "故鏡雖幸重圓, 思之尚為可懼。"
> 則克曰: "陳舊頑梗, 流弊必多。今當維新之時局, 且行維新之政治。以情愛為共和, 以嫁娶為平權。吾竭吾力, 盡卿之歡, 雖死亦無遺憾。"
> 加得母來德曰: "世界上有情眷屬, 夫夫婦婦, 咸能臻此家道和, 而國家自然亦進於富強矣! 豈不快哉! 豈不快哉!"

This reform-minded notion of an ideal conjugal relationship was generated from Xue and Shoupeng's life experience and reflected in their open debate on reform issues. By publicizing their debates in the preface of each of their co-authored and co-translated books—*Foreign Women*, *Around the World in Eighty Days*, *China Sea Directory*, and *A Double Thread*—they challenged the conventional dictum that "inner words do not go outside." Beneath Xue's open "quarrelsomeness"—one of the "seven offenses"—is her attempt to "partake in [Shoupeng's] world in a public capacity."[23]

Of course, without Shoupeng's understanding and cooperation, Xue would not have been able to change her role from a conventionally obedient wife into an independent thinker of equal standing with her husband. Xue's self-repositioning, therefore, benefited from and reflected the changing gender relationship in the reform era. This personal experience led her to design education for her children in direct correlation with the larger social and cultural contexts of the time.

The Role of a Mother

Xue and Shoupeng had five children, including three sons—Chen Keng (1883–95), Chen Qiang (b. 1890), and Chen Ying (b. 1899)—and two daughters—Chen Yun (1885–1911) and Chen Hong (b. 1892).[24] Shoupeng's constant absence left the task of educating the children entirely to Xue, in addition to her busy routine of taking care of their daily life. Xue taught sons and daughters with equal attention. While following the same peda- gogical principles, she designed two different curricula, epitomized in the twenty poems on "Lecturing My Sons" and the ten poems on "Instructing My Daughters" ("Xunnü shi" 訓女詩). Xue composed the two series re- spectively in 1903 and 1904, when the Qing court was in the midst of a new wave of civil examination reform. Benjamin Elman remarks: "In August 1901, for the first time since 1664–67, the abolition of eight-legged essays was approved by the court and obeyed by the Ministry of Rites," and local examiners could now expect candidates "to answer questions dealing with both Chinese and Western learning."[25] Shoupeng, one of the few Fuzhou Naval Academy graduates who had persistently tried to pass the *keju*, fin- ished thirtieth in the 1902 Fujian provincial examination.[26] We can assume that he benefited from the new examination curriculum that better fit his new knowledge base. Under these circumstances, Xue's task was to create an education suited to the needs of her children.

Judging from these two poetic series, Xue's pedagogic and curricula con- cerns went far beyond the *keju* regime that had dominated Chinese elite life for so long and been so close to the traditions of Xue's family. In her preface to "Lecturing My Sons," Xue wrote:

> While my husband has been far away from home, our son Qiang has grown up. Although he is well versed in literary composition and capable of con- tinuing the family learning, he has a slight tendency to go in for trendy fash- ions and has brought some baseless wording into his writing, possibly because in his reading he has not yet exhaustively understood true principles (*li*).[27]

外子遠出, 鏘兒差長, 雖能為文傳家學, 然微好時趨, 往往有不根字 面, 闌入筆端, 殆讀書窮理未至耳。

What does Xue consider to be the "family learning" that Qiang, then age twelve, has inherited and from whom? Xue and Shoupeng's eldest son Keng's education at the same age may serve as a reference. Keng was twelve when he died in the summer of 1895. His younger siblings recalled that he "was refined in the principles of mathematics (*suan*) and well versed in the techniques of astronomy and astrology (*butian zhanxing*)."[28] So Keng must have inherited family learning from both parents, inasmuch as Shoupeng learned mathematics and astronomy at the Naval Navigation School and Xue, like her father, was an astrologer. In other words, Keng had inherited a "family learning" that comprised both Chinese and Western traditions, and Qiang must have received a similar education.

At first sight, Xue seems to have wanted her sons to pursue the Neo-Confucian *li*, for she composed this series rhyming after the twenty penta-syllabic old-style poems of "Thoughts from My Studio Life" ("Zhaiju ganxing" 齋居感興) by the Song Neo-Confucian Zhu Xi (1130–1200).[29] In this series Zhu Xi expresses his understanding of *li* as the "constant and unalterable" principle "according to which the process of creation unfolded in the medium of *qi*."[30] Yet Xue expands the meaning of *li* beyond the Neo-Confucian realm. In poem 16 of "Lecturing My Sons" she says: "Most important is to exhaustively understand true principles; / Read books so you can express the nature [of all things]" (要之在窮理, 盡性且讀書).[31] This couplet clarifies that the purpose of reading books is for "*qiongli jinxing*" (窮理盡性), a phrase taken from the *Book of Changes* that means "to exhaustively understand (*qiong*) the profound and sophisticated principles (*li*) of myriad things, and to fully express (*jin*) the nature (*xing*) of all sentient beings."[32]

Poem 16 promotes learning poetry and takes Su Shi as a major mentor; hence it adopts Su Shi's somewhat more Daoist construction of *li* as the principles of things and *xing* as the nature-endowed features of each individual. In order to understand the Dao, one has to study closely the myriad things through exhaustive learning and capture their profundity and subtlety using highly refined poetic words. Under the common denominators of *li* and *xing*, Xue designed curricula respectively for her sons and daughters. Both entailed a triadic process of learning, from knowledge acquisition, to spiritual power formation, and to world transformation, all within a metaphysical structure "in which Heaven and man, Way and Potency, have their places and functions."[33]

Scholars before Xue had commented that Zhu Xi structured his "Thoughts" series following the "Principle of the Mean": "He discusses one *li* at the beginning, spreads it into myriad things, and gathers the series into one *li* again."[34] Xue's "Lecturing My Sons" uses the same rhyme words as Zhu Xi and adopts a similar structure. The twenty poems can be divided into three sections. The first four poems draw upon a variety of classics, primarily the Four Books, to elaborate the pedagogical principle of self-cultivation. The second section specifies the curriculum in twelve poems. The final four poems summarize ideas about education in general.

Whereas Zhu Xi devotes his series to *li*, Xue highlights *cheng* (integrity, integral, integrate). She opens the series locating her sons firmly in *cheng* and concludes the series encouraging her sons "to keep being the most integral unceasingly" (至誠此無息). And her understanding of *cheng* follows the *Doctrine of the Mean* (*Zhongyong*), which states:

> Integrity (*cheng*) is heaven's Way; integrating is the human Way. One who is integral attains centrality without striving, apprehends without thinking, and is effortlessly on the Way; hence the sage. One who integrates chooses what is good and holds on to it firmly. This involves broad learning, extensive inquiry, careful thought, clear discrimination, and earnest practice. . . .
>
> Only the world's most integral may be deemed capable of giving full play to their nature. Being able to give full play to one's nature, one is able to give full play to the natures of other human beings; being able to give full play to the natures of other human beings, one is able to give full play to the natures of other living things. Being able to give full play to the natures of other living things, one can assist in the transforming and nourishing powers of heaven and earth; being able to assist in the transforming and nourishing powers of heaven and earth, one can form a triad with heaven and earth.[35]

> 誠者, 天之道也; 誠之者, 人之道也。誠者, 不勉而中, 不思而得, 從容中道, 聖人也。誠之者, 擇善而固執之者也。博學之, 審問之, 慎思之, 明辨之, 篤行之 ...?
> 唯天下至誠、為能盡其性; 能盡其性、則能盡人之性; 能盡人之性、則能盡物之性; 能盡物之性、則可以贊天地之化育; 可以贊天地之化育、則可以與天地參矣。

Cheng is at the center of the Confucian sage ideal. While the sage, as the emblem of the heavenly Way, embraces *cheng* effortlessly, a human being has to acquire it through learning. In the process, *cheng* connects one's nature with the natures of other human beings and other living things. Through this communication, one can then join heaven and earth to transform the world.

In explaining the function of *cheng*, Xue begins the first poem by identifying "integrating intentions" as the most important learning process of the eight-step "classic account" in the *Great Learning*. The first two steps, "investigating things" and "perfecting knowledge," are for cultivating one's capability of "integrating intentions," allowing one to "choose what is good and hold on to it firmly." Only then can one proceed to the next five steps. In this sense, *cheng*'s position in the sage ideal is equivalent to that of *shen* (spirit) in the perfected-person ideal, which Xue also highlights in her series (poems 14 and 17); both result from one's self-cultivation and both are deployed as the spiritual power in one's attempt to transform the world.

Equating *cheng* with *shen*, Xue shows that she prefers each individual to act according to his/her self-motivated, autonomous spiritual power rather than to an abstract heavenly principle. Moreover, as A. C. Graham points out, "In the 'Doctrine of the Mean' the Mencian theory of the goodness of human nature is extended to a universal reconciliation of nature and morality."[36] In her two poetic series on educating children, Xue frequently ties Confucian morality with Daoist naturalness, and hence finds a reconciliation of the Confucian/Neo-Confucian sage ideal and the Daoist/abstruse perfected-person ideal. With such a smooth, eclectic synthesis of intellectual resources, Xue brings tradition to meet current challenges, as in the first poem in "Lecturing My Sons":

On looking within, if I find myself in the right,	自反若能縮，
I will go forward alone even against thousands of men.[37]	萬人吾獨往。
Even if Confucius's Way is high and hard to reach,	所際縱高堅，
You should try with all your might to bore into it and emulate it.[38]	竭力事鑽仰。
To dwell in benevolence and to follow righteousness,[39]	居仁與由義，
All of a sudden your mind will become open and luminous.	豁然心爽朗。
A superior person should not allow any self-deception,[40]	君子勿自欺，
Nor be bewildered by foreign aggression.	外侮不可罔。
From here, embark on your life path,	即此循程途，
Which will be as clear as [the lines] in your own palm.[41]	示斯指其掌。

Grounded firmly in *cheng* and with a broad mind/heart that "integrates" all goodness, one may move forward to accomplish difficult tasks, even if fighting alone against myriad enemies. Xue then emphasizes the point that living according to the benevolent spirit and righteousness of the Confucian sage will cause one's mind to be as "open and luminous" as that of a perfected person. These combined Confucian and Daoist qualities enable a clear response to any foreign challenge. To acquire these qualities, Xue argues in the following three poems, one must persist in learning (poem 2) and obtain knowledge from both heaven and the phenomenal world (poem 3). Walking along this path, even the clumsiest person will be able to take the eight steps to complete success (poem 4).

Xue then moves to the second section to detail the actual curriculum. In addition to the Four Books already covered in the first four poems, poems 5 to 9 discuss the purpose of learning the Five Classics: The *Changes* sets up the proper path for self-cultivation; the *Documents* indicates how to order the state and pacify the world; the *Songs* helps regulate the family; the *Ritual* assists in ruling; and the *Spring and Autumn Annals* stresses the praise-and-blame purpose of writing histories. Each of poems 10 to 16 directs the study of specific topics, including *Songs of Chu* (*Chuci* 楚辭), the philosophers (*zhuzi* 諸子), the One Hundred Schools (*baijia* 百家), empirical learning (*puxue* 樸學), minor talks or fiction (*xiaoshuo* 小說), ancient-style prose (*guwen* 古文), and poetry (*shi* 詩). All these subjects, especially *xiaoshuo*, go well beyond the then-current examination curriculum that focused on classical learning and political policies.[42]

In specifying each kind of learning, Xue instructs her children: "Please do not identify yourself with a cramped scholar, / Who is confined within only one field" (幸勿等曲士, 拘墟守一疆) (poem 6). This instruction draws upon the "Autumn Floods" ("Qiushui" 秋水) chapter of the *Zhuangzi*. That chapter recounts how the Lord of the Yellow River had believed that "all the beauty in the world belonged to him alone" until he reached the North Sea and exclaimed in awe at its "unfathomable vastness." The god of the North Sea, Ruo, responded:

You can't discuss the ocean with a well frog—he's limited by the space he lives in. You can't discuss ice with a summer insect—he's bound to a single season. You can't discuss the Way with a cramped scholar—he's shackled by his doctrines. Now you have come out beyond your banks and borders and have seen the great sea—so you realize your own limits. From now on it will be possible to talk to you about the Great Principle.[43]

北海若曰: "井鼃不可以語於海者, 拘於虛也; 夏蟲不可以語於冰者, 篤於時也, 曲士不可以語於道者, 束於教也。今爾出於崖涘, 觀於大海, 乃知爾醜, 爾將可與語大理矣。"

Thus, although Xue did not specify Western learning in her curriculum, it is implied in this reference to reaching the ocean, both literally and metaphorically, and exemplified in the "family learning" that both Xue and Shoupeng cultivated with their broad repertoire of knowledge.

In the last section Xue provides methodologies of learning. Poem 17 urges hard work, regardless of one's financial means. Poem 18 recommends enlarging one's vision through broad reading and traveling. Poem 19 advises concentrating on learning and resisting distraction by material temptations. The final poem connects knowledge acquisition to self-cultivation that combines Confucian/Neo-Confucian integrity with the Daoist free spirit:

With a mind serene, quietly digest your knowledge;	靜心但默會,
How can you hear the clatter of the human world?	那聞人世喧。
You won't notice the departure of spring—	不知春已去,
Quickly the morning replaces the evening.	忽忽自晨昏。
Be the most integral, without ceasing!	至誠此無息,
Be simple but wondrous, no redundancy!	簡妙亦非繁。
Learning should adopt this standard:	為學宜准此,
Look for the foundation and pursue the origin.[44]	探本以窮原。

This poem advises an approach to life similar to what *Zhuangzi* argues in the "Free Roaming" chapter: upon fulfilling a task, a perfected person should claim no profit, no merit, and no fame,[45] as Xue argues by alluding to the lines of Tao Qian (*zi* Yuanming, 365–427):

I built my hut in a place where people live,	結廬在人境,
and yet there's no clatter of carriage or horse.	而無車馬喧。
You ask, how could that be?	問君何能爾?
With a mind remote, the region too grows distant.[46]	心遠地自偏。

Tao abandoned his career as an official to return to his home in the country, where he lived a poor farmer's life following the course of nature.[47] Advising her sons to follow in Tao's footsteps, Xue seems to have a far-sighted vision for her sons' education under the current sociopolitical situation, with the possibility that her sons would pursue a path other than *keju*. (Jitong sent his only son, Shi'er, to a French school in Shanghai, and the son eventually had a career in the military.) At this uncertain moment, Xue concludes, her sons should engage in learning in its most fundamental sense, as the *Doctrine of the Mean* instructs: "Only the most integral under heaven can manage the great order under heaven, establish the great foundation under heaven, and comprehend the transformation of heaven and earth."[48]

Just as she underscores *cheng*, integrity, in "Lecturing My Sons," Xue features *shen*, spirit, in "Instructing My Daughters." She explains in poem 7 of the series:

As your pure Bamboo Grove aura is activated,	林下清風動,
It spreads your fragrant reputation in the neighborhood.	里黨揚芳聲。
Ban Zhao, who did not dazzle people with a beautiful face,	班昭靡艷色,

Completed the *Han History* and wrote the *Eastern Expedition*.	續史賦東征。
Meng Guang, who equaled her husband in virtue and wisdom,	孟光能舉案,
Did not have an elegant face and a slim figure.	顏狀非亭亭。
Uncarved jade contains rich inner essences;	璞玉蘊內質,
Limpid waves can rinse the strings of one's cap.	浪滄清濯纓。
Consult women's classics to use the past as your mirror;	鑑古稽女典,
Cultivate your graceful nature with the Six Classics.	淑性陶六經。
Be gentle, prevent yourself from being shrewish and brutal;	溫柔戒暴厲,
Despise sharp weapons for they are inauspicious.	不祥噬佳兵。
Your ice-and-snow complexion surpasses powdered faces;	冰雪勝膏沐,
With solemn manners you guard the inner chamber.	正色守閨楹。
Mutual respect between spouses results from accumulated virtue;	敬為德所聚,
Good names will be passed down by the red-tube brush.[49]	彤管存令名。

Although the word *shen* does not appear in the poem, it is implied in the allusions to the "Bamboo Grove aura" and the "ice-and-snow complexion"— both are metonymically related to *shen*. The former characterizes Xie Daoyun's "relaxed and luminous spirit" in the *Shishuo* "Xianyuan," and the latter depicts the spiritual person in the *Zhuangzi* "Free Roaming" chapter whose spiritual power "can protect creatures from sickness and plague and make the harvest bountiful." Xue highlights *shen* in this poem on womanly bearing because she believes that *shen*, having a transformative power similar to *cheng*, reveals one's inner talent and virtue in one's appearance, making these inner qualities known to others, so one can properly and sensitively communicate with the world.

We can, therefore, understand why Xue modeled "Instructing My Daughters" on the "Miscellaneous Poems" ("Zashi" 雜詩) by the Jin poet Zhang Xie 張協 (d. ca. 307). In this series Zhang uses "skillfully structured words of similitude" (巧構形似之言) to construct natural images, altering shapes, colors, and scents in close interaction with changing human moods. Because of Zhang Xie's "flowery and pure poetic style" (*wenti huajing* 文體華淨), Zhong Rong (468–518) ranked him among the best poets in the *Poetry Grading* (*Shipin*) and stressed his influence on the landscape poet Xie Lingyun.[50] Xue adopted Zhang's pentasyllabic old-poetry style, borrowing his every rhyme word and implanting Zhang's naturalness into her design of women's role as protectors and nurturers of life.

The ten poems in "Instructing My Daughters" can be divided into three groups. The first three consider a woman's roles as a daughter, a wife, and a mother, constructed with Confucian and Daoist theories that reconcile women's moral roles with the natural order.[51] Poem 1 begins with the birth of a daughter: "Men and women are born of the same natural process; / One *qi* is divided into the translucent and the opaque" (男女同化生, 一氣分清濁). Opaqueness associates women with earth, making "the female Way one of firmness and constancy" (坤道履堅貞). It enables a young woman to "Guard sternly her person as pure jade, / And solemnly maintain a superior person's integrity, even in seclusion" (如玉嚴守身, 君子凜幽獨). Such a girl will stand out as does an evergreen tree from myriad flowers, spreading green shade to shelter others.

Poem 2 builds an equal, dynamic relationship between husband and wife based on a series of hexagrams. The poem opens with: "A girl is sent to her marital family based on the hexagram of Development (*jian*)" (女歸本漸卦). The couple consummate the marriage just as "heaven mates with earth, as manifested in the hexagram Peace (*Tai*)" (天地象泰交). From this intercourse new lives are "Arousing (*Zhen*), as green as young bamboos" (震則蒼筤竹). The Family (*jiaren* 家人) is hence formed, "pure and harmonious like fragrant chrysanthemums" (純和比芳菊).[52] Poem 3 eulogizes the role of the mother: "The Dao of earth is the mother of myriad things; / Producing and reproducing, without end" (地道萬物母, 生生無盡期). It celebrates the mother's fertility alluding to the *Book of Songs*: "Dolichos creepers and young gourds / Thickly grow and widely spread" (葛藟與瓜瓞, 緜緜成蕃滋).[53] The mother should begin educating her children when they are young, for "They can continue the family line and carry on loyalty and filial piety, / All because of the mother's care and education in their childhood" (克家事忠孝, 悉出鞠育時).

Part two, poems 4 to 9, details women's proper behavior.[54] Poem 4 points out the correlation between self-cultivation and constant learning: "Womanly virtue knows no bounds; / Diligent learning exposes our limitations" (婦德亦無極, 力學知不足). Poem 5 addresses kitchen management, where women prepare for ceremonial sacrifices and should be thrifty: "Noble intent is revealed after shedding away extravagant desires, / Gods and ghosts will see and understand" (志以淡泊明, 鬼神具體察). Poem 6 advises how to find the right path for "the rough journey in the world." Trapped in "places of sorrow, calamity, danger, and uncertainty" (憂患危疑地) and lost among "forests of right and wrong, gain and loss" (是非得失林), one should make quick decisions "in order to avoid shame and fear" (但求免愧怍). "To anticipate what lies ahead in one thousand years, / All depends on a sincere, integrated mind" (領取千秋意, 全凴一片心). This capacity of making good judgments and foretelling the future is an important component of the spiritual power of the perfected person/*xianyuan*. Poem 8 paints a happy picture of womanly work framed in a serene natural environment.

Poem 9 concludes part two by reiterating the purpose of learning: "Let us read books to understand meanings and principles; / Thus we make education for women subtle and profound" (讀書識義理, 女教微而深); "Brightness and intelligence need cultivation; / Learn the principles and you will become thoughtful and composed" (聰明必涵養, 學理潛以沉). Xue then reminds her daughters: "Compose poetry and prose after your other engagements; / Your father is after all a Confucian scholar" (詩文餘緒耳, 而父原儒林).[55] This admonition, seemingly uncharacteristic of Xue the passionate poet, has an aggressive connotation. She expects her daughters to acquire the "family learning" from their father, who has added to his "Confucian scholarship" the most up-to-date knowledge, Chinese and Western, of the humanities and sciences.

Poem 10 is the grand finale of the series.[56] Xue instructs her daughters on how to position themselves in a variety of spaces—domestic and public, historical and global—with appropriate moral behavior grounded in intellectual principles. Within the household, "tenderly conforming [to nature]" will keep one in an amicable relationship with one's family. In society, "Treat those under you with motherly love and kindness; / Spread care for others and understand their feelings as your own" (慈祥以待下, 推愛而準情). In history, being worthy and intelligent (*xianming*) will allow one to align with the traditional exemplary women who left images of their beautiful figures on painted scrolls. In the world, "The straight Way enables the masses to walk; / Harmonious music rarely involves jarring sounds" (道直可容眾, 樂和稀促聲). The poem concludes:

The sage and the worthy people treasure substantial meanings;	聖賢踐實義,
Women look down upon empty names.	婦女薄虛名。
Inscribe my words on your scarves.	書紳記吾語,
You will be proud of being born to heaven and earth![57]	何慚天地生?

To be sure, mother's teaching was not a new concept in the reform era but an important component of the Min writing-women culture. What is new here is that Xue reinforced this role by incorporating all that could strengthen her children's self-fashioning in a contemporary context.

The Role of a Sister and a Sister-in-Law

Xue had two elder sisters, Shenhui (d. 1876) and Sihui (b. 1859), as well as an elder brother, Yukun (b. 1863). Losing their parents early, the Xue siblings kept lifelong close ties, and their relationship was deeply rooted in a common interest in learning. The eldest sister, Shenhui, married young and died soon after, and Yukun studied away from home. Xue Shaohui was therefore closer to Sihui than to her other siblings. In her essay, "Dedication to the Third Sister Yingyu [Sihui's *zi*] on Her Fiftieth Birthday" ("Yingyu sanzi wushi shouyan" 英玉三姊五十壽言), Xue details how Sihui brought her up. Xue portrays Sihui as a refined girl since childhood:

Her gentle quality improves day by day;	淑質日新,
Her pure mind resembles lustrous jade.	清心玉映,
She composed a poem comparable to Consort Xu Hui's "Little Hill"	徐惠妃小山之作,
Before she came of age (*jinian*);	未及笄年;
She rhymed after Xie Daoyun's willow-catkin chanting	謝道韞詠絮之吟,
With a different elegance.[58]	別饒幽致。

Sihui began tutoring Xue when Xue was barely two, telling her bedtime stories from the classics every night.[59] After their mother died, Sihui took care of her aging father and younger siblings, so that

Every evening, after the inner chamber became quiet,	每當璇閨人靜,
Under the dim light on the desk,	棐几燈昏,
She taught me womanly work	課我女紅,
And instructed me about the woman's Way.[60]	導我婦道。

Sihui kept in close contact with Xue even after she married: "Sending me poems and replying to mine, her maidservants were running up and down the street" (贈詩和詩, 接婢媼於道上).[61] Using her own experiences, Sihui taught Xue how to behave in the marital family. Xue records:

She cuts up the cloth on the loom to urge her children to study,[62]	斷織勗學,
And cooks the egg-laying hen (*ci*) to treat her husband.[63]	烹雌佐餐。

She ascends the hall to greet the parents-in-law following the eldest sister-in-law;	隨冢婦升堂，
And puts on a veil to debate in her younger brother-in-law's place.	為小郎施障。
She gets up at the crowing of the cock with utensils ready at hand,	雞鳴佩用，
Attending at the door of the parents-in-law's bedroom.[64]	侍立寢門；
Day and night she works diligently,	夙夜執勤，
Taking care of everything with her own hands.[65]	必成手迹 。
She helps her husband (haozhen) to rank first among the junior scholars,	薦砧既冠童子之軍，
So he is able to enter the Imperial Academy of Learning;[66]	遂得成均入貢；
Although she sends sons and daughters to study with teachers outside,	兒女雖就外傅之讀，
She still transmits to them knowledge from rare books.[67]	猶傳口授秘書。

All her life Xue regarded Sihui as a mentor and a surrogate mother. From Sihui she received a typical Min writing-women education that featured the *xianyuan* agenda and local Guanglu poetics. The records are insufficient to show whether Sihui and Yukun participated in the late Qing reforms. They did, however, support Xue's writing career and her reform activities, not the least by helping Shoupeng preserve and publish Xue's *Posthumously Collected Writings from Black-Jade Rhythm Tower*. In their prefaces to Xue's *Collected Prose* and *Collected Song-Lyrics*, Sihui and Yukun recount how they were entrusted with the manuscripts amid the chaos of late 1911 and how they treasured these writings as more important than their own lives.

In 1880, the fourteen-year-old Xue married into the Chen household, which at this time comprised the eldest brother, Chen Botao; his wife, Lady Ye; their children; and Jitong's wife, Lady Liu. Xue quickly embarked on a daily routine with her in-laws. Her children later recollected:

Our father's family was poor and had a tradition of thrift, yet our late mother happily settled in. Getting up early in the morning, finishing with her toilet, and dusting the house thoroughly, she would then visit her sisters-in-law. She spent the afternoon on embroidery and sewing. At night she read books by the light with our father, like two mutually respectful friends.[68]

In addition to her daily chores, Xue "developed a deep friendship through literary creation" with the Chen women and girls, such as Chen Botao and his wife Lady Ye's two daughters, Lei and Rong.[69] This friendship moved the Chen women into a cooperative effort to continue the women's literate tradition. For instance, Xue would complete Rong's *Collection of Women's Song-Lyrics through the Ages* after Rong passed away in 1901. And Xue and her daughter Chen Yun would together document the achievements of Qing women poets (see Chapter One). Chen Botao and his wife were so impressed by Xue's personality and creativity that they also took a liking to Xue's elder brother Yukun and married Lei and Rong to him consecutively.[70]

With her female in-laws Xue continued the Min writing-women tradition that combined household management with literary creation. With Jitong, Xue followed a *Shishuo* example and subverted conventional norms that instructed "sister-in-law and brother-in-law not to exchange inquiries directly with each other" (嫂叔不通問).[71] Xue regarded Jitong as a spiritual mentor and role model who inspired her to become a reformer. In reciprocation, Xue relentlessly defended Jitong's reputation and openly voiced her admiration for him. Rarely had such a close rapport between a sister- and a brother-in-law been expressed in writing for a public occasion. Jitong's Western education and the changing social environment of the reform era might have contributed to this new type of gender relationship. More importantly, I believe, the two built their mutual admiration and understanding upon the perfected-person/*xianyuan* ideal. When Jitong first saw Xue in the spring of 1883, he commented: "The bride has a graceful and dignified manner. Isn't this what it is meant by the Bamboo Grove aura?" (新婦度態雍穆, 殆所謂林下風歟?).[72] Xue, for her part, would evaluate Jitong drawing on the same intellectual resources from the *Shishuo* discourse, as typified in her "Call for Poetic Contributions" to celebrate Jitong's fiftieth birthday.[73]

Jitong's fiftieth birthday was in the first lunar month of 1901.[74] The Chen family took this opportunity to honor Jitong's life and to clear his name, which had been unfairly tarnished in the early 1890s (as introduced in Chapter Three). For this purpose, Xue declared: "His deeds deserve to be inscribed on gold and metal, so we call far and wide for outstanding compositions based on solid facts; / His life needs to be fully recounted, thus we can happily borrow those words to toast his longevity" (合揚金石, 廣徵摭實之英詞; 如說生平, 藉作稱觴之歡洽).[75] The family agreed with Xue and entrusted to her the job of soliciting poems to celebrate Jitong's life. They assigned Xue this task because of her writing talent. It might also have been Jitong's own idea; he believed that Xue understood him better than anyone else. This was neither the first nor the last time that the Chens asked Xue to write on their behalf. The year before, she had written a letter to the Korean king for a relief group led by Jitong. In August 1905, she would draft the "Editorial Introduction" for the *Official Daily of the Southern Ports*. Also in the fall of 1905, she would draft an essay in celebration of the seventieth birthday of the Chen brothers' boss, the superintendent of the Southern Ports, Zhou Fu, and his wife.[76] But whereas Xue wrote all these documents on behalf of others, she signed the "Call for Poetic Contributions" with her own name.

Xue structured the "Call for Poetic Contributions" within a *Shishuo* framework, summarizing Jitong's personal qualities and achievements under five rubrics. The first two are adopted directly from the *Shishuo* categories, namely, "Literature and Scholarship" ("Wenxue" 文學) and "Virtuous Conduct" ("Dexing" 德行). The third expands the original "Political Affairs" ("Zhengshi" 政事) into "Politics and Economics" ("Jingji" 經濟) to adapt to the changing sociopolitical situation. To these three, Xue adds "Friendly Relations" ("Jiaoyi" 交誼), which covers a variety of the *Shishuo* categories on human relationships, and "Aura and Feelings" ("Fenghuai" 風懷), which synthesizes the *Shishuo* categories on one's disposition and feelings. In her essay, Xue draws extensively upon the *Shishuo* terminology and personalities and so assimilates into the presentation of Jitong the perfected-person ideal that permeates the *Shishuo*.

Xue, however, changes the original *Shishuo* order by arranging the first three categories following the idea of an "outward extension from oneself." She begins by promoting "Literature and Scholarship" from its original fourth place to the first in accordance with Jitong's argument that literature is the basis for fashioning culture and its participants (as discussed in Chapter Two). She recounts Jitong's literary and scholarly achievements as follows:

Our lord brother was born with a special disposition	兄公生具岐嶷,
And an outstanding capacity of understanding.	少多穎悟。
At 9, he studied the three books of the *Ritual*.	就傅之年, 已通三禮;
At 12, he could explicate a [Confucian] classic.	舞勺而後, 自講一經。
As he galloped through the four directions	比及馳騁四國,
And traveled the five continents,	遊覽五洲,
He expanded his poetic ideas in the great wilderness	拓詩思於大荒,
And refined his literary mind in the vast ocean.	鍊文心於窮海。
. . .	. . .

There is also his knowledge of foreign languages,	又不僅旁通梵字,
Of which he knows thirty-six,	解三十六國語言;
And with which he has translated rare books,	繙緝異書,
Six hundred classics in total.[77]	成六百餘部經典。

As Xue indicates, Jitong's self-cultivation accords with the perfected-person ideal. Standing solidly on his cultural roots, Jitong has increased his knowledge and strengthened his poetic creativity as he expands his contacts with the world. In the process, he translates alien cultures for Chinese reference. (Jitong could not possibly have known thirty-six foreign languages nor could he have translated six hundred classics, of course. This kind of "birthday" text tended to use hyperbole.)

Xue relegates the leading *Shishuo* category "Virtuous Conduct" to second place, defining it primarily in terms of Jitong's devotion to his family and his clan. Jitong "has dispersed his salary among family and friends, thus all look up to him for a means of living; / He enjoys richness and thrift with the clan, so all rely upon his fraternal cooking fire" (祿秩散之親故, 四方仰續命之田; 豐儉共于鄉家, 九族借同功之火).[78] Xue then moves to the third category, "Politics and Economics." Here we see Jitong putting his broad learning into full use, from advising on state policies and constructing irrigation systems to renovating businesses, proposing military strategies, and leading a relief group to the devastated North. She makes a special point of emphasizing Jitong's contribution to China's diplomacy: "With great eloquence, he served as an envoy on special missions; / Neither too proud nor too humble, he kept his country from falling into factionalism" (況有辨給之才, 嘗充專對之使。不亢不卑, 無偏無黨).[79] Xue understands Jitong's diplomatic principles in terms of the Confucian teaching that a "superior person" (*junzi*) "should not form cliques" (*budang*).[80] Jitong maintained the dignity of China as the *junzi* among nations, insisting on a diplomacy that would not ally China with one country against another.

Fourth, Xue discusses Jitong's friendship with people in China and throughout the world. Jitong enjoys such respect that "People wish to see his dashing appearance, so much that they feel seeing him amounts to receiving a large fiefdom; / Admirers, often including envoys from Western countries, come to greet him" (故願瞻丰采, 如膺萬戶侯封; 拜問起居, 時有摩訶使者).[81] Finally, Xue tries to defend Jitong's somewhat decadent lifestyle with references to a series of romantic figures in China's distant past. In the face of adversity, Jitong sometimes seeks spiritual comfort from talented courtesans, just like Bai Juyi, who "at the end of the sky felt deeply for a lute player" (天涯深感琵琶),[82] and Su Shi, who in his banishment "conversed with the zitherist Qincao on Buddhist meanings in the human realm" (人境轉參琴操).[83] Jitong's indulgence in music and beauties does not affect his serving the country and the people with his talent, just as in the case of Xie An, for whom "String and pipe music in the Eastern Mountains / Does not obstruct a genius from spreading copious rain" (東山絲竹, 無妨霖雨奇才).[84]

Xue paints a Jitong who has devoted all his might to his family, his people, and his country during China's most tumultuous decades. Charming, handsome, talented, generous, and responsible, Jitong exemplifies the ideal construct of a new intellectual of the reform era. To praise such a brother-in-law, Xue writes without reservation. Although speaking for the entire Chen clan, Xue declares her name at the end:

I, Shaohui, a cypress vine clinging to the tree of marriage,	紹徽託蔦蘿為姻婭,
Follow closely the footsteps of the Chen brothers.	隨棠棣以趨蹌。
A humble bride who wishes to marry the brother-in-law	新婦參軍,
Feels embarrassed to bring inner words across the boundary.	愧內言之踰越;
Yet this is only to wish Brother Sha and Sister-in-law Cui	沙哥崔嫂,
A ceaseless longevity.[85]	願上壽而綿長。

Xue reveals her identity to align her position with that of Zhong Yan, another major character in the *Shishuo* "Xianyuan," who joked that she could have borne a better son had she married her brother-in-law.[86] Zhong Yan's daring comments were condemned by some later imperial scholars. Zhang Xuecheng accused her—along with Xie Daoyun—of "wiping out moral teachings" (see also Chapter One),[87] and Li Ciming (1830–94) referred to her remarks as "dirty and heretical words" (*huiyu wangyan*).[88] These criticisms notwithstanding, Xue emulates Zhong Yan and goes even further: whereas Zhong Yan kept her words within the inner chamber, Xue publicizes hers to the world.

Xue is more daring than Zhong Yan because she knows that she stands on the solid moral ground of the *xianyuan* tradition, which had been revitalized in the reform era. The *Shishuo* authors enlisted Zhong Yan as a leading *xianyuan*, and early Tang historians quoted Zhong Yan's "dirty and heretical words" in the "Lienü zhuan" of the *History of the Jin*, showing that scholars close to her time understood she was elevating the Wei-Jin values embodied by the brother-in-law.[89] The same *xianyuan* spirit encourages Xue to vocalize her admiration for Jitong, who has displayed the values embedded in the perfected-person ideal. Even her "feeling embarrassed" is intended to intensify—rather than apologize for—her eagerness to praise Jitong. Ending the "Call for Poetic Contributions" in her own name allows Xue the freedom to portray Jitong from perspectives that transcend the conventional formulae of birthday-celebration writing.

Continuing the Min writing-women tradition, Xue positioned herself solidly on learning. Seizing on the changing sociopolitical and cultural opportunities in the reform era, Xue rebuilt learning, redefined the meaning of intellectualism, and refashioned gender relationships by sorting through a variety of values. Equipped with new knowledge, she brought women's roles across the inner-outer boundaries, making the originally male-dominated polity a shared realm of the two sexes. Throughout the process, Xue maintained the conventional "outward extension," starting from the family. This solid rooting of women's self-positioning in the family would mark the fundamental difference between the emancipation discourse of women who favored reform and women who favored revolution (see the Conclusion).

EIGHT

Xue's Literary Response
to the Late Qing Reforms

The bloody termination of the Hundred Days and its repressive aftermath only urged Xue into a more profound contemplation of the purpose and practice of the reform, and she naturally rendered her response in poetic forms that transformed passion into reason. One major issue that immediately preoccupied her was the proper position of women with and within the *guo* amid the reconceptualization of the *guo* as state, country, and nation-state during the reform era. Xue would apply related ideas to her portrayal of women in the 1900 Boxer Rebellion. These ideals would eventually prompt Xue to deliberate on the ideal political system for China in her last poems, composed in the New Policy era (1901–11).

Xue's Response to the Hundred Days

As reformers in Shanghai successfully carried out the campaign for women's education, leading reformers Kang Youwei and Liang Qichao, in Beijing, the capital, convinced Emperor Guangxu to speed up political reform and thus offended Empress Dowager Cixi. On 21 September 1898, Cixi terminated the reforms. On 28 September, six leading reformers were executed, including Kang Guangren, one of the eight initiators of the 1897–98 campaign for women's education and the financial executive of the Shanghai Girls' School, Tan Sitong, an active supporter of the project, and Lin Xu, a neighbor and family friend of the Chen brothers.[1] Shocked and devastated on hearing of Cixi's coup d'état, Xue nevertheless kept up an unabated spirit of reform as reflected in her poem "Reading History on the Night of the Mid-Autumn Festival" ("Zhongqiu ye dushi zuo" 仲秋夜讀史作), written on 30 September. Despite the deadly blow dealt to the reformers, Xue contended that the "chess game" was not yet over, and the future of China still looked as bright as the autumn moon.[2] This poem represented the voice of a much broader range of reformers who were not directly involved in the politics of the Hundred Day reforms and did not equate the reform enterprise as a whole with one skirmish over power in the capital. A temporary halt only offered them time to prepare for further reform operations.

Xue's optimism notwithstanding, she and her family undoubtedly felt great sorrow over the tragic death of the six reform martyrs, especially Lin Xu. Under the circumstances, though, they, even Lin Xu's father-in-law, Shen Yuqing, could only express their grief implicitly.[3] Xue also managed to express hers. A song-lyric she composed during this period, "Tomb of the Righteous Woman" ("Yifu zhong" 義婦冢), to the tune "Slow Song of Zhu Yingtai" ("Zhu Yingtai ji" 祝英台近) looks like a possible elegy for Lin Xu and his wife, Shen Queying, who died soon after him. Xue often composed song-lyrics to a tune related to the theme, and the theme of this one is identical to that of the origin of the tune—a song about the Eastern Jin girl Zhu Yingtai.[4] Xue probably adopted the details of her story from her townsman Liang Zhangju's *Continued Collection of a Wanderer's Talks* (*Langji xutan*) and the *Prefectural Gazetteer* (*Fuzhi*) of Ningbo, Zhejiang province, where the tomb was located and where Xue and her family lived from early 1898 to early 1902. According to these sources, Zhu disguised herself as a young man in order to study at a boys' school. There she befriended a classmate, Liang Shanbo. Having learned that Yingtai was a woman, Shanbo proposed to her, but Yingtai was already betrothed to another man. The heartbroken Shanbo soon died and was buried on the Pure-Way Mound (Qingdaoyuan) to the west of Maocheng county (in suburban Ningbo). On her wedding day, Yingtai passed by Shanbo's tomb and cried the tomb open. She jumped into the tomb and buried herself with Shanbo. Their spirits were transformed into butterflies, roaming freely into legend. Later the Eastern Jin prime minister Xie An named the site "Tomb of the Righteous Woman," hence Xue's title of the song-lyric.[5]

Grass soughing, and breeze sighing,	草蕭蕭, 風惻惻,
Nine out of ten days it is rainy and windy.	十日九風雨。
The sky clears on the Cold-Food Day,	寒食初晴,
Orioles chirp at dusk in this desolate temple.	荒寺暮鶯語。
Ashes of the mourning paper float to the sky	紙灰飄上遙空,
And transform into butterflies,	化爲蝴蝶。
Looking like the two lovers still dancing,	算猶是, 兩情飛舞,
Hearts tied together.	同心縷。
The mourners who offer wine at the site	轉令澆酒人來,
Look up to the tall trees in front of the tomb arch.	高瞻墓門樹。
The fragrant souls, so stubbornly in love,	癡魂香魄,
Now happily reunite underground.	地下共歡聚。
To this day, by the Pure-Way Mound,	只今清道原邊,
Cold waves roar as in the old days.	寒濤依舊。
Their spirits must roam freely, till the end of the world.[6]	想靈爽, 優游終古。

Xue composed the "Tomb of the Righteous Woman" between the fall of 1898 and June 1901, coinciding with the last years of Shen Queying's life.[7] One may wonder whether Xue was drawing a parallel between the Liang-Zhu story and Queying's relentless devotion to Lin Xu. Not only were both couples classmates and soul mates but also the word *hantao*, or "cold waves," reminds the reader of the Shen family shrine, the Roaring-Wave Garden, where the heroic spirit of Lady Lin Puqing, the source of her granddaughter Queying's moral strength and intellectual brilliance, dwells. This being the case, Xue must have written the song-lyric on the Cold-Food Day—a festival in early April for remembering the dead—either in 1899 after Queying's rumored suicide or in 1901 after her eventual death in May 1900.[8]

This mourning mood in Xue's song-lyric was reinforced by a poem by her daughter Chen Yun, written at the same time and bearing the same title:

The song-lyric tune "Zhu Yingtai,"	詞調祝英台,
The Music Bureau ballad "Huashan ji,"	樂府華山幾。
Decaying skirt transforms into butterflies;	壞裙化蛺蝶,
Still flying with the spring wind.[9]	猶逐春風飛。

Chen Yun alludes to two stories similar to the Liang-Zhu legend. The "Huashan ji" ballad tells of a Liu-Song scholar who was smitten with a girl and died of lovesickness. As his coffin passed by the girl's door, the girl cried

the coffin open and buried herself with the man.[10] The "decaying skirt" alludes to the tragic love between scholar Han Ping and his wife during the
Warring States period (770–476 BCE). King Kang of Song took Han Ping's
wife by force, leading Han Ping to kill himself. His wife threw herself down
a terrace in front of the king. The attendants rushed to catch her, only to
see the shreds of her skirt transform into butterflies.[11] Allowing a not-yet-
betrothed daughter to write about such intense spousal attachment seems
uncharacteristic for a gentry family unless the mother and the daughter had
a higher cause embedded in the title, *Yifu*, "Righteous Woman."

Xue and Chen Yun surely understand that calling Zhu Yingtai an *yifu*
defies the Confucian definition of *yi*. How can a daughter be praised as
"righteous" when she rejects a marriage arranged by her parents—the very
foundation of a stable Confucian society? Given that it was Xie An, Xie
Daoyun's supportive uncle, who labeled Zhu a "righteous woman," Xue
and Chen Yun must have deciphered this *yi* in terms of Wei-Jin *xianyuans*'
demands for equal and passionate gender relationships. Seen in this light,
it was very possible that Xue and Chen Yun composed the "Tomb of the
Righteous Woman" to commemorate Shen Queying, who died not as a
subservient widow upholding the cult of chastity but as a reform-minded
comrade of her martyred husband. Indeed, Queying lamented in her last
days that "no one recognizes my secret regrets" (幽恨無人省),[12] and her regrets should have resulted from the couple's unfulfilled hope for reform, not
from a widow's hopeless life. It was on such a noble basis that the maiden
Chen Yun dared praise spousal love and devotion. Xue's poems in response
to the Hundred Days, though only a few, are numerous enough to show her
unfading support for the reform movement.

Repositioning Women with and within the
Guo (Country, State, and/or Nation)

After the Hundred Days, Xue continued to be the leading contributor to
the *Nü xuebao*. The pause in the reform movement allowed Xue time for
thoroughly reflecting on issues prompted by the campaign for women's education. One imperative question for her was how to define women's proper
position on their own terms, both with and within the *guo*. "*Guo*" in the
late Qing reform era had complex connotations. It might mean the "state,"
referring to a sovereign political entity; the "country," which combined a geographical region, a sovereign territory, and a cultural tradition; or the "nation-

state," which emerged from the process of Western modernization. In any meaning, *guo* became a central concept women had to deal with as they participated in public affairs. Xue addressed this question in three parallel-prose essays, namely, "A Letter to Ms. Shen" ("Fu Shen nüshi shu" 覆沈女士書), "On Xi Shi" ("Xizi lun" 西子論), and "On Li Qingzhao and Zhu Shuzhen" ("Li Qingzhao Zhu Shuzhen lun" 李清照朱淑貞論), published very likely in the *Nü xuebao* during this difficult time.[13] In writing these essays, Xue invoked "women's lived bodily experiences" to dispute "the cultural meanings inscribed on the female body."[14] Here "cultural meanings" refer specifically to a variety of patriarchal—Confucian and/or nationalistic—implications that reify the female body into a force subversive to the male political order.

"On Xi Shi" deals with the most complex correlations among the female body, patriarchal decorum, and state politics. Male rulers always warn against women's enticing power to manipulate the state order, yet they often recruit enticing women to undermine their political enemies. Either way, women are condemned. The Xi Shi story is one of the earliest to entail such political complexities. The legendary beauty Xi Shi lived in the state of Yue during the late Spring and Autumn period. She was sent by her king, Goujian, to beguile the Wu king Fuchai. Having helped Yue destroy Wu, Xi Shi went into reclusion "in fear of [suffering the same destiny as] a hunting dog" (*wei gonggou*), which was often cooked with the hare it had caught. One of Xue's "Miscellaneous Poems from Ningbo" composed in the spring of 1898 adapted this conventional narrative.[15] Xue, however, soon subverted this image of Xi Shi as a state-destroyer, as she argues at the very outset of "On Xi Shi":

A city or a state was ruined
    Not by an intelligent woman able to beguile [the ruler];
	夫傾城傾國，
	    非哲婦之能妖；

A ruler infatuated with [a woman]
    Had only his own wantonness to blame.
	而君寵君憐，
	    實王心之自蕩。

Had he been able to manage the male order, The female order would also have been well founded.	倘乾綱果然克振， 則地道必底於成。
How, then, could it end up that deer ascended the Su Palace Terrace,	奚至鹿上蘇臺，
Weeds covered secluded paths, The ruler lost his hegemonic ambition, And caused the beauty to lose her life?[16]	草埋幽徑， 失霸業之雄圖， 貽佳人之薄命哉？

Xue challenges the famous accusation against women from the *Book of Songs* that states "An intelligent man builds up the city wall; / An intelligent woman ruins it" (哲夫成城, 哲婦傾城) with "An intelligent woman has a long tongue, / And it is a stepping-stone to disaster" (婦有長舌, 維厲之階).[17] Since the Han, the Confucian patriarchy had used the "ruining-the-city" verdict to ban women from state affairs. Liu Xiang, for instance, quoted this poem to condemn "Vicious and Depraved Women" in the *Lienü zhuan*.[18] To clear the path for women's participation in politics, Xue felt it urgent to dispute this long-standing disparagement.

Xue therefore consciously worked out a different version of the Xi Shi story based on earlier historical records and filled in details drawing upon "women's lived bodily experiences." Xi Shi was born an innocent girl, without the slightest idea of political intrigue:

Happily she accompanied her sisters to wash silk, And returned home behind the closed door of a thatched abode;	笑伴浣紗姊妹, 掩此蓬門;
How could she know that the vengeful ruler and ministers Would recruit her as an unusual commodity?[19]	詎知嘗膽君臣, 居為奇貨?

Yue sent Xi Shi to Wu against her will. There "the king treated her with tenderness from beginning to end; / How could she forget to return it with respect and love?" (終老溫柔, 敢忘敬愛?). Their harmonious life ended in tragedy as Wu fell. Yet Xue insists that Xi Shi had no part in Yue's dark tactics against Wu—"She followed the Yue order to attend the Wu king; / Of course she would devote herself to serving her lord husband" (既奉命以來嬪, 當委身而事主). In this sense, "If she did not even betray Wu, / How dared she betray Yue?" (其無負於吳者, 胡敢貳心於越耶?).[20] Xi Shi's loyalty from a woman's standpoint transcends the borders of states: she kept her promise to Yue to be a dutiful wife of Wu. Xue's redefinition of loyalty stands in sharp contrast to the male-made political rules that demand loyalty to the state at all cost, even at the expense of the closest human relationships.

Xue rejects the broadly circulated ending of Xi Shi: to avoid a "hunting dog" destiny, she retreated into the mist of Lake Wuhu with the Yue statesman Fan Li. "What was the need for Xi Shi to bear the humiliation of a remarriage simply for survival?" (奚必隱忍偷生, 蒙恥再醮乎?),[21] Xue asks, for she would surely die for her husband. In conclusion, Xue laments:

Alas, the one who destroyed Wu was Yue Not Xi Shi;	嗟嗟, 破吳者越也, 非西子也;

| The one who ruined the Wu was Wu | 亡吳者吳也, |
| Not Xi Shi![22] | 非西子也 |

As for Xi Shi, "her last-day integrity spreads such a sweet scent that only the autumn appearance of Tao [Qian]'s chrysanthemums are comparable" (晚節能香, 剩陶菊之秋容得似).[23] Tao Qian, the founder of pastoral poetry, infused Daoist ideals into the chrysanthemum imagery that embodies nature's purity, plainness, and forbearance in the face of a harsh environment.[24]

Xue reinforces her defense of women like Xi Shi in a song-lyric on Zhang Lihua (559–89), the notorious concubine of the last ruler of the Chen dynasty (557–89), Chen Shubao (r. 583–89), composed later, in early 1905, in Nanjing. Official histories portrayed Zhang as a typical "intelligent woman" who "ruined the city." Beautiful and talented, she beguiled the ruler and intervened in state affairs, causing "the state order to become murky and chaotic" (*gangji maoluan* 綱紀瞀亂).[25] As the Sui troops entered the Chen capital of Jiankang (today's Nanjing) in 589, they spared Chen Shubao but executed Zhang Lihua, fearing she might cast a spell on the newly established Sui ruler.[26] Xue nonetheless offers an alternate reading of her life:

I recall that old osmanthus tree, in the opulent palace,	遙思老桂璇宮,
Waking up from a short dream fermented in red millet:	醒一夢紅粱,
[The emperor] summoned his men of letters	宣進詞客。
To compose beautiful songs for his Moon Fairy Chang E.	嫦娥曲美,
Moreover, sitting on his knees	更膝上,
She was capable of analyzing court memos and military reports.	奏記軍書能識。
The fragrant face died for the country;	芳容殉國,
Even if incense is still burnt for her, she deserves more tender regards.	卜香火已堪憐惜。
Yet the misty tide has put off the smoke and washed off her shrine,	況渺茫潮打烟沉,
Leaving no sight of her beautiful and divine traces.[27]	不見艷痕靈跡。

Full of "tender regard," Xue and Shoupeng are searching for the wretched soul of Zhang Lihua along Green Brook, where she was beheaded. Xue describes her stunning beauty but praises more her talent in helping the ruler by "analyzing court memos and military reports." While this detail has been taken by male historians as one of the causes that led to toppling the "city wall," Xue reads it as Zhang's contribution to the state. The Sui general killed her fearing not her beauty but her talent, which might help the Chen rise again. Xue therefore applauds Zhang Lihua for having "died for her country" (*xunguo* 殉國), the noblest sacrifice to the state and the people.

Xue associates Zhang Lihua with Xi Shi more explicitly and sympathetically in the rhyme-prose "Qinhuai" ("Qinhuai fu" 秦淮賦), also composed in early 1905. At the floodgate connecting the Qinhuai River to Green Brook, Xue asks who would show pity for this woman: "Only the weeping water still flows after a thousand years, / But for whom to wash silk by its side?" (留得千秋嗚咽水, 更與何人作浣紗?).[28] No record shows that Zhang, though of humble origins, ever washed silk by the river. Assuming Zhang was once a washing girl, Xue aligns her with Xi Shi under the common denominator of *huansha* 浣紗, washing silk for weaving, which symbolizes feminine purity and women's attentiveness to their work. Once the washing girls were dragged into the bloody abyss of male politics, however, they could not survive dark power struggles. Who would weep for their tragic destiny but the water that once witnessed their youthful innocence? Centering on the metaphor "washing silk," Xue weaves a discursive defense to clear the much maligned names of Xi Shi and Zhang Lihua and to redefine their relationship with the state on women's own terms: as loving daughters and wives, Xi Shi was loyal to her native state and her husband's kingdom, and Zhang Lihua gave her state her talent and eventually her life.

"On Li Qingzhao and Zhu Shuzhen" pointedly disputes the late imperial statement on female chastity, "having no talent is women's virtue." Zhu and Li were both "famous women poets of song-lyrics of the Zhao-Song dynasty."[29] Although poetic achievements may bring fame, for women they often lead to defamatory voyeurism into a poet's private life; hence "their great reputation caused slander; / their innocent sentiments aroused suspicion" (負盛名以致謗; 因清怨而生疑).[30] Even during the Shanghai campaign for women's education, there were still arguments that singled out Li Qingzhao to demonstrate how a woman poet "undermined her moral integrity with her excessive talent."[31] Xue contends:

Wagging long tongues to pave steps to disaster	長舌厲階,
Is indeed the business of the nosy men of letters;	實文人之好事;
We abominate slander that destroys good behavior,[32]	聖［聖］讒殄行,
And vilifies gentle ladies with massive slurs.	致淑媛以厚誣。
Black and white are confused;	黑白既淆,

Chastity and lust cannot be differentiated.	貞淫莫辨,
All this makes us women wring wrists in sorrow.	竟使深閨扼腕。
Attentively reading their remnant works,	抱讀遺編,
I am willing to spread the radiance of their red-tube brushes,	願教彤管揚輝,
To glorify their writings as trustworthy history.[33]	昭為信史。

The term "long tongue" was originally used in the *Book of Songs* to characterize "an intelligent woman" who toppled men's political order. Xue reverses it to accuse some "intelligent men" of sullying women's moral order.

Xue then proceeds to clarify what she believes to be men's malicious rumors about Li's remarriage and Zhu's secret love affair. While details of their lives remain debatable, what matters is why they were vilified. It is because, Xue maintains, "as one's Dao becomes lofty, slander follows" (*daogao huilai* 道高毀來). Taking Li, for example, Xue solemnly declares her Dao to be *aiguo* 愛國: "Willing to cross the Huai River, [Li] still maintained a sincere love for the *guo*" (願過淮水, 猶存愛國之忱).[34] This line alludes to Li's rhyme-prose "Horse Chess" ("Dama fu" 打馬賦) composed in her later years in Lin'an (Hangzhou), the "temporarily settled" capital of the newly established Southern Song. Having lost her home, her husband, and the couple's lifelong collection of books and antiques after the Northern Song fell to the Jurchens, an ailing Li still hoped to recover the lost land:

Foli [referring to the Jurchen invaders] will surely die in the year *yimao*;	佛狸定見卯年死。
Yet nobles and commoners are all running for their lives.	貴賤紛紛尚流徙,
Horses after horses, of all kinds, full in my sight.	滿眼驊騮雜騄駬,
Has the situation really fallen into such devastating straits?	時危安得真至此?
Only Mulan, the outstanding woman, holds her spear.[35]	木蘭橫戈好女子。
Old, who still has the ambition to gallop a thousand *li*?	老矣誰能志千里?
Let's cross the Huai River, fighting back to the north![36]	但願相將過淮水。

Li's *aiguo* boasts not only heroic emulation of Mulan, who goes to the battlefield to protect her country and family, but also courageous criticism of the cowardly Southern Song ruler, as Xue elaborates: "Comparing the current gentry with Wang Dao, [Li] accused them of mistaking Hangzhou for Bianzhou" (衣冠王導, 斥將杭作汴之非).[37] Here Xue alludes to Li's couplet: "Among the gentlemen fleeing to the south, none resembles Wang Dao; / Of the messages from the north, few tell about Liu Kun" (南渡衣冠欠王導, 北來消息少劉琨).[38] After the Western Jin (265–317) fell to the nomads, Minister Wang Dao helped move the Jin regime to the south and safeguarded the people, and General Liu Kun continued fighting the invaders in the north. Recalling these precedents, Li utters her profound disappointment with the current situation. "Hangzhou" and "Bianzhou" refer to a line from the Southern Song poet Lin Sheng's 林升 "Inscribed on a Lin'an Inn" ("Ti Lin'an di" 題臨安邸) that echoes Li's frustration:

Green mountains beyond green mountains, and towers beyond towers,	山外青山樓外樓,
When will they stop singing and dancing by the West Lake?	西湖歌舞幾時休?
A cozy breeze intoxicates visitors wandering about—	暖風熏得游人醉,
They just take Hangzhou for [the old capital] Bianzhou![39]	直把杭州作汴州!

Li's open criticism undoubtedly offended the Southern Song authorities who, out of self-interest, never wanted to recover the land and people lost to the invaders. Li thus made "the evil and treacherous men feel ashamed and fly into a rage" (姦黠者轉羞成怒), and they subsequently "slandered the frosty inner chamber widow after her death" (謗霜閨於身後).[40]

In interpreting Li Qingzhao's life, Xue has conceptualized the ideal of *aiguo* as first and foremost love for the land, the people, and the culture, and in this sense *aiguo* can be best rendered as "love for the country," which includes but goes far beyond a sovereign political entity. More importantly, based on this love, one should accept the responsibility of criticizing a sovereign who fails to protect the country and subjects his people to misery. Xue's concept of *aiguo* follows a central principle of traditional Chinese political ethics that "people are more important than the ruler."[41] This principle has repeatedly justified dynastic change in China's history, as Xue recognizes: "Kings and marquises are long gone; / The Han and the Song left not a single inch of land" (王兮侯兮成千古, 漢宋於今無寸土).[42] What remains unchanged is the land and attached to it the people and the culture. *Aiguo* should, therefore, put all these components of a *guo* before its sovereign.

This is about the first time that *aiguo* was applied to a reading of Li Qingzhao,[43] and it shows Xue's sensitivity to the concept of *aiguo* that loomed large in the 1898 reform discourse when China's sovereignty was facing threats from abroad. Indeed, *aiguo* had been a focal topic in the 1898 *Nü xuebao*, but, as in Xue's essay on Li Qingzhao, women reformers hardly took a nationalistic stand. Lu Cui's "On Women's Patriotism" ("Nüzi aiguo shuo" 女子愛國說), the first essay on this theme, considered *aiguo* as women's equal political and educational rights. She argued:

> Our country is now increasingly endangered by foreign imperialist invasions. Whoever has a voice should heave a sigh! Last month His Majesty decreed that each of his people might present his/her opinions. Since "people" should include both male and female, we women should also present a collectively signed memorial to the emperor with our candid views, so that we will not regret being Chinese women who stand [equally with men] under heaven and on the earth.[44]

Lu Cui then lists systematic requests to the emperor, asking him to open girls' schools, publish women's journals, build libraries and reading clubs for female readers, patronize art exhibitions for female artists, establish gynecological and obstetric hospitals, and even organize beauty pageants. The most solemn request Lu Cui puts forward is to establish an educational bureau for women to hold female civil examinations and select members for a female parliament. Lu Cui's requests resonate with Xue's historical account of women's broad range of political service to the state, built upon their talent and learning.[45]

Some historians credit Liang Qichao with minting the term *aiguo* in his "On *Aiguo*" ("Aiguo lun") published in February 1899.[46] Yet the women contributors to the 1898 *Nü xuebao* had conceptualized *aiguo* even earlier, in August 1898. Whereas Liang's *aiguo* bears a strong nationalistic connotation that places sovereignty before people's well-being and can be best rendered as love for the nation-state,[47] women's *aiguo* is humanitarianly and culturally oriented. It places women's self-cultivation ahead of the nation's empowerment so as to nurture and protect the country as a whole, including its families, its people, and its culture.

"A Letter to Ms. Shen" disputes the current nationalistic condemnation of women's footbinding as a major cause of China's backwardness. Yang Nianqun notes that the 1898 anti-footbinding movement was largely a "male discourse" that lacked substantial participation by women.[48] Indeed, leading women reformers such as Xue Shaohui, although no supporter of footbinding, refused to treat it a sensational issue at the expense of more fundamental issues of women's rights. Xue's point, as Dorothy Ko summarizes with great insight, "is that footbinding is a trivial, private matter; bound or unbound, a woman's foot is simply irrelevant to her mission in life and her contributions to the nation."[49] Xue contends:

Generals and ministers never rise from fixed family backgrounds;	將相本無定種;
Writing poetry and learning classics can strengthen us.	詩書即可自強。
Women are born with genuineness;	婦女固有其真,
Tenderly conforming [to the course of nature] is their proper principle.	柔順始為正則。
Depending on the ten fingers, We pull needles and thread year after year;	全憑十指, 壓針線於連年;
Striving to be of one mind with our spouse, We supervise cooking in the kitchen.	黽勉同心, 課米鹽於中饋。
By cultivating female virtue, We can then complete women's Way.	女德能修, 婦道乃備。
All those theories on [fortifying] the weakened race, empowering the *guo*,	凡所謂弱種強國、
Prospering business, and managing the household,	興業持家之說,
Lie in this [women's self-strengthening] not in that [abolishing footbinding].[50]	又在此不在彼矣。

The last three lines indicate that Ms. Shen's letter (unseen so far) must have drawn upon the anti-footbinding discourse widely circulated by male reformers, which ties the eradication of this malpractice closely to the reform purpose of empowering the *guo*. "*Guo*" in this context, with "race" in the foreground, clearly refers to the newly imported concept of the nation-state. Though aware of the subtle changes to the connotations of the *guo*, Xue does not yield to nationalistic patriarchal prejudice against women's self-strengthening. On the contrary, she sets up even higher demands: through education, women should be able to become generals and ministers of state. When peasants revolted against the Qin, they shouted: "Do kings, barons, generals, and ministers rise from only a fixed family background?" (王侯將相寧有種乎).[51] "Family background" for them might only indicate class differences, and they certainly did not have women in mind. Now Xue gendered this typical male political ambition to be women's.

Xue's design for women's ambitions, however, far exceeded men's designs, which concentrated largely on public affairs. She expects women to carry out the "women's Way" (*fudao*), the same mission of "mothering the world" as she had suggested in the "Preface to the *Nü xuebao*," which, as Xue elaborates in her letter to Ms. Shen, involves activities from household chores to state management, from culture to politics. To fulfill this task, women should "tenderly conform to the course of nature" (*roushun* 柔順), a principle generated from the perfected-person discourse. Xiang Xiu in his commentary on the "Free Roaming" chapter of *Zhuangzi* compares the feminine features of the perfected person to those of a young girl, saying: "Such a young girl has an open and peaceful mind, and she tenderly conforms [to the course of nature] (*roushun*). She is harmonious with nature without disturbing it. She does not ask for help from others but is asked to help others" (時女虛靜柔順, 和而不喧, 未嘗求人而爲人所求也).[52] Such is the model Xue sets up for women to conduct their much-enlarged sociopolitical role.

Dorothy Ko points out that Xue in her letter to Ms. Shen was "to introduce a vantage point that had been missing in the gigantic histories: a subjective view from inside the woman's body."[53] This comment is also applicable to the other two essays. With these three works, Xue cleared women of the political stigma that Chinese patriarchies, past and present, had inscribed on the female body, from the tongue to the feet. Her intention, therefore, was to pave the way for women to participate in public affairs, from which they had long been excluded.

Portraying Women in the Boxer Rebellion

In 1900, when Xue and Shoupeng were in Ningbo writing and translating, the Boxer Rebellion broke out. From then on, Xue wrote at least six long poems that depicted the lives of women of the time and expressed their opinions about the incident. With these poems, Xue demonstrated women's strength and role in China's sociopolitical life across a wide class spectrum and hence reinforced their collective will to participate in public affairs.

In "Reading the Song History" ("Du Songshi" 讀宋史) (1900) and the "Eulogy to His Majesty Returning to the Capital" ("Huiluan song" 回鑾頌) (1901), Xue delivered a real-time response to the Boxer Rebellion. Comparing the current situation to historical precedents, Xue accused the Qing regime of manipulating the Boxers for its own political and diplomatic purposes, only causing "bodies to fill in the Guarding-Dragon River" (積屍填滿護龍河) and "the five-colored banners [of the Eight Powers] to compete for the Chinese throne" (五采旛爭窺象闕).[54] Though utterly critical, Xue still hoped that Guangxu and Cixi, who had fled the capital, would return to Beijing and resume the reform: "Enlisting heavenly talents and benefiting from the geographic situation, / the Zhou state [11th century–221 BCE] may reform its system" (取擇天材地利, 周邦儘可維新).[55]

It took great courage to make such a suggestion at this sensitive moment. Cixi's intention to force Guangxu to abdicate after her coup d'état aroused strong opposition from the gentry, led by none other than the Chen brothers' close associate Jing Yuanshan. The court detained Jing for over a year in an attempt to silence the reformers.[56] Out of frustration, Jitong voiced his open support for Guangxu regaining his power by printing "Restore Emperor Guangxu to his position!" (光緒皇覆任) on the cover of his book *The Chinese Empire, Past and Present*, published in Chicago in 1900 (Figure 8.1). Although even radical scholar-officials were cautious at this moment,[57] Xue frankly defended the reform-minded emperor and continued to advocate reform. In a sense, these two poetic works represent Xue's own image as a gentry housewife who has, as she puts in the "Eulogy to His Majesty," "diligently obeyed the instruction that inner words should not go out."[58] Now she breaks this Confucian injunction and openly expresses her opinions regarding state affairs.

Xue recalled women's efforts to ease people's sufferings in the aftermath of the Boxer Rebellion in the "Song of the Old Courtesan" ("Laoji xing" 老妓行) (1902) and "Inscribed on Wu Zhiying's Calligraphy Scroll in Cursive Style" ("Ti Wu Zhiying caoshu hengfu" 題吳芝瑛草書橫幅) (1905). The "Old Courtesan" recounts the legendary life of Fu Caiyun (aka Sai Jinhua). A young singing girl from Suzhou, Caiyun later became the concubine of the late Qing diplomat Hong Jun (1839–93) and capably assisted him during his mission in Europe. There, with her talent in foreign languages and good manners, Caiyun won the respect of the Western courts. When the Eight-Power Allied Forces occupied Beijing, Caiyun walked ahead to protect women, again using her talent in foreign languages:

Soldiers assaulted women on the capital's streets.	捕卒六街擾婦女
In their orchid inner chambers, virtuous ladies hid like mice.	蘭閨淑媛伏如鼠
Only the courtesan Dong'er courageously stepped forward.[59]	偏有冬兒慷慨前
Wearing rustic clothes, but speaking foreign languages.[60]	短衣縛袴能胡語

Despite Caiyun's humble origins and controversial reputation (caused mainly by her rumored sexual relationship with the commander of the Eight-Power Allied Forces, the German general Waldersee), Xue contends her conduct fits *fudao*.[61] Xue points out in Caiyun's case that "the women's Way should focus on virtue and proper manners" (婦道要論容德美).[62] Caiyun behaved properly on diplomatic occasions and should be acknowledged as having good manners. She courageously rescued people at her own risk and hence demonstrated virtue. Xue's open-minded approach to Caiyun's life follows her definition of *fudao* as "mothering the world." Her compilation of foreign women's experience in the *Biographies of Foreign Women* also helped her to expand women's moral space beyond the late imperial cult of chastity.[63]

Figure 8.1. Cover of *The Chinese Empire*, by Tcheng-Ki-Tong and John Henry Gray (Chicago: Rand, McNally, 1900). The Chinese characters read: "Restore Emperor Guangxu to his position!" (光緒皇覆任).

Xue composed the poem inscribed on a calligraphy scroll by Wu Zhi-ying (1868–1934) in 1905 to commemorate Zhiying's contribution to a relief operation that Jitong conducted in the most devastated areas of Tianjin and Beijing in the fall of 1900.[64] (Xue herself also joined the effort. At Jitong's request, she sent the Korean king a letter in parallel prose, pleading for him to assist in the safe passage of the relief group.[65]) Jitong recorded the mission in a sorrowful poem with such lines as: "Extravagant mansions have not even three tiles left; / Residents have fled into the nine states" (華屋不留三片瓦, 良民散作九州人).[66] Zhiying rhymed after Jitong with two poems and inscribed them on a scroll in cursive style. She wielded her brush with such vigor that, as Xue depicts it, "her valiant calligraphy startles the wind and rain" (筆陣蒼茫動風雨). She wrote in such sympathy for the people that "her tender wrist sends out bitter cries like those of sad swans" (腕底哀鴻哭聲苦).[67] Zhiying created this scroll, Xue indicates, to raise money—a new social practice of charity that would soon gain popularity among women and girl students in China.[68] Using Wu Zhiying's and her own experience as examples, Xue again showcases the great contribution of women's poetic and artistic talent to public affairs: calling attention to people's misery and, specifically in the current situation, relieving the suffering in the North.

After the family moved to Beijing in 1907, Xue had more direct access to Boxer Rebellion remembrances. She composed two poems that examined women's lives in 1900 from the extremes at both ends of the class spectrum. The "Melody of the Golden Well" ("Jinjing qu" 金井曲) (1908) recounts the tragic death of Zhenfei 珍妃 (1876–1900), Emperor Guangxu's favorite concubine, upon the invasion of the Eight-Power Allied Forces, and the "Song of the Old Woman from Fengtai" ("Fengtai lao'ao ge" 豐臺老媼歌) (1909) records the incident from the perspective of a wet-nurse who had served Manchu nobles.

In the first part of the "Golden Well" Xue emphasizes that Zhenfei was loved by Guangxu because she assisted in state affairs—"Palace Lady Zuo excelled in literary composition; / [Zhang] Lihua on his knees could analyze court memos" (宮中左女善文辭, 膝上麗華通奏記).[69] Imperial favor, however, caused jealousy among powerful families (implying those related to Guangxu's wife, Empress Longyu 隆裕). Zhenfei was reprimanded by the empress dowager and confined within "clay circles and myriad walls as if deep down in the ocean" (圜土重垣似海深) and not allowed to see the emperor again.[70] Then the Boxer Rebellion erupted and the Eight Powers savaged China's capital:

Suddenly, alerting smoke broke war drums;	狼煙一夕喧鼙鼓,
Brutal Boxers danced to the tune of heavenly demons.	老拳毒手天魔舞。
Banners of the Eight Powers stirred the dust around the palace;	八國旗翻闕下塵,
Bones of myriad families were disposed of along the road.	萬家骨暴道旁土。
I heard chanting about the Five Lords shedding emerald blood;[71]	側聞碧血詠五公,
Who could pacify the vicinity of the capital using the Yellow Map?[72]	誰把黃圖靖三輔?
Panting imperial guards marched into Tong Pass;	厖頭噴霧入潼關,
Glittering flowery canopies rushed out the Water Margin.[73]	華蓋馳輝出水滸。

The incompetent regime unjustly executed five statesmen for their anti-Boxer position but could not find any means of protecting the capital from the foreign invasion. The imperial household escaped, abandoning its people, including Zhenfei, to the ravages of war:

Palace ladies and eunuchs dispersed like snowflakes;	青娥阿監散如雲,
Cannon shells and gunshots spread like a rain storm.	礮石槍聲急似雨。
On Jian Terrace Lady Jiang received no tallied summons from her lord;[74]	漸臺未召姜女符,
In the east tower the suffering Plum Spirit was alone left.[75]	樓東空剩梅精苦。
Lost and speechless, her tears were streaming down;	蒼茫無語淚滂沱,
The dry well, so deep, no water there to stir a ripple.	枯井深沉水不波。
Dragons coiled their way into Liang Garden, turning up the whirling spring.	龍盤梁苑迴瀾湧,
A jade seal fell into Zhengong Well, vaporizing colorful vigor.[76]	璽落甄官綵氣多。

Despite the broadly circulated version, which depicted Cixi ordering Zhen-fei's death by casting her into a palace well,[77] Xue portrays a forlorn yet heroic Zhenfei who jumped into the well to die for the emperor and the country. In life and in death, Zhenfei acted on her own volition. As if not wanting Zhenfei to die in vain, Xue adds a jade-seal detail to her suicide: When the southern warlord Sun Jian (155–91) entered the capital Luoyang to pacify the Yellow Turbans, he saw "five-colored vapor" (*wuse qi*) rising from Zhenguan Well and thence retrieved the Han imperial seal, which was tied to the body of a palace lady who had apparently jumped into the well to protect this imperial symbol.[78] Xue employs this legend to eulogize Zhenfei for having defended the legitimacy and dignity of the dynasty. Her spirit touched heaven, thus the five dragons carved on the seal called the water back to the dry well and protected her body.

After the imperial household returned, the emperor "tried but nowhere could find the fragrant soul" (欲覓芳魂不知處), just like Emperor Xuanzong's desperate search for Yang Guifei depicted in Bai Juyi's "Unending Sorrow" ("Changhen ge" 長恨歌). Whereas Bai has a Daoist priest locating Yang's soul in the immortal world, Xue soberly indicates no such magic priest was present at the current imperial service. The poem ends with a lament:

Alas!	吁嗟乎!
The Jade Spring flows around the Western Mountain,	玉泉縈帶西山璞,
In the palace of our august dynasty, ladies are chaste and sincere.	熙朝宮闈皆貞確。
The profoundly benevolent emperor is loving and passionate;	深仁龍種自多情,
Tender beauty should not be slandered by rumors.	婉孌美人莫諑訴。
The sun shines over the silver bottle dangling in the well;	日照銀缾蕩漾中,
The jade tiger pulls the silk string, conducting her feelings to him.	玉虎牽絲宛轉通。
On Mount Jiuyi, his tears stain the bamboo by the empty river;	九嶷淚洒空江竹,
Atop the one-hundred-foot-tall *wutong* tree, her soul returns.[79]	百尺魂歸金井桐。

This last stanza combines several enigmatic allusions to the image of a well. The "silver bottle" alludes to "Old Sentiments" ("Guyi"), by Chang Jian 常建 (*js.* 727), which describes a fairy flying to heaven from her crystal cave in a well.[80] The "jade tiger" refers to the heart-wrenching "Untitled" ("Wuti" 無題) poem by Li Shangyin 李商隱 (ca. 813–ca. 858): At night the woman burns incense waiting for her lover to come; at dawn the man has to leave at hearing the jade tiger pulling the silver bottle from the well. "Never let your heart open with the spring flowers" (春心莫共花爭發), the poet warns, for "one inch of love is an inch of ashes" (一寸相思一寸灰).[81] For Guangxu, the woman who used to burn incense waiting for his arrival now dwells in a crystal cave. He wishes her to fly out of the well, or at least send him a message using the silver bottle tied to the jade tiger. Knowing all is in vain, he can but shed tears. The last couplet brings in the legend of the sage king Shun: Upon hearing that Shun died in the Jiuyi Mountains, his two wives rushed to his side, and their tears stained the bamboo along the Xiang River.[82] Xue reverses this gender and class order by spreading Guanxu's tears on the bamboo and thus summons back Zhenfei's soul. She returns like a noble phoenix to her nest in the pure *wutong* tree.[83]

"The Old Woman from Fengtai" recounts the Boxer Rebellion from a peasant woman's perspective and blames it on the stupid, self-interested Manchu nobles. The narrator served in a Manchu nobleman's household nursing his little daughter. The Boxers in Beijing "claimed they could empower China, / and defeat the strong barbaric enemies" (謂能大中國, 可以退強虜). The delighted nobleman invited them to be his "mind and arms" (*xinlü* 心膂), and even his little daughter was mesmerized:

There was also Fairy Number Two,	更有二仙姑,
Named Sacred Mother of Yellow Lotus.	黃蓮稱聖姥。
She could teach little girls	能教小女兒,
To raise up red lanterns,	紅燈自高舉。
And burn down foreign embassies and churches,	使館與教堂,
Easily in one single torch fire.	何難殲一炬?
My little missy, young and naive,	格格尚嬌癡,
Would also like to learn their tricks.	亦愛傳其緒。
I exhorted her with earnest words,	我亟苦口勸,
So she did not join their clique.[84]	乃未入儔侶。

Despite the evident absurdity of the Boxers' claims, the nobleman trusted them and together they instigated the chaos. The uprising finally backfired and destroyed the nobleman's own family. Why could not the nobleman see the oncoming disaster? Xue, through the voice of the Old Woman, points out that "to be content with one's own position is a blessing" (安分即多祐). Unfortunately, however, the nobleman did not have the wisdom to see what even a countrywoman could see, for he was blinded by his lust for power.

Xue's other poem composed in 1909, "The Extra Space in My New Residence Is Full of Elm Trees" ("Xinju yudi duo yumu" 新居餘地多榆木), seems an allegory also targeting the Manchu nobles:

Dark green leaves are all over branches;	蒼蒼葉滿枝,
Worm threads are densely hanging from the tree.	垂垂蟲吐絲。
These worms cannot make cocoons:	既不能作繭,
How can their threads be woven on a loom?	安能上杼機?
They have done no good to benefit the world;	于世總無益,

They have nibbled away others' territory, regardless of criticism.	弗恤蠶食譏。
They gather the clan to live in the high place,	聚族居高位，
And bully vegetables and flowers below.	下把蔬花欺。
They sometimes transform into white butterflies	或化白蝴蝶，
Flying far and near with the wind.	隨風近遠飛。
They lay eggs to breed offspring,	遺卵種子孫，
Who again suck the syrup of the tree.	再剝樹膏脂。
Once the West wind blows,	一朝西風來，
Who will lament the fallen tree?[85]	樹倒誰為悲？

Xue is obviously worried about the predictable consequences of the racial tension between the Manchu ruling class and the common Chinese. The Manchus nibbled away at the land that originally belonged to the Chinese. They could not produce anything but only live upon others. Their greed weakened China, and its downfall would come with incessant Western aggression. Xue wrote these two poems also with clear reference to the ongoing dispute between the Manchu regime and the Chinese gentry over which constitutional model to follow—the central issue of the New Policy campaign.

Reflections on the "New Policies"

Startled by the invasion of the Eight Powers, Cixi initiated the "New Policies," which literally continued the 1898 agenda. The year 1904 saw a substantial turn in the campaign. Stimulated by Japan's recent victory in its war with Russia—a result of Japan's adaptation of the constitutional system, as the Chinese generally believed—high-ranking officials joined the chorus advocating "constitutional construction" (*lixian*). The superintendent of the Southern Ports, Zhou Fu, for one, along with Zhang Zhidong and Yuan Shikai (1859–1916), proposed to the court in July 1904 that China be transformed into a constitutional state within twelve years.[86] The Chen brothers were then serving on the Southern Ports staff in Nanjing. Given their intimate knowledge of the constitutional system they had acquired from the West, it is possible that they helped Zhou with the proposal.

In the summer of 1905, the Qing regime began seriously tackling the possibility of adopting a constitutional monarchy. In order to communicate between the regime and the general public, the Chen brothers inaugurated the *Official Daily of the Southern Ports* (*Nanyang riri guanbao*) on 1 August 1905 to complement the *Official Journal of the Southern Ports* (*Nanyang guanbao*), which had also been in their charge.[87] The editorial board invited Xue to pen the "Editorial Introduction" to the *Daily* on their behalf, even though the ports flocked with talented men. This brought Xue directly into the constitutional reform movement. Clearly, they knew that they could trust her literary talent, up-to-date knowledge, and, above all, relentless commitment to reform.

Xue begins the "Introduction" with a briefing on the current situation in China: "The ruler on high is considering good plans for invigorating the country, / And the masses below expect civilized governing" (上思振作之良圖, 群仰文明之盛治). The function of the news media, Xue maintains, is to open a space for "declaring the ruler's will and conveying the people's demands" (宣上德而通下情). The eventual purpose is for both sides to work together on "political reforms."[88] Although Jitong had defined the news media as one more historical genre, with the traditional function of mirroring right and wrong (see Chapter Two), Xue made it clear that the media should "pen the news according to what is heard of, / without praise or blame, exhortation or condemnation" (據所聞以載筆, 非立意褒貶勸懲) and should not "intentionally judge right from wrong, black from white" (故作是非黑白). This neutral, objective position sets up journalists as a third party between the ruler and the people, offering both sides quick and objective information—a healthy structure in which a society can function.[89]

Constitutional reform then proceeded quickly. In 1906, five statesmen were sent to inspect Western political systems for a half year, and on 6 November 1906, the court declared a reform of the civil service system.[90] Shoupeng was appointed to a position in the newly established Ministry of Posts and Communications (Youchuan bu) and moved to Beijing with his family in 1907. There Xue spent her last four years in close observation of the New Policy reforms. Her 1907 "Miscellaneous Poems about Beijing" began with a joyful scene in which people of all classes welcomed the reform: "The spring breeze wafts to the heart's content of the Five Lords and Seven Nobles; / The splendid moonlight shines into myriad doors of common households" (五侯七貴春風暢, 萬戶千門夜月多). Xue then detailed the current political changes undertaken by the court:

I recall, since the war drums cleared up the wolf smoke,	憶從鼙鼓靖狼煙,
The dragon chariot has returned to the east and begun changing the old ways.	龍馭東歸作改弦。
The *Zhou Rituals* sets up the official system to accommodate reform;	周禮設官通變法,

Xun Qing studied abroad, happily like a rising immortal.	荀卿遊學笑登仙。
Soldiers compete for training under the order of the Minister of the Army;	府兵爭練大司馬，
The Minister of Music sends for the singer Little Crying Sky.	樂部猶傳小叫天。
Who would continue writing Huan Kuan's *Treatise on Salt and Iron*,	誰續桓寬鹽鐵論，
So that the Minister of Finance can enrich the state's wealth?[91]	度支來裕水衡錢？

Xue happily sees that the reformers' appeal to continue the 1898 reforms, which she called for in her "Eulogy to His Majesty," has received a positive response from the Qing regime. The court has embarked on changing the government's offices—originally set up in the *Zhou Rituals* (*Zhouli*)[92]—to accommodate constitutional reform (line 3) and inspecting Western political systems (line 4). For instance, the Ministry of War (Bingbu) has become the Ministry of the Army (Lujun bu), in charge of reorganizing the Chinese army on Western lines (line 5).[93] While all this is laudable, Xue shows some unease about the motivation and sincerity of the Qing ruler's reforms with the phrase *gaixian* 改絃, "changing the old ways," which alludes to the admonition of the Chen minister Fu Zai 傅縡 (531–85) to his wanton ruler, Chen Shubao. If the emperor does not change his old ways, Fu warns, the Chen dynasty will fall and "wild deer will again roam on the palace terrace" (麋鹿復遊於姑蘇臺).[94] For Xue, it seems, the regime has agreed to reform only out of fear of losing its power, rather than for the purpose of improving people's well-being, and the Five Statesmen abroad (compared to Xun Qing [313?–238? BCE] studying in the state of Qi) were merely enjoying themselves like immortals rather than gathering political ideas (line 4).[95] She criticizes the Ministry of Music (Yuebu) for failing to fulfill its important duty of focusing on state ceremonies but instead attending to the Empress Dowager's personal indulgence in Peking Opera ("Little Crying Sky" refers to Cixi's favorite singer, Tan Xinpei, 1847–1917) (line 6). Xue also wishes that the state financial system would be seriously discussed following the model of Han scholars as recorded in the *Treatise on Salt and Iron* (*Yantie lun*) by Huan Kuan (fl. first century BCE) (lines 7–8),[96] implying the court has failed to improve its financial situation.

Xue's worry intensified as constitutional reform was evolving, and she expressed anxiety in her last long song, "Viewing the Lantern Gathering at the

Front Gate of the Capital" ("Qianmen guan denghui ge" 前門觀燈會歌),
composed on 6 November 1910, a half year before her death. On that day
students in Beijing gathered to celebrate two imperial edicts, respectively
declared on 4 and 5 November. These two edicts proclaimed the opening of
parliament in 1913 and appointed courtiers to draft a constitution and organize the cabinet.[97] People were contented that "luckily a date is set up for
the Zhou to reform the mandate of heaven" (周命維新幸有期).[98] Yet Xue's
comparison of the Qing reform to that of the good old state of Zhou—the
third time in her major reform writings in ten years—connotes complicated meanings.[99] If previously Xue expressed the general hope that the old
state would reform, this time she draws the allusion with clear pertinence
to the "Court Sanctioned Outline of the Constitution" ("Qinding xianfa
dagang" 欽定憲法大綱), announced on 27 August 1908. The Qing regime
composed this outline with the "declared intention to imitate the Japanese
system," which "served the purposes of the oligarchy."[100] The court's explicit
desire to garner even greater power than the Japanese had disappointed the
Chinese constitutionalists, for most of them favored the British parliamentary system, a "republicanism with a nominal monarch" (xujun gonghe 虛君
共和).[101] (Hence Xue derided the greedy Manchu nobles in her 1909 "Old
Woman from Fengtai" and "Elm Trees.") Qin Hui observes:

> There existed a fundamental difference between the late Qing court and the
> Chinese constitutionalists. The court wanted a constitution in the "Japa-
> nese style." The Meiji Restoration retrieved power from shoguns and re-
> turned it to the central government so as to empower the emperor. . . . In
> the eyes of the Chinese constitutionalists, the Meiji Restoration looked just
> like a Westernized "change from the Zhou to the Qin," that is, from feudal-
> ism to an imperial oligarchy. It transformed the Japanese emperor from a
> nominal ruler similar to the King of the Zhou into one with real power like
> the First Emperor of the Qin. . . . Yet for the Chinese constitutionalists,
> [the] constitutional movement was not to walk out of the Zhou but to walk
> out of the Qin.[102]

Seen in this light, Xue's repeated emphasis on the Zhou system sets up a stark
contrast between the Confucian ideal of wangdao 王道 (kingly way of benevolence) and the imperial ideal of badao 霸道 (hegemonic way of force), in
both traditional and contemporary senses. Traditionally, pre-Qin Confucians
upheld wangdao as the core value of the Zhou polity, as typified in Mencius's
argument, "When people are able to care for those who are alive and bury
those who are dead, they will have no regrets. This is the first step along

the kingly way" (養生喪死無憾, 王道之始也).[103] *Wangdao* plus Zhou feudalism seems to resemble "republicanism with a nominal monarch." As for *badao*, this Legalist ideal enabled the Qin unification of China and initiated China's imperial autocracy and therefore seems to resemble modern Western imperialism once practiced by Napoléon and then by Japan.

The current lantern gathering reminds Xue of a Shanghai lantern show in 1906, when "People were celebrating the hundred-year democracy of France, / But no one there called attention to its once hegemonic ambitions" (百年民政法蘭西, 不見遺風號霸王).[104] At that event, Xue also composed a poem celebrating French democracy and criticizing Napoléon's dream of empire: "By expanding the territory the little Yelang [referring to the Napoléonic France] bragged about its greatness, / Yet its onetime glory now looks like the floating lights, misty and lost" (闢土雖教大夜郎, 浮空燈彩看迷茫).[105] Japan's constant military aggression against China was only repeating Napoléonic vanity. China should not, Xue argues, copy their mistakes. Xue would of course like to propose an ideal political system for China by combining Chinese *wangdao* with French democracy, which goes even further than the British constitutional monarchy. For a smooth transition on the people's behalf, however, Xue resolves to work with the current regime: "Ruler and people should always form a grand righteousness in unison; / Managing millet, rice, hemp, and silk, each fulfills their tasks" (君民從來合大義, 粟米麻絲盡所事).[106] This system of "grand righteousness" should ensure the fundamental welfare that the Chinese people have expected for so long.

Xue ends this celebratory poem in a heavy tone: "A piercingly cold wind suddenly arises, and snowflakes whirl down; / Stars disappear, the moon sets, and lanterns are extinguished" (酸風倏起雪花下, 星殘月落燈光謝).[107] Seeing the discrepancy between the Qing ruler and the people, the poet must have sensed the difficulty in transforming China in peace as she had always hoped. On 26 July 1911, Xue died after an illness. Four months later, the Republican revolution took place. The Chinese intellectual elite replaced a highly refined imperial system with an instant republic, one more radical than had been originally proposed by Kang and Liang.

To be sure, Chinese writing women had long embraced the ideal of the "poet-historian," especially in the late Ming and late Qing, when women were deeply involved in the nation's upheavals. Some of them, in Wai-yee Li's words, realized their poetic self-definition "in witnessing, remembering, and understanding the momentous changes and challenges that China faced at critical junctures."[108] Xue Shaohui and her female colleagues followed as well as developed this tradition: they were not only witnesses to history but also enthusiastic participants in late Qing politics. Taking advantage of the reform era, they crossed gender boundaries and stood on equal terms with men reformers as independent thinkers, activists, and critics. Through the news media and new printing technologies, their voices were quickly heard, leaving their alternate versions of late Qing history and their alternate visions for China's future.

Conclusion

Despite their significant contributions to the late Qing reforms, Xue Shao-hui and those in her intellectual networks were all but forgotten by the end of the dynasty. The near-total eradication of their memory began as early as 1907, when the republican revolutionary journalist Chen Yiyi (also known as Chen Zhiqun, 1889–1962) attributed the "birth" of women's journalism in China to *Xuchu Nübao* (A continuation of *Woman's Journal*)/*Nü xue-bao*), "published at the turn of 1902 to 1903" by Chen Xiefen (1883–1923).[1] This misremembrance was officially endorsed by the *Collected Catalogue of Modern Chinese Periodicals* (*Zhongguo jindai qikan bianmu huilu*) in 1965, which touted the 1902–3 *Xuchu Nübao*/*Nü xuebao* as "the first Chinese peri-odical for women"[2]—even though two 1963 articles in the *Journal of Library Science* (*Tushuguan*) had already detailed the contents of the twelve issues of the 1898 *Nü xuebao* that were then available.[3]

For nearly a century, this neglect of the 1898 *Nü xuebao* continued,[4] caused by the rapidly growing nationalism of Chinese intellectuals, which increasingly took revolutionary forms. As Joseph Levenson noted long ago, when nationalism "began to flourish in Chinese intellectual circles in the earliest years of the twentieth century," the question became: What should be the goal of progressive change? Levenson, looking back at the period and recognizing its social-Darwinist preoccupations, saw an obvious answer:

> The end of change . . . [must be] the strengthening of the nation. For if the nation, not the culture, has the highest claim on the individual, then the abandonment of traditional values, if they seem to be indefensible, is a cheerful duty, not a painful wrench. And the laws of evolution, not Confucian now but social-Darwinist, exalt the nation as the highest unit in the struggle for existence, and proclaim that the past must die and should never be lamented.[5]

Viewing the matter from another angle, it is clear that the broad education advocated by Xue and her colleagues ran counter to a growing conviction on the part of late Qing intellectuals that "with modern [Western] technology, new techniques of political participation . . . and new forms of knowledge," China's economic and political problems could be solved.[6] From this standpoint, as Thomas Metzger has argued, "the Western promise of material progress was welcomed not [simply] by people with . . . the normal desire for rising living standards but by people for whom the question of 'the people's livelihood' was philosophically of the utmost importance." The result was that, "as transformative action in the 'outer' realm [of the economy and politics] appeared ever more feasible to modern Chinese, the search for transformative power within the mind was relaxed." The "beginnings of [Chinese] nationalism turned late Ch'ing [Qing] reformers toward the goal of 'wealth and power,'" leading them to accept the view that "technology in its most refined form" was the answer not only to China's political and military problems but also to its spiritual problems.[7] This "Panglossian optimism," as Metzger describes it, undercut the position of Xue and her colleagues philosophically as well as practically.

Displaying a certain Panglossian optimism of their own, Xue and her colleagues refused to surrender to a narrow construction of Chinese nationalism. They were patriotic, to be sure, and they certainly appreciated the virtues of science and technology, but they persisted in believing that women's learning should be as broadly based as possible. They also believed in the need to reach a wide audience. As a result, women reformers expressed themselves in writing in all kinds of genres, employing the news media to disseminate their reform ideas, and translating Western science, literature, and history for a Chinese readership. They debated at the very outset whether to use classical or vernacular Chinese for their women's journal, eventually deciding to use both so that they could continue with familiar traditional literary forms while gradually expanding to more popular forms. And, as I have tried to show, they did this with uncommon success.

Yet their moderate approach could not keep pace with the anti-traditional torrent. In 1902, for instance, Jiang Zhiyou (1865–1929) gave a speech at the opening ceremony of the Patriotic Girls' School (Aiguo nüxuexiao), which was published in Chen Xiefen's *Xuchu Nübao* 9 (30 December 1902). In it, Jiang recounted the humiliations that China had recently endured as a result of foreign imperialism:

> The 1894 Sino-Japanese War, in which China was defeated by Japan, cost us an indemnity of two hundred million taels of silver; the 1900 Boxer Rebellion, in which China was defeated by the Eight-Power Allied Forces, cost us four hundred million taels of silver. [In the meantime,] Lüshun was lost to Russia, Jiaozhou was lost to Germany, Weihaiwei and Kowloon were lost to Britain, and Taiwan was lost to Japan. Now even the Yangzi River valley, where we are living, is about to be occupied by foreign powers and is no longer our territory![8]

Against this backdrop, Jiang emphasized that a new course of study, a course for learning to be national "heroines" (*nüjie*, or *nüxia*), should be established at the girls' school. To explain why, he posited three types of human communities—*shenjia zhuyi* (family-ism), *guojia zhuyi* (nationalism), and *shijie zhuyi* (globalism); the first, he argued, belonged to the past, the third to the future, and the second to the present. Contemporary needs thus demanded the education of young women to be enlightened exponents of modern Chinese nationalism. "The past employed the old way," he said, "and today we [must] promote the new way."[9]

That same year, Chen Xiefen's *Xuchu Nübao* condemned women poets who worked in traditional styles as "literary goblins" (*wenyao*).[10] This negative attitude only accelerated in subsequent years. During the New Culture movement (ca. 1915–25), scholars such as Hu Shi condemned women's traditional poetry in even harsher terms than Liang had. In his preface to Shan Shili's (1858–1945) *Bibliographic Treatise of Qing Women Writers* (*Qing guixiu yiwen lüe*), which covered 3,333 titles by 2,787 Qing women, mostly poetry, Hu sweepingly asserted that "few of these works are of any value."[11] As Joan Judge comments on the 1898 women reformers in her recent state-of-the-field review for the *Journal of Women's History*, it was this "erudite redeployment of historical cultural practices" that "rendered these women invisible in conventional narratives of modern Chinese history."[12]

Underlying the rift between culturalism and nationalism in China was a persistent patriarchy. Xue and her colleagues were undoubtedly correct in arguing that male discourses on the "women problem" in China were the result of men projecting onto women their own anxiety and frustration in the wake of the Sino-Japanese War—especially with the palpable deterioration of China's position in East Asia and the problems that followed. But the response of these women was not simply to blame men; rather, they sought a healthy cooperation with their anxious and frustrated brethren.

In the end, however, the "modernizing" Chinese patriarchy chose to write out Xue and her fellow reformers, preferring instead the views of their more radical "daughters"—represented by Chen Xiefen—who proved to be more sympathetic to men's nationalistic solutions than to "women's problems." What could have been more satisfying to Chinese men than the idea, expressed by Chen, that Chinese women should "invigorate" themselves by taking the opportunity—while males were promoting women's education— "to unite with these hot-blooded men, so that we can take on the responsibility of rescuing our nation (*guo*) and our race (*zhong*)"?[13]

Thus it was, as I have discussed at length elsewhere, that in the space of just a few years, the moderate reformism of the 1898 "mother" *Nü xuebao* was replaced by the far more radical program of the 1902–3 "daughter" *Xuchu Nübao/Nü xuebao*.[14] Unlike the former publication, which exalted the writing-women tradition, the *Xuchu Nübao/Nü xuebao* valorized a heroine model, informed by a male-oriented perspective on China's modern needs—one that emphasized military power and patriotic self-sacrifice above all. Advocates of this view, who celebrated the exploits of individuals such as the flamboyant late-Qing female revolutionary Qiu Jin, naturally preferred the more nationalistically oriented "daughter" to the more culturally focused "mother."[15]

In short, the 1902–3 *Xuchu Nübao/Nü xuebao* and its later promoters such as Chen Yiyi rejected the expressions of feminine subjectivity in the 1898 *Nü xuebao* in favor of, in the well-chosen words of Joan Judge, the "submersion of selfhood in the pursuit of nationhood." This marked what Judge describes as "the first phase in a broader cultural critique that would inform radical politics throughout the twentieth century."[16] This critique, with its reductive nationalist discourse, effectively silenced the more nuanced approach to reform advocated by Xue and her broad-minded associates.

The twentieth-century's radical politics left little room for the memory of the 1898 women reformers. From the standpoint of perceived national priorities, many of the central ideas of Xue and her circle were either too ide-alistic, too metaphysical, or too slow to meet China's pressing needs. These women most assuredly wanted China to be strong and self-sufficient but not at the expense of their own vision of womanhood. Although Xue and her colleagues were among the most determined and inventive reformers of their time, they were not so radical as to abandon tradition as a rich source of ideas and strategies for building a new China. They upheld the lofty goal of harmonizing the world but insisted on doing it according the eight-step process outlined in the *Great Learning*—an enduring model for linking the self to the transformation of Chinese society and ultimately "all under heaven." They expected to reform China into a democratic republic but one that evolved gradually so as to give the common people a smooth transition without disturbing their life routine.

As we have seen, the sophisticated position of Xue and her circle stemmed from the resourceful perfected-person/*xianyuan* model, which offered, in their view, an ideal paradigm for comprehensive reform. This paradigm re-sulted from the long-term interaction of a variety of philosophical schools—Confucianism, Daoism, and Buddhism, as well as their hybrid variants, Abstruse Learning (Xuanxue) and Neo-Confucianism. It opened a creative space that allowed ideas to flow freely into one another and to embrace those from other sources, creating new formulations designed to transform the world. This transformative process occurred on two levels—metaphysi-cal and experiential. Metaphysically, it focused on the concept of a powerful spiritual self confronting a rapidly changing world. The human agents in this process were sensitive to temporal and spatial changes and differences but not bound by them. Experientially, it emphasized engaging and employ-ing all relevant knowledge, regardless of the source, and remaining open to all possibilities.

Sustained by these beliefs and experiences, and buoyed by unabated self-confidence, the members of Xue's networks were quick to avail themselves of all opportunities and resources in pursuit of their goals. They seized upon every possible opportunity to promote their reform ideals: from the Self-strengthening movement from the 1860s to the 1890s, to the constitutional campaign at the beginning of the twentieth century. The 1897–98 campaign for women's education provided an especially powerful demonstration of their collective capacity, as they made this campaign into a triadic enter-prise for women to achieve equal rights in education as well as in social and political life. In knowledge acquisition, they did not discriminate between

Chinese and Western ideas or between their roles as either the foundation (*ti*) or the practical application (*yong*). Rather, they let their desire for learning evolve naturally, according to the times.

Xue and her cohorts therefore opted for a richly nuanced culturalism rather than a strategically oriented nationalism. But, as indicated above, there was little room for this particular vision of women's culture after 1900 because nationalism, in its many forms, dominated Chinese discourse throughout the twentieth century, as it does to this day. Yet despite the power of nationalism and the growth of radical politics in twentieth-century China, late Qing women reformers were not totally effaced. During the last decade or so, through painstaking research in multiple archives, Asian and Western scholars, myself included, have come to appreciate the multifaceted historical role of Chinese writing women. More work remains to be done, of course, through the careful excavation and sifting of historical evidence—much of it still to be mined.

By listening carefully to the voices of these heretofore marginalized groups and individuals, however, we can reconstruct a world in which wide-ranging debates between men and women contributed to a far more vital and vibrant cultural environment in China than was once imagined, even if eventually one or another discourse came to be dominant. My hope is that this case study of Xue and her networks will not only provoke further explorations into the dynamism and variety of late Qing intellectual and social life but also serve as a reminder of the value of poetry as a research tool. Above all, I hope that I have shown that "Chinese tradition" is by no means a simple thing. Rather, it is and has always been multidimensional, resilient, tolerant, and capable of incorporating other traditions into its vast repertoire. With this guiding notion we may aspire to produce ever more diversified and complex narratives of modern Chinese history.

Reference Matter

Notes

Introduction

All translations from other languages into English are mine unless otherwise stated.

1. Chen Qiang et al., "Xianbi Xue gongren nianpu," in Xue Shaohui, *Daiyunlou yiji*, 1b.

2. For background, see Pong, *Shen Pao-chen*, 1, 107–33; and Lin Chongyong, *Shen Baozhen*, 241–82.

3. Pong, *Shen Pao-chen*, 226.

4. Li Hongzhang, "Chouyi zhizao lunchuan weike caiche zhe" 籌議製造輪船未可裁撤折 (Memo on not abandoning the manufacture of ships) (20 June 1872) (in *Li Hongzhang quanji, juan* 19, 2:45a).

5. Morse, *The International Relations of the Chinese Empire*, 3:132.

6. See, for instance, Tang Zhijun, *Wuxu bianfa shi*, and *Kang Youwei yu Wuxu bianfa*. Both works present solid research, but they are framed by the typical conservative/reform and tradition/modernity binary paradigms. Standard PRC textbooks maintained this sort of narrative into the 1990s; see Li Shiyue et al., *Zhongguo jindai shi*, 233–73 for the 1898 reforms, and 369–83 for the New Policy reforms. This textbook received a first prize from the Ministry of Education.

7. Cohen, *Discovering History in China*, 3.

8. See Liang Qichao, "Lun nüxue," *Shiwu bao* 25:2b; Lin Lezhi [Young J. Allen], "Zhuxing nüxue lun."

9. Duara, "The Regime of Authenticity," 298.

10. See Tang, *Wuxu bianfa shi*, 106–7, 203, 205–6, and 268–69.

11. See Wang Xiaoqiu, ed., *Wuxu weixin yu jindai Zhongguo de gaige*.

12. Dorothy Ko's comments on Wang Zheng, *Women in the Chinese Enlightenment*, book jacket.

13. Wang, *Women in the Chinese Enlightenment*, 36.

14. See Ip et al., "The Plurality of Chinese Modernity," 499.

15. Zarrow, "Introduction," in *Creating Chinese Modernity*, 1.

16. The title of Cohen's pioneering book, *Discovering History in China*.

17. Duara, *Rescuing History from the Nation*, 4; see also Luo Zhitian, *Quanshi zhuanyi*, 8; Qian et al., eds., *Different Worlds of Discourse*, esp. the Introduction.

18. See, for instance, Luo, *Quanshi zhuanyi*, 115–60, on Hunan scholars Wang

Xianqian (1842–1917) and Ye Dehui (1864–1927); Wang Yi, "Wuxu weixin yu wan-Qing shehui biange."

19. See Wang, "Wuxu weixin yu wan-Qing shehui biange."

20. Works generated from expanded research on late Qing women include Luo Suwen, *Nüxing yu jindai Zhongguo shehui*; and Xia Xiaohong, *Wan-Qing wenren funü guan* and *Wan-Qing nüxing yu jindai Zhongguo*.

21. Karl and Zarrow, "Introduction," in *Rethinking the 1898 Reform Period*, 13.

22. Karl, "'Slavery,' Citizenship, and Gender in Late Qing China's Global Context," 212.

23. Ip et al., "The Plurality of Chinese Modernity," 499.

24. Mann, *Precious Records*, 8.

25. Ko, *Teachers of the Inner Chambers*, 4.

26. Ibid., 3, 4.

27. Ibid., 4.

28. Ibid., 9; Mann, *Precious Records*, 3.

29. On Xue as a translator, see Guo Yanli, "Nüxing zai 20 shiji chuqi de wenxue fanyi chengjiu," 38.

30. See Karl and Zarrow, "Introduction," *Rethinking the 1898 Reform Period*, 8. See also Qian et al., eds. *Different Worlds of Discourse*, for some case studies.

31. Wasserman and Faust, *Social Network Analysis*, 11, as quoted in Chao, "Chen Duxiu's Early Years," 8.

32. Knoke, *Political Networks*, 68, as quoted in Chao, "Chen Duxiu's Early Years," 8.

33. Smith, *China's Cultural Heritage*, 64.

34. Ibid., 64–65.

35. See the cover pages of Xue, *Daiyunlou yiji*, *Shiji*, *Ciji*, and *Wenji*.

36. *Tong-Guang ti* refers to the poetic styles and fashions of the Tongzhi (1862–74) and Guangxu (1875–1908) reigns. Qian Zhonglian, however, notes that it should be more appropriately named the *Guang-Xuan ti*, for its major poets were active during the Guangxu and Xuantong (1909–11) eras; see Qian Zhonglian, "Lun Tong-Guang ti," 114.

37. See Chen Shoupeng, "Wangqi Xue gongren zhuanlüe"; and Chen et al., "Xianbi Xue gongren nianpu."

38. On Chen Jitong's married life, see Chapters Three and Seven.

39. Zheng advocated education for Chinese women as early as 1893 in his reform thesis *Shengshi weiyan*. Its abridged version is included in Jing Yuanshan, ed., *Nüxue jiyi chubian*, 54a–55b. For a detailed discussion of Zheng's reform ideas on women's education, see Yamazaki Jun'ichi, "Shinmatsu hempōron dankai no joshi dōtokuron to kyōikuron," 2–5.

40. Zarrow, "Introduction," in *Creating Chinese Modernity*, 13.

41. For the Wei-Jin conceptualization of *xianyuan* and its connection with the *Shishuo xinyu*, see Qian, *Spirit and Self in Medieval China*, 142–48.

42. For the Han definition of *xian*, see ibid., 144, and 415n109. For the Wei-Jin redefinition of *Dao*, *de*, and *xian*, see ibid., 126–28. See also A. C. Graham on the

redefinition of *de* by the Wei scholar Wang Bi (226–54), in Graham, *Disputers of the Tao*, 13, 497.

43. See Smith, *Fathoming the Cosmos and Ordering the World*, 36–37. Smith also expounds on the connection between spirit (*shen*) and heart/mind (*xin*) in the following terms: "'Spirit,' in late Zhou usage, had a wide range of meanings, as it does in contemporary English. But whereas in English the term almost invariably implies a sharp contrast with the material body, in classical Chinese discourse the distinction was never so clear. Spirit was viewed as an entity within the body that was responsible for consciousness, combining what Westerners would generally distinguish as 'heart' and 'mind.' In other words, the spiritual essence of human beings came to be viewed in terms of 'the interface between the sentient and insentient, or the psychological and physical,' uniting both aspects rather than insisting on boundaries" (Smith, *The I Ching*, 53; see also ibid., 228n5).

44. See Smith, *Fortune-Tellers & Philosophers*, 272.

45. Metzger, *Escape from Predicament*, 93.

46. See ibid., 215; and Smith, *Fortune-Tellers & Philosophers*, 272.

47. Zhi Daolin [Zhi Dun], "Da Xiao ping duibi yaochao xu," *juan* 8, 299.

48. For Su Shi's invocation of the perfected person (*zhiren*), see *Su Shi shiji*, *juan* 1, 1:28; *juan* 3, 1:109; *juan* 3, 1:111; *juan* 4, 1:174; *juan* 4, 1:182; *juan* 6, 1:290; *juan* 15, 3:745; *juan* 19, 3:990; *juan* 31, 5:1667–68; *juan* 37, 6:2002. For Su Shi's inheritance of the perfected-person ideal, see Ge Xiaoyin, "Lun Su Shi shiwen zhong de liqu."

49. *Han Fei zi*, "Jie Lao" 解老 (Expounding the Laozi), quoted by Guo Shaoyu to interpret Su Shi's Dao in Guo's *Zhongguo wenxue piping shi*, 168. For a thorough discussion of Su Shi's understanding of the Dao, see Smith et al., *Sung Dynasty Uses of the I Ching*, 72–81.

50. Su Shi, "Riyu" 日喻 (On finding an analogy for the sun), in *Su Shi wenji*, *juan* 64, 5:1981; see also Peter Bol's discussion in *"This Culture of Ours,"* 276.

51. Su Shi, "Yu Xie Minshi tuiguan shu" 與謝民師推官書 (Letter to Judge Xie Minshi), in *Su Shi wenji*, *juan* 49, 4:1418.

52. From fall 1899 to spring 1900, Chen Jitong and his poet-friends Fan Dangshi (1854–1905), Shen Yuqing, and Zhang Jian (1853–1926) organized a poetry club in Shanghai and dedicated one gathering to Su Shi's birthday at which they identified themselves as Su Shi's disciples (*dizi*); see Fan Dangshi, *Fan Bozi shiji*, *juan* 12, 15b–16a. On Su Shi's influence on Chen Jitong's poetic styles, see Qian, "Qianyan" (Foreword) to Chen Jitong, *Xue Jia yin*, 23–24; on Su's influence on Chen Jitong's calligraphy, see Huang Dun, "Xu" to *Xue Jia yin*, 1–5.

53. See Liang Qichao, "Xiaoshuo yu qunzhi zhi guanxi" and "Gao xiaoshuo jia," in *Zhongguo lidai wenlun xuan*. For major studies of late Qing fiction see, for instance, Wang, *Fin-de-siècle Splendor*.

54. See, for instance, Part Three in Qian et al., eds., *Different Worlds of Discourse*, 225–382.

55. See Kowallis, *The Subtle Revolution*; and Yan, *Qingshi shi*.

56. David Der-wei Wang's comments on Wu, in *Modern Archaics*, book jacket.

57. Furth, "Poetry and Women's Culture," 8.

58. Robertson, "The Meaning of Literary Authorship for 17th and 18th Century Governing-Class Women," 14.

59. *China Perspectives*, http://chinaperspectives.revues.org/document4752.html (accessed 21 Mar. 2014).

60. As Graham puts it in *Disputers of the Tao*, the "social order derives through the family from the self-cultivation of the individual" (132). See also *Liji* [*zhengyi*], *Daxue, juan* 60, 2:1673.

61. See Xue Shaohui, "*Nü xuebao* xu," *Nü xuebao* 1 (24 July 1898): 3a.

62. *Liji* [*zhengyi*], *Daxue, juan* 60, 2:1674.

63. See Xue, "*Nü xuebao* xu," 3a.

64. Graham, *Disputers of the Tao*, 133.

65. See Xue, "*Nü xuebao* xu," 3a.

Chapter One

1. Liang Zhangju's *Minchuan guixiu shihua* records 103 Min poetesses from the Ming to the Qing; *Xuxiu siku quanshu* edn., vol. 1705.

2. Xue Shaohui, "Ti *Minchuan guixiu shihua*" 題閩川閨秀詩話 (Inscribed on the *Remarks on Women's Poetry from Min Rivers*), *Daiyunlou yiji, Shiji, juan* 1, 1b.

3. As Ko points out, an example of summoning the Confucian canon in justifying women's poetic creation "was the argument that the *Book of Odes* [*Shijing*] was full of works by women poets. The fact that the Sage himself selected these poems from a pool of three thousand must mean that he liked and approved of verses written by women. This argument was so widespread that it became a convention in introducing collections of women's poetry in the seventeenth and eighteenth centuries" (Ko, "Pursuing Talent and Virtue," 30).

4. On the life and work of Xu Can and Ji A'nan (under Ji Yinghuai), see Chang and Saussy, eds., *Women Writers of Traditional China*, 337–50, and 366–69, respectively.

5. Ding Yun's *Minchuan guixiu shihua xubian* adds another 130 Qing names to the list of Min writing women in Liang's *Minchuan guixiu shihua*.

6. For a detailed study of Xie Daoyun's dates, see Zeng Caihua, "Xie Daoyun shengzu nian buzheng."

7. See Xue's "Xu" (Preface) to Ding, *Minchuan guixiu shihua xubian*, 1a–2a.

8. Liu Zhiji, *Shitong* [*tongshi*], *juan* 8, 1:238.

9. He Liangjun, *Yulin*, "Xianyuan," *juan* 22, 12a.

10. Zhang Xuecheng, *Wenshi tongyi* [*jiaozhu*], "Fuxue," *juan* 5, 1:532, 1:534.

11. See Furth's paraphrase of Mann on Zhang Xuecheng, in Furth, "Poetry and Women's Culture," 3–4; see also Zhang, *Wenshi tongyi* [*jiaozhu*], 1:532–34; and Mann, *Precious Records*, 86–92.

12. See Fan Ye, *Hou-Han shu*, "Lienü zhuan," *juan* 84, 10:2781, 2800–03.

13. For Xue's comments on Cai and Xie, see her "Xu" to Ding, *Minchuan guixiu shihua xubian*, 1a.

14. For the Chinese text of the *Shishuo*, see Liu Yiqing, *Shishuo xinyu* [*jianshu*],

commentary by Yu Jiaxi (1884–1955); quoted from Mather, trans., *A New Account of Tales of the World*, 64, modified.

15. See Fang Xuanling et al., *Jinshu*, "Lienü zhuan," *juan* 96, 8:2516.

16. See Liu, *Shishuo xinyu* [*jianshu*], 19/30; also Yu Jiaxi's commentary on this episode, ibid., 2:698.

17. See Zürcher, *The Buddhist Conquest of China*, 1:46.

18. For background, see Liu, *Shishuo xinyu* [*jianshu*], and Mather, trans., *A New Account of Tales of the World*. For the connections between the Wei-Jin Xuanxue and the *Shishuo xinyu*, see Qian, *Spirit and Self*, chaps. 1–3.

19. See *Zhuangzi* [*jishi*], "Xiaoyao you" 逍遙遊 (Free roaming), *juan* 1A, 1:17, 28; the *shu* 疏 commentary by Cheng Xuanying 成玄英 on the *Zhuangzi* "Xiaoyao you" points out that the *zhiren* 至人, the *shenren* 神人, and the *shengren* 聖人 "are in fact one" (*qishi yiye* 其實一也); ibid., *juan* 1A, 1:22. See also Watson, trans., *Complete Works of Chuang Tzu*, 32–33.

20. Zhi Daolin [Zhi Dun], "Da Xiao ping duibi yaochao xu," *juan* 8, 300–301. On the Wei-Jin understanding of *shen* 神, see Qian, *Spirit and Self*, 152–55.

21. On Wei-Jin women's participation in Xuanxue activities, see Qian, "Women's Roles in Wei-Chin Character Appraisal."

22. See Liu, *Shishuo xinyu* [*jianshu*], 19/26, and Fang et al., *Jinshu*, "Lienü zhuan," *juan* 96, 8:2516.

23. Xue's "Xu" to Ding, *Minchuan guixiu shihua xubian*, 2a.

24. Zhong Xing's "Xu" to *Mingyuan shigui*, 1a.

25. On *ziran* as the fundamental principle of Wei-Jin Xuanxue, see Qian, *Spirit and Self*, 53–54, 58, 411n62.

26. The phrase "zhengshi" first appeared in the "Shi daxu" 詩大序 (Grand preface to the *Book of Songs*), which maintains that the poems collected in the "Zhounan" 周南 and "Shaonan" 召南 sections in the *Book of Songs* are "the Dao of correct beginnings and the foundation of princely transformations" (正始之道, 王化之基). Because later imperial Chinese women writers generally believed that these two sections contained poems mostly composed by women, Wanyan Yun Zhu titled her collection of Qing women's poetry the "Guochao guixiu zhengshi ji." See *Mao Shi* [*zhengyi*], "Shi dauxu," in *Shisanjing zhushu*, *juan* 1, 1:273; and Wanyan Yun Zhu's "Bianyan" 弁言 (Foreword) to the *Guochao guixiu zhengshi ji*, 1b–2a.

27. According to Chen Shoupeng, "Wangqi Xue gongren zhuanlüe," Xue did not finish editing the *Nü wenyuan xiaozhuan* 女文苑小傳 (4a). Xue's fellow townsman Jiang Yujing 江畬經, in his 1944 preface to Hu Wenkai, *Lidai funü zhuzuo kao*, however, cites Xue's *Nü wenyuan* and the two *Guixiu yiwen zhi* 閨秀藝文志 (Bibliographic treatise of women) respectively by two other women scholars, Shan Shouzi 單受玆 and Xian Yuqing 冼玉清, as the three major references that Hu may have used, indicating that Xue "copied and collected over six hundred works by women" (2); possibly Xue's unfinished manuscript was still extant at the time.

28. *Xiao daixuan lunshi shi* has 221 poems and over one thousand biographical notes, mostly on Qing women's poetry.

29. Chen Yun, *Xiao daixuan lunshi shi*, *juan* A, 5a.

30. Liang, *Minchuan guixiu shihua, juan* 1, 14b–16a.

31. See Xue's "Xu" to Ding, *Minchuan guixiu shihua xubian*, 1a.

32. On the lives and poetic achievements of Huang Ren and his two daughters, see Zheng, *Quan Min shihua*, "Huang Ren," *Xuxiu siku quanshu* edn., vol. 1702, *juan* 9, 38b–42a; "Huang Shutiao and Shuwan," *juan* 10, 30a–30b. See also Chen Yan, *Shiyishi shihua*, vol. 1, *juan* 26, 349–51; Chen Shirong, *Fuzhou Xihu Wanzaitang shikan zhenglu*, 2:690–97; and Chen Qingyuan, *Fujian wenxue fazhan shi*, 425–35. On Huang Ren's relationship with the Xus, see Chen, *Fujian wenxue fazhan shi*, 432. On the connection of Huang's Fragrant-Grass Studio to Xu You's Ink Studio, see "Huang Ren guju" (Old residence of Huang Ren), http://fuzhou .fznews.com.cn /sfqx/fxjz/2007-8-31/2007831hb4na6gv__165131.shtml (accessed 9 Mar. 2014).

33. On Huang Tansheng's age (believed to be seventy-eight at the time of her death), see Lin Changyi, *Sheyinglou shihua, Xuxiu siku quanshu* edn., vol. 1706, *juan* 16, 6a.

34. Zhuang, *Jiuwan guwen* 九畹古文 (Jiuwan's classical prose), quoted in Zheng Fangkun's biographic sketch of his mother, Huang Tansheng, in *Quan Min shihua, juan* 10, 30b–31b.

35. See Liang, *Minchuan guixiu shihua, juan* 2, 5b; Lin, *Sheyinglou shihua, juan* 16, 6a; Ding, *Minchuan guixiu shihua xubian, juan* 4, 1b–2b; Shen and Chen, *Fujian tongzhi*, "Lienü zhuan," "Biantong" 辯通 (Eloquence and erudition), *juan* 6, 15b; and Chen Yan, *Min-Hou xian zhi*, "Lienü zhuan," "Biantong" I, "Minxian," *juan* 100, 2a–2b.

36. Liang, *Minchuan guixiu shihua, juan* 2, 5b.

37. Chen, *Min-Hou xian zhi*, "Lienü zhuan," "Biantong" II, "Houguan," *juan* 101, 1b.

38. The couple was happily married: "When Liao Shuchou and Xu Jun painted a large scroll with flowering plums, Xu Jun displayed the branches, and Shuchou drew the flowers. The prime minister Chen Hongmou [1696–1771] felt that their collaborative works emanated an aura and a taste no less than those by the famous Yuan dynasty couple of Guan Daosheng and Zhao Mengfu" (Chen, *Min-Hou xian zhi*, "Lienü zhuan," "Biantong" II, "Houguan," *juan* 101, 1b).

39. For instance, Huang Tansheng prefaced the poetic collections of Ding Yu and Lin Yingpei, Lin reciprocally wrote a foreword to Huang Tansheng's *Xiaoranju ji* 蕭然居集 (Collection from Leisure Residence), which was collected and preserved by Huang's granddaughter Zheng Hanchun, and Zhuang Jiuwan compiled Huang Tansheng's biographic sketch (Chen, *Min-Hou xian zhi*, "Lienü zhuan," "Biantong" I, "Minxian," *juan* 100, 2a). Also, Huang Ren prefaced Zhuang Jiuwan's *Qiugu ji* 秋穀集 (*Collection of Autumn Grains*) (ibid., "Biantong" II, "Houguan," *juan* 101, 1b), and Huang Tansheng's son Zheng Fangkun composed the *Quan Min shihua*, which documented the lives of Min poetic talents, including a chapter on forty women from the Tang to his time; *juan* 10, 2b–31b.

40. Xue's "Xu" to Ding, *Minchuan guixiu shihua xubian*, 1a.

41. For a study of Min women's literary works compiling while they sojourned

throughout the Qing Empire and how these works contributed to the Min writing-women culture, see Li, "Imagining History and the State."

42. Liang, *Minchuan guixiu shihua, juan* 3, 3a–3b.

43. Ibid., *juan* 3, 2b.

44. See ibid., *juan* 3, 2b–3a. On the life of Meng Chaoran 孟超然, see his biography in Zhao Erxun et al., *Qingshi gao*, "Rulin" 儒林 (Confucian scholars), *juan* 480, 43:13151–52.

45. Liang, *Minchuan guixiu shihua, juan* 3, 11a.

46. Ibid., 17b–18a.

47. See Wei Xiuren, *Gainan shanguan shihua* 陔南山館詩話 (Remarks on poetry from Gainan Heights), quoted in Ding, *Minchuan guixiu shihua xubian, juan* 2, 7b.

48. See Chen Dequan 陳德銓, "Xushinü muzhiming" 許氏女墓誌銘 (Epitaph to Daughter Xu), quoted by Wei Xiuren in *Gainan shanguan shihua*, which in turn is quoted in Ding, *Minchuan guixiu shihua xubian, juan* 2, 7b–9a.

49. Since Wei was the author of the *Huayue hen*, the first Chinese novel that focused on courtesan-poetesses, Xu Tingting might have been this sort of woman. On Wei Xiuren's life and works, see Du Weimo, "Jiaodian houji," in Wei Xiuren, *Huayue hen*, 447–54.

50. See Ding, *Minchuan guixiu shihua xubian, juan* 1, 2b–3a on Lin; 3b–6a on Shao; *juan* 2, 13a–13b on Wang.

51. See Xue's "Xu" to Ding, *Minchuan guixiu shihua xubian*, 1b–2a.

52. See Ibid., 1a–2a.

53. Zheng, *Quan Min shihua, juan* 10, 23a–23b. See also Liang, *Minchuan guixiu shihua, juan* 1, 11a–11b.

54. For a study of *Zaisheng yuan* 再生緣 (Love reincarnate) by Chen Duansheng 陳端生, see Chen Yinke, "Lun Zaisheng yuan," 1–96; for Chen Zhaolun 陳兆侖 and Chen Duansheng's dates, see ibid., 35–37.

55. Chen, *Shiyishi shihua, juan* 26, 351.

56. Liang, *Minchuan guixiu shihua, juan* 2, 9a; Shen and Chen, *Fujian tongzhi*, "Lienü zhuan," "Biantong," *juan* 6, 21b.

57. Liang, *Minchuan guixiu shihua, juan* 2, 9b.

58. Ibid., *juan* 3, 9a. Men in the Liang lineage also consciously promoted *xianyuan* values. Liang Zhangju's male cousin Liang Yunchang (*js.* 1799), for instance, wrote two poems titled "Ji kujie" 紀苦節 (On bitter chastity), which argued fervently against a widow's self-mutilation and planned suicide. In pleading for this woman to reconsider her restricted definition of wifely virtue, Liang employed the concept of *xianmingyuan* 賢明媛 (worthy and intelligent lady), a variant of *xianyuan* 賢媛, to indicate unambiguously that a woman's life had a much broader significance (see ibid., *juan* 4, 4b–6b).

59. Ding, *Minchuan guixiu shihua xubian, juan* 2, 17a–17b.

60. Chen Dequan, "Xushinü muzhiming," in Ding, *Minchuan guixiu shihua xubian, juan* 2, 8a. Late imperial women assimilated the *Book of Songs* as their own "Flowery Classic."

61. For Daoyun's comments, see Fang et al., *Jinshu*, "Lienü zhuan," *juan* 96, 8:2516;

the line is from *Mao Shi [zhengyi]*, "Daya" 大雅 (Great elegantiae), "Zhengmin" 蒸民 (People), in *Shisanjing zhushu*, *juan* 18, 1:569.

62. Liang, *Minchuan guixiu shihua*, *juan* 1, 8a, *juan* 4, 8b–9a; Chen, *Min-Hou xian zhi*, "Lienü zhuan," "Biantong" I, "Minxian," *juan* 100, 4a, 1b.

63. Shen and Chen, *Fujian tongzhi*, "Lienü zhuan," "Biantong," *juan* 6, 9b.

64. Ding, *Minchuan guixiu shihua xubian*, *juan* 2, 13b; see also Liu, *Shishuo xinyu [jianshu]*, 19/26.

65. Chen, *Min-Hou xian zhi*, "Lienü zhuan," "Biantong" II, "Houguan," *juan* 101, 3a–3b.

66. Shen Queying, "Yi Tangzixiang xiaolou" 憶堂子巷小樓 (Recalling my little tower in Tangzi Alley), to the tune "Zhegu tian" 鷓鴣天 (Partridge sky), *Yanlou ci*, in *Yanlou yigao*, appended to Lin Xu, *Wancuixuan shi*, 6b.

67. Xiao Daoguan, "Zhongzhu xiaoji" 種竹小記 (A brief record on planting bamboo), *Dao'anshi zawen*, in *Xiao Daoguan ji*, 1a.

68. See Chen Qiang et al., "Xianbi Xue gongren nianpu," 6a.

69. See Xue, *Daiyunlou yiji*, *Shiji*, *juan* 2, 5b–6a.

70. See Xue, "Ti Huaxi nüshi *Fushi jixue tu*" 題花谿女士富士霽雪圖 (Inscribed on Ms. Hanakei's *Sun Shine after Snow on Mount Fuji*), in ibid., *juan* 2, 18a–18b.

71. Xue, "Daini Xumu Lin taiyiren liushi shouxu" 代擬許母林太宜人六十壽序 (Dedication to Grand Lady Lin, the Mother of the Xus, on Her Sixtieth Birthday, on behalf [of the Chens]), *Daiyunlou yiji*, *Wenji*, *juan* B, 13b. Here, Xue alludes to another *Shishuo* account about Xie An, who educated the Xie girls and boys "like growing orchids and jade trees in the courtyard" (*Shishuo xinyu [jianshu]*, 2/92).

72. *Guixiu* 閨秀 originated from the same *Shishuo* episode (19/30) that coded Xie Daoyun's "Bamboo Grove aura." This episode relates that Daoyun's younger brother Xie Xuan and his friend Zhang Xuan matched each of their sisters against the other. People asked Nun Ji, a friend of both families, which of the two women was superior and which was inferior. Nun Ji commented that the Zhang sister represented the "full flowering of the inner chamber" (*guifang zhi xiu* 閨房之秀, later *guixiu*), which was admirable, to be sure, but she still conformed to Han Confucian moral norms rather than exhibiting a broader form of self-cultivation. In comparison, Daoyun possessed the Bamboo Grove aura, and was therefore judged superior. Over forty titles use the phrase *guixiu* as against only one using *xianyuan* in the two hundred or so anthologies of Ming-Qing women's writings documented in Hu, *Lidai funü zhuzuo kao*, "Zongmu" 總目 (General contents), 50–55.

73. Chen Yan comments: "Shaohui was diligent in study. Always with books in hand, she was extensively learned. She wrote fluently and could fully express her mind. She did not intentionally seek profundity and subtlety (*shenwei* 深微), and no one could pinpoint whose style she resembled" (Shen and Chen, *Fujian tongzhi*, "Yiwen zhi" 藝文志 [Bibliographic treatise], *juan* 66, 27b–28a).

74. For a survey of the conventional late Qing poetics, see Zeng, "Lun Tong-Guang ti shi"; Qian Zhonglian, "Lun Tong-Guang ti," and "Qianyan" to Huang Zunxian, *Renjinglu shicao [jianzhu]*.

75. "*Wanzai*" alludes to *Mao Shi [zhengyi]*, "Qinfeng" 秦風 (Air of Qin), "Jianjia"

蒹葭 (Rush leaves), in Ruan Yuan, ed., *Shisanjing zhushu, juan* 6, 1:372. This poem depicts the frustrating pursuit of a beloved one, who floats elusively in mid-water. Borrowing this poetic image, Min poets built Wanzaitang in the West Lake of Fuzhou to enshrine their poetic icons who had long gone, leaving only their lingering spirits.

76. For the conventional version of Min poetics, see Chen Yan, "Buding *Minshi lu* xu" 補訂《閩詩錄》序 (Preface to the complemented version of the *Records of the Min Poetry*), *Minshi lu*, ed. Zheng Jie, complemented by Chen Yan, *Xuxiu siku quanshu* edn., vol. 1687. For a detailed study of the Wanzaitang tradition, see Chen, *Fuzhou Xihu Wanzaitang shikan zhenglu*. Wanzaitang collapsed in the Guangxu era. Chen Yan and Shen Yuqing rebuilt the hall in 1913–14 and increased the enshrined poets to thirty-two; see Chen, *Shiyishi shihua, juan* 21, 285–86.

77. Xue, *Daiyunlou yiji, Shiji, juan* 1, 6a.

78. See Zheng, *Quan Min shihua, juan* 1, 30a–45a; see also Chen, *Fujian wenxue fazhan shi*, 80–83.

79. Ge Lifang 葛立方 (?–1164) mentions in his *Yunyu yangqiu* 韻語陽秋 (Critical remarks on poetry) that "the one hundred poems in Han Wo's *Xianglian ji* all belong to *yanti*" (quoted in Zheng, *Quan Min shihua, juan* 1, 36a).

80. Qian Qianyi, ed., *Liechao shiji, Runji, Xuxiu siku quanshu* edn., vol. 1624, *juan* 4, 24b.

81. Ibid.; quoted from Pei-kai Cheng, trans., in Chang and Saussy, eds., *Women Writers of Traditional China*, 151, modified.

82. Pei-kai Cheng's introductory note to his translation of Zhang Hongqiao's poems, in ibid., 150.

83. Respectively in Fang Hui 方回 (1227–1306), *Yingkui lüsui* 瀛奎律髓 (Essence of the regulated poems from immortal constellations), and Chu Renhuo 褚人獲 (fl. 1681), *Jianhu ji* 堅瓠集 (Collection from Hard Gorge), quoted in Zheng, *Quan Min shihua, juan* 1, 36b, 43a.

84. Liu was the first to detail the Zhang-Lin love story in her biography of Zhang, in Qian, ed., *Liechao shiji, Runji, juan* 4, 23b–24a. This favorable record of Zhang and Lin, along with the whole corpus of their poetic exchanges, was then extensively quoted in Min records such as Zheng, *Quan Min shihua, juan* 10, 16a–19a; Shen and Chen, *Fujian tongzhi*, "Lienü zhuan," "Biantong," *juan* 6, 7a–8b. Zheng also quoted Zhang and Lin's song-lyric exchanges from the *Ciyuan congtan* 詞苑叢談 (Forest of talks from the *Ci*-Lyric Garden) edited by Xu Qiu 徐釚 (1636–1708). The *Siku* compilers, however, questioned the authenticity of the Zhang-Lin correspondence and its inclusion in Lin's *Mingsheng ji* 鳴盛集 (Collected works singing the prosperity); see Yongrong and Ji Yun et al., eds., *Siku quanshu zongmu*, "Jibu" 集部 (Collected works), "Biejilei" 別集類 (Separate collections) 22, *juan* 169, 2:1473.

85. Qian Qianyi, *Liechao shiji xiaozhuan*, 1:180–81.

86. See Zheng, *Quan Min shihua*, "Sun Daoxuan," *juan* 10, 7b–9b. "Tying hearts with a willow twig" (*Liu jie tongxin* 柳結同心) alludes to a *ci*-lyric to the tune of "Yi Qin E" 憶秦娥 (In memory of Qin E), written by another Lady Sun of the Song but attributed to Sun Daoxuan by mistake; see Tang Guizhang, ed., *Quan Song ci*, 5:3539.

87. Xue's "Xu" to Ding, *Minchuan guixiu shihua xubian*, 1a. "Fish darting in the

spring water" (*Yu you chunshui* 魚游春水) is the tune of a song-lyric written by Ruan Yi's daughter, no longer extant; see Tang, ed., *Quan Song ci*, 1:203.

88. For the Fujian elite Jiang Caiping was a real historical figure and a source of local pride. Zheng Fangkun based his biographical sketch of Jiang on *Meifei zhuan*, a Song fictitious work (*Quan Min shihua*, "Meifei," *juan* 10, 2b–4a). See also Shen and Chen, *Fujian tongzhi*, "Lienü zhuan," *juan* 6, 1a–2b.

89. See Zheng, *Quan Min shihua*, "Chen Jinfeng," *juan* 10, 5a–5b.

90. Xue's "Xu" to Ding, *Minchuan guixiu shihua xubian*, 1a.

91. See Zheng, *Quan Min shihua*, "Chen Jinfeng," *juan* 10, 5a–5b.

92. Han Wo's "Zixu" (Self-preface) to *Xianglian ji*, quoted in Zheng, *Quan Min shihua*, *juan* 1, 34a.

93. Liu, *Shishuo xinyu* [*jianshu*], 17/4; quoted from Mather, trans., *A New Account of Tales of the World*, 324, modified.

94. Qian, ed., *Liechao shiji*, *Runji*, *juan* 4, 25b; also quoted in Zheng, *Quan Min shihua*, *juan* 10, 18b.

95. Referring to the *Lanwan ji* 蘭畹集 (Collected song-lyrics from Orchid Garden), a collection of the song-lyrics from the Tang to the Northern Song, compiled by the Song scholar Kong Fangping 孔方平, and the *Caotang shiyu* 草堂詩餘 (Song-lyrics from Grass Hall), a four *juan* collection of song-lyrics compiled in the Southern Song.

96. Xue, to the tune of "Die lian hua" 蝶戀花 (Butterflies lingering over flowers), *Daiyunlou yiji*, *Ciji*, *juan* B, 10b–11a.

97. Xue, "Yu Yingzi lun ci" 與英姊論詞 (Discussion of the song-lyric with Sister Ying), *Daiyunlou yiji*, *Shiji*, I, 4b.

98. See, for instance, Wang Mingqing, *Yuzhao xinzhi*, *Siku quanshu* edn., vol. 1038, *juan* 5, 18a.

99. *Liji* [*zhengyi*], "Jingjie" 經解 (Interpreting classics): "Its people are tender and sincere, a result of the teaching of the *Book of Songs*" (其為人也, 溫柔敦厚, 詩教也), in Ruan, ed., *Shisanjing zhushu*, *juan* 50, 2:1609.

100. The *Zhuangzi* "Xiaoyao you" uses "*naoyue*" 淖約 to describe the spiritual person, one of the variants of the perfected person; Cheng Xuanying's *shu* commentary notes *naoyue* as *rou ruo* 柔弱 meaning "tender and soft"; see *Zhuangzi* [*jishi*], "Zaiyou" 在宥 (Let it be), *juan* 4B, 2:372.

101. Xue, *Daiyunlou yiji*, *Shiji*, *juan* 2, 5b.

102. Ibid., 5b–6a.

103. *Laozi*, chap. 28, *Laozi Dao De jing* [*zhu*], in Wang Bi, *Wang Bi ji* [*jiaoshi*], 1:74. *Laozi zhu*, attributed to Heshang gong 河上公 (early Han), comments on this chapter, saying: "Taking away the strong and aggressive features of masculinity and adopting the tender and harmonious (*rou he*) qualities of femininity, all under heaven will go to this person, as water flows into the deep ravine" (去雄之強梁, 就雌之柔和, 如是, 則天下歸之如水流入深谿也) (*Laozi zhu*, *Siku quanshu* edn., vol. 1055, *juan* A, 17a–17b).

104. Liu, *Shishuo xinyu* [*jianshu*], 11/3; quoted from Mather, trans., *A New Account of Tales of the World*, 293, modified.

105. Upon Wan'er's birth, her mother dreamed that the girl would grow up to measure the talents under heaven. Wan'er later served under Empress Wu Zetian 武則天 (624–705) and Emperor Zhongzong 中宗 (r. 705–10), handling political affairs. Zhongzong often held poetic gatherings at court and assigned Wan'er to evaluate the poems by the courtiers; see Ouyang Xiu and Song Qi, *Xin Tangshu*, "Houfei liezhuan" 后妃列傳 (Biographies of royal consorts), *juan* 76, 11:3488–89.

106. Jason M. Miller defines "aesthetic subjectivity" as referring "generally to the status of the individual subject in the context of aesthetic theory." He interprets Hegelian aesthetic theory as one that reconciles the subjective, experiential aspect of art with its objective, content-oriented, expressive aspect. Thus Miller elaborates the Hegelian definition of "aesthetic subjectivity" into one that consists of three elements—experience, imagination, and interpretation—that work together in a "*reflexive interaction* between the spectator and the work of art" (Miller, "Subjectivity in Hegel's Aesthetics," 20). This close connection between aesthetic subjectivity, social, historical, natural, and cultural contexts, and works of art is relevant in understanding the formation of Xue's aesthetic ideal.

107. Chen, *Xiao daixuan lunshi shi, juan* A, 8b.

108. Yin Yun 殷芸 (471–529), *Xiaoshuo*: "To the east of the Heavenly River lives the Weaving Girl, daughter of the Heavenly God. For years she has worked hard on weaving colored brocades with clouds as heavenly clothes" (天河之東有織女，天帝之子也。年年機杼勞役，織成雲錦天衣), quoted in Feng Yingjing, *Yueling guangji*, "Qiyue ling" 七月令 (The seventh month), *juan* 14, 11b.

109. Chen, *Xiao daixuan lunshi shi, juan* B, 18b.

110. Chen, *Chen Xiaonü yiji*, appended to Xue, *Daiyunlou yiji, juan* A, 8a and 9a.

111. See Chen, *Xiao daixuan lunshi shi, juan* B, 33 a.

112. Liang, *Minchuan guixiu shihua, juan* 4, 11a–11b.

113. See *Zhuangzi*, "Qiwu lun," *Zhuangzi [jishi], juan* 1B, 1:112.

114. See Chen, *Xiao daixuan lunshi shi, juan* B, 19a.

115. Ding, *Minchuan guixiu shihua xubian, juan* 2,1b.

116. Liang, *Minchuan guixiu shihua, juan* 3, 5b–6b.

117. Ibid., 5b.

118. Bai, *Bai Juyi ji, juan* 22, 2:493.

119. See, for instance, Liu, *Shishuo xinyu [jianshu]*, 1/3, 7; 2/24; 4/46; 8/23, 32, 107, 111; 23/25; 25/21; 26/22; 33/14. For discussions of the function of the water image in character appraisal, see Qian, *Spirit and Self*, 62–63, and chapters 4 and 5.

120. Liang, *Minchuan guixiu shihua, juan* 2, 16b–17a.

121. Ibid., *juan* 2, 17a. On Yao's heroic death, see Zhao et al., *Qingshi gao*, "Zhongyi" 忠義 (Biographies of the loyal and the righteous) 8, *juan* 494, 45:13665–66.

122. This commander was Zhang Chaofa (1788–1840), who was in fact fatally wounded at the same battle and was therefore defeated by the British invaders. Zhang died soon afterward (see Zhao et al., *Qingshi gao*, "Liezhuan" [Biographies] 159, *juan* 372, 38:11534). Possibly for this reason, Sa Lianru did not reveal his name in the poem.

123. Chen, *Min-Hou xian zhi*, "Lienü zhuan," "Biantong" II, "Houguan," *juan* 101, 7a. Shen Baozhen's mother was Lin Zexu's younger sister. David Pong attri-

butes Puqing's "devotion as a wife and as an assistant to Shen" to her relationship with Shen as cousins and childhood playmates; see Pong, *Shen Pao-chen*, 30.

124. Ding, *Minchuan guixiu shihua xubian*, juan 2, 14a–15b.

125. Pong, *Shen Pao-chen*, 51.

126. Ding, *Minchuan guixiu shihua xubian*, juan 2, 15a.

127. Xu Yuan 許遠 (709–57) and Zhang Xun 張巡 (709–57) died together in defending Suiyang against the An Lushan Rebellion (755–57). Lin Puqing in this letter invokes their spirit based on the comments of Han Yu (768–824) in his "Zhang Zhongcheng zhuan houxu" 張中丞傳後序 (Postscript to the *Biography of Governor Zhang* [Xun]), in *Han Changli wenji* [*jiaozhu*], juan 2, 73–78. On Zhang Xun's and Xu Yuan's heroic deeds, see Ouyang and Song, *Xin Tangshu*, "Zhongyi zhuan," juan 192, 18:5534–42.

128. Ding, *Minchuan guixiu shihua xubian*, juan 2, 15a–15b.

129. The second stanza of Xue, "Taoyuan," to the tune "Huafa Qinyuan chun" 花發沁園春 (Flowers bloom in spring in the Qin Garden), *Daiyunlou yiji, Ciji*, juan B, 7a.

130. Including women such as the Eastern Jin general Zhu Xu's mother Lady Han, who helped her son protect Xiangyang by leading women to build a city wall against the attack by the Former Qin ruler Fu Jian (r. 357–85); see Fang et al., *Jinshu*, "Zhu Xu zhuan," juan 81, 7:2133; Princess Pingyang of the Tang, who organized a troop of women to help her father, Li Yuan, the founder of the Tang, rise up against the Sui regime; see Ouyang and Song, *Xin Tangshu*, "Zhudi gongzhu" (Princesses), juan 83, 12:3643; and Lady Liang, the wife of the Southern Song general Han Shizhong (1089–1151), who "drummed up support for the campaign" (*qincao fugu*) to help her husband resist the invasion of the Jurchens; see Tuotuo et al., *Songshi*, "Han Shizhong zhuan," juan 364, 32:11361.

131. Chen Yun, "Taoyuan," *Chen Xiaonü yiji*, juan B, 18a–18b.

132. See Shen Yuqing's preface to his poem "Taoyuan," in Qian Zhonglian, ed., *Qingshi jishi*, 19:13124. Shen indicates that the garden had been Xu You's villa, which he bought in 1880 to enshrine his father.

133. Chen Yun recorded the poetic lineage from Lin Puqing to her female descendants in *Xiao daixuan lunshi shi*, juan A, 27a. Chen Yun, however, mistook Li Shenrong for Lin Puqing's granddaughter; see Table 3.2 for the Shen-Li lineage connections.

Chapter Two

1. Wakeman, Review of John L. Rawlinson, *China's Struggle for Naval Development, 1839–1895*, 604.

2. Liu Kwang-ching, "Shijiu shiji moye zhishi fenzi de bianfa sixiang," 44.

3. Elman, "Naval Warfare," 326.

4. Pong, *Shen Pao-chen*, 114.

5. Ibid., 113.

6. Lin Chongyong, *Shen Baozhen*, 273, 285; quoted from *Shen wensu gong zhengshu* 沈文肅公政書 (Shen Baozhen on governing), "Chuanzheng renshi riq-

izhe" 船政任事日期摺 (Memorandum on assuming the directorship of the navy yard) (18 July 1867), *juan* 4.

7. Pong, *Shen Pao-chen*, 318.

8. Ibid.

9. Elman, "Naval Warfare," 299.

10. Lin, *Shen Baozhen*, 474, 480.

11. Pong, *Shen Pao-chen*, 321.

12. Lin, *Shen Baozhen*, 476.

13. Ibid.

14. See ibid.

15. See Chen Qiang et al., "Xianbi Xue gongren nianpu," 4b, 11b. Similarly, "Classical learning was continued in the Jiangnan Arsenal. . . . It remained separate from the Translation Department in the hope that its graduates would go on to pass the more prestigious civil examinations. Hence, the school attracted the sons of Shanghai merchants and Christian converts in a more foreign environment. Arsenal students were also drilled in the 8-legged essay at the same time that mathematics was given high priority" (Elman, "Naval Warfare," 293).

16. Giquel, *Foochow Arsenal*, 9; see also Lin, *Shen Baozhen*, 247; Pong, *Shen Pao-chen*, 120–21. Prosper Giquel was a lieutenant on leave from the French navy and then serving as the commissioner of customs at Ningpo when Zuo Zongtang invited him to help build the Fuzhou Navy Yard in 1864. He assumed the directorship in 1866. See Pong, *Shen Pao-chen*, 110, 134–36.

17. Giquel, *Foochow Arsenal*, 17. See also Lin, *Shen Baozhen*, 472–73; Pong, *Shen Pao-chen*, 230–34.

18. Giquel, *Foochow Arsenal*, 18.

19. Pong, *Shen Pao-chen*, 231.

20. Giquel, *Foochow Arsenal*, 29–30.

21. Ibid., 21–22; see also Pong, *Shen Pao-chen*, 231–32.

22. See Lin, *Shen Baozhen*, 492–93.

23. See Giquel, *Foochow Arsenal*, on the students of naval construction, 19; of design, 21–22; and of naval navigation, 32.

24. Lin, *Shen Baozhen*, 505–6.

25. See ibid., 509–11.

26. On the one hundred twenty young boys' studies in the United States, see Rhoads, *Stepping Forth into the World*; and Leibovitz and Miller, *Fortunate Sons*.

27. See Lin, *Shen Baozhen*, 508–9, 521–29.

28. Liu Xiang was a native of the Minxian district of Fuzhou and the younger brother of the famous Min poet Liu Jiamou (1814–53); Liu Shaogang was Liu Xiang's cousin from the same paternal origin (*congdi*) but was from Houguan (see Chen Qiang et al., "Xianbi Xue gongren nianpu," 5a–5b; Liu Rongping, "Juhongxie changhe kaolun," 108). The Chinese call a parent's male cousins of the same generation from the same clan "uncles." On Chen Xi's name, see Gu Tinglong, ed., *Qingdai zhujuan jicheng*, "Lin Daren," 340:88. Lin Daren (b. 1880, *jr.* 1902), a great grandson of Lin Zexu's, married Chen Jitong's second daughter and so listed the

four-generation genealogy of the Chen family in his examination paper. Since there is no clear indication whether Jitong's sonless first wife, Lady Liu, had a daughter, I have temporarily entered Chen Chao (*zi* Banxian, b. 1885?), Jitong and Maria-Adèle Lardanchet's second daughter, as Lin Daren's wife in Tables 3.1 and 3.2.

29. Jitong was so familiar with the *Hanshu* that he could recite it on request; see Shen Yuqing, "Chen Jitong shilüe," *juan* 39, 70b. Shoupeng, too, was familiar with classics. Both brothers became well-established poets; see Qian Zhonglian, *Qingshi jishi*, 20:14172–73 for Shoupeng, 20:14669–71 for Jitong.

30. Chen Jitong indicated their parents' early death in dedicating his *Contes Chinois* to Shoupeng ("Dédicace," i). No records show when their parents died. The father would have been alive as late as Jitong's ninth birthday in 1860, when he took Jitong for a visit to a Buddhist temple; see Tcheng-Ki-Tong, *Les plaisirs en Chine*, 77–80. The two brothers were raised by their eldest brother, Chen Botao (*zi* Youru, 1837?–99) and his wife, Lady Ye (d. 1896); see Jitong's poem "Fuzhou laidian jingzhi dasao xianshi" 福州來電驚知大嫂仙逝 (Shocked to know from a Fuzhou telegram that my eldest sister-in-law has passed away), in Chen Jitong, *Xue Jia yin*, 39. On Chen Botao's name, see Gu, ed., *Qingdai zhujuan jicheng*, 340:89. Pong is incorrect in asserting that Jitong was among a few "students from wealthy backgrounds" (*Shen Pao-chen*, 228).

31. See Li Huachuan, *Wan-Qing yige waijiao guan de wenhua licheng*, 158; Giquel, *Foochow Arsenal*, 17. On Chen Jitong's life, see Shen Yuqing, "Chen Jitong shilüe," *juan* 39, 70b–72b; Yeh, "The Life Style of Four *Wenren*"; Huang Xingtao, "Yige bugai bei yiwang de wenhua ren," the introduction to Chen Jitong, *Zhongguo ren zihua xiang*, a Chinese translation of Chen Jitong's *Les Chinois peints par eux memes* and *Les plaisirs en Chine*, i–xi; Sang Bing, "Chen Jitong shulun"; Li, *Wan-Qing yige waijiao guan*; and Qian Nanxiu, "Qianyan" to Chen, *Xue Jia yin*, 1–35.

32. Bryois, "Le Général Tcheng-Ki-Tong," 289.

33. See Liu, "Juhongxie changhe kaolun," 108.

34. Shen, "Chen Jitong shilüe," *juan* 39, 70b.

35. See ibid.; Li, *Wan-Qing yige waijiao guan*, 13, 161. Li dates Jitong's graduation based on Zhang Xia et al., *Qingmo haijun shiliao*, 434–35.

36. Shen, "Chen Jitong shilüe," *juan* 39, 71a.

37. Basidi [Marianne Bastid-Bruguière], "Qingmo fu Ou de liuxuesheng men," 193.

38. Shen, "Chen Jitong shilüe," *juan* 39, 71a.

39. See Bryois, "Le Général Tcheng-Ki-Tong," 290; Lin, *Shen Baozhen*, 519–20; and Li, *Wan-Qing yige waijiao guan*, 14.

40. Li Hongzhang, "Minchang xuesheng chuyang xuexi zhe" 閩廠學生出洋學習摺 (Memo on Fuzhou Naval Academy students studying abroad) and attached "Xuanpai chuanzheng shengtu chuyang yiye zhangcheng shanju qingzhe" 選派船政生徒出洋肄業章程繕具清摺 (Memo on the regulations of selecting naval academy students to study abroad) (*Li Hongzhang quanji*, *juan* 28, 2:21a, 2:25a).

41. See Li Hongzhang, "Chuyang jiandu xinfei ji shengtu jingfei qingzhe" 出洋監督薪費及生徒經費清摺 (Memo on the salary of the supervisors and funds for

students abroad) (*Li Hongzhang quanji, juan* 28, 2:28a). As Guo Songtao recorded in his diary on 25 March 1878, Li Fengbao showed him Li Hongzhang's letter that instructed "to send Ma Jianzhong and Chen Jitong to [French] national schools in Paris to learn international and some other applicable laws, as well as English language and literature" (quoted in Li, *Wan-Qing yige waijiao guan*, 165).

42. See Li, *Wan-Qing yige waijiao guan*, 14.

43. See Lin, *Shen Baozhen*, 522–24.

44. See Bryois, "Le Général Tcheng-Ki-Tong," 290 (Bryois mistakes 1876 for 1877); Shen, "Chen Jitong shilüe," *juan* 39, 71a; Li, *Wan-Qing yige waijiao guan*, 164.

45. *Qian haijun jiudang junxue lei* 前海軍舊檔軍學類 (Old archives of the former navy, category of military learning), quoted in Lin, *Shen Baozhen*, 524.

46. See Bryois, "Le Général Tcheng-Ki-Tong," 290–91.

47. See Li, *Wan-Qing yige waijiao guan*, 198.

48. Bryois, "Le Général Tcheng-Ki-Tong," 291. Although Bryois did not specify which of Le Play's theories had interested Jitong, Jitong must have been attracted by Le Play's 1871 work *L'Organisation de la famille*, for a comparative study of Chinese and French family structures was a focus of Jitong's works in French; see, for instance, Tcheng-Ki-Tong, *Les Parisiens peints par un Chinois*, 231–40.

49. See Bury, *Gambetta and the Making of the Third Republic*, 6–7.

50. Bryois, "Le Général Tcheng-Ki-Tong," 291.

51. See Chen et al., "Xianbi Xue gongren nianpu," 4b.

52. As Xue indicates in "Jingru xionggong wushi shouchen zhengshi qi" 敬如兄公五十壽辰徵詩啓 (Call for poetic contributions in celebration of the fiftieth birthday of our Lord Brother Jingru [Jitong's courtesy name]) (*Daiyunlou yiji, Wenji, juan* B, 17b–18a).

53. See Chen Qiang et al., "Xianbi Xue gongren nianpu," 7a–7b.

54. *Le théâtre des Chinois* surveys Chinese drama; *Les contes Chinois* briefs Chinese fiction through an abridged translation of *Liaozhai zhiyi* 聊齋志異 (Strange tales from Make-Do Studio) by Pu Songling蒲松齡 (1640–1715); *Le roman de l'homme jaune* (1890) is Jitong's trial fictional writing, adapted from the account by Jiang Fang 蔣防 (fl. 809–28) of the tragic life of the Tang courtesan Huo Xiaoyu 霍小玉. Jitong even tried drama writing in his last French work, "L'amour héroïque, vaudeville-Chinois en un acte" (Heroic love: a Chinese light comedy in one act) (*Figaro illustré* 9 [1891]: 1–6). He notes that fiction, though the most popular literary genre in Europe, has yet to attract adequate attention in China, where "the gentry has favored more poetry, history, and philosophy" (*Les Parisiens peints par un Chinois*, 215). Huangshanke 黃衫客 is a character in the Tang tale *Huo Xiaoyu zhuan* 霍小玉傳 (The tale of Huo Xiaoyu), after which Chen Jitong created *Le roman de l'homme jaune*. Chen's French title plays on the epithet of the character, which has been variously translated as "Yellow Robe," "The Man in Yellow," and so on. Li Huachuan translated *Le roman de l'homme jaune* as *Huangshanke chuanqi* 黃衫客傳奇 (literally, *The Legend of the Man in Yellow*), for the same reason, I believe.

55. See Savarese, "The Experience of the Difference," 46–47.

56. Li, *Wan-Qing yige waijiao guan*, 45.

57. "Gleaner," "Monthly Notes: Literature," 78.

58. "The Chinese as They Are," 184.

59. *Appletons' Annual Cyclopædia and Register of Important Events of the Year*, 436.

60. Yeh, "The Life Style of Four *Wenren*," 436.

61. Ibid., 449.

62. See Ke Ren, "Painting China with a French Brush," 24–29.

63. See Meng Hua, "Qianyan," 5.

64. See Tcheng-Ki-Tong, "Avant-Propos," *Le théâtre des Chinois*, i–ii.

65. Ibid., vii–viii.

66. Ibid., ix; Jitong notes that he quoted this line from Vauvenargues.

67. Ibid.

68. See ibid., vii.

69. Ibid.

70. See ibid., ii–iii.

71. Tcheng-Ki-Tong, *Les Parisiens peints par un Chinois*, 218.

72. Zeng Pu, "Zeng xiansheng dashu," *juan* 8, 3:1127–31. Zeng's letter was written on 16 March 1928, thirty years after he first met Chen Jitong at a party seeing off Tan Sitong to Beijing on the eve of the Hundred Days.

73. Sang Bing also notes Jitong's focus on the function of literature in communicating China to the West; see *Guoxue yu Hanxue*, 104–8. Jing Tsu also points out that Jitong's "vision of world literature and recognition of language as the key contact point between cultures put him ahead of many of his colleagues, who would not come to fully recognize the strategic importance of revamping Chinese literature until after China's disastrous defeat by Japan in 1895" (*Sound and Script in Chinese Diaspora*, 125). I believe, however, rather than treating world literature as an open access "prerequisite to a deeper, more strategic engagement," that is, "to elevate national interests under the guise of transcending them" (ibid.), Jitong intended world literature to communicate among all peoples so as to reach his utopian ideal of world harmony.

74. See Tcheng-Ki-Tong, "Avant-Propos," *Le théâtre des Chinois*, ii–iii, v–vi.

75. Tcheng-Ki-Tong, *Le théâtre des Chinois*, 60.

76. The *Ping Shan Leng Yan* was translated into French by Stanislas Julien under the title *Les Deux Jeunes Filles Lettrées* (ibid., 60). For a discussion of the authorship and the Chinese editions of the novel, see Feng Weimin, "Biaodian houji," to the *Ping Shan Leng Yan*, 261–64.

77. *Ping Shan Leng Yan*, 94.

78. Ibid. See also Tcheng-Ki-Tong, *Le théâtre des Chinois*, 60–61; and Chen Jitong, *Zhongguo ren de xiju*, a Chinese translation of *Le théâtre des Chinois*, 41–42.

79. Tcheng-Ki-Tong, *Bits of China*, 135–36.

80. See Qian Nanxiu, "Qianyan" to Chen, *Xue Jia yin*, 21–22.

81. Li, *Wan-Qing yige waijiao guan*, 15.

82. Rolland, *Le cloître de la rue d'Ulm*, 276–77.

83. See Zhao Erxun et al., *Qingshi gao*, "Yufu zhi" 輿服志 (Treatise of chariots and clothing), II, *juan* 103, 11:3055–57; see also Garrett, *Chinese Dress*, 64–82.

84. The five photos, all by Studio Nardar, I acquired from Bibliothèque Nationale de France portray Chen Jitong wearing three different outfits: one a civil official robe, one a military uniform, and the third in his two close cuts looks like the same one in his portrait in the *Bits of China*.

85. *Compact Edition of the Oxford English Dictionary* (Oxford: Oxford University Press, 1971), s.v. "Purple."

86. Rolland, *Le cloître de la rue d'Ulm*, 277.

87. Ibid., 276.

88. Tcheng-Ki-Tong, *Les Parisiens peints par un Chinois*, 26.

89. Tcheng-Ki-Tong, *Les plaisirs en Chine*, 142–43.

90. Tcheng-Ki-Tong, "La Chine vue par un artiste," *Revue bleue* XLVI, 1890, 686; quoted in Ren, "Painting China with a French Brush," 24.

91. For instance, "La Femme," in Tcheng-Ki-Tong, *Les Chinois peints par eux-mêmes*, 56–67; trans., idem, *The Chinese Painted by Themselves*, 45–52; "Les Bas-bleus, en Chine," in *Les Parisiens peints par un Chinois*, 271–82; "La Soubrette," in *Le théâtre des Chinois*, 243–62; and so forth.

92. Tcheng-Ki-Tong, *Les Parisiens peints par un Chinois*, 275.

93. See Tcheng-Ki-Tong, *Les Chinois peints par eux-mêmes*, 56–67, and *The Chinese Painted by Themselves*, 45–52.

94. Tcheng-Ki-Tong, *Le théâtre des Chinois*, 247.

95. Ibid., 246.

96. Tcheng-Ki-Tong, *Les Chinois peints par eux-mêmes*, 57, and *The Chinese Painted by Themselves*, 46.

97. Tcheng-Ki-Tong, *Le théâtre des Chinois*, 247.

98. Tcheng-Ki-Tong, *Les Parisiens peints par un Chinois*, 274, 276. For the whole chapter, see 271–82.

99. Tcheng-Ki-Tong, *Mon pays*, 78.

100. Ibid., 75.

101. Ibid., 75–76.

102. Bury, *Gambetta and the Making of the Third Republic*, 54, 56.

103. Ibid., 54.

104. Tcheng-Ki-Tong, *Les Chinois peints par eux-mêmes*, 97, and *The Chinese Painted by Themselves*, 72.

105. Tcheng-Ki-Tong, *Les Parisiens peints par un Chinois*, 177.

106. Tcheng-Ki-Tong, Les Chinois peints par eux-mêmes, 97, and *The Chinese Painted by Themselves*, 72.

107. Li, *Wan-Qing yige waijiao guan*, 106–7.

108. Ibid., 55, 45.

109. Chen Jitong, "*Qiushi bao* xu," 1a.

110. Judge, *Print and Politics*, 17.

111. See, for instance, Xu Songrong's introduction to the column "Zhongwai baoyi" 中外報譯 (Translated items from the foreign press in China and abroad) in the *Shiwu bao* (Xu Songrong, *Weixin pai yu jindai baokan*, 75–76).

112. Referring to the opening of the five "treaty ports" of Canton, Amoy,

Foochow, Ningpo, and Shanghai in 1842. Many more such ports were opened from the 1860s onward. See *Cambridge History of China, Late Ch'ing [Qing], 1800–1911*, ed. John K. Fairbank, 10:211–12.

113. *Qiushi bao* 1 (30 Sept. 1897), "Xilü xinyi" column, 1a.

114. Yan Fu, Fayi 法意 (*Spirit of the Laws*), bk. XI, p. 8; translated and quoted in Schwartz, *In Search of Wealth and Power*, 151. Schwartz comments on Yan Fu: "The individual in question has been chosen because he related himself with peculiar directness to the confrontation of traditional China with the ideas of eighteenth- and nineteenth-century Europe. Like many of his predecessors and contemporaries he is profoundly concerned with the secrets of Western military, economic, and political power, but unlike them he is profoundly interested in what Western thinkers have thought about these matters. He is the first Chinese literatus who relates himself seriously, rigorously, and in a sustained fashion to modern Western thought" (3). The same observations can be applied to Jitong's understanding of political and legal systems as the foundation of Western wealth and power. Both were pioneers in their understanding of law and politics in the West. Their efforts together show the central role of the Fuzhou Navy Yard culture in the late Qing reforms.

115. See Lin, *Shen Baozhen*, 522–27, passim; and Li, *Wan-Qing yige waijiao guan*, 164–65.

116. See Schwartz, *In Search of Wealth and Power*, 149.

117. In fact, Chen Jitong was "so familiar with French politics and the Code Napoléon that even very learned scholars of French law could not get the better of him" (Shen, "Chen Jitong shilüe," *juan* 39, 71a).

118. *Qiushi bao* 1, "Xilü xinyi," 1a.

119. See *Code Napoléon, or, The French Civil Code*, trans. George Spence, "Contents," iii–xix.

120. Chen Jitong's published translation of the *Code Napoléon* covers only its "Preliminary Title," Articles 1–6, and Book I, Articles 7–209 (1–58), under the "Qijia lü," in "Xilü xinyi," *Qiushi bao* 4 (30 Oct. 1897), 5 (9 Nov. 1897), 6 (19 Nov. 1897), 7 (28 Nov. 1897), 9 (18 Dec. 1897), and 11 (15 Feb. 1898).

121. *Qiushi bao* 1, "Xilü xinyi," 1b. For the French original of the *Lois Constitutionnelles de la République Française*, see Bard and Robiquet, *Droit constitutionnel comparé*, "Appendice," 389–94. The *Lois* consists of three chapters. The chapter "Loi relative à l'organisation des pouvoirs publics" (Law on the organization of the public powers) has nine articles (deliberated 25 Jan., 3 and 25 Feb. 1875; promulgated in the *Journal officiel* of 28 Feb. 1875) (389–90); its Chinese translation by Chen Jitong appears in *Qiushi bao* 1, "Xilü xinyi," 1b–2b. The chapter "Loi sur l'organisation du Sénat" (Law on the organization of the Senate) has ten articles (deliberated 24 Feb. 1875; promulgated in the *Journal officiel* of 28 Feb. 1875) (390–92); its Chinese translation by Chen Jitong appears in *Qiushi bao* 1, "Xilü xinyi," 2b–3a. The chapter "Loi sur les rapports des pouvoirs publics" (Law on the reports of the public powers) has fourteen articles (deliberated 22 June, 7 and 16 July 1873; promulgated in the *Journal officiel* of 18 July 1875) (392–94); Chen Jitong's Chinese translation of Articles 1–7 in *Qiushi bao* 1, "Xilü xinyi," 3a–3b; Articles 8–14 in *Qiushi bao* 2 (10 Oct. 1897), "Xilü xinyi," 4a–4b.

122. See *Compact Edition of the Oxford English Dictionary*, s.v. "Democracy."

123. As in *Shangshu*, "Duofang" 多方 (Numerous regions): "Heaven on this sought a *true* lord for the people [*minzhu*], and made its distinguishing and favouring decree light on T'ang the Successful" (天惟時求民主, 乃大降顯休命于成湯) (*Shangshu* [*zhengyi*], *juan* 17, 1:228; trans. Legge, *The Shoo King*, in Legge, trans., *The Chinese Classics*, 3:497).

124. For instance, in an early issue of his journal the *République Française*, Gambetta recognized the provincial press's contribution to Republican electoral success, saying, "Our thoughts accompany and would wish to encourage these devoted groups, this unknown France, the hope and strength of democracy" (quoted in Bury, *Gambetta and the Making of the Third Republic*, 62).

125. On the presidentialism of the Third Republic, see Bell, *French Constitutional Law*, 14. On the late Qing translation, introduction, and usage of Western political concepts such as republic, democracy, and presidency, see Xiong Yuezhi, "Wan-Qing jige zhengzhi cihui de fanyi yu shiyong"; and Lackner et al., eds., *New Terms for New Ideas*.

126. *Qiushi bao* 1, "Xilü xinyi," 1b.

127. See Bury, *Gambetta and the Making of the Third Republic*, 9, 147–48, 175, 233–35.

128. See Shen, "Chen Jitong shilüe," *juan* 39, 72a.

129. See *Liji* [*zhengyi*], *Daxue*, *juan* 60, 2:1673.

130. See, for instance, the *Code Napoléon*, Book I, Articles 75 (22–23), 76 (23), 124 (37), 139, 140 (42), 190 (54), 196 (55), 197 (56), translated respectively in *Qiushi bao* 6 (19 Nov. 1897), "Xilü xinyi," 7a–7b; *Qiushi bao* 7 (28 Nov. 1897), "Xilü xinyi," 11a, 12a; *Qiushi bao* 11 (15 Feb. 1898), "Xilü xinyi," 1b, 2a.

131. See *Qiushi bao* 8 (8 Dec. 1897), "Xilü xinyi" column, 1a.

132. See "Xilü xinyi," in *Qiushi bao* 8, 10 (28 Dec. 1897); and 12 (7 Mar. 1898); see also Grattier, *Commentaire sur les Lois de la presse et des autres moyens de publication*, 1:19–115, 302–542, passim.

133. Kuhn, *The Media in France*, 16.

134. See ibid., 16–17.

135. Schwartz, *In Search of Wealth and Power*, 244.

136. Ibid.

137. Tcheng-Ki-Tong, *Les Parisiens peints par un Chinois*, 121–22.

138. Tcheng-Ki-Tong, *Mon pays*, 239; see also Li, *Wan-Qing yige waijiao guan*, 145.

139. For a detailed discussion of Jitong's ideal of making "all under heaven into one family," see Li, *Wan-Qing yige waijiao guan*, 142–50. In addition to the examples Li has listed from Jitong's French publications, I have also found similar expressions in Jitong's Chinese poems collected in his manuscript *Xue Jia yin*. In "Ren gui yin erlü" 人鬼吟二律 (Chanting on human and ghost, two regulated poems), which Jitong composed on his trip to inspect the new mining industries in Guizhou, he celebrated the welcome he and two French technicians received from the local minority people: "Now all under heaven has become one family" (天下而今已一家). In another poem, Jitong compares the Guizhou Miao ethnic custom of

dancing to the moon (*tiaoyue* 跳月) to Western balls, both offering young people an opportunity for courtship. Jitong concludes: "Chinese and Western peoples are apart by a thousand miles, / Speaking different languages and wearing different clothes. / Only in the grand relationship between men and women, / We follow the same rules of dancing and mating" (中西相距三萬里, 言語不通服飾異。獨於 男女之大倫, 跳舞合歡能一理) (Chen, *Xue Jia yin*, 8–9).

Chapter Three

1. See Chen Qiang et al., "Xianbi Xue gongren nianpu," 1a–1b. Xue's mother, Lady Shao, was "well versed in literature and scholarship," according to Shen and Chen, *Fujian tongzhi*, "Lienü zhuan," "Biantong," *juan* 6, 50a; and Chen Yan, *Min-Hou xian zhi*, "Lienü zhuan," "Biantong" II, *juan* 101, 6a. Lady Shao's mentor, the famed Minxian woman poet Lin Peifang (fl. 1840), enjoys an extensive entry in Ding Yun, *Minchuan guixiu shihua xubian*, *juan* 1, 14a–15a; see also *Min-Hou xian zhi*, "Lienü zhuan," "Biantong" I, *juan* 100, 5a.

2. Referring to Confucius, Yan Hui, Mencius, and Zeng Shen; cf. *Sishi xue* 四 氏學 in *Ciyuan*, s.v. "*Si*."

3. See Chen et al., "Xianbi Xue gongren nianpu," 1a–5a, which also indicates that the poetry bell was invented by Shoupeng's father and his fellow poets in the Flying Society (Feishe) in the Daoguang reign (1821–50) (see ibid., 5a–5b). For a detailed introduction to the practice of the poetry bell, see Wu, *Modern Archaics*, 203–17.

4. Wen Chu, a native of Changzhou (today's Suzhou, Jiangsu), was skilled in flowers, insects, and rocks; Chen Shu, a native of Xiushui (today's Jiaxing, Zhejiang), was skilled in plants, birds, and insects; see Weidner et al., *Views from Jade Terrace*, 88–91 and 117–20, respectively.

5. Chen Shoupeng, "Wangqi Xue gongren zhuanlüe," 3a.

6. See ibid., 2b–3a.

7. Chen et al., "Xianbi Xue gongren nianpu," 4b–5b.

8. Xue Shaohui, *Daiyunlou yiji*, *Shiji*, *juan* 1, 1b–2a.

9. Like those in the "Wusheng gequ" 吳聲歌曲 (Wu songs) in Guo Maoqian, ed., *Yuefu shiji*, *juan* 44–45, 2:639–55.

10. For puns conventionally used in Chinese amatory poetry, see Frankel, *The Flowering Plum and the Palace Lady*, 58.

11. For "Shuixian diao" (aka "Shuixian cao") and Boya's 伯牙 friendship with Zhong Ziqi 鍾子期, see Zhu Changwen, *Qinshi*, vol. 839, *juan* 2, 9b–11a.

12. Feng Yansi 馮延巳, "Changming nü": "On a spring Feast, / One cup of green wine and a song. / Bowing twice, I present three wishes: / First wish, one thousand years to my young lord; / Second wish, lasting health to thy maidservant; / Third wish, like the swallows on the beam, / We'll see each other year after year" (春日宴, 綠酒一杯歌一遍, 再拜陳三願: 一願郎君千歲, 二願妾身常健, 三願 如同梁上燕, 歲歲長相見) (in Feng, *Yangchun ji* 陽春集 [Collection of the sunny spring], vol. 1722, *juan* 1, 16a).

13. For a detailed introduction to the *fuji* divination, see Smith, *Fortune-Tellers & Philosophers*, 225–30.

14. See Yao Yuanzhi, *Zhuyeting zaji, juan* 6, 135.

15. Xue, *Daiyunlou yiji, Ciji, juan* A, 7a.

16. *Shenxian zhuan*, "Fan Furen" 樊夫人 (Lady Fan), vol. 1059, *juan* 6, 9b–10a.

17. See Li E, *Yutai shushi*, vol. 1084, *juan* 44, 19b–24b.

18. See Liang Zhangju, *Langji congtan, Xutan, Santan, Xutang, juan* 5, 343.

19. See the preface by Guo Boyin (1807–84) to Zhao Xin, *Xu Liuqiu guo zhilüe*, 1a–1b.

20. The dragon flag, in a triangular shape, was adopted as China's national symbol in 1862 and then was changed to a rectangular shape in 1888; see Liu Zuozhong, "Zhongguo jindai guoqi xiaoshi."

21. James Alden Barber's introduction to propellers may help us understand the function of the counterclockwise propeller as depicted by Xue. Barber writes: "Most single-screw propellers rotate in a clockwise direction, as viewed from the stern. Ships with two or four shafts generally have out-turn screws, that is, when going ahead the starboard screw rotates clockwise and the port screw rotates counterclockwise as seen from astern" (*Naval Shiphandler's Guide*, 35). As for shells, note that the Buddhist definition of "right-turning" or "left-turning" coiled shells clashes with the science of biology. Biologically, "the majority (over 90%) of gastropod species have dextral (right-handed [clockwise]) shells in their coiling, but a small minority of species and genera are virtually always sinistral (left-handed [counterclockwise]). . . . In species that are almost always dextral, very rarely a sinistral specimen will be produced, and these oddities are avidly sought after by some shell collectors" (http://en.wikipedia.org/wiki/Gastropod_shell, accessed 16 July 2011). The right-turning conch shell, *youxuan luo*, that appears in the title of Xue's song-lyric is precisely such a rare, counterclockwise sinistral shell. See also "Conch Shell in Buddhism" (www.religionfacts.com/buddhism/symbols/conch.htm, accessed 16 July 2011).

22. Xue, *Daiyunlou yiji, Ciji, juan* A, 7b–8a.

23. Luonü (Snail Girl), is a Houguan fairy first recorded in *Soushen houji*, "Bai-shui sunü" 白水素女 (The pure maiden of the White Waters), *juan* 5, 30.

24. Xue, "Jiwai" 寄外 (To my husband), *Daiyunlou yiji, Shiji, juan* 1, 5b.

25. Chen et al., "Xianbi Xue gongren nianpu," 8b.

26. See Liu Yiqing, *Shishuo xinyu* [*jianshu*], 19/23, text proper, and Yu Jiaxi's commentary, 2:694–95.

27. Such an episode can be found in the *Shishuo*, chapter "Huoni" 惑溺 (Delusion and infatuation): "Wang Rong's wife always addressed Rong with the familiar pronoun 'you' [*qing*]. Rong said to her, 'For a wife to address her husband as 'you' is disrespectful according to the rules of etiquette [*li*]. Hereafter don't call me that again.' His wife replied, 'But I'm intimate with you and I love you, so I address you as "you." If I didn't address you as "you," who else would address you as "you"?' After that he always tolerated [this usage]" (35/6); quoted from Mather, trans., *A New Account of Tales of the World*, 488, modified. Yu Ying-shih suggests that the wife's remarks reveal a growing jealousy among Wei-Jin women as well as an increasing intimacy between husbands and wives. See his *Zhongguo zhishi jieceng shilun*, 346. See also Qian, *Spirit and Self*, chap. 4.

28. Xue, "Songwai zhi Riben" 送外之日本 (Seeing my husband off to Japan) (1883), *Daiyunlou yiji, Shiji, juan* 1, 3a.

29. Xue, "Jiwai" 寄外 (To my husband), ibid., *juan* 1, 5a.

30. I wonder if these rubbings are of the hieroglyphs inscribed on the Egyptian stones in the British Museum such as the Rosetta Stone (Ptolemaic Period, 196 BCE), which has been exhibited in the museum since 1802 (www.britishmuseum. org/explore/highlights/highlight_objects/aes/t/the_rosetta_stone.aspx, accessed 11 May 2014). No record shows that Shoupeng ever visited Egypt.

31. "Rao foge," in Xue, *Daiyunlou yiji, Ciji, juan* A, 9a.

32. "Mu husha," in ibid., *juan* A, 9b.

33. Ibid., *juan* A, 15b–16a, following the same rule of Liu Yong's "Shier shi"; see Tang Guizhang, ed., *Quan Song ci*, 1:55. Lin Yi notes the tune as "Shier shi man" 十二時慢 (Twelve double-hours, slower); see Xue Shaohui, *Xue Shaohui ji*, 82.

34. Xue, *Daiyunlou yiji, Ciji, juan* A, 14a–15b.

35. See Sima Qian, *Shiji*, "Song Weizi shijia" 宋微子世家 (Hereditary house of Song Weizi), *juan* 38, 5:1620–21.

36. Xue, To the tune "Jinlü qu" 金縷曲 (Melody of a gold strand), *Daiyunlou yiji, Ciji, juan* B, 6b.

37. Ibid., *juan* A, 23b. Liu Ling was one of the Seven Worthies of the Bamboo Grove; his "Jiude song" 酒德頌 (Eulogy to the virtue of wine) exudes the spirit of the perfected person; see Liu, *Shishuo xinyu* [*jianshu*], 4/69.

38. The Jin general Zu Ti 祖逖 (266–321) "beat his oars in mid-current" (*zhongliu jiji* 中流擊楫) in vowing to recover the Central Plains; see Fang Xuanling et al., *Jinshu*, "Zu Ti zhuan," *juan* 62, 6:1695.

39. Xue, *Daiyunlou yiji, Ciji, juan* B, 5a.

40. On the Battle of Dadonggou, see Paine, *The Sino-Japanese War of 1894–1895*, 179–95.

41. Xue, To the tune "Dian jiangchun" 點絳唇 (Touching up crimson lips), *Daiyunlou yiji, Ciji, juan* B, 9b.

42. On the establishment of the Republic of Taiwan and Chen Jitong's role in it, see Lamley, "The 1895 Taiwan Republic"; see also Shen Yuqing, "Chen Jitong shilüe," *juan* 39, 72a.

43. Chen Jitong, *Xue Jia yin*, 151–52. See also a variant version in Qian Zhonglian, ed., *Qingshi jishi*, 20:14670.

44. Xue, *Daiyunlou yiji, Ciji, juan* B, 10a. On the Woman of Qishi, see Liu Xiang, [*Gu*] *Lienü zhuan*, "Renzhi" 仁智 (Benevolence and wisdom), *juan* 3, 101:87–88; cf. O'Hara, trans., *The Position of Woman in Early China*, 95–97. See also *Liezi*, "Tianrui" 天瑞 (Auspicious omen of heaven): "In the state of Qi there was once a man who worried that heaven and earth might collapse and he would lose his lodging. He was so anxious that he could not eat or sleep" (*Liezi zhu, juan* 1, 8). Xue here changes the idiomatic expression "Qiren youtian" 杞人憂天 (The man of Qi worries about heaven) into "weitian you Qi" 為天憂杞 (One worries about Qi on behalf of heaven), thus transforming the Man of Qi's unnecessary panic into the Woman of Qishi's justifiable concern for Lu.

45. See Mann, "The Lady and the State," 285.

46. Quoted in ibid., 394. Mann notes that the translation is from O'Hara, *The Position of Women in Early China*, 96.

47. Xue, "Ti Yiru fuzi hutian zhangjian zhaoxiang" 題繹如夫子胡天仗劍照相 (Inscribed on a photo of Master Yiru wearing a sword), to the tune "Yan Qingdu" 宴清都 (Banquet in the pure capital), *Daiyunlou yiji, Ciji, juan* A, 10a–10b. For the Ganjiang Moye story, see Zhao Ye (fl. 25–56), *Wu-Yue chunqiu, juan* 4, 20–21.

48. Chen, *Xue Jia yin*, 34.

49. Chen et al., "Xianbi Xue gongren nianpu," 10a.

50. *Xinwen bao* (24 November 1897); Jing Yuanshan, *Nüxue jiyi chubian*, 6b.

51. Shen, "Chen Jitong shilüe," *juan* 39, 72b.

52. See Li Huachuan, *Wan-Qing yige waijiao guan*, 36–44.

53. On Jitong's imprisonment from 1891 to 1892, and Jitong's and Shoupeng's activities from 1892 to 1895, see Chen et al., "Xianbi Xue gongren nianpu," 8b–9b. On Jitong's wives and children living in the Chen household in Fuzhou, see Chen Chao, "Lun nianqing de xin yibian," 3b–4a. According to this essay, Jitong's family lived with the extended Chen household at least until late 1895 or early 1896, when Chen Chao was about ten or eleven years old.

54. See Chen Yun, "Jinling bie Cha Ban liangzi" 金陵別槎、班兩姊 (Farewell to Cousins Qian and Chao in Jingling [Nanjing]) (Autumn 1905), *Chen Xiaonü yiji, juan* B, 3b–4a.

55. Chen et al., "Xianbi Xue gongren nianpu," 7a–7b, 8a–8b, 9b, 11b, 12a. For an interpretation of the poem "Shi'er" and a detailed discussion of the women and children in the Chen household, see Qian's introduction to Chen, *Xue Jia yin*, 10–19.

56. Plauchut, *China and the Chinese*, 57.

57. Tang Caichang, *Tang Caichang ji*, 102. See also Huang Xingtao, "Yige bugai bei yiwang de wenhua ren," i.

58. Zeng Pu, *Niehai hua*, 303. Zeng recollected Jitong's decisive influence on his career as a novelist in his letter to Hu Shi on 16 March 1928; see Zeng Pu, "Zeng xiansheng dashu," *juan* 8, 3:1125–39.

59. Chen Shuping and Chen Shujing, "Houji" (Postscript) to Chen, *Xue Jia yin*, 178–79.

60. Hart, *The I. G. in Peking*, 2:849, Letter 802 (emphasis added). Robert Hart served from 1863 to 1911 as the second Inspector General of China's Imperial Maritime Custom Service.

61. Guerville, *Au Japon*, 89; see also Tsu, *Sound and Script in Chinese Diaspora*, 263n18.

62. Sherard, *Twenty Years in Paris*, 303.

63. Zeng, *Niehai hua*, 302.

64. Tcheng-Ki-Tong, *The Chinese Painted by Themselves*, 51; the entire discussion (49–52) was reprinted in Tcheng-Ki-Tong and Gray, *The Chinese Empire*, 174–76. Jitong also discussed concubinage and its dramatization in *Le théâtre des Chinois*, 223–42.

65. Tcheng-Ki-Tong, *The Chinese Painted by Themselves*, 50–52, passim.

66. Xue, *Daiyunlou yiji, Wenji, juan* B, 18b.

67. See Ban Gu, *Hanshu*, "Su Wu zhuan," *juan* 54, 8:2459–69. When Han emperor Xuandi (r. 73–49 BCE) inquired about Su Wu's descendents, he reported to the court that he had a son by his "foreign wife" (*Hufu* 胡婦) (see *juan* 54, 8:2468).

68. Chen et al., "Xianbi Xue gongren nianpu," 7b.

69. Chen, *Xue Jia yin*, 57.

70. Xue, *Daiyunlou yiji, Wenji, juan* B, 17b.

71. There was a copyright dispute between Jitong and his erstwhile French tutor Foucault de Mondion over the authorship of *Les Chinois peints par eux-mêmes* and *Le théâtre des Chinois*. After a meticulous investigation, Li Huachuan suggests coauthorship; see *Wan-Qing yige waijiao guan*, 27–35. I rather believe that Mondion at most helped fine-tune the manuscripts. First, Mondion did not have any background in Chinese culture, which would have been crucial for writing the two books. Second, Mondion alleged Jitong's incompetence in French, yet a great deal of evidence shows the opposite (see also ibid.). Finally, Maria-Adèle would certainly have offered help.

72. Jitong officially married Maria-Adèle Lardanchet on 12 April 1890, in her hometown Desnes (Jura), France, as announced in *Le Temps* (18 April 1890): 3, "Faits Divers" column. See also Li Huachuan, "Qingmo Zhongguo ren chuangzuo de Fawen xiaoshuo," 72–73. The *Le Temps* report hastened to add, however: "Their Chinese wedding had been celebrated in Beijing several years ago." This report was published in at least two other journals, *T'oung pao* 1 (Leiden, 1890): 160; and *Annales de l'Etrême Orient et de l'Afrique* 8.1 (Paris, 1890): 287. I have found no record of the Beijing wedding so far, and the couple might just have made up the story to tone down the awkward fact that they had had two daughters before tying the knot.

73. Chen, *Xue Jia yin*, 45.

74. "Nüluo" 女蘿 (usnea lichen) alludes to Li Bai, "Guyi": "My lord, you are an usnea lichen; / I am a cuscuta flower. / . . . We attach to the tall pine tree, / Tenderly we entangle into one family" (君為女蘿草, 妾作菟絲花。. . . 百丈托遠松, 纏綿成一家) (*Li Taibai quanji, juan* 8, 1:453).

75. Chen Jitong, "You ji Feiren" 又寄妃人 (Again to Feiren), *Xue Jia yin*, 12.

76. Chen Jitong, "Zhimeng" 志夢 (Record of a dream), *Xue Jia yin*, 66.

77. Recorded in Benas, "The Ethics and Poetry of the Chinese."

78. An elder sister of Chen Yan's was married to Shen Baozhen's eldest son, Shen Weiqing (d. 1880); see Chen Yan, "Shu Zhongrong liujie shi" 書仲容六姐事 (Memories of my sixth elder sister, Zhongrong), in *Chen Shiyi ji*, 1:461; see also Liu Jianping, "Lun Shen Queying de shici chuangzuo," 84.

79. Hu Wenkai, "Xiao Daoguan." Her broad reading list covers Tang and Song poetry and prose and fiction, including titles such as *Tangren shuohui* 唐人說薈 (Assorted Tang minor talks), *Honglou meng* 紅樓夢 (Dream of the Red Chamber), and *Liaozhai zhiyi*. See Xiao Daoguan, *Xiao Daoguan ji, Ping'anshi zaji*, 1a.

80. Xiao Daoguan, *Xiao Daoguan ji, Ping'anshi zaji*, 1b.

81. Including *Dao'anshi zawen* (1 *juan*), *Xiaoxiantang yishi* (1 *juan*), *Daihua ping'anshi ci* (1 *juan*), and *Ping'anshi zaji* (1 *juan*).

82. See Xiao, *Xiao Daoguan ji*, *Ping'anshi zaji*, 1a; Chen Yan, "Dao'anshi shilüe," 2a–2b; both in *Shiyishi congshuben edn.*

83. See Ling Hongxun, *Zhonghua tielu shi*, 72.

84. Xiao Daoguan, "Wei tielu zaoqiao ji Mengxia heshen wen" 為鐵路造橋祭艋舺河神文 (Sacrificial oration to the Mangkah River God for constructing the railroad bridge), *Xiao Daoguan ji*, *Dao'anshi zawen*, 2b–3a.

85. Xiao, *Xiao Daoguan ji*, *Ping'anshi zaji*, 4a–4b.

86. Chen Shengji and Wang Zhen, eds., *Shiyi xiansheng nianpu*, *juan* 4, 14b–15a.

87. Chen Yan, *Shiyishi shiji*, *juan* 3, 11a.

88. Qian, ed., *Qingshi jishi*, 22:16005.

89. In his *Principles of Biology*, vol. 1, published in 1864, Spencer coined the axiom "survival of the fittest." He states, for instance: "This survival of the fittest, which I have here sought to express in mechanical terms, is that which Mr. Darwin has called 'natural selection, or the preservation of favoured races in the struggle for life'" (444–45). This "natural selection," Spencer continues, "must be a process of equilibration, since it results in the production of organisms that are in equilibrium with their environments; and at the outset of this chapter, something was done towards showing how this continual survival of the fittest, may be understood as the progressive establishment of a balance between inner and outer forces" (457).

90. Yan Fu translated Huxley's *Evolution and Ethics* into *Tianyan lun* first in 1895 with a revised version in 1898. The translation had a great impact on the Chinese intellectual elite; see Billy K. L. So, "You fa wu tian?," 5–6.

91. See ibid., 3–12. See also Dikötter, *The Discourse of Race in Modern China*, 67–69.

92. See Chen Yan, "Dao'anshi shilüe," 1a–2b.

93. See Hu, "Xiao Daoguan."

94. Chen Yan, *Shiyishi shihua*, *juan* 18, 254.

95. Shen and Chen, "Shen Que[ying] shilüe" 沈鵲[應]事略 (Biographic sketch of Shen Que[ying]), *Fujian tongzhi*, "Lienü zhuan," "Biantong," 6:50b; Chen, *Min-Hou xian zhi*, "Lienü zhuan," "Biantong" II, 101:6b.

96. Chen Yan, "Shen Que[ying] shilüe," *Min-Hou xian zhi*, 101: 6b, records that Queying "learned poetry and prose from Chen Shu and Chen Yan." Liu Jianping indicates that, from 1894 to 1898, Lin Xu and Shen Queying studied poetry under the guidance of Chen Shu; see Liu, "Lin Xu Wancuixuan shiji tanxi," 65. Both Lin Xu and Shen Queying address Chen Shu as *"shi"* or *"xiansheng"* (teacher, mentor, master) in their poems; see Lin Xu, *Wancuixuan shi*, and Shen Queying, *Yanlou yigao*, ed. Li Xuangong. Li's grandmother was Shen Baozhen's daughter and Li himself was Lin Xu's close friend. He collected and published several editions of Lin Xu's and Shen Queying's works after their death. The 1936 edition is the latest and most complete version. See Li's preface to Lin Xu, *Wancuixuan shi*; see also Lin Ning, "Li Xuangong de jiashi yu shengping."

97. See Shen Queying, "Dongpo 'Dule yuan shi,' jia daren, Feng'an shi jun

ciyun, suitong Jilan sanmei" 東坡《獨樂園詩》, 家大人、馮庵師均次韻, 遂
同季蘭三妹 (My father and my mentor Feng'an [Chen Shu] both followed the
rhyme of Dongpo's "Poem from the Happy-alone Garden"; so I also wrote one
along with Third Sister Jilan) (*Yanlou shi*, in *Yanlou yigao*, 1a–1b). Qian Zhonglian
points out that the Min school "imitated ancient poets starting with Han Yu and
Meng Jiao . . . and Shen Yuqing especially favored Su Shi" ("Lun Tong-Guang ti,"
115).

98. Shen Queying, "Dongpo 'Dule yuan shi,'" *Yanlou shi*, in *Yanlou yigao*, 1b.

99. Shen Queying, *Yanlou ci*, in *Yanlou yigao*, 6b–7a.

100. See Du Guangting 杜光庭 (850–933), "Qiuranke zhuan," in Wang Pijiang,
ed., *Tangren xiaoshuo*, 178–84.

101. The expression *kuijian xiongwang* 葵踐兄亡, literally, "climbing spinaches
were tramped across, and my elder brother died," alludes to Liu Xiang, [*Gu*] *Lienü
zhuan*, "Renzhi": "The Woman from Qishi of Lu said: 'In the past, a guest tied
his horse in our garden. The horse ran away and tramped across the climbing spinaches, causing me not to have enough to eat for the entire year. Our neighbor's
daughter eloped with a man. Her family asked my elder brother to fetch her. On
the way my elder brother encountered a rising flood and drowned in the current,
so I did not have an elder brother all my life. I have heard that as the river swells
for nine *li*, so does it expand three hundred steps wider. Now the Ruler of Lu is
old and muddled in his head, and the crown prince is young and ignorant. Stupid-
ity and insincerity increase daily. If the Kingdom of Lu has a disaster, its ruler and
ministers, fathers and sons will all suffer from humiliation, and misfortune will
befall the common people. I am very worried! Why are you telling me that women
have nothing to do with all this?'" (魯漆室之女曰: "昔有客繫馬園中, 馬逸, 踐
葵, 使予終歲不飽葵。鄰人女奔隨人亡, 其家倩吾兄行追之。逢霖水出, 溺
流而死。令吾終身無兄。吾聞河潤九里, 漸洳三百步。今魯君老悖, 太子少
愚, 愚偽日起。夫魯國有患者, 君臣父子皆被其辱, 禍及眾庶, 婦人獨安所避
乎! 吾甚憂之。子乃曰婦人無與者, 何哉!") (*juan* 3, 101:87–88).

102. Shen Queying, to the tune "Yanshan ting" 燕山亭 (Tower on the Yan
Mountain), *Yanlou ci*, in *Yanlou yigao*, 7a.

103. Mann, "The Lady and the State," 285.

104. For the Woman of Wuyan (aka Zhongli Chun 鍾離春), see Liu, [*Gu*] *Lienü
zhuan*, "Biantong," *juan* 6, 101:173–76.

105. See, for instance, Deng Hongmei, *Nüxing cishi*, 562; and Liu, "Lun Shen
Queying de shici chuangzuo," 86.

106. See Shen, *Yanlou ci*, in *Yanlou yigao*, 8b–9b. *Yanlou yigao* appears to have
been edited in chronological order. At least we can tell that the song-lyric right
before these last five, titled "Chongjiu" 重九 (Double ninth) and to the tune "Duji-
ang yun" 渡江雲 (Clouds ferrying the river), heavily alludes to Li Qingzhao's same
titled song-lyric to the tune "Zui huayin" 醉花蔭 (Drunk in the shade of flowers),
which expresses Li's longing for a faraway yet still alive husband. See Shen, *Yanlou
ci*, 8b, and Li Qingzhao, *Li Qingzhao ji* [*jiaozhu*], *juan* 1, 34–35.

107. Chen, *Min-Hou xian zhi*, "Lienü zhuan," "Biantong," *juan* 100, 5b.

108. See ibid., *juan* 100, 5b–6a. For the founding date of the Quanshan Girls' School, see Lai Maogong, "Shi Bingzhang sheji Luhaijun dayuanshuai jiuzhi jinian youpiao kao," 3. Shi Bingzhang is the son of Shi Yumin's youngest brother, Shi Jingcheng.

109. See Zheng Zhenlin, "Fuzhou nannü liang shikan."

110. See Chen et al., "Xianbi Xue gongren nianpu," 10a–14a.

Chapter Four

1. As pointed out by Noriko Kamachi at the 1975 Harvard workshop on late Qing reforms. See *Reform in Nineteenth-Century China*, eds. Paul A. Cohen and John E. Schrecker, 248.

2. See Qian, "Revitalizing the *Xianyuan* (Worthy Ladies) Tradition."

3. For a report on the first meeting of the society, see "Jinguo duocai" 巾幗多才 (Many talents among women), *Xinwen bao* (7 Dec. 1897).

4. The *Chinese Girl's Progress* is the original English title that appears on the front page of every issue of the *Nü xuebao*. Studies on this first Chinese women's journal include Pan Tianzhen, "Tan Zhongguo jindai diyifen nübao"; Du Jikun, "Zai tan *Nü xuebao*"; and Yu Fuyuan, "Guanyu *Nü xuebao* de kanqi he kanxingqi." Twelve issues of the 1898 *Nü xuebao* seem to have been published; all were extant as late as 1963 (Du, 55; Yu, 52–53). Only the first eight issues can be found in the Wuxi Library, Jiangsu. I also acquired a photocopy of the ninth issue with the help of Professor Xia Xiaohong. Xu Chuying and Jiao Lizhi record an additional issue published on 6 March 1899, not numbered. See their "Zhongguo jindai funü qikan jianjie," 4:681.

5. Western missionary schools for girls already existed, such as the one in Ningbo established in 1844 by an English woman missionary, Miss Aldersey; see Burton, *Education of Women in China*, 35; Xiong Yuezhi, *Xixue dongjian yu wan-Qing shehui*, 287–92; and Xia Xiaohong, *Wan-Qing wenren funü guan*, 18. Although there were earlier girls' schools established by the Chinese in Suzhou and other places, historians tend to consider the Nü xuetang as a pathbreaker because of its clear reform agenda, thoroughly thought-out management, well-constructed curricula, and high-profile publicity; see Xia, *Wan-Qing nüxing yu jindai Zhongguo*, 4. On the opening date of the Nü xuetang, see the announcements in *Xinwen bao* (30 May and 8 June 1898) and the poems by the school's faculty in *Xinwen bao* (4 June 1898). The school had various names, including Zhongguo nü xuetang 中國女學堂, Jingzheng nüxue 經正女學, Shanghai Guishuli nü xuetang 上海桂墅里女學堂, Shanghai xinshe Zhongguo nü xuetang 上海新設中國女學堂, Guishuli nü xuehui shushu 桂墅里女學會書塾, and Zhongguo nü xuehui shushu 中國女學會書塾.

6. For works introducing the 1897–98 Shanghai campaign for women's education, see Xia, *Wan-Qing wenren funü guan*, 16–46; Ma Gengcun, *Zhongguo jindai funü shi*, 67–75; Luo Suwen, *Nüxing yu jindai Zhongguo shehui*, 113–20; and particularly Xia Xiaohong, "Zhong Xi hebi de Shanghai 'Zhongguo Nü xuetang.'" These works represent the campaign mostly as a men's project without detailed

analysis of women reformers' autonomous voices. Only Ma Gengcun acknowledges that "women reformers actively joined the campaign, crying for their rights. They appeared more radical than the leading [men] reformers such as Kang Youwei and Liang Qichao in pursuing equality with men" (74); he has not provided the grounds for this conclusion, however.

7. Variants include *xianfu* 賢婦 (worthy women), *xianmu* 賢母 (worthy mothers), *xianshu furen* 賢淑夫人 (worthy and gentle wives), and *xianshu mingyuan* 賢淑名媛 (famous worthy and gentle ladies). See essays and reports on women's gatherings in Jing Yuanshan, ed., *Nüxue jiyi chubian*, 8b, 10a–10b, 12a, 15b, 34a, and the "Wei gongren shu" 魏恭人書 (Letter from Lady Wei), front pages of the *Nüxue jiyi chubian*, 2a. The Western translators Young J. Allen and Timothy Richard also adopted these terms in writing about Chinese women reformers; see, for instance, Jing, ed., *Nüxue jiyi chubian*, 50b, 51a–51b; see also women's poems, using related terms, in ibid., 47a; and in *Xinwen bao*, 5, 7, 10, 12 June 1898 and 4 July 1898; *Xinwen bao*, "Fuzhang" 附張 (Appended pages), 13, 19 June 1898.

8. Liang Qichao, "Lun nüxue," *Shiwu bao* 23, 1a.

9. Li Timotai [Timothy Richard], "Shengli fenli zhi fa"; Liang, "Lun nüxue," *Shiwu bao* 23: 1a–3b.

10. *Xinwen bao* (19 Nov. 1897); reprinted in Jing, ed., *Nüxue jiyi chubian*, 1a–2b.

11. *Xinwen bao* (19 Nov. 1897); reprinted in Jing, ed., *Nüxue jiyi chubian*, 2b–3b.

12. *Shiwu bao* 45 (15 Nov. 1897): 3a–4a.

13. *Xinwen bao* (18 Nov. 1897). For publication details of the "Provisional Regulations," see under Liang Qichao et al., "Nü xuetang shiban lüezhang" in the Bibliography; see also Xia, "Zhong Xi hebi de Shanghai 'Zhongguo Nü xuetang,'" 58–59. Xia attributes this document to Liang Qichao, citing Jing Yuanshan's statement that "drafting the 'Announcement,' settling the 'Regulations,' and initiating the fundraising, all came from Master Liang's grand talents" (Jing, ed., *Nüxue jiyi chubian*, 53a). I, however, consider it a collective work that was only finalized by Liang, for he never signed this document (unlike the "Announcement"). Later, when the final version of the "Regulations" was published in the spring of 1898, it was signed by Maria-Adèle Lardanchet (under Lai Mayi) and Shen Ying (under Shen Heqing), the two "superintendents" of the new Girls' School (*Xiangbao* 64 [19 May 1898]: 254a–55a).

14. Xia, "Zhong Xi hebi de Shanghai 'Zhongguo Nü xuetang,'" 58–60; on men reformers seeking publicity for the Girls' School through the news media, see 58–71.

15. Jing, ed., *Nüxue jiyi chubian*, 22a–28a.

16. Jing Yuanshan, "Yuanqi" 緣起 (Memorial on the motivation and purpose), *Nüxue jiyi chubian*, 1a.

17. Ibid., 1a–2a. Only about thirty-six gentlemen signed up for the Beijing branch of Kang Youwei's Qiangxue hui 強學會 (Higher Study Society), and another thirty for its Shanghai branch; no women seem ever to have participated in either (see Tang Zhijun, *Wuxu bianfa shi*, 139–40, 161–62).

18. *Xinwen bao* (7, 9–12 Dec. 1897); reprinted in Jing, ed., *Nüxue jiyi chubian*, 12a–18a.

19. See Jing, ed., *Nüxue jiyi chubian*, 3a, 49a–52a; Richard, *Forty-five Years in China*, 261; Burton, *Education of Women in China*, 100–111; Cameron, *Reform Movement in China*, 83.

20. Liang, "Lun nüxue," *Shiwu bao* 23, 2b.

21. Jing, ed., *Nüxue jiyi chubian*, 25a–26a.

22. "Wei gongren shu," in ibid., 1b–2b. On Long Zehou's relationship with Kang Youwei and the 1898 reform, see Tang, *Wuxu bianfa shi*, 71, 73, 159, 161, 203.

23. Lin Lezhi [Young J. Allen], "Zhuxing nüxue lun," 21b; reprinted in Jing, ed., *Nüxue jiyi chubian*, 50b–51a.

24. See Jing, "Yuanqi," *Nüxue jiyi chubian*, 2a–5b.

25. *Xinwen bao* (3 Dec. 1897); reprinted in Jing, ed., *Nüxue jiyi chubian*, 10a.

26. *Xinwen bao* (12 Dec. 1897); reprinted in Jing, ed., *Nüxue jiyi chubian*, 15a.

27. Jing, ed., *Nüxue jiyi chubian*, 20a.

28. *Xinwen bao* (12 Dec. 1897); reprinted in Jing, ed., *Nüxue jiyi chubian*, 15b.

29. Jing, ed., *Nüxue jiyi chubian*, 15b, 20b–21a, 44b–45a, 46b–47b.

30. See *Xinwen bao* (4, 5, 7, 9, 10, 12 June 1898); *Nü xuebao* 5 (27 Aug. 1898): 3b; 8 (Sept. 1898): 3b; *Wanguo gongbao* 115 (Aug. 1898): 29a.

31. See *Xinwen bao* (13, 19 June, 4 July 1898). Men reformers responded primarily with letters and essays. The only poem of which I am aware is by Lin Shu (pen name "Weiluzi" 畏盧子): "Xing nüxue: mei shengju ye" 興女學: 美盛舉也 (Advocating women's education: Praising the grand deed), in his series titled *Minzhong xin yuefu* 閩中新樂府 (New music bureau poetry of the Min area), *Zhixin bao* 46 (13 Mar. 1898): 2b.

32. Jing, ed., *Nüxue jiyi chubian*, 15b, 20b, 47b; *Nü xuebao* 5 (27 Aug. 1898): 3b.

33. Jing, ed., *Nüxue jiyi chubian*, 47a, 20b.

34. *Xinwen bao* (4 June 1898).

35. *Xinwen bao* (4, 5, 7, 9, 10, 12 June 1898).

36. Jing, ed., *Nüxue jiyi chubian*, 44b.

37. Liang, "Lun nüxue," *Shiwu bao* 23, 1a.

38. Jing, ed., *Nüxue jiyi chubian*, 47b.

39. Lin, "Zhuxing nüxue lun"; reprinted in Jing, ed., *Nüxue jiyi chubian*, 50a–b.

40. Lin, "Zhuxing nüxue lun," 22a; reprinted in Jing, ed., *Nüxue jiyi chubian*, 51b. These events were enthusiastically covered by the Western news media in Shanghai. For instance, in addition to Allen's "Zhuxing nüxue lun," in *Wanguo gongbao*, the *Yixin xibao* reported the dinner party by the Spanish consul's wife and the first meeting of the Nü xuehui under the title "On [Establishing] Schools for Women in China" ("Lun Zhongguo nüxue") (31 Dec. 1897); reprinted in Jing, ed., *Nüxue jiyi chubian*, 49a–49b.

41. *Xinwen bao* (9 Dec. 1897); reprinted in Jing, ed., *Nüxue jiyi chubian*, 12a.

42. See *Xinwen bao* (18 Nov. 1897); *Qiushi bao* 9 (18 Dec. 1897): 5b.

43. Chen Qian and Chen Chao not only enthusiastically participated in the 1897–98 campaign for women's education, but they would also continue participating in late Qing reforms such as by contributing to a later women's journal edited and published by the woman revolutionary journalist Chen Xiefen (1883–1923)

from 1902 to 1903; see Qian, "The Mother *Nü Xuebao* versus the Daughter *Nü Xuebao.*"

44. See *Xinwen bao* (3, 7, 9 Dec. 1897); reprinted in Jing, ed., *Nüxue jiyi chubian*, 9a, 16a, 18b.

45. Jing, ed., *Nüxue jiyi chubian*, 20b.

46. See *Lunyu*, 11.26 (chap. 11, entry 26), *Lunyu* [*yizhu*], annotation and translation from classical into modern Chinese by Yang Bojun (1909–92), 119.

47. *Xinwen bao* (4 June 1898).

48. See Burton, *Education of Women in China*, 106–9; see also "Shanghai chuangshe Zhongguo Nü xuetang ji."

49. Burton, *Education of Women in China*, 110.

50. Ibid., 106–7, 110.

51. Ibid., 110–11.

52. Shen Ying et al., "Zhongguo Nüxue ni zengshe baoguan gaobai"; *Zhixin bao* 55 (9 June 1898): 26b; *Xiangbao* 87 (15 June 1898).

53. Shen Ying et al., "Zhongguo Nü xuehui zhi houguan Xue nüshi Shaohui shu."

54. The extant issues (the initial nine) show that the editorial board of the *Nü xuebao* enlisted thirty Chinese women altogether, although there was frequent turnover; Xue remained the first on the list.

55. Shen et al., "Zhongguo Nüxue ni zengshe baoguan gaobai."

56. Pan, "Shanghai *Nü xuebao* yuanqi," *Nü xuebau* 2:3a.

57. Shen et al., "Zhongguo Nü xuehui zhi houguan Xue nüshi," 8b.

58. See Chen Pingyuan, *Chumo lishi yu jinru wusi*, 81.

59. Richard, *Forty-five Years in China*, 260.

60. Xue Shaohui, "*Nü xuebao* xu," 3a.

61. Pan, "Shanghai *Nü xuebao* yuanqi," *Nü xuebau* 2:2b.

62. *Nü xuebao* 3 (15 Aug. 1898): 2b.

63. *Nü xuebao* 9 (Oct. 1898): 4a.

64. Their titles are provided by Du, "Zai tan *Nü xuebao*," 55–56.

65. See ibid., 56.

66. See *Nü xuebao* 8 (Sept. 1898): 1a.

67. See Du, "Zai tan *Nü xuebao*," 55–56; and Yu, "Guanyu *Nü xuebao* de kanqi he kanxingqi," 53.

68. Jing Yuanshan, "Da Yuankou Wenyi jun wen" (Reply to Mr. Haraguchi Bun'ichi) (6 Nov. 1900), in *Juyi chuji, juan* 2, 63b; Luo, *Nüxing yu jindai Zhongguo shehui*, 119.

69. Xue, "*Nü xuebao* xu," 3a.

70. Pan Xuan, "Lun *Nü xuebao* nanchu," 2b. The earliest and most authoritative demarcation between the *nei*, inner domain, and the *wai*, outer domain, was delineated in the "Neize" 內則 (Inner principles) of the *Liji*: "Men should not speak of domestic affairs, and women should not speak of public affairs" (*nan buyan nei, nü buyan wai* 男不言內, 女不言外), and again "inner words should not go out, and outer words should not go in" (*neiyan buchu, waiyan buru* 內言不出, 外言不入); *Liji* [*zhengyi*], *juan* 27, 2:1462. Zheng Xuan (127–200) com-

ments that this demarcation indicates "the allotment of responsibilities [for men and women]" (ibid.).

71. *Xinwen bao* (24 Nov. 1897); reprinted in Jing, ed., *Nüxue jiyi chubian*, 6b.

72. Xue's "Suggestions" has at least two versions. One was published in *Qiushi bao* 9 (18 Dec. 1897): 6a–7b; and 10 (28 Dec. 1897): 8a–b. A revised version with five more suggestions, titled "Yu Hu Jin'an Xue nüshi shang Nüxue tangdong tiaoyi bing xu," was published consecutively in the *Xinwen bao* (14–17 Jan. 1898). My discussion cites both but focuses on the former because of its immediate influence.

73. Xue wrote at the outset of her "Suggestions" that Chen Jitong brought her the "Provisional Regulations" on 24 November 1897 ("Chuangshe Nü xuetang tiaoyi bing xu," *Qiushi bao* 9, 6a). She must have drafted the "Suggestions" soon thereafter, and it should be considered the earliest (and surely the most thorough) woman's response to the campaign. It was also among the first writings by a woman in the reform era to be widely circulated by the modern news media. Others are Kang Tongwei, "Nüxue libi shuo" (preliminary version in *Xinwen bao* [3 Dec. 1897]; revised in *Nü xuebao* 7 [Sept. 1898]); Zheng Qimei, "Zhongguo yi zhengxing nüshu shuo" (On the necessity of establishing girls' schools in China, 1897; quoted in *Xinwen bao* editorial, "Lun nü xuetang" [9 Dec. 1897]); Pan Daofang, "Lun Zhongguo yi chuangshe nü yixue" (On the necessity of establishing public girls' schools in China, *Xianggang xunhuan bao* [18 Nov. 1897]; reprinted in Jing, ed., *Nüxue jiyi chubian*, 36a–37b).

74. Liang Qichao, "Changshe nü xuetang qi,"3b; see also Jing, ed., *Nüxue jiyi chubian*, 38b, 39a, 40a.

75. Xue, "Chuangshe Nü xuetang tiaoyi bing xu," *Qiushi bao* 9, 6a–6b.

76. *Nü xuebao* 1 (24 July 1898): 3a.

77. Ibid.

78. Ibid.

79. See Lackner and Vittinghoff, eds., *Mapping Meanings*, for a discussion of the "New Learning" as a "disunified occupation," marked by encounters between Chinese and Western thinkers that were reciprocal and transcultural, blurring the distinction between what was "indigenous" and what was "foreign." See also the insightful review of this volume by Susan Mann in the *China Review International* 12.1 (Spring 2005): 147–51.

80. Cf. Vittinghoff: "The nativisation of Western knowledge in China was influenced, restricted, or engendered by such diverging factors as institutional frameworks, structures of classifying knowledge, ideological interests and indigenous exigencies. However, as many of the contributions in this volume show, a large part of these alternative ways of perceiving and actualizing the new and foreign in a familiar context, have largely been obliterated by the ideological radicalization in the early twentieth century, which established intellectual homogenization and did not allow for ambivalences" (in Lackner and Vittinghoff, eds., *Mapping Meanings*, 4).

81. *Liji* [*zhengyi*], *Daxue*: "On Tang's bathtub were engraved the following words: 'If you can one day renovate yourself, then do so from day to day! Always

keep renovating yourself!' The 'Decree of Kang' instructs: 'Encourage people to renovate themselves!' The *Book of Songs* has the following lines: 'Although Zhou is an old state, it is destined for self-renewal.' Therefore, the superior man (*junzi*) tries his utmost to do everything he can [to renovate himself]" (湯之《盤銘》曰: "苟日新, 日日新, 又日新。"《康誥》曰: "作新民。"《詩》曰: "周雖舊邦, 其命惟新。"是故君子無所不用其極) (in Ruan Yuan, ed., *Shisanjing zhushu, juan* 60, 2:1673; cf. *The Great Learning*, Legge, trans., *The Chinese Classics*, 1:361–62).

82. Xue, "Chuangshe Nü xuetang tiaoyi bing xu," *Qiushi bao* 9, 6b.

83. *Side* was first systematically defined in Ban Zhao's *Nüjie*, in which she advised: "To guard carefully her chastity, to control circumspectly her behavior, in every motion to exhibit modesty, and to model each act on the best usage—this is womanly virtue. To choose her words with care, to avoid vulgar language, to speak at appropriate times, and not to weary others with much conversation may be called the characteristics of womanly words. To wash and scrub filth away, to keep clothes and ornaments fresh and clean, to wash the head and bathe the body regularly, and to keep the person free from disgraceful filth may be called the characteristics of womanly bearing. With wholehearted devotion to sew and to weave, to love not gossip and silly laughter, in cleanliness and order to prepare the wine and food for serving guests may be called the characteristics of womanly work. These four qualifications characterize the greatest virtue of a woman. No woman can afford to be without them" (清閑貞靜, 守節整齊, 行己有恥, 動靜有法, 是謂婦德。擇辭而說, 不道惡語, 時然後言, 不厭於人, 是謂婦言。盥浣塵穢, 服飾鮮絜, 沐浴以時, 身不垢辱, 是謂婦容。專心紡績, 不好戲笑, 絜齊酒食, 以奉賓客, 是謂婦功。此四者, 女人之大德, 而不可乏之者也) (Ban Zhao, *Nüjie*, quoted in Fan Ye, *Hou-Han shu*, "Lienü zhuan," *juan* 84, 10:2789; Swann, trans., "Lessons for Women," 537–38).

84. Xue, "Chuangshe Nü xuetang tiaoyi bing xu," *Qiushi bao* 9, 6b–7a.

85. Wanyan Yun Zhu, comp., *Guochao guixiu zhengshiji*, "Bianyan," 1a.

86. On these traditions, see Ko, *Teachers of the Inner Chamber*; and Mann, *Precious Records*. On Yun Zhu's compilation of the *Guochao guixiu zhengshi ji* and its connection to women's literary culture, see Mann, *Precious Records*, 94–117. See also Xiaorong Li, "Gender and Textual Politics during the Qing Dynasty."

87. For a discussion of the origin and development of "having no talent is women's virtue" in the Ming-Qing period, see Liu Yongcong [Clara Wing-chung Ho], *De, cai, se, quan*, 165–252.

88. Liang, "Lun Nüxue," *Shiwu bao* 23, 2a.

89. See Jing, ed., *Nüxue jiyi chubian*, 4a, 41a.

90. Judge, "Reforming the Feminine," 165.

91. As recounted by Xue's daughter Chen Yun in her preface to *Xiao daixuan lunshi shi*, 1b.

92. See Xue, "Chuangshe Nü xuetang tiaoyi bing xu," *Qiushi bao* 9, 7a–7b.

93. Ibid., 6b–7b; 10 (28 Dec. 1897): 8a–8b; Xue, "Yu Hu Jin'an Xue nüshi shang Nüxue tangdong tiaoyi bing xu," *Xinwen bao* (17 Jan. 1898).

94. Xue, "Chuangshe Nü xuetang tiaoyi bing xu," *Qiushi bao* 9, 7b.

95. Xue, "Yu Hu Jin'an Xue nüshi shang Nüxue tangdong tiaoyi bing xu," *Xinwen bao* (17 Jan. 1898).

96. Xue, "Chuangshe Nü xuetang tiaoyi bing xu," *Qiushi bao* 10, 8b.

97. *Xinwen bao* (3 Dec. 1897).

98. Lai and Shen, "Zhongguo Nü xuehui shushu zhangcheng," *Xinwen bao* (17, 19, 20 Mar. 1898).

99. Jing, ed., *Nüxue jiyi chubian*, "Yuanqi," 3b–4a.

100. Liang Qichao et al., "Nü xuetang shiban lüezhang."

101. Huters, "A New Way of Writing," 245.

102. Xie Zirong [M. E. Sheffield], "Taixi zhi xue youyi yu Zhonghua lun," 7a. Sheffield attended the Third Triennial Meeting of the Educational Association of China, held in Shanghai in May 1899. There he strongly urged Western women to support the education of Chinese women, to encourage them to "stand on their feet"; see *Records of the Third Triennial Meeting of the Educational Association of China*, 163.

103. "Lun Zhongguo nüxue," 49a.

104. Xue, "Chuangshe Nü xuetang tiaoyi bing xu," *Qiushi bao* 9, 6b–7a.

105. See ibid., 7a–7b; "Yu Hu Jin'an Xue nüshi shang Nüxue tangdong tiaoyi bing xu," *Xinwen bao* (15–16 Jan. 1898).

106. See, for instance, Jing, ed., *Nüxue jiyi chubian*, 4a.

107. See *Xinwen bao* (5, 7, and 9 June, 1898), "Fuzhang" (21 Apr. 1898).

108. Fang Xuanling et al., *Jinshu*, "Lienü zhuan": "Wei Cheng's mother, Song . . . was born into a Confucian family. Her mother died while she was young. Her father raised her and taught her to read and interpret the *Zhou Rituals* (*Zhouguan*). . . . [The late Qin ruler Fu Jian (r. 365–83)] set up a lecture hall at her home and enrolled 120 students under her [supervision]. She lectured them behind a gauze curtain" (*juan* 96, 8:2521–22).

109. Alluding to the mother and wife of King Wen, who educated future sages with their virtuous, admirable voices (*huyini* 徽音); see *Mao Shi* [*zhengyi*], "Daya," "Siqi" 思齊 (Emulation), in *Shisanjing zhushu, juan* 16, 1:516.

110. *Chongyi*, literally, "multiple translations," refers to foreign countries of different cultures; see Sima Qian, *Shiji*, "Taishi gong zixu" 太史公自序 (Autobiography of the Grand Historian), *juan* 130, 10:3299.

111. See Ban Gu, *Hanshu*, "Yang Xiong zhuan" 揚雄傳: "[Yang Xiong] was poor but was addicted to wine. . . . Some curious people brought wine and food to befriend him and to study with him" (*juan* 87, 11:3585).

112. Jing, ed., *Nüxue jiyi chubian*, 44b.

113. On the life and work of Lady Zheng, wife of the Tang minister Houmochen Miao 侯莫陳邈, see Yongrong, Ji Yun et al., eds., *Siku quanshu zongmu tiyao*, "Zibu" 子部 (Philosophers), "Rujialei" 儒家類 (Confucian school), "Cunmu" 存目 (Preserved titles), *juan* 95, 1:801. On the life and work of Song Ruoshen 宋若莘, see Liu Xu et al., *Jiu Tangshu*, "Houfei zhuan" 后妃傳 (Biographies of imperial consorts and concubines), *juan* 52, 7:2198; Ouyang Xiu and Song Qi, *Xin Tangshu*, "Houfei zhuan," *juan* 77, 11:3508. On the life and work of Empress Xu, wife of Emperor Chengzu of the Ming (r. 1403–24), see Zhang Tingyu et al., *Mingshi*, "Houfei zhuan," *juan* 113,

12:3509–11. On the life and work of Lady Liu, mother of Wang Xiang (*js.* 1521) who edited the *Nü sishu* as well as a detailed study of the *Nü sishu* and the *Nü Xiaojing*, see Yamazaki Jun'ichi, *Kyōiku kara mita Chūgoku joseishi shiryō no kenkyū.*

114. See Liu Kunyi, "Guangxu ershsi nian qiyue ershjiu ri liangjiang zongdu Liu Kunyi pian" 光緒二十四年七月二十九日兩江總督劉坤一片 (The governor-general of Jiangsu, Anhui, and Jiangxi, Liu Kunyi's memorandum to the court, 14 Sept. 1898), in Zhu Youhuan, ed., *Zhongguo jindai xuezhi shiliao*, 2:904; "Shanghai chuangshe Zhongguo Nü xuetang ji," 1b.

115. See "Shanghai chuangshe Zhongguo Nü xuetang ji," 1b–2a; Burton, *Education of Women in China*, 108–9.

116. Kang and Shi are named as possible instructors of Western knowledge in Section 27 of the "Provisional Regulations"; see Liang et al., "Nü xuetang shiban lüezhang."

117. Liang Qichao, "Ji Jiangxi Kang nüshi," 2b.

118. See ibid., 2b–3a; Hu, *Tales of Translation*, 124–25. On the significance of Kang Aide's career to China's modernity, see ibid. Hu probes several sources of information on Kang's life, including Liang Qichao's biography, but does not examine Kang's direct response to Liang.

119. The idea that Confucius sought to reestablish the Three Dynasties' educational institutions for women was often repeated in male reformist discourse; see, for instance, Liang, "Changshe nü xuetang qi," 4a; and Section 1 of Liang et al., "Nü xuetang shiban lüezhang."

120. *Lunyu* 17.25, *Lunyu* [*yizhu*], 191.

121. Kahn and Stone, "Correspondence to the Report 'The New Chinese Girls' School,'" 17.

122. The report and the translation of the "Provisional Regulations" are in *North China Herald and Supreme Court and Consular Gazette*, 59.1586 (24 Dec. 1897): 1123–24 and 1138–39, respectively.

123. Kahn and Stone, "Correspondence to the Report 'The New Chinese Girls' School,'" 16. Xia Xiaohong suggests that Kang and Shi were reluctant because of their Christian faith (see "Zhong Xi hebi de Shanghai 'Zhongguo Nü xuetang,'" 79). They themselves declared, however: "We have seen other countries and learned of the Sages of other ancient lands . . . yet we can truly say that we honour none as we do our own Confucius." But they also pointed out that "honour to the best of human beings is not an unmixed blessing when it creates an idol and holds the eyes of the devotees down to earth. We do not think it the sentiment that will make the education of women successful or even safe" ("Correspondence," 17).

124. See Hu, "Naming the First 'New Woman,'" 205. Hu points out that women's missionary work "gained momentum in conjunction with abolition: the correlation between the biblical arguments in support of women's work ('female reform') and against slavery (abolitionism) strengthened both causes. Indeed, it was soon after the Civil War that the Women's Foreign Missionary Society was formed (1870); Gertrude Howe became one of the first missionaries to China (1873) under its auspices" (205–6).

125. Liang, "Changshe nü xuetang qi," 3b.

126. Section 1 of Liang et al., "Nü xuetang shiban lüezhang."

127. Liang et al., "Nü xuetang shiban lüezhang."

128. Xue, "Chuangshe Nü xuetang tiaoyi bing xu," *Qiushi bao* 10, 8a.

129. *Nü xuebao* 5 (27 Aug. 1898): 2a–2b. On the theoretical basis of Wang Chunh lin's argument, see *Zhuangzi* [*jishi*], "Xiaoyao you," and the commentary of Guo Xiang (fl. late third century) on "free roaming" as "self-contentment" (*zizu*), in *Zhuangzi* [*jishi*], *juan* 1A, 1:1.

130. *Nü xuebao* 5 (27 Aug. 1898): 3a.

131. *Nü xuebao* 8 (Sept. 1898): 2a–2b.

132. Howe, trans., "The Provisional Prospectus of the Chinese Girls' School," a variant translation of the "Nü xuetang shiban lüezhang," 54.

133. *Xinwen bao* (28 Nov. 1897).

134. See, for example, the lists of those attending the first meeting of the Nü xue-hui on 6 December 1897 (*Xinwen bao* [9 Dec. 1897]) and those subscribing to the Nü xuetang fund (*Xinwen bao* [18 Nov. 1897]). That men reformers wished women to sign their names in this traditional way is made clear in Section 23 of the "Provisional Regulations" (Liang et al., "Nü xuetang shiban lüezhang").

135. *Dianshi zhai huabao*, Category "Li" 利, 5.39, under the title "Qunchai dahui" 裙釵大會 (A grand meeting of ladies). For a full translation of the caption, see Yeh, "The Life Style of Four *Wenren* in Late Qing Shanghai," 446.

136. *Nü xuebao* 3 (15 Aug. 1898): 2a. Similarly, Sui Nianqu's essay "Suishi tanbing" 睢氏論兵 (Sui on military affairs) argued that women were equally capable of acting in this typically male domain; see *Nü xuebao* 6 (6 Sept. 1898): 2a–3a.

Chapter Five

1. Guo Yanli believes that Xue understood foreign languages; see his *Zhongguo jindai fanyi wenxue gailun*, 168–69. Xue herself, however, stated as late as 1892 that she "knows no Western words" (Xue Shaohui, *Daiyunlou yiji, Ciji, juan* B, 6a). Chen Shoupeng acknowledges that "in writing classical Chinese, I am far inferior to my wife" ("Wangqi Xue gongren zhuanlüe," 1a). Chen Qiang et al., "Xianbi Xue gongren nianpu," also records how Chen's friends joked about his indebtedness to his "inner-chamber assistant" (*neizhu* 內助) in essay writing (6a).

2. See Xue Shaohui and Chen Shoupeng, *Waiguo lienü zhuan*, frontispiece, Xue's "Xu," 1a–1b, and Chen's "Yili" (Translation notes), 1a; Chen et al., "Xianbi Xue gongren nianpu," 11a. Reference to the influence of the *Waiguo lienü zhuan* (hereafter *WGLNZ*) awaits more research. We know, at least, the post-Mao era *Renmin ribao* 人民日報 (People's daily) (13 Jan. 1981) credited it for the earliest introduction to the American woman writer Harriet Beecher Stowe (1811–96), the author of *Uncle Tom's Cabin*.

3. See Xue, "Chuangshe Nü xuetang tiaoyi bing xu," *Qiushi bao* 9 (18 Dec. 1897): 6b.

4. *WGLNZ*, Xue's "Xu," 1a.

5. Ibid., 1a.

6. Chen et al., "Xianbi Xue gongren nianpu," 11a.

7. *WGLNZ*, Xue's "Xu," 1a–1b, Chen's "Yili," 1a–2a, and "Zongmu" (General contents).

8. As shown in the entry of Deborah, wife of Lapidoth and a Hebrew prophet, in *WGLNZ, juan* 8, 1a; see also the Bible, *Book of Judges*, chaps. 4 and 5.

9. The *WGLNZ* follows Elwood for the lives of Mary Wortley Montagu (1690 [1689]–1762; standard dating follows the Library of Congress catalogue, bracketed here and in text below); Elizabeth Carter (1717–1806); Sarah Trimmer (1741–1810); Anne Letitia Barbauld (1743–1825); Anne Grant (1755–1838); Ann Ward Radcliffe (1764–1823); Jane Austen (1776 [1775]–1817); and Felicia Dorothea Hemans (1793–1835).

10. Some recognizable cases of this sort include: Behn, *All the Histories and Novels Written by the Late Ingenious Mrs. Behn*; Montagu, *The Letters and Works of Lady Mary Wortley Montagu*, edited and published by her great-grandson, Lord Wharncliffe, in 1837; Barbauld, *The Works of Anna Letitia Barbauld* (1825 edn.); Staël-Holstein, *Œuvres Complètes de Mme. La Baronne de Staël, publiées par son fils* (1820 edn.); Hemans, *The Works of Mrs. Hemans. with a Memoir by Her Sister, and an Essay on Her Genius by Mrs. Sigourney* (1840 edn.); Bremer, *Life, Letters, and Posthumous Works of Fredrika Bremer*, edited by her sister Charlotte Bremer (1868 edn.); Martineau, *Harriet Martineau's Autobiography, with Memorials by Maria Weston Chapman* (1877 edn.); Landon, *Life and Literary Remains of L.E.L. [Letitia Elizabeth Landon]*, edited by Laman Blanchard (1804–45) (1841 edn.); Howe, *Margaret Fuller (Marchesa Ossoli)* (1883 edn.); Somerville, *Personal Recollections, from Early Life to Old Age, of Mary Somerville*, edited by her daughter, Martha Somerville (1874 edn.); du Deffand, *Letters of the Marquise du Deffand to the Hon. Horace Walpole*, published from the originals at Strawberry Hill (1810 edn.); Lespinasse, *Lettres de Mademoiselle de Lespinasse* (1809 edn.); and so forth.

11. As far as I can tell, most of the English and French biographical works on women by the late 1800s include at most dozens of entries; the only comparable one is Sarah Josepha Buell Hale, *Woman's Record* (1860), containing about 1,800 entries. Xue and Chen cited it as Hale's major work in her *WGLNZ* entry but did not use it as a source.

12. For instance, Lynn M. Osen states in her 1974 *Women in Mathematics*: "Much has been written about the compelling problems of women in political and economic fields; less attention has centered on women in mathematics and the 'hard sciences'" (ix). Yet five out of eight women in Osen's work had entries in the *WGLNZ*, in full recognition of their scientific contributions and accomplishments. Similarly, Madeleine Mary Henry observes in her 1995 *Prisoner of History* that the historical possibilities for Aspasia's life and the ebb and surge of her biographical tradition "have never before been seriously and comprehensively examined; they are the subject of my study. It is time to remember Aspasia's place in the history of women and of feminist epistemology" (3). Aspasia, however, has an extensive entry in the *WGLNZ* (*juan* 7, 1a–1b), written in a strongly feminist tone.

13. Mann, *Precious Records*, 2.

14. According to its earliest extant version, edited by the Song scholar Wang Hui in 1063, the categories of Liu Xiang's *Lienü zhuan* include: 1) *Muyi* 母儀 (Maternal rectitude); 2) *Xianming* 賢明 (Worthiness and intelligence); 3) *Renzhi* 仁智 (Benevolence and wisdom); 4) *Zhenshun* 貞順 (Chastity and subservience); 5) *Jieyi* 節義 (Integrity and righteousness); 6) *Biantong* 辯通 (Eloquence and erudition); and 7) *Niebi* 孽嬖 (Vicious and depraved women) (Liu Xiang, [*Gu*] *Lienü zhuan*, 101: 673–74). Translation of the first and the seventh titles follows Raphals, *Sharing the Light*, 263, 266.

15. *WGLNZ*, Chen's "Yili," 1a.

16. See ibid., 1a–1b. Chen's observation may have come from his reading experience. Western biographic works of women rarely adopt moral categories, as shown in Strickland, *Lives of the Queens* (1840–48); Elwood, *Memoirs of the Literary Ladies* (1843); Goodrich, *World-Famous Women* (1879); Goodrich, *Lives of Celebrated Women* (1844); Parton et al., *Eminent Women of the Age* (1869); and so forth.

17. *WGLNZ*, Chen's "Yili," 1b–2a.

18. Ibid., Xue's "Xu," 1a, 1b.

19. Ibid., 1b.

20. Emperor Taizong of the Tang said: "We use bronze as a mirror to straighten our clothes and cap, the past as a mirror to understand the rise and fall of states, and a person as a mirror to recognize our merits and faults. I have always maintained these three mirrors to prevent myself from making mistakes"; Liu Su, *Sui-Tang jiahua*, 7; quoted from Wechsler, trans., *Mirror to the Son of Heaven*, vi, modified.

21. *WGLNZ*, Xue's "Xu," 1b, and Chen's "Yili," 1a.

22. For a detailed discussion of Xue's redefinition of female virtue in reference to Western women's lives, see also Qian, "'Borrowing Foreign Mirrors and Candles to Illuminate Chinese Civilization.'"

23. *WGLNZ*, Chen's "Yili," 1b.

24. Ko, *Teachers of the Inner Chambers*, 123.

25. William Smith recounts: "Statues were erected to Corinna in different parts of Greece, and she was ranked as the first and most distinguished of the nine lyrical Muses. She was surnamed Μυῖα (the Fly)" (in *Dictionary of Greek and Roman Biography and Mythology*, 1:852). For Pausanias and Pindar, see also ibid., 3:157–59, 367–70.

26. Cao Pi, *Dianlun*, juan 52, 3:720.

27. As termed in the *Xunzi*, "Zhengming" 正名 (Rectifying names): "To speak with a benevolent mind (*renxin*); to listen with a diligent mind (*xuexin*); to discern with a fair mind (*gongxin*)" (以仁心說, 以學心聽, 以公心辨) (*Xunzi* [*jijie*], juan 16, 282).

28. See Guo, *Zhongguo jindai fanyi wenxue gailun*, 22–31.

29. Yan Fu and Xia Zengyou 夏曾佑, "Benguan fuyin shuobu yuanqi" 本館附印說部緣起, *Guowen bao* (10 Nov.–11 Dec. 1897), quoted in Chen Pingyuan and Xia Xiaohong, eds., *Ershi shiji Zhongguo xiaoshuo lilun ziliao*, 1:12. See also Guo, *Zhongguo jindai fanyi wenxue gailun*, 28.

30. See Zeng Pu, "Zeng xiansheng dashu."

31. Ban Gu, *Hanshu*, "Yiwen zhi," juan 30, 6:1745. J. A. Cuddon defines fiction

as "a vague and general term for an imaginative work, usually in prose. At any rate, it does not normally cover poetry and drama though both are a form of fiction in that they are molded and contrived—or feigned. Fiction is now used in general of the novel, the short story, the *novella* (*qq.v.*) and related genres" (*A Dictionary of Literary Terms* [Penguin Books, 1982, 1987], s.v. "Fiction"). For the evolution of the concept of *xiaoshuo*, see Wang Qizhou, "Zhongguo xiaoshuo qiyuan tanji," 12–23; and Laura Hua Wu, "From *Xiaoshuo* to Fiction," 339–71.

32. For reasons unknown, Xue included Sappho in this group, obviously mistaking her for a man.

33. Cf. Elwood, *Memoirs of the Literary Ladies*, 2:185; Scott, "Miss Austen's Novels," *Miscellaneous Prose Works*, 18:209–49.

34. Xue's definition of scholarly achievements follows the traditional *liuyi* 六藝 (six subjects) as defined in the *Zhouli* 周禮 (Zhou rituals), including *li* 禮 (ritual), *yue* 樂 (music), *she* 射 (archery), *yu* 御 (charioteering), *shu* 書 (writing), and *shu* 數 (mathematics); see *Zhouli* [*zhushu*], "Diguan" 地官 (Official of earth), "Baoshi" 保氏 (Grand guardian) (*juan* 14, 1:731).

35. Smith, *Dictionary*, 1:391.

36. Such as the German astronomer Caroline Lucretia Herschel (1750–1848) (*juan* 3, 3b), the English scholar Elizabeth Carter, the Scottish poet Joanne Baillie (1762–1851) (*juan* 4, 6b–7a), the Irish writer Maria Edgeworth (1767–1849) (*juan* 4, 8b–9a), the English novelist Jane Austen, the English writer Elizabeth Braddon (1827 [1837]–[1915]) (*juan* 4, 25b–26a), and the American doctor Elizabeth Blackwell (1821–[1910]) (*juan* 5, 4b–5a).

37. As Xue records, Émilie du Châtelet's major achievement was her French translation of the works of Sir Isaac Newton (1642–1727) (*juan* 4, 3b–4a).

38. See the entries on the French writers Anne-Louise-Germaine Staël-Holstein, *juan* 4, 7b–8a, and Amantine Lucile Aurore Dudevant (aka George Sand, 1804–1876), *juan* 4, 17b–18a; and the German writer Luise Aston (1814–71), *juan* 4, 24b.

39. For the *qichu/qi zhitiao* 七出／棄之條, see, for example, He Xiu's commentary on the sentence, "to be divorced is termed 'to come back'" (大歸曰來歸), in *Chunqiu Gongyang zhuan* [*zhushu*], the twenty-seventh year of the reign of Duke Zhuang, *juan* 8, 2:2239.

40. Except for the Wei-Jin, when social norms for women were less restrictive than in other times, as Ge Hong noted: "Today's women . . . abandon their domestic responsibilities and socialize with people" (今俗婦女, . . . 舍中饋之事, 修周旋之好) (*Baopu zi*, "Waipian" 外篇 [Outer chapters], "Jimiu" 疾謬 [Reprimanding faux pas], *juan* 25, 148).

41. See, for instance, Mme. du Deffand's life sketch included in *Letters of the Marquise du Deffand to the Hon. Horace Walpole*, xix–lxv. Xue and Chen cited this work in the *WGLNZ* and followed its details about Mme. du Deffand as well as about Julie de Lespinasse.

42. See also Smith, *Dictionary*, 1:386, s.v. "Aspasia"; and Plutarch, *Lives*, "Pericles," 317ff. Xue and Chen also cited Thucydides' *The History of the Peloponnesian War* for background reference.

43. For Xue's poems related to late Ming Qinhuai courtesans, see Xue, *Daiyun-lou yiji, Shiji, juan* 2, 8b–9a, 10a–10b; for Sai Jinhua, see ibid., *juan* 2, 6b–8b.

44. Scott, "Mrs. Ann Radcliffe," *Miscellaneous Prose Works*, 3:355.

45. Toland, *Hypatia*, frontispiece.

46. For the rising frenzy about *nüjie* that quickly superseded *cainü* at the turn of the twentieth century, see Qian, "The Mother *Nü Xuebao* Versus the Daughter *Nü Xuebao.*"

47. Xia Xiaohong, "Yingci nüjie qin chuaimo," 88.

48. Dobson, *Four Frenchwomen*, 35–36. This is about the closest reference to the *WGLNZ* account of Madame Roland in terms of the publication date and content.

49. Liang Qichao, "Luolan furen zhuan," 6:1; trans. quoted from Hu, *Tales of Translation*, 172, modified.

50. Yao Feng 么鳳, "Yongshi bashou" 詠史八首 (Chanting on history, eight poems), no. 7, in *Zhongguo xinnüjie zazhi* 中國新女界雜誌 (Journal of new Chinese women) 3 (Apr. 1907), quoted in Xia, "Yingci nüjie qin chuaimo," 90.

51. Dobson, *Four Frenchwomen*, 59.

52. As termed by Katie Conboy, "Introduction," in Conboy et al., eds., *Writing on the Body*, 7.

53. Xue's account is similar to that in Smith, *Dictionary*, 2:658–59.

54. Xue, "Nü xuebao xu," 3a. *Laozi Dao de jing* [*zhu*], chap. 25: "[Dao] can be taken as the mother of all under heaven" (1:63).

55. Xue never fails to specify the Greek heritage of other goddesses in Roman mythology; she points out that, for instance, Venus is in fact Aphrodite and "Minerva in Rome is similar to Athena in Greece" (*WGLNZ, juan* 8, 5b, 12b).

56. Xue seems unhappy with Hera being described as ox-eyed, which is, however, merely a typical Homeric epithet for Hera, as in the *Iliad*, "Then the goddess the Ox-eyed lady Hera answered" (Homer, *Iliad*, 73).

57. Nemesis is the goddess of vengeance (*Compact Edition of the Oxford English Dictionary* [Oxford: Oxford University Press, 1971], s.v. "Nemesis"), but Xue avoids mentioning this, possibly because she does not want this negative identity to undermine the overall positive images established in the chapter on goddesses.

58. Smith, *Dictionary*, 1:398.

59. *Laozi Dao de jing* [*zhu*], chaps. 6 and 10, 1:16, 23; translation by Lau, trans., *Lao Tzu Tao Te Ching*, 62, 66.

60. *Compact Edition of The Oxford English Dictionary* (1971), s.v. "Nymph": "1. Myth. One of a numerous class of semi-divine beings, imagined as beautiful maidens inhabiting the sea, rivers, fountains, hills, woods, or trees, and frequently introduced by the poets as attendants on a superior deity."

61. *WGLNZ*, Xue's "Xu," 1b–2a.

Chapter Six

1. For a rough reference, among the poems of 871 men and 65 women from the Tongzhi to the Xuantong reigns collected in Qian Zhonglian, *Qingshi jishi*, vols. 17–22, only seven poems are about modern science and technology. As for parallel

prose, of the sixty-seven essays by the leading late Qing *pianwen* essayists collected in Shen Zongqi, ed., *Lian'an pianti wenxuan*, none is on science or technology.

2. Xue Shaohui and Chen Shoupeng, trans., *Bashi ri huanyou ji*, Chen's "Xu," 1a.

3. Xue Shaohui, *Daiyunlou yiji*, *Wenji*, Xue Sihui's "Xu," 1b.

4. Liu Xie, *Wenxin diaolong* [*zhu*], "Shilei" 事類 (Allusions), commentary by Fan Wenlan, *juan* 8, 2:614.

5. Ibid., "Lici" 麗辭 (Parallelism), *juan* 7, 2:588. See also Liu Hsieh, *The Literary Mind and the Carving of Dragons*, 369.

6. Liu Xie, *Wenxin diaolong* [*zhu*], "Shilei," *juan* 8, 2:615.

7. Shen Zongqi, a leading late Qing man of letters himself, aligned Xue with the best late Qing parallel-prose writers, all men, by including two of her parallel-prose essays, "Huiluan song" (1901) and "Fu Shen nüshi shu" (1898?), in his *Lian'an pianti wenxuan*, *juan* 3, 28a–31b. For a close reading of these two essays, see Chapter Eight.

8. Chen Shoupeng, trans., *Zhongguo jianghai xianyao tuzhi*, "Zixu" 自敍 (Self-preface), 5b. The "Zixu" was dated early 1900 after Shoupeng completed the translation, which was first published in 1901 by Jingshi wenshe in Shanghai.

9. Ibid., "Juanshou" 卷首 (frontispiece), Xue's "Houxu" 後序 (postscript), 7b; also in Xue, *Daiyunlou yiji*, *Wenji*, *juan* B, 2b. Chinese text follows *Wenji*.

10. See *Chunqiu Zuozhuan* [*zhengyi*], the twenty-third year of Duke Xi 僖, *juan* 15, 2:1815.

11. Shen Yue, *Songshu*, "Zang Zhi zhuan" 臧質傳, *juan* 74, 7:1912.

12. See Chen, trans., *Zhongguo jianghai xianyao tuzhi*, "Juanshou," Xue's "Houxu," 7b–8b; also in Xue, *Daiyunlou yiji*, *Wenji*, *juan* B, 3a–5a.

13. *Laozi*, chap. 5: "Is not the space between heaven and earth like a bellows? It is empty without being exhausted: The more it works the more comes out" (天地之間, 其猶橐籥乎? 虛而不屈, 動而愈出); chap. 39: "Heaven in virtue of the One is pure; Earth in virtue of the One is peaceful; . . . the myriad creatures in virtue of the One are alive" (天得一以清, 地得一以寧 . . . 萬物得一以生) (*Laozi Dao de jing* [*zhu*], 1:14, 106; translation by Lau, *Lao Tzu Tao Te Ching*, 61, 100 [modified]).

14. Xue's "Houxu," 7b, in Chen, trans., *Zhongguo jianghai xianyao tuzhi*; also in Xue, *Daiyunlou yiji*, *Wenji*, *juan* B, 3a.

15. See Fan Ye, *Hou-Han shu*, "Zhang Heng zhuan" 張衡傳, *juan* 59, 7:1897–98.

16. Liu Xu et al., *Jiu Tangshu*, "Tianwen zhi" 天文志 (Treatise on astronomy) I, *juan* 35, 4:1304, 1307.

17. Referring to Li Ye 李冶 (1192–1279), *Ceyuan haijing* 測圓海鏡, which is "the first systematic work" on "the 'celestial element' (*tianyuan* 天元) method," for "finding the diameters of circles inscribed in or cutting the sides of right-angled triangles from the lengths of the sides" (Li and Du, *Chinese Mathematics*, 114).

18. Referring to Liu Hui 劉徽 (fl. 263), *Haidao suanjing* 海島算經, which uses the method of "double differences" (*chongcha* 重差) "for finding heights or surveying great depths while knowing the distances" (Li and Du, *Chinese Mathematics*, 75).

19. Xue's "Houxu," 7b–8a, in Chen, trans., *Zhongguo jianghai xianyao tuzhi*; also in Xue, *Daiyunlou yiji*, *Wenji*, *juan* B, 3a–3b.

20. Xue's "Houxu," 8b, in Chen, trans., *Zhongguo jianghai xianyao tuzhi*; also in Xue, *Daiyunlou yiji, Wenji, juan* B, 4b–5a. The last couplet refers to *Lunyu*, 1.10: "When the Master arrives in a state, he invariably gets to know its government" (*Lunyu* [*yizhu*], 6; quoted from Lau, trans., *Confucius: The Analects*, 60).

21. For "*polan*," see Tuotuo et al., *Songshi*, "Shihuo zhi xia ba" 食貨志下八 (Treatise on economics and finances, B, 8): "The Hu people count 300 *jin* [1 *jin* = ca. 500 grams] as one *polan*. The biggest ship is called Duqiang and may carry one thousand polan" (*juan* 186, 13:4565). For "Kunlun zhi bo," Ōmi no Mifune records that in 750 Monk Jianzhen arrived in Guangzhou en route to Japan and saw "in the river numerous ships from India, Persia, Kunlun, etc., all loaded with fragrances, herbs, and treasures, piled up like mountains" (*Tang Da heshang dongzheng ji*, 74).

22. Xue's "Houxu," 8b, in Chen, trans., *Zhongguo jianghai xianyao tuzhi*; also in Xue, *Daiyunlou yiji, Wenji, juan* B, 5a.

23. Xue's "Houxu," 8a, in Chen, trans., *Zhongguo jianghai xianyao tuzhi*; also in Xue, *Daiyunlou yiji, Wenji, juan* B, 4a.

24. Xue's "Houxu," 8a, in Chen, trans., *Zhongguo jianghai xianyao tuzhi*; also in Xue, *Daiyunlou yiji, Wenji, juan* B, 4a.

25. In Wang Wei, *Wang Wei ji* [*jiaozhu*], *juan* 2, 1:191.

26. See also Mather, trans., *A New Account of Tales of the World*, 71.

27. "Fish" alludes to *Yuefu shiji*, "Xianghe geci" 相和歌辭 (Songs of harmony), "Yinma changcheng ku xing" 飲馬長城窟行 (Watering horses at the breech in the Great Wall): "Telling my son to cook the carp, / We see inside of the fish a letter on a piece of white silk" (呼兒烹鯉魚, 中有尺素書) (*juan* 38, 2:556). "Geese" alludes to Ban Gu, *Hanshu*, "Su Wu zhuan": "[A subordinate of Su Wu] told the Han envoy to tell the Chanyu [of the Huns] that the Han emperor shot down a goose in the imperial garden, with a letter on silk attached to its foot" (*juan* 54, 8:2466).

28. Xue, "*Nanyang riri guanbao* xuli," *Nanyang riri guanbao* (2 Aug. 1905): front page; also in Xue, *Daiyunlou yiji, Wenji, juan* B, 7a.

29. *Laozi*, chap. 36, *Lao zi Dao de jing* [*zhu*], 1:89.

30. See Liu Linsheng, *Zhongguo pianwen shi*, 123–44.

31. See Xue and Chen, trans., *Bashi ri huanyou ji*, Chen's "Xu," 1. William Butcher confirms that the first English translation "of high quality" of *Le tour du monde en quatre-vingts jours* into *Around the World in Eighty Days* was by George M. Towle and N. d'Anvers (London: Sampson Low, 1873); see Verne, *The Extraordinary Journeys*, xl. The earliest Sampson Low edition (1874) I have located so far only has Towle as the translator. Discussion in this chapter will cite the chapter and page numbers of this edition and the *juan* and page numbers of Xue and Chen's Chinese translation.

32. Guo Yanli, "Nüxing zai 20 shiji chuqi de wenxue fanyi chengjiu," 39.

33. In *Xin xiaoshuo* 新小說 (New fiction) 17 (1905), collected in Chen Pingyuan and Xia Xiaohong, eds., *Ershi shiji Zhongguo xiaoshuo lilun ziliao*, 1:154.

34. See Jin Tianyu, *Tianfanglou shiji*, attached to his *Tianfanglou wenyan*, 2a–2b.

35. Xue and Chen, trans., *Bashi ri huanyou ji*, Xue's "Xu," 2a–2b; also in Xue, *Daiyunlou yiji, Wenji, juan* A, 13a–14a.

36. Xue and Chen, trans., *Bashi ri huanyou ji*, Chen's "Xu," 1.

37. Ibid.

38. Recorded in Liu Fu, *Qingsuo gaoyi, juan* 6, 61.

39. Smith, *Mapping China*, 83.

40. Calcutta (Kolkata) is located on the east bank of the Hooghly River, a distributary of the Ganges River. Xue here only indicates the Ganges (Henghe) for it is more familiar to the Chinese through Buddhism.

41. See Ling Hongxun, *Zhonghua tielu shi*, 4–10. In their annotations to the railroad construction in America, Xue and Shoupeng did not mention the participation of Chinese workers, possibly because they did not consider it relevant. Undoubtedly Xue and her circles were the earliest among the Chinese elite to recognize the importance of railroads, as shown in Xiao Daoguan's "Sacrificial Oration to the Mangkah River God for Constructing the Railroad Bridge" written in 1887, which I discussed in Chapter Three.

42. Pomeroy Tucker, *Origin, Rise, and Progress of Mormonism: Biography of Its Founders and History of Its Church* (New York: D. Appleton, 1867), might have been a possible source on Mormon history for Xue and Chen.

43. Guo, "Nüxing zai 20 shiji chuqi de wenxue fanyi chengjiu," 39.

44. Among the few scholars who have studied Xue Shaohui's translational works, Luo Lie insightfully discussed Xue's reconstruction of Aouda's subjectivity in the *Bashi ri huanyou ji*. Luo, however, asserts that Xue, as "a female intellectual who obstinately guarded old morality," intentionally twisted Aouda's "seizing" Fogg's hand into "seeing" his hand in order to keep Aouda within the bounds of traditional Chinese female virtue and docility. Luo therefore cannot explain why, in the ensuing scene (which Luo did not mention in her article), Xue not only honestly translated that Aouda "seized his [Fogg's] hand and pressed it to her heart," but she also made Aouda demand: "Do not break your pledge!" See Luo, "Nü fanyi jia Xue Shaohui yu *Bashi ri huanyou ji* zhong nüxing xingxiang de chonggou."

45. Elman, *A Cultural History of Modern Science in China*, 1.

46. Wang Hui, "The Fate of 'Mr. Science' in China," 1.

Chapter Seven

1. Mann, *Precious Records*, 204–5.

2. Ibid., 205.

3. The sequence of the Five Classics, *Yi* 易 (Book of changes), *Shu* 書 (Book of documents), *Shi* 詩 (Book of songs), *Li* 禮 (Books of ritual, including *Yili* 儀禮 [Book of etiquette and ceremonial], *Liji* 禮記 [Records of ritual], and *Zhouli* 周禮 [Zhou rituals]), *Chunqiu* 春秋 (Spring and autumn annals), follows Xue's list in her "Lecturing My Sons" ("Ke'er shi" 課兒詩) (*Daiyunlou yiji, Shiji, juan* 2, 13a–16b), which reflects the Eastern Han Archaic Script (*guwen* 古文) order instead of that of "Modern Script texts" (*jinwen* 今文), which were "transcribed in the clerical script in current use during Western Han" (Nylan, *The Five "Confucian" Classics*, 128 and 204).

4. Ko, *Teachers of the Inner Chambers*, 183.

5. Ibid.

6. *Chengyi* is translated as "integrating the intentions" and *cheng* is translated as "integrity," following Graham, *Disputers of the Tao*, 133–34.

7. The eight-step "classic account" is detailed in the opening passage of the *Daxue*; see *Liji* [*zhengyi*], *Daxue*, *juan* 60, 2:1673; for a translation, see Graham, *Disputers of the Tao*, 132–33.

8. *Liji* [*zhengyi*], *Zhongyong* 中庸 (Doctrine of the Mean), *juan* 53, 2:1626.

9. Xue Shaohui, "*Nü xuebao xu*."

10. Xue, *Daiyunlou yiji*, *Shiji*, *juan* 2, 14a.

11. *Lunyu*, 3.14: "Confucius said, 'The Zhou is resplendent in culture, having before it the example of the two previous dynasties [the Xia and the Yin]. I am for the Zhou'" (周監於二代, 郁郁乎文哉! 吾從周) (*Lunyu* [*yizhu*], 28; translation from Lau, trans., *Confucius: The Analects*, 69, modified). For "xianwang zhidao," see *Lunyu* 1.12; *Lunyu* [*yizhu*], 8.

12. Xue, *Daiyunlou yiji*, *Shiji*, *juan* 2, 14a.

13. *Jiaoshi Yilin* [*jiaolüe*], collation by Zhai Yunsheng (*js*. 1822), *juan* 9, 1a. For a brief discussion of this work, see Smith, *Fathoming the Cosmos and Ordering the World*, 72.

14. *Zhouyi* [*zhu*], "Tuan" 彖 (judgment) on *Kun*, in *Wang Bi, Wang Bi ji* [*jiaoshi*], 1:226; translation from Lynn, trans., *The Classic of Changes*, 143.

15. Xue, *Daiyunlou yiji*, *Shiji*, *juan* 2, 14b.

16. Xue, *Daiyunlou yiji*, *Ciji*, *juan* B, 6b.

17. See Xue, "Nüjiao yu zhidao xiangguan shuo," *Nü xuebao* 3, 2a.

18. Xue, *Daiyunlou yiji*, *Shiji*, *juan* 3, 16b.

19. Xue Shaohui and Chen Shoupeng, trans., *Shuangxian ji*, Xue's "Xu," 1a; also in Xue, *Daiyunlou yiji*, *Wenji*, *juan* A, 10b–11a.

20. Xue and Chen, trans., *Shuangxian ji*, Xue's "Xu," 2a; also in Xue, *Daiyunlou yiji*, *Wenji*, *juan* A, 12b. On the non-discriminative attitude of Jizha 季札 (fl. 557 BCE) toward music, see *Chunqiu Zuozhuan* [*zhengyi*], the 29th year of Duke Xiang 襄, *juan* 39, 2:2006–8. On Confucius's compilation of the *Book of Songs*, see Sima Qian, *Shiji*, "Kongzi shijia" 孔子世家 (The hereditary house of Confucius), *juan* 47, 6:1936–37.

21. Fowler, *A Double Thread*, 418.

22. Xue and Chen, trans., *Shuangxian ji*, *juan* 6, 17b.

23. As in Ko's words, *Teachers of the Inner Chambers*, 183.

24. See Chen Qiang et al., "Xianbi Xue gongren nianpu," 6a, 7a, 8a, 8b, 9b, 11a, 14a. The couple had a sixth child, a boy named Chen Jin who was born in the early 1898 and died five months later (see ibid., 10b).

25. Elman, *A Cultural History of Civil Examinations in Late Imperial China*, 595.

26. Shoupeng started taking the provincial examination as soon as he graduated from the Fuzhou Naval Academy in 1879. See Chen et al., "Xianbi Xue gongren nianpu," 4b. Another naval academy graduate, Yan Fu, was not so lucky. He failed the provincial examination four times, in 1885, 1888, 1889, and 1893. See Elman, *A Cultural History of Civil Examinations in Late Imperial China*, 585.

27. Xue, *Daiyunlou yiji*, *Shiji*, *juan* 2, 13a.

28. Chen et al., "Xianbi Xue gongren nianpu," 9b.

29. For Zhu Xi's "Zhaiju ganxing," see *Zhuzi wenji, juan* 4, 1:146–51.

30. Peter Bol's interpretation of the Cheng brothers' and Zhu Xi's understanding of *li*; see his *Neo-Confucianism in History*, 163–64. Bol defines *qi* as "a combination of matter (condensed solid as in stone, liquid as in water, rarified as in air) and the energy inherent in matter, thus the common translation of *qi* as 'material force'" (161).

31. Xue, *Daiyunlou yiji, Shiji, juan* 2, 15b.

32. See the *shu* interpretation of the phrase "*qiongli jinxing*" (Kong Yingda, *Zhouyi zhengyi*, "Shuokua" [Explaining the trigrams], *juan* 9, 1:93).

33. To borrow Graham's phrasing, *Disputers of the Tao*, 204.

34. Hu Bingwen, "*Ganxing shi tong* xu," *juan* 3, 3b. For a study of Hu's *Ganxing shi tong*, see Shi Zhentao, "Cong *Ganxing shi tong* lun Hu Bingwen dui Zhuxue de jicheng yu fazhan."

35. *Liji* [*zhengyi*], *Zhongyong, juan* 53, 2:1632; trans. based on de Bary and Bloom, *Sources of Chinese Tradition*, 1:338; and Graham, *Disputers of the Tao*, 135–36. *Cheng* here is translated as "integrity," "integral," or "integrate" following Graham, while de Bary and Bloom render it conventionally as "sincerity" or "sincere."

36. Graham, *Disputers of the Tao*, 136.

37. *Mengzi*, 3.2: If "one finds oneself in the right, one goes forward even against men in the thousands" (自反而縮, 雖千萬人吾往矣) (*Mengzi* [*yizhu*], 1:61; translation from Lau, trans., *Mencius*, 77).

38. *Lunyu*, 9.11, "Yan Yuan, heaving a sigh, said, 'The more I look up at it [Confucius's Way] the higher it appears. The more I bore into it the harder it becomes. . . .'" (顏淵喟然歎曰: "仰之彌高, 鑽之彌堅 . . . .") (*Lunyu* [*yizhu*], 90; translation from Lau, trans., *Confucius: The Analects*, 97, modified).

39. *Mengzi*, 13.33: "To dwell in benevolence and to follow righteousness constitutes the sum total of a great person" (居仁由義, 大人之事備矣) (*Mengzi* [*yizhu*], 2:316; translation from Lau, trans., *Mencius*, 189, modified).

40. *Liji* [*zhengyi*], *Daxue*: "What is called 'integrating intentions' is to allow no self-deception" (所謂誠其意者, 毋自欺也) (*juan* 60, 2:1673; translation from Legge, trans., *Li Chi*, 2:413, modified).

41. Xue, *Daiyunlou yiji, Shiji, juan* 2, 13a–13b. *Lunyu*, 3.11: "Someone asked about the theory of the *ti* sacrifice. Confucius said, 'It is not something I understand, for whoever understands it will be able to manage all under heaven as easily as if he had it here,' pointing to his palm" (或問禘之説。子曰: "不知也。知其説者之於天下也, 其如示诸斯乎?" 指其掌) (*Lunyu* [*yizhu*], 27, translation from Lau, trans., *Confucius: The Analects*, 69, modified).

42. See Elman's table "Format of provincial and metropolitan civil service examinations during the Late Ch'ing [Qing] dynasty, after the 1901 reform (abolished in 1905)" (*A Cultural History of Civil Examinations in Late Imperial China*, 596).

43. *Zhuangzi* [*jishi*], *juan* 6B, 3:561–63; translation from Watson, trans., *Complete Works of Chuang Tzu*, 175–76, modified.

44. Xue, *Daiyunlou yiji, Shiji, juan* 2, 16a–b. *Liji* [*zhengyi*], *Zhongyong*: "The mean is the great foundation of all under heaven" (中也者, 天下之大本也), *juan* 52, 2:1625.

45. *Zhuangzi* [*jishi*], "Xiaoyao you": "The perfected person (*zhiren*) has no self; the spiritual person (*shenren*) has no merit; the sage (*shengren*) has no fame" (至人 無己, 神人無功, 聖人無名) (*juan* 1A, 1:17; translation from Watson, trans., *Complete Works of Chuang Tzu*, 32, modified).

46. Tao Yuanming, "Yinjiu" 飲酒 (Drinking wine), no. 5, in Tao Qian, *Tao Yuanming ji, juan* 3, 89; translation from Watson, *The Columbia Books of Chinese Poetry*, 135, modified.

47. See Tao, *Tao Yuanming ji*, passim.

48. *Liji* [*zhengyi*], *Zhongyong, juan* 53, 2:1635.

49. Xue, *Daiyunlou yiji, Shiji, juan* 2, 20a–20b.

50. Zhong Rong, *Shipin* [*zhu*], *juan* A, 27, 29.

51. In Xue, *Daiyunlou yiji, Shiji, juan* 2, 19a–19b.

52. See, respectively, *Zhouyi* [*zhu*], hexagrams *Jian* 漸 (Development), *Tai* 泰 (Peace), *Zhen* 震 (Arousing), and *Jiaren* 家人 (Family), in Wang Bi, *Wang Bi ji* [*jiaoshi*], 2:483, 1:276, 2:579, and 2:401.

53. Alluding to *Shijing*, "Wangfeng" 王風 (Wind of the king), "Gelei" 葛藟 (Dolichos creepers), and "Daya," "Mian" 緜 (Thickly growing) (*Mao Shi* [*zhengyi*], *juan* 4, 1:132–33, and *juan* 16, 1:509–12).

54. In Xue, *Daiyunlou yiji, Shiji, juan* 2, 19b–21a.

55. *Lunyu*, 1.6: "If you have extra energy, then you can devote it to making yourself cultivated" (行有餘力, 則以學文) (*Lunyu* [*yizhu*], 5); see also Lau, trans., *Confucius: The Analects*, 60.

56. In Xue, *Daiyunlou yiji, Shiji, juan* 2, 21a.

57. Ibid., *juan* 2, 21a.

58. Xue, "Yingyu sanzi wushi shouyan," *Daiyunlou yiji, Wenji, juan* B, 14a–14b. Xu Hui was Emperor Tang Taizong's concubine. She imitated the *Lisao* 離騷 (Encountering sorrow) and composed the poem "Xiaoshan" (Little hill) at seven. See Ouyang Xiu and Song Qi, *Xin Tangshu*, "Houfei" I, "Taizong Xianfei Xu Hui" 太宗賢妃徐惠 (Taizong's Worthy Concubine Xu Hui), *juan* 76, 11:3472–73. "*Jinian*" refers to the year (*nian*) when a girl came of age with her hair tied up using a hairpin (*ji*), which should be at fifteen *sui* (fourteen years old); see *Liji* [*zhengyi*], "Neize," *juan* 28, 2:1471.

59. Chen et al., "Xianbi Xue gongren nianpu," 2a.

60. Xue, "Yingyu sanzi wushi shouyan," *Daiyunlou yiji, Wenji, juan* B, 14b.

61. Ibid., 15a.

62. Mencius's mother cut up the cloth on her loom to show Mencius the dangers of stopping learning. See Liu Xiang, [*Gu*] *Lienü zhuan*, "Muyi," "Zou Meng Ke mu" 鄒孟軻母 (Mother of Meng Ke of Zou), *juan* 1, 21–24.

63. Bali Xi 百里奚, a scholar of the Spring and Autumn period, became the prime minster of the state of Qin. His newly hired washerwoman offered to play the zither for his guests. In the zither song, she asked Baili Xi if he still remembered his wife, who cooked an egg-laying hen for him when he left home. Baili recognized that the woman was none other than his wife, and the two reunited. Xue alludes to this story to praise Sihui's virtue for doing all she can for her husband. See

Ying Shao 應劭 (fl. late Han), *Fengsu tongyi* [*jiaozhu*], "Yiwen" 佚文 (Lost texts), "Qingyu" 情遇 (Passionate meeting), 592–93.

64. A son and his wife should get up at the first crowing of the cock, suspend from their girdles the articles they will need to use and wait at the door of the parents' bedroom to attend to their needs. See *Liji* [*zhengyi*], "Neize," *juan* 27, 2:1461; see also Legge, trans., *Li Chi*, 1:449–50.

65. Ban Zhao, *Nüjie*: "That which must be done, let her finish with her own hands completely and tidily; then she may be said to be industrious" (所作必成, 手迹整理, 是谓执勤也) *juan* 84, 10:2787; translation from Swann, trans., "Lessons for Women," 535, modified.

66. *Haozhen* 薅砧 is an euphemistic expression for "husband" used in Southern Dynasties *yuefu* folksongs, such as the song titled "Gu jueju: Haozhen jin hezai" 古绝句: 薅砧今何在 (Old quatrain: Where is my husband?). See Xu Ling, *Yutai xinyong* [*jianzhu*], *juan* 10, 2:469.

67. Xue, "Yingyu sanzi wushi shouyan," *Daiyunlou yiji, Wenji, juan* B, 15a.

68. Chen et al., "Xianbi Xue gongren nianpu," 5b.

69. Ibid., 7a. Chen Botao and Lady Ye had at least two daughters, Lei and Rong, and at least five sons, with the fifth, Chen Chengfen (b. 1886?), given by adoption to Chen Jitong. See Qian's introduction to Chen Jitong, *Xue Jia yin*, 10–12, and Table 3.1.

70. See Chen et al., "Xianbi Xue gongren nianpu," 7a–8b.

71. Quoted in the commentary by Liu Jun 劉峻 (462–521) on Liu Yiqing's *Shishuo xinyu*, 23/7; translation from Legge, *Li Ki* I, 77, quoted in Mather, trans., *A New Account of Tales of the World*, 374n2 to 23/7 (which recounts that Ruan Ji and his sister-in-law together defied this norm by "exchanging inquiries directly with each other"), modified.

72. Chen et al., "Xianbi Xue gongren nianpu," 6a.

73. See Xue, "Jingru xionggong wushi shouchen zhengshi qi," *Daiyunlou yiji, Wenji, juan* B, 16b–19a.

74. Western libraries, such as the Bibliothèque Nationale in France and the Library of Congress in the United States, give 1851–1907 as the dates for Chen Jitong (under Tcheng-Ki-Tong). In this case, the celebration of his fiftieth birthday following the Chinese custom should have been held in the first lunar month of 1900. Yet according to Xue's "Jingru xionggong wushi shouchen zhengshi qi," she composed this essay after Jitong led the relief group to Tianjin and Beijing in the fall of 1900 (see *Daiyunlou yiji, Wenji, juan* B, 18a). Thus, Jitong's date of birth recorded in Western bibliographies was possibly based on his own reckoning following Chinese tradition—one year of age (*sui*) at birth—and hence the year should be 1852 rather than 1851. Mainly based on Xue's account Li Huachuan deduces that Jitong was born on 12 March 1852, and based on some other sources, he puts Jitong's death as 22 January 1907 (see Li, *Wan-Qing yige waijiao guan*, 154 and 235–36, respectively). I follow Li Huachuan's dating.

75. Xue, "Jingru xionggong wushi shouchen zhengshi qi," *Daiyunlou yiji, Wenji, juan* B, 17a.

76. See Xue, *Daiyunlou yiji, Wenji, juan* B, 19a–20b, 6a–8a, 8a–12a, respectively.

77. Ibid., 17b.

78. Ibid., 17b–18a.

79. Ibid., 18a.

80. *Lunyu*, 15.22 (*Lunyu* [*yizhu*], 166).

81. Xue, *Daiyunlou yiji, Wenji, juan* B, 18b.

82. See Bai Juyi, "Pipa xing" 琵琶行 (Song of the lute), in *Bai Juyi ji, juan* 12, 1:241–43, under the title "Pipa yin" 琵琶引. For a translation of this poem, see Watson, *The Columbia Book of Chinese Poetry*, 249–52.

83. See Wu Zeng, *Nenggaizhai manlu, juan* 16, 483.

84. Xue, *Daiyunlou yiji, Wenji, juan* B, 18b. On Xie An, see Liu, *Shishuo xinyu* [*jianshu*], 2/62, 19/23, 25/26; for translation of these episodes and Liu Jun's commentary, see Mather, trans., *A New Account of Tales of the World*, 61, 353–54, 412.

85. Xue, *Daiyunlou yiji, Wenji, juan* B, 18b–19a.

86. See Liu, *Shishuo xinyu* [*jianshu*], 25/8.

87. Zhang Xuecheng, *Wenshi tongyi* [*jiaozhu*], "Fuxue," *juan* 5, 1:534.

88. Quoted in Yu Jiaxi's commentary on Liu, *Shishuo xinyu* [*jianshu*], 2:789.

89. Liu Jun comments on Zhong Yan's brother-in-law Wang Lun, quoting from the *Wangshi jiapu* 王氏家譜 (Genealogy of the Wang clan): "[Wang Lun was] pure, plain, and lofty. He valued the learning of the *Laozi* and the *Zhuangzi*, and was detached from mundane affairs" ([王淪] 醇粹簡遠, 貴老、莊之學, 用心淡如也) (Liu, *Shishuo xinyu* [*jianshu*], 2:788). Thus Wang Lun typified the abstruse aura of the Seven Worthies of the Bamboo Grove.

Chapter Eight

1. The causes of the bloody termination of the Hundred Days to this day remain debatable. My account follows the conventional narrative in Tang Zhijun, *Wuxu bianfa shi*, 421–23; and Kwong, *A Mosaic of the Hundred Days*, 201–24. A 2008 Beijing conference commemorating the 110th anniversary of 1898 focused on this topic; see Wang Yi, "Wuxu weixin yu wan-Qing shehui biange," 134–38.

2. See Xue Shaohui, *Daiyunlou yiji, Shiji, juan* 2, 3b.

3. Only Fan Dangshi presented a poem to Shen on the first anniversary of Lin Xu's execution, and a poem to Jitong with a line, "Shedding blood, let's finish with the burial of the dead" (灑血且完前死事) but still under the disguise of mourning the death of Jitong's elder brother. See *Fan Bozi shiji, juan* 12, 3a–3b. Lin Xu's other friends commemorated his death much later; see Lin Xu, *Wancuixuan ji*, "Fulu" 附錄 (Appendix), 1a–7a.

4. See Mao Xianshu 毛先舒 (1620–88), *Tianci mingjie* 填詞名解 (Interpretations to the tune-titles of song-lyrics), quoted in Long Yusheng, *Tang-Song ci gelü*, 99–100.

5. Liang's account and the *Ningbo fuzhi* record are basically the same, except that Liang's contains Xie An's memo and the *Ningbo fuzhi* ends with the fantastic butterfly legend. For Liang's account, see his *Langji congtan, Xutan, Santan, Xutan, juan* 6, 353. The *Ningbo fuzhi* account is quoted in Yin Zhanhua, "Liang Zhu gushi qiyuan yu liuchuan de zai kaocha," 56. For a thorough study of the evolution of this story, see Idema, *The Butterfly Lovers*.

6. Xue, *Daiyunlou yiji, Ciji, juan* B, 13a.

7. Xue lists the "Yifu zhong" after a song-lyric about the autumn scene in Ningbo in the fall of 1898 at the earliest and before a mourning song for the death of her brother's wife in June 1901. See ibid., 12b–14a.

8. Liang Qichao asserts in "Lin Xu zhuan," written between 1898 and 1899, that Queying poisoned herself to death soon after Lin Xu's execution, apparently based on a rumor widely circulated at the time. See Liang, "Lin Xu zhuan," 103. Shen Chenghu et al., "Shen Jingyu gong nianpu," records Queying's death as follows: "In the fourth month [of the year gengzi (ca. May 1900)], daughter Queying pined away to death after [her husband]" ([庚子]四月女鵲應毀殉) (232). See also Chen Yan, "Shen Que[ying] shilüe," *Min-Hou xian zhi, juan* 101, 6b.

9. Chen Yun, *Chen Xiaonü yiji, juan* B, 15b.

10. See Guo Maoqian, ed., *Yuefu shiji, juan* 46, 2:669.

11. This story is recorded in Gan Bao, *Soushen ji*, but the butterfly part seems to have been added later, in the Song, along with the spread of the Liang-Zhu story. See *Soushen ji*, commentary by Wang Shaoying, *juan* 11, 141–42, text and commentary.

12. Shen Queying, to the tune "Pusa man" 菩薩蠻 (Deva-like barbarian), *Yanlou ci*, in *Yanlou yigao*, 9a.

13. I consider these three essays to have appeared in the last three issues of the 1898 *Nü xuebao*, which were published in October 1898 but have yet to be located (see Yu Fuyuan, "Guanyu *Nü xuebao* de kanqi he kanxingqi," 52–53), for three reasons: 1) Xue's *Wenji* collected nineteen *pianwen* essays; sixteen were written after 1900 according to their contents. The remaining are these three that bear no clear indication of the dates. Xue Sihui's preface to Xue's *Wenji* indicates that Xue sent her "newly written *pianwen* essays published in newspapers" after moving to Shanghai in 1897, and these three were very likely among them. 2) From 1897 to 1898, Xue published in three periodicals, namely, *Qiushi bao, Xinwen bao*, and *Nü xuebao*. I searched through all twelve issues of the *Qiushi bao* (30 September 1897–7 March 1898) and the whole stack of *Xinwen bao* from 1897 to 1898, but found no *pianwen* essays by Xue; hence *Nü xuebao* was the only possible place for these three essays. 3) All three essays were on women and therefore fit for *Nü xuebao*.

14. Katie Conboy states: "At first glance, the answer to Simone de Beauvoir's question—'What is a woman?'—appears simple, for is the female body not the marker of womanhood? The body has, however, been at the center of feminist theory precisely because it offers no such 'natural' foundation for our pervasive cultural assumptions about femininity. Indeed, there is a tension between women's lived bodily experiences and the cultural meanings inscribed on the female body that always mediate those experiences" ("Introduction," in Conboy et al., eds., *Writing on the Body*, 1).

15. Xue, "Yongshang zashi" 甬上雜詩 (Miscellaneous poems of Ningbo), *Daiyunlou yiji, Shiji, juan* 2, 2b.

16. Xue, *Daiyunlou yiji, Wenji, juan* B, 22a.

17. *Mao Shi [zhengyi]*, "Daya," "Zhanyang" 瞻卬 (Looking up), *juan* 18, 1:577.

18. See Liu Xiang, [*Gu*] *Lienü zhuan, juan* 7, 101:189–90.

19. Xue, *Daiyunlou yiji, Wenji, juan* B, 22b.

20. Ibid., 22b–23a.

21. Ibid., 23a.

22. Ibid., 23b.

23. Ibid.

24. See Tao Qian, *Tao Yuanming ji, juan* 3, 89.

25. Yao Silian et al., *Chenshu,* "Zhang Lihua zhuan," *juan* 7, 1:133.

26. See ibid., 1:131; see also Wei Zheng et al., *Suishu,* "Gao Jiong zhuan" 高熲傳, *juan* 41, 4:1181.

27. Xue, "Xie Yiru fan Qingxi mi Zhang Lihua ci bude" ("Boating with Yiru along Green Brook to Look for the Shrine of Zhang Lihua, to No Avail"), to the tune "Yaohua" ("Jade Flower"), *Daiyunlou yiji, Ciji, juan* B, 18b.

28. Xue, *Daiyunlou yiji, Wenji, juan* A, 4a.

29. Xue, "Li Qingzhao Zhu Shuzhen lun," *Daiyunlou yiji, Wenji, juan* B, 24a.

30. Ibid.

31. Jing Yuanshan, ed., *Nüxue jiyi chubian,* 4a.

32. *Shangshu* [*zhengyi*], "Shundian" 舜典 (Cannon of Shun): "We abominate slander that destroys good behavior" (朕聖讒說殄行), *juan* 1, 1:132.

33. Xue, "Li Qingzhao Zhu Shuzhen lun," *Daiyunlou yiji, Wenji, juan* B, 24a.

34. Ibid., 25a.

35. Wang Zhongwen points out that this line only appears in the version in Li Qingzhao's *Maxi tupu* 馬戲圖譜 (Diagrams of *Horse Chess*) and in Yu Zhengxie 俞正燮 (1775–1840), *Guisi leigao* 癸巳類稿 (Categorized draft of the year 1833). See Li Qingzhao, *Li Qingzhao ji* [*jiaozhu*], 151.

36. Ibid.; translation based on Wang's commentary, 158–59.

37. Xue, "Li Qingzhao Zhu Shuzhen lun," *Daiyunlou yiji, Wenji, juan* B, 25a.

38. Li Qingzhao, "Shiti" 失題 (Title lost), in *Li Qingzhao ji* [*jiaozhu*], 137.

39. In Cheng Qianfan, ed., *Songshi jingxuan,* 270.

40. Xue, "Li Qingzhao Zhu Shuzhen lun," *Daiyunlou yiji, Wenji, juan* B, 25a. Li Qingzhao's remarriage had not been in dispute until the Ming-Qing period, as Li's literary reputation rose to equal that of leading male poets and the number of women writers quickly increased. In order to set up a righteous model for writing women, scholars had to dismiss Li's remarriage as fabricated or dismiss Li herself as an unqualified role model. Either way, Li's marital status became a major issue in Ming-Qing discussions of her life. For a detailed discussion, see Qian Nanxiu, "Li Qingzhao de jiaguo qinghuai." For a recently published thorough study of Li Qingzhao, see Egan, *The Burden of Female Talent,* especially chap. 8, "Saving the Widow, Denying the Remarriage: Reception during the Ming and Qing," 237–82.

41. *Mengzi* 14.14: "The people are of supreme importance; the altars to the gods of earth and grain come next; last comes the ruler" (民為貴, 社稷次之, 君為輕) (*Mengzi* [*yizhu*], 2:328; translation from Lau, trans., *Mencius,* 196).

42. Xue, "Ti Yue Wumu caoshu Zhuge Zhongwu qianhou 'Chushi biao' shike hou" 題岳武穆草書諸葛忠武前後出師表石刻後 (Inscribed after the robins of

Yue Fei's cursive calligraphy of the *Former and Latter Memos of Military Campaigns by* Zhuge Liang) (1909), *Daiyunlou yiji, Shiji, juan* 4, 6a–6b.

43. *Aiguo* would become indispensable to the study of Li Qingzhao in modern times, although its actual meaning has never been clarified. See Qian, "Li Qingzhao de jiaguo qinghuai," 222–24.

44. Lu Cui, "Nüzi aiguo shuo," 2b.

45. See ibid., 2b–3a.

46. See Zheng Shiqu, "Liang Qichao de aiguo lun," 175.

47. Hao Chang believes that Liang's concept of *qun* in his 1897 essay "Shuo qun" 說羣 (On grouping) indicates "an implicit but ambivalent acceptance of the ideal of the nation-state" (*Liang Ch'i-ch'ao and Intellectual Transition in China,* 111).

48. See Yang Nianqun, "Lun Wuxu weixin shidai guanyu 'xixing' gaizao de gouxiang jiqi yiyi," 210.

49. Ko, *Cinderella's Sisters,* 39. For a thorough discussion of this letter, see 38–40.

50. Xue, "Fu Shen nüshi shu," *Daiyunlou yiji, Wenji, juan* B, 21a–21b.

51. Sima Qian, *Shiji,* "Chen She shijia" 陳涉世家 (Hereditary house of Chen She), *juan* 48, 6:1952.

52. Quoted in *Zhuangzi jishi,* "Xiaoyao you," *juan* 1A, 31.

53. Ko, *Cinderella's Sisters,* 39.

54. Xue, "Du Songshi," *Daiyunlou yiji, Shiji, juan* 2, 4b; Xue, preface to "Huiluan song," *Daiyunlou yiji, Wenji, juan* 1, 5a–5b.

55. Ibid., 7b.

56. See Jing Yuanshan, *Juyi chuji, juan* 1, 1a–1b; *juan* 2, 47a–49b, 53a–59b.

57. For example, Huang Zunxian never explicitly discussed reform in his poems about Cixi and Guangxu in the Boxer Rebellion; see *Renjinglu shicao* [*jianzhu*], *juan* 10–11.

58. Xue, *Daiyunlou yiji, Wenji, juan* A, 8a.

59. "Dong'er" alludes to the major character in Wu Weiye, "Linhuai laoji xing" 臨淮老妓行 (Old courtesan from Linhuai), who witnessed the tumult of the Ming-Qing transition and helped with military affairs; see *Wu Meicun quanji, juan* 11, 1:285–87.

60. Xue, *Daiyunlou yiji, Shiji, juan* 2, 8a.

61. For a more detailed discussion of Xue's "Laoji xing" and controversies surrounding Fu Caiyun's life, see Qian, "Xue Shaohui and Her Poetic Chronicle of Late Qing Reforms," 362–66.

62. Xue, "Laoji xing," *Daiyunlou yiji, Shiji, juan* 2, 8b.

63. On Xue's application of her new standards of female virtue, rewritten with reference to foreign women's lives, to Fu Caiyun's life, see Qian, "Borrowing Foreign Mirrors," 95–99.

64. See Shen Yuqing, "Chen Jitong shilüe," *juan* 39, 72a–72b; Li Huachuan, *Wan-Qing yige waijiao guan,* 226–29.

65. Xue, "Dai jiuji shanhui ni zhi Gaoli guowang shu" 代救濟善會擬致高麗國王書 (Letter to the king of Korea, on behalf of the relief group), *Daiyunlou yiji, Wenji, juan* B, 20a–20b.

66. Jitong's original poem, titled "Tianjin ganshi" 天津感事 (Thoughts on Tianjin), quot. in Lu Shufan, "Gengzi quanbian hou Jing-Jin jian zhi canzhuang," 445.

67. Xue, *Daiyunlou yiji, Shiji, juan* 3, 7a–7b.

68. See, for instance, Chen Pingyuan, "Male Gaze/Female Students," esp. 328–30.

69. Xue, *Daiyunlou yiji, Shiji, juan* 3, 22b. "Gongzhong Zuonü" (Palace Lady Zuo) refers to Zuo Fen 左芬 (d. 300), concubine of Emperor Wudi of the Jin (r. 266–90), a famed woman of talent. See Fang Xuanling et al., *Jinshu*, "Houfei shang" 后妃上 (Imperial consorts, A), *juan* 31, 4:957–62.

70. Xue, *Daiyunlou yiji, Shiji, juan* 3, 22b.

71. "Wugong" 五公 (Five Lords) refers to Yuan Chang 袁昶 (1848–1900), Xu Jingcheng 許景澄 (1845–1900), Xu Yongyi 徐用儀 (1826–1900), Lianyuan 聯元 (1838–1900), and Lishan 立山 (1843?–1900); all were accused of opposing the Boxers and executed in the summer of 1900; see Yun Yuding, "Chongling chuanxin lu."

72. *Sanfu huangtu* 三輔黃圖 (Yellow map of the vicinity of the capital) is a geographic classic about the Qin and Han capitals; see He Qinggu's introduction to the *Sanfu huangtu* [*jiaoshi*], 1.

73. Xue, *Daiyunlou yiji, Shiji, juan* 3, 22b–23a.

74. See Liu Xiang, [*Gu*] *Lienü zhuan*, "Zhenshun," about Lady Jiang, the wife of King Zhao of Chu, who refused to leave the soon-to-be-flooded Jian Terrace and eventually drowned as she did not receive a tallied summon from the king (*juan* 4, 101:109–10).

75. Meijing 梅精 (Plum Spirit) refers to Meifei, Emperor Tang Xuanzong's Plum Consort, who was left alone and eventually killed by rebels during the An Lushan Rebellion (755–57). See Shen Yuqing and Chen Yan, *Fujian tongzhi*, "Lienü zhuan," "Biantong," *juan* 6, 1a–2b.

76. Xue, *Daiyunlou yiji, Shiji, juan* 3, 23a.

77. See, for instance, Yun, "Chongling chuanxin lu," 1:53.

78. See *Wushu* 吳書 (History of the Wu), quoted in the commentary of Pei Songzhi (372–451) on Chen Shou (233–97), *Sanguo zhi, Wushu*, "Sun Jian zhuan" 孫堅傳, *juan* 46, 5:1099. See also Luo Guanzhong, *Sanguo yanyi*, 1:53.

79. Xue, *Daiyunlou yiji, Shiji, juan* 3, 23a–23b.

80. See *Quan Tang shi, juan* 144, 4:1461.

81. Li Shangyin, *Li Shangyin shige* [*jijie*], commentary by Liu Xuekai and Yu Shucheng, 4:1467; translation from Graham, trans., *Poems of the Late T'ang*, 146.

82. See *Shuyi ji*, attributed to Ren Fang, *juan* A, 5b–6a.

83. See *Zhuangzi* [*jishi*], "Qiushui" 秋水 (Autumn floods): "The phoenix rises up from the South Sea and flies to the North Sea, and it will rest on nothing but the *wutong* tree, eat nothing but the fruit of bamboo, and drink only from springs of sweet water" (夫鵷鶵，發於南海而飛於北海，非梧桐不止，非練實不食，非醴泉不飲) (*juan* 6B, 3:605); translation from Watson, trans., *Complete Works of Chuang Tzu*, 188, modified.

84. Xue, *Daiyunlou yiji, Shiji, juan* 4, 1b–2a.

85. Ibid., 5b–6a.

86. See Zhang Peitian and Chen Jinquan, "Qingmo yubei lixian de shishi kaolun," 81.

87. The *Nanyang riri guanbao* prints the French title of the *Nanyang guanbao*, *Journal officiel de Nan Yang*, under its Chinese title, showing its connection with the *Journal*.

88. Xue, "*Nanyang riri guanbao* xuli," front page; also in Xue, *Daiyunlou yiji*, *Wenji*, juan B, 6a–6b.

89. Xue, "*Nanyang riri guanbao* xuli"; also in Xue, *Daiyunlou yiji*, *Wenji*, juan B, 7b. This role of journalism as the "middle realm," a "new arena of negotiation between ruler and ruled," was envisaged by many late Qing journalists; see Judge, *Print and Politics*, esp. 54–75.

90. The imperial edict on sending statesmen abroad on a political inspection tour was issued on 16 July 1905, and the inspection took place in early 1906. For related documents, see Gugong bowuyuan dang'anbu, *Qingmo choubei lixian dang'an shiliao*, 1:1–41. Dai Hongci 戴鴻慈 (1853–1910) and Duanfang 端方 (1861–1911), two of the five statesmen sent abroad, presented the eight suggestions for reforming the civil service system on 25 August 1906. This proposal even mentioned that women secretaries served efficiently at government offices in foreign counties (see ibid., 1:380). The imperial edict on this reform was issued on 6 November 1906 (see ibid., 1:471–72).

91. Xue, *Daiyunlou yiji*, *Shiji*, juan 3, 16a.

92. See *Zhouli* [*zhushu*], 1:631–940.

93. See Gugong bowuyuan dang'anbu, *Qingmo choubei lixian dang'an shiliao*, 1:471–72.

94. Yao Silian et al., *Chenshu*, "Fu Zai zhuan," juan 30, 2:406–7.

95. See Sima Qian, *Shiji*, "Mengzi Xun Qing liezhuan" 孟子荀卿列傳, juan 74, 7:2348. In their memos to the court, the Five Statesmen depicted how they were warmly received by Western governments and people (see Gugong bowuyuan dang'anbu, *Qingmo choubei lixian dang'an shiliao*, 1:6–41, passim). This, and the five's lack of Western learning, might have aroused suspicion in Xue as how well they could fulfill their task.

96. See Huan Kuan, *Yantie lun* [*jiaozhu*].

97. See Guo Tingyi, ed., *Jindai Zhongguo shishi rizhi*, 2:1372–73.

98. Xue, *Daiyunlou yiji*, *Shiji*, juan 4, 15a. *Mao Shi* [*zhengyi*], "Daya," "Wenwang" 文王 (King Wen): "Although Zhou is an old state, / Heaven bestows on it a new mandate" (周邦雖舊, 其命維新) (juan 16, 1:503).

99. Xue had stated in "Huiluan song" (1901): "The state of Zhou may reform its system"; and in Xue, "*Nanyang riri guanbao* xuli" (1905): "Although Zhou is an old state, it may reform itself" (also in *Daiyunlou yiji*, *Wenji*, juan B, 6b).

100. Gasster, "Reform and Revolution in China's Political Modernization," 76. On late Qing constitutional reform and its Japanese sources, see Shang Xiaoming, "Liu Ri xuesheng yu Qingmo xianzheng gaige." On the *Qinding xianfa dagang*, see Xianzheng bianchaguan, *Qingmo Minchu xianzheng shiliao jikan*, 2:329–35.

101. See Hou Yijie, *Ershi shiji chu Zhongguo zhengzhi gaige fengchao*, 557.

102. Qin Hui, "Qin Hui tan xinhai."

103. *Mengzi*, 1.3 (*Mengzi* [*yizhu*], 1:5); see Lau, trans., *Mencius*, 51.

104. Xue, "Qianmen guan denghui ge," *Daiyunlou yiji, Shiji, juan* 4, 15a.

105. Xue, "Huangputan guandeng ge" 黃埔灘觀燈歌 (Viewing lamps on the Huangpu River), *Daiyunlou yiji, Shiji, juan* 3, 11a–11b. Yelang was a small state southwest of Han China, yet its ruler thought Yelang was bigger than Han. See Sima Qian, *Shiji*, "Xi'nan yi liezhuan" 西南夷列傳 (Biographies of the southwestern minority peoples), *juan* 116, 9:2996.

106. Xue, "Qianmen guan denghui ge," *Daiyunlou yiji, Shiji, juan* 4, 15a.

107. Ibid.

108. Li, "Women Writers and Gender Boundaries during the Ming-Qing Transition," 213. For pioneer studies in this regard, see also Hu, "The Daughter's Vision of National Crisis," and Kang-i Sun Chang, "Women's Poetic Witnessing: Late Ming and Late Qing Examples."

Conclusion

1. Chen Yiyi, "*Shenzhou nübao* fakanci," 9; also see Chen Yiyi, "Nübaojie zuixin diaochabiao," which listed thirteen women's journals published by 1909. On Chen Yiyi's life, see Xia Xiaohong, "Wan-Qing nüxing de xingbie guanzhao," 45–52.

2. *Zhongguo jindai qikan bianmu huilu*, s.v. *Nübao, Nü xuebao*, footnote to the entry, which indicates that Chen Xiefen started the journal as the *Nübao* in 1899, continued it in 1902 under the title of *Xuchu Nübao*, and retitled it *Nü xuebao* in 1903. This catalogue only records the 1902–3 *Xuchu Nübao/Nü xuebao*. The 1899 *Nübao* has not yet been found.

3. These two articles are Pan Tianzhen, "Tan Zhongguo jindai diyifen nübao–*Nü xuebao*"; and Du Jikun, "Zai tan *Nü xuebao*."

4. Since the late 1990s, scholarship in Chinese has acknowledged the existence of the 1898 *Nü xuebao* but mostly based on secondary sources. My article, "Revitalizing the *Xianyuan*," was the first English-language study of this pioneering women's journal based on its eight extant issues. As for the 1902–3 *Xuchu Nübao/Nü xuebao*, no detailed study appeared until my 2008 essay, "The Mother *Nü Xuebao* Versus the Daughter *Nü Xuebao*." In a recent study, Xia Xiaohong has found some traces of Chen Xiefen's 1899 *Nübao*, although the journal itself is yet to be discovered; see Xia, "Wan-Qing liangfen *Nü xuebao* de qianshi jinsheng."

5. Levenson, *Confucian China and Its Modern Fate*, 98.

6. Metzger, *Escape from Predicament*, 214.

7. Ibid., 215–17.

8. Jiang Zhiyou, "Aiguo nü xuexiao kaixiao yanshuo," 3a.

9. Ibid., 2b.

10. Anonymous, *Aiguo nü'er chuanqi*. 2b–3a.

11. Hu Shi, "Sanbai nian zhong de nü zuojia," 4:588. For a critique of Hu's biases, see Chen Pingyuan, *Zhongguo xiandai xueshu zhi jianli*, 226. For a detailed introduction to *Qing guixiu yiwen lüe* 清閨秀藝文略 by Shan Shili 單士釐, see Huang Xiangjin, "Nanguo nüzi jie nengshi."

12. Judge, "Chinese Women's History," 227.

13. Chen Xiefen, "Nannü dou yaokan," 2a–2b.

14. See Qian, "The Mother *Nü Xuebao* Versus the Daughter *Nü Xuebao*."

15. In his "Foreword" to the first issue of *Shenzhou nübao* (Dec. 1907), Chen Yiyi declared that he established the journal "in grand memory of the bloodshed of the Mirror-Lake Heroine Qiu Jin," who was executed by the Qing court on 15 July 1907. It was against this background that Chen Yiyi credited Chen Xiefen with inaugurating the first Chinese women's journal "during 1902–3, when women in China yet lived in darkness and ignorance" and praised the journal as "the only light shone through that awakened women to their desolate situation" ("*Shenzhou nübao* fakanci," in *Nülun*, 9).

16. Judge, "Reforming the Feminine," 178.

Glossary of Chinese Names, Terms, and Titles of Works

aiguo 愛國

Aofeng shuyuan 鰲峰書院

badao 霸道

baobian 褒貶

baobing 暴病

baoguo, baozhong, baojiao 保國, 保種, 保教

bei'ai koubai 悲哀口白

beifen zhi zuo 悲憤之作

Beiyang xuetang 北洋學堂

buren 不忍

butian zhanxing 卜天占星

cai 才

Cai Yan 蔡琰 (aka Cai Wenji 蔡文姬)

cainü 才女

caiyi 才藝

cesuan 測算

chan 禪

Chen Hongmou 陳宏謀

Chen Jidong 陳驥東

Chen Ruolan 陳若蘭

Chen Sanli 陳三立

Chen Shu 陳書

Chen Shubao 陳叔寶

cheng 誠

Cheng Shimeng 程師孟

Cheng Yi 程漪

chengyi 誠意

chiguo 治國

Chong'er 重耳

ci 詞

ci 慈

cigong gebei 詞工格卑

Cixi 慈禧

congdi 從弟

Dao 道

datong 大同

Daxue 大學

dianbao 電報

diaochong xiaoji 雕蟲小技

Ding Suqing 丁素清

dizi 弟子

Duji 妒記

Fan Li 范蠡

Fang Boqian 方伯謙

Feishe 飛社

fengshui 風水

fengwei dierao 蜂圍蝶繞

Foli 佛貍

Fu Caiyun 傅彩雲 (aka Sai Jinhua 賽金花)

Fuchai 夫差

fudao 婦道

fugong 婦工

fuji/fuluan 扶乩/扶鸞

Fujian 符堅

fuqiang 富強

furong 婦容

fusheng danxian 輔聖誕賢

Fuxue 婦學

gangrou bingji 剛柔並濟

Ganjiang 干將

Gaofeng yipin furen Bali Laishi 誥封一品夫人巴黎賴氏

gaoxian shunü 高賢淑女

gewu 格物

Gezhi zhenggui 格致正軌

gongxin 公心

Gu'an 固安

Guan Daosheng 管道昇

Guang fangyan guan 廣方言館

guanhua 官話

guankui li'ce 管窺蠡測

guixiu 閨秀

guizhong shuangfeng 閨中雙鳳

Guizu lianyin 貴族聯姻

Guo Songtao 郭嵩燾

guojia zhuyi 國家主義

guwen 古文

Han Ping 韓凴

Han Wo 韓偓

hao 號

Henghe 恆河

Hong Jun 洪鈞

Hongfu nü 紅拂女

Honglou meng 紅樓夢

Honglou yinshe 紅樓吟社

Hongze 洪澤

Huai'an 淮安

Huang Qian 黃謙

Huang Youfan 黃幼繁

Huang Youzao 黃幼藻

huiyu wangyan 穢語妄言

huntian yi 渾天儀

ji 記

Ji Yinghuai 紀映淮 (aka Ji A'nan 紀阿男)

jian 鑒

Jiang Kui 姜夔

Jiang Lan 蔣蘭 (*zi* Wanfang 畹芳)

Jiangnan zhizaoju 江南製造局

Jiankang 建康

jiaoshe gongfa 交涉公法

jifeng buying 繫風捕影

jin 斤

jingzhu 鏡燭

jinian 笄年

jinshi 進士

jiqing 寄情

junzi 君子

junzi budang 君子不黨

juren 舉人

jushi zhishu 據事直書

Kang Guangren 康廣仁

Kangxi 康熙

kaoju 考據

keju 科舉

kujie 苦節

kundao 坤道

Kunqu 昆曲

Leng Jiangxue 冷絳雪

li 理

Li Ciming 李慈銘

Li Duanhui 李端蕙

Li Fengbao 李鳳苞

Li Jing 李靖

Li Shimin 李世民

Li Zongxi 李宗羲

lienü 烈女

Lin Hong 林鴻

Lin Malai 林瑪萊 (Mary Louise Allen)

linxia fengqi 林下風氣

Liu Buchan 劉步蟾

Liu Kunyi 劉坤一

Liu Mingchuan 劉銘傳

Liu Renlan 劉紉蘭

Liu Shi 柳是 (aka Liu Rushi 柳如是)

Liu Yong 柳永

liuqi 六氣

liuxu zhi ci 柳絮之辭

lixian 立憲

Long Zehou 龍澤厚

luandang 亂黨

Lujun bu 陸軍部

lunce 論策

Luo Fenglu 羅豐祿

Ma Jianzhong 馬建中

Ma Yuanyu 馬元馭

Maocheng 鄮城

Meifei 梅妃

meishan wuhan 美善無憾

Meng Jiao 孟郊

ming 名

mingli 明理

miyue 蜜月

Moye 莫邪

Mozhai 墨齋

mudao 母道

Nanyang dachen 南洋大臣

Neixun 內訓

Neize yanyi 內則衍義

Ningbo 寧波

Nü Lunyu 女論語

Nü sishu 女四書

Nü Xiaojing 女孝經

nü zongtong 女總統

Nüfan jielu 女範捷錄

nügong 女工

nüjie 女傑

Nüjie 女誡

Nüjie zhong 女界鐘

nüxia 女俠

Nüxue 女學

nüzong 女宗

Pan Daofang 潘道芳

Peng Jiyun 彭寄雲

pianguan pianyin 偏官偏印

pianwen 駢文

piaoran yuanyin erqu 飄然遠引而去

ping tianxia 平天下

pingdeng 平等

poxin 婆心

puchen 鋪陳

puxue 樸學

qijia 齊家

Qingliu 清流

qiong 窮

Qiu Jin 秋瑾

Qiu Yufang 裘毓芳

Qiu Yunfang 邱韻芳

qiyu 綺語

Qu Yufen 瞿玉芬

Quanshan 泉山

Rao Tingxuan 饒廷選

renjing 人鏡

rou 柔

roushun 柔順

rouyin manjie 柔音曼節

ru bao chizi 如保赤子

ruorou qiangshi 弱肉強食

Sa Zhenbing 薩鎮冰

Sang-Pu huiji 桑濮穢跡

Shan Dai 山黛

shanchuan lingxiu 山川靈秀

shanggu qi nüzi 上古奇女子

Shangguan Wan'er 上官婉兒

Shao Feifei 邵飛飛

shen 神

Shen Cuiying 沈翠英

Sheng Xuanhuai 盛宣懷

Shengji 生計

shengren 聖人

shenlang 神朗

shenqing sanlang 神情散朗

shenren 神人

shi 詩

shi 士

shi daifu 士大夫

Shi Jingcheng 施景澄

Shi Yumin 施毓敏

Shibao 時報

Shijian 識鑒

shijiao 詩教

shijie zhuyi 世界主義

shiqing 石青

shiqing 詩情

Shiwu xiao haojie 十五小豪傑

shixue 實學

shizhong 詩鐘

Shuchang guan 庶常館

shude 淑德

Shuihu zhuan 水滸傳

Shunzhi 順治

side 四德

sifu 私婦

Song Ruoshen 宋若莘

Sui Nianqu 眭念劬

Suiyang 睢陽

Sun En 孫恩

Sun Jian 孫堅

Sun Yun 孫蘊

Taiwu 太武

Tan Sitong 譚嗣同

tanben zhilun 探本之論

taoxie xingqing 陶寫性情

tian 天

Tong-Guang ti 同光體

Tongwenguan 同文館

Tongzhi 同治

Tuoba Tao 拓跋燾

tuqi 吐氣

Wang Ningzhi 王凝之

Wang Rong 王戎

Wang Xizhi 王羲之

Wang Yanjun 王延鈞

Wang Zhenxian 王貞仙

wangdao 王道

wei gonggou 畏功狗

Wei-Jin 魏晉

Weixin pai 維新派

wen 文

Wen Chu 文俶

Wen Tingshi 文廷式

wenming 文明

wenren 文人

wenyao 文妖

wu 物

Wu Cailuan 吳彩鸞

Wu Yi 吳逸

Wubei yuan 武備院

wujing tianze 物競天擇

wuru shengjiao 吾儒盛教

wuse qi 五色氣

Xi Shi 西施

xian 賢

xiangcao yihui 香草遺徽

xianming 賢明

xianmu xianfu 賢母賢婦

xianshu mingyuan 賢淑名媛

xianyuan 賢媛

xiao 孝

xiaoshuo 小説

Xiaozhuang 孝莊

Xie Lingyun 謝靈運

Xie Zhi 謝芝

xieyi 寫意

xiezhen 寫真

xing 性

xinmin 新民

xinmin zhi zhi 新民之旨

xinxue 新學

xinzheng 新政

xiushen 修身

Xiyou ji 西遊記

Xu Deying 徐德英

Xu Fu 許孚

Xu Tingting 許亭亭

Xu Yi'e 徐一鶚

Xuantong 宣統

Xuanxue 玄學

Xuanye 玄燁

xuanyin 玄音

xue 學

Xue Fucheng 薛福成

xueyi jiancan 學藝兼參

yan 艷

Yan Fu 嚴復

Yang Lanzhen 楊蘭貞

yangwu 洋務

yanli 艷麗

yanqing 艷情

yanti 艷體

yasan suqi 雅三俗七

Ye Bojun 葉伯鋆

yi 藝

yifu 義婦

yili 義理

yinxie zhi nian 淫邪之念

Yipuliu suipian shi 懿浦留碎篇詩

Yixing 一行

yongbi 用筆

yongwu 詠物

Youchuan bu 郵傳部

youji xiaoqian 幽寂消遣

Youxue xuzhi jujie 幼學須知句解

yuanyin 元音

Yue Fei 岳飛

yufu 愚婦

Yun Bing 惲冰

Yun Shouping 惲壽平

Yushan 玉山

Zeng Guofan 曾國藩

Zeng Yangdong 曾仰東

zhaifen cuosu/difen cuosu 摘粉搓酥/
滴粉搓酥

Zhang Heng 張衡

Zhang Hongqiao 張紅橋

Zhang Jian 張謇

Zhang Jiliang 張際亮

Zhang Jingyi 張靜儀 (*zi* Yunhua
蘊華)

Zhang Zhidong 張之洞

zhanghui xiaoshuo 章回小説

Zhao Mengfu 趙孟頫

Zhao Mingcheng 趙明誠

zheng 正

Zheng Guanying 鄭觀應

Zheng Hunbing 鄭渾冰

Zheng Jiangxia 鄭絳霞

Zheng Xiaoxu 鄭孝胥

Zheng-Wei zhi feng 鄭衛之風

zhengxin 正心

zhidao 治道

zhiren 至人

zhiyin 知音

Zhiyun nüshi 織雲女史

zhizhi 致知

Zhong Xi hecan 中西合參

Zhong Yan 鍾琰

Zhou Fu 周馥

Zhou Yuanxiang 周遠香

Zhoubi suanjing 周髀算經

Zhu Fanghui 朱芳徽

Zhu Shilan 朱蒔蘭

zhuangyan 莊嚴

zhubi 主筆

zhufu 主婦

Zhulin qixian 竹林七賢

zi 字

zide zhi quan 自得之權

ziqiang 自強

ziran 自然

ziwei 自慰

ziyu 自娛

zizhu 自主

zizu 自足

Zongli yamen 總理衙門

Zuo Zongtang 左宗棠

Bibliography

Anonymous. *Aiguo nü'er chuanqi* 愛國女兒傳奇 (Legend of patriotic girls). *Xuchu Nübao* 6 (2 Oct. 1902). The Nübao Fujian 女報附件 (Appendix) column, 1a–3a.

Appletons' Annual Cyclopædia and Register of Important Events of the Year: Literature, Continental, in 1891. New York: D. Appleton and Company, 1892.

Bai Juyi 白居易 (772–846). *Bai Juyi ji* 白居易集 (Collected works of Bai Juyi). 4 vols. Beijing: Zhonghua shuju, 1979.

Ban Gu 班固 (32–92). *Hanshu* 漢書 (History of the Han). Commentary by Yan Shigu 顏師古 (581–645). 12 vols. Beijing: Zhonghua shuju, 1962.

Ban Zhao 班昭 (ca. 45–ca. 116). *Nüjie* 女誡 (Admonitions for women). Quoted in Fan Ye, *Hou-Han shu*, "Lienü zhuan," *juan* 84, 10:2786–92.

Barbauld, Anna Letitia (1743–1825). *The Works of Anna Letitia Barbauld*. London: Longman, Hurst, Rees, Orme, Brown, and Green, 1825.

Barber, James A. *Naval Shiphandler's Guide*. Annapolis, MD: Naval Institute Press, 2005.

Bard, Alphonse (b. 1850), and Paul Robiquet (1848–1928). *Droit constitutionnel comparé: la Constitution française de 1875 étudiée dans ses rapports avec les constitutions étrangères*. Paris: E. Thorin, 1876.

Basidi 巴斯蒂 [Marianne Bastid-Bruguière]. "Qingmo fu Ou de liuxuesheng men—Fujian chuanzhengju yinjin jindai jishu de qianqian houhou" 清末赴歐的留學生們──福建船政局引進近代技術的前前後後 (Late Qing Chinese students in Europe: About the Fujian Navy Yard's import of modern technology). Trans. from French by Zhang Fuqiang 張富強 and Zhao Jun 趙軍. *Xinhai geming shi congkan* 辛亥革命史叢刊 (Serial journals of the history of the 1911 Republican Revolution) 8 (1991): 189–202.

Behn, Aphra (1640–89). *All the Histories and Novels Written by the Late Ingenious Mrs. Behn, together with the History of the Life and Memoirs of Mrs. Behn*. 5th edn. London: Printed for R. Wellington, 1705.

Bell, John. *French Constitutional Law*. Oxford: Clarendon Press, 1992.

Benas, B. L. "The Ethics and Poetry of the Chinese, with Phases in Their History." *Proceedings of the Literary and Philosophical Society of Liverpool, during the Seventy-ninth Session, 1889–90*, no. XLIV. London: Longmans, Green, Reader & Dyer; Liverpool: D. Marples & Co. Limited, 1890. 103–166.

Bol, Peter. *Neo-Confucianism in History*. Cambridge, MA: Harvard University Asia Center, 2008.

———. *"This Culture of Ours": Intellectual Transitions in T'ang and Sung China*. Stanford, CA: Stanford University Press, 1992.

Bremer, Fredrika (1801–65). *Life, Letters, and Posthumous Works of Fredrika Bremer*. Ed. Charlotte Bremer. New York: Hurd and Houghton, 1868.

Brunnert, H. S., and V. V. Hagelstrom. *Present Day Political Organization of China*. Revised by N. Th. Kolessoff. Trans. from Russian by A. Beltchenko and E. E. Moran. Taipei: Book World Co., 1911.

Bryois, Henri. "Le Général Tcheng-Ki-Tong." *Revue illustrée* 128 (April 1891): 289–92.

Burton, Margaret E. *The Education of Women in China*. New York: Fleming H. Revell, 1911.

Bury, J. P. T. *Gambetta and the Making of the Third Republic*. London: Longman, 1973.

Cameron, Meribeth E. *The Reform Movement in China, 1898–1912*. Stanford, CA: Stanford University Press, 1931.

Cambridge History of China. 15 vols. Vols. 10–11, *Late Ch'ing, 1800–1911*. Ed. John K. Fairbank. Cambridge: Cambridge University Press, 1978.

Cao Pi 曹丕 (187–226). *Dianlun* 典論 (On classics). "Lunwen" 論文 (On literature). In Xiao Tong 蕭統 (501–31), ed., *Wenxuan* 文選 (Selections of refined literature). 3 vols. Beijing: Zhonghua shuju, 1977. *Juan* 52, 3:720–21.

Chang, Hao. *Liang Ch'i-ch'ao and Intellectual Transition in China 1890–1907*. Cambridge, MA: Harvard University Press, 1971.

Chang, Kang-i Sun. "Women's Poetic Witnessing: Late Ming and Late Qing Examples." In Wang and Shang, eds., *Dynastic Crisis and Cultural Innovation*, 504–22.

Chang, Kang-i Sun, and Haun Saussy, eds. *Women Writers of Traditional China: An Anthology of Poetry and Criticism*. Stanford, CA: Stanford University Press, 1999.

Chao, Anne S. "Chen Duxiu's Early Years: The Importance of Personal Connections in the Social and Intellectual Transformation of China 1895–1920." PhD dissertation. Rice University, 2009.

Chen Chao. "Lun nianqing de xin yibian" 論年輕的心易變 (On youthful minds are easy to change). *Xuchu Nübao* 2 (6 June 1902). "*Nübao* yanshuo" 女報演説 (Vernacular speeches in the *Woman's Journal*) column: 3a–4a.

Chen Jitong 陳季同 (1852–1907) [See also Tcheng-Ki-Tong]. *Bali yinxiang ji* 巴黎印象記. Trans. Duan Yinghong 段映虹. Guilin: Guangxi shifan daxue chubanshe, 2006. [A translation of Tcheng-Ki-Tong, *Les Parisiens peints par un Chinois*.]

———. *Huangshanke chuanqi* 黃衫客傳奇. Trans. Li Huachuan. Beijing: Renmin wenxue chubanshe, 2010. [A translation of Tcheng-Ki-Tong, *Le roman de l'homme jaune*.]

———. "*Qiushi bao* xu" 求是報序 (Preface to the *International Review*). *Qiushi bao* 1 (30 Sept. 1897): 1a.

———. *Wuguo* 吾國. Trans. Li Huachuan. Guilin: Guangxi shifan daxue chubanshe, 2006. [A translation of Tcheng-Ki-Tong, *Mon pays, la Chine d'aujourd'hui*.]

———. *Xue Jia yin* 學賈吟 (Chanting after Jia [Yi]). Ed. Qian Nanxiu 錢南秀. Shanghai: Shanghai guji chubanshe, 2005.

———. *Zhongguo ren de kuaile* 中國人的快樂. Appended to *Zhongguo ren zihua xiang*, a translation of Tcheng-Ki-Tong, *Les Chinois peints par eux mêmes* and *Les plaisirs en Chine*.

———. *Zhongguo ren de xiju* 中國人的戲劇. Trans. Li Huachuan 李華川 and Ling Min 凌敏. Guilin: Guangxi shifan daxue chubanshe, 2006. [A translation of Tcheng-Ki-Tong, *Le théâtre des Chinois*.]

———. *Zhongguo ren zihua xiang* 中國人自畫像. Trans. Huang Xingtao 黃興濤 et al. Guiyang: Guizhou renmin chubanshe, 1998. [A translation of Tcheng-Ki-Tong, *Les Chinois peints par eux memes* and *Les plaisirs en Chine*.]

Chen Pingyuan 陳平原. *Chumo lishi yu jinru wusi* 觸摸歷史與進入五四 (Touching history and walking into May Fourth). Beijing: Beijing daxue chubanshe, 2005.

———. "Male Gaze/Female Students: Late Qing Education for Women as Portrayed in Beijing Pictorials, 1902–08." In Qian, Fong, and Smith, eds., *Different Worlds of Discourse*, 315–47.

———. *Zhongguo xiandai xueshu zhi jianli: Yi Zhang Taiyan, Hu Shizhi wei zhongxin* 中國現代學術之建立: 以章太炎、胡適之為中心 (The establishment of modern Chinese learning: Centering on Zhang Taiyan [Binglin] and Hu Shizhi [Shi]). Beijing: Beijing daxue chubanshe, 1998.

Chen Pingyuan and Xia Xiaohong, eds. *Ershi shiji Zhongguo xiaoshuo lilun ziliao* 二十世紀中國小説理論資料 (Theoretical sources of twentieth-century Chinese fiction). Vol. 1. Beijing: Beijing daxue chubanshe, 1997.

Chen Qiang 陳鏘 (b. 1890), Chen Ying 陳瑩 (b. 1899), and Chen Hong 陳紅 (b. 1892). "Xianbi Xue gongren nianpu" 先妣薛恭人年譜 (Biographic chronology of our late mother, Lady Xue). In Xue, *Daiyunlou yiji*.

Chen Qingyuan 陳慶元. *Fujian wenxue fazhan shi* 福建文學發展史 (History of the development of Fujian literature). Fuzhou: Fujian jiaoyu chubanshe, 1996.

Chen Shengji 陳聲暨 (1877–1925) and Wang Zhen 王真 (1904–71), eds. *Shiyi xiansheng nianpu* 石遺先生年譜 (Biographic chronology of Master Remnant-Stone [Chen Yan]). *Jindai Zhongguo shiliao congkan* 近代中國史料叢刊 (Serial publications of historical materials of Modern China) edn. Taipei xian Yonghe zhen: Wenhai chubanshe, 1968.

Chen Shirong 陳世鎔 (1899–1962). *Fuzhou Xihu Wanzaitang shikan zhenglu* 福州西湖宛在堂詩龕徵錄 (Tested records of the Hall of Elusive Existence Shrine of Poets in Fuzhou's West Lake). 2 vols. Fuzhou: Fujian renmin chubanshe, 2007.

Chen Shou 陳壽 (233–97). *Sanguo zhi* 三國志 (Records of the three kingdoms). Commentary by Pei Songzhi 裴松之 (372–451). 5 vols. Beijing: Zhonghua shuju, 1959.

Chen Shoupeng 陳壽彭 (1857–ca. 1928). "Wangqi Xue gongren zhuanlüe" 亡妻薛恭人傳略 (A brief biography of my late wife, Lady Xue). In Xue, *Daiyunlou yiji*.

———. trans. *Wanguo shilüe* 萬國史略. Nanjing: Jiangchu bianyi guanshuju, 1906. [A translation of Samuel G. Goodrich, *A History of All Nations*.]

———. trans. *Zhongguo jianghai xianyao tuzhi* 中國江海險要圖誌 (from the *China Sea Directory*, 3rd edn., by the Hydrographic Department, Great Britain). 14 vols. 1901; rprt. Guangzhou: Guangya shuju, 1907.

Chen Xiefen 陳擷芬 (1883–1923). "Nannü dou yaokan" 男女都要看 (Both men and women should read this essay). *Xuchu Nübao* 8 (30 Nov. 1902): 2a–3b.

Chen Yan 陳衍 (1856–1937). *Chen Shiyi ji* 陳石遺集 (Collected works of Chen Shiyi [Yan]). 3 vols. Fuzhou: Fujian renmin chubanshe, 2001.

———. *Chen Yan shilun heji* 陳衍詩論合集 (Chen Yan's collected commentaries on poetry). 2 vols. Fuzhou: Fujian renmin chubanshe, 1999.

———. "Dao'anshi shilüe" 道安室事略 (Biographic sketch of the Dao'an Studio Scholar). In Xiao, *Xiao Daoguan ji.*

———. *Min-Hou xian zhi* 閩侯縣誌 (Gazetteer of the Minxian and Houguan districts [of Fuzhou]). 106 *juan*. Min-Hou xian: Min-Hou xian difangzhi bianzuan weiyuanhui, 1933.

———. *Shiyishi shihua* 石遺室詩話 (Remarks on poetry from Remnant-Stone Studio). In Zhang Yinpeng 張寅彭, ed., *Minguo shihua congbian* 民國詩話叢編 (Serial collections of remarks on poetry of the Minguo era). 6 vols. Shanghai: Shanghai shudian, 2002. Vol. 1.

———. *Shiyishi shiji* 石遺室詩集 (Collected poems from Remnant-Stone Studio). Wuchang: Chen Yan's family edition, 1905.

Chen Yinke 陳寅恪 (1890–1969). "Lun Zaisheng yuan" 論《再生緣》(On *Love reincarnate*). In idem, *Hanliutang ji* 寒柳堂集 (Collected works from Cold-Willow Hall). Shanghai: Shanghai guji chubanshe, 1980. 1–96.

Chen Yiyi 陳以益 [Chen Zhiqun 陳志群]. "Nübaojie zuixin diaochabiao" 女報界最新調查表 (Most up-to-date investigation of periodicals for women). *Shenzhou Nübao* 3 (Feb. 1908). Reprinted in *Nülun* 女論 (On women), a special issue of *Nübao* (28 Sept. 1909): 11–12.

———. "*Shenzhou nübao* fakanci" 神州女報發刊詞 (Foreword to the *Shenzhou nübao*). *Shenzhou nübao* 1 (Dec. 1907). Reprinted in *Nülun*, 9–10.

Chen Yun 陳芸. *Chen Xiaonü yiji* 陳孝女遺集 (Posthumously collected writings by the Filial Daughter Chen), originally titiled *Xiao daixuan shiji* 小黛軒詩集 (Collected poems from Little Black-Jade Pavilion), 2 *juan*. Appended to Xue, *Daiyunlou yiji.*

———. *Xiao daixuan lunshi shi* 小黛軒論詩詩 (Poems on poetics from Little Black-Jade Pavilion), 2 *juan*. Appended to Xue, *Daiyunlou yiji.*

Cheng Qianfan 程千帆 (1913–2000), ed. *Songshi jingxuan* 宋詩精選 (Refined selections of Song poetry). Nanjing: Jiangsu guji chubanshe, 1993.

"The Chinese as They Are." *Literary World: A Fortnightly Review of Current Literature* 16.10 (30 May 1885): 184.

Chunqiu Gongyang zhuan [*zhushu*] 春秋公羊傳[註疏] ([Commentary on the] *Gongyang Commentary on the Spring and Autumn Annals*). *Jiegu* 解詁 commentary by He Xiu 何休 (129–82), and *shu* commentary by Xu Yan 徐彥 (ninth century?). In Ruan Yuan, ed., *Shisanjing zhushu*, 2:2189–2355.

Chunqiu Zuozhuan [*zhengyi*] 春秋左傳[正義] ([Orthodox commentary on the]

Zuo Commentary on the Spring and Autumn Annals). *Zhu* 註 commentary by Du Yu 杜預 (222–85), and *shu* 疏 commentary by Kong Yingda 孔穎達 (574–648). In Ruan Yuan, ed., *Shisanjing zhushu*, 2:1697–2188.

Clergue, Helen. *The Salon: A Study of French Society and Personalities in the Eighteenth Century*. New York: G. P. Putnam, 1907.

Code Napoléon, or, The French Civil Code. Literally translated by George Spence, from the original and official edition, published at Paris, in 1804. Baton Rouge: Claitor's Book Store, 1960.

Cohen, Paul A. *Discovering History in China: American Historical Writing on the Recent Chinese Past*. New York: Columbia University Press, 1984.

Cohen, Paul A., and John E. Schrecker, eds. *Reform in Nineteenth-Century China*. Cambridge, MA: Harvard University East Asian Research Center, 1976.

Conboy, Katie et al., eds. *Writing on the Body: Female Embodiment and Feminist Theory*. New York: Columbia University Press, 1997.

De Bary, William Theodore, and Irene Bloom. *Sources of Chinese Tradition*. 2 vols. New York: Columbia University Press, 1999–2000.

Deng Hongmei 鄧紅梅. *Nüxing cishi* 女性詞史 (History of song-lyrics by women). Ji'nan: Shandong jiaoyu chubanshe, 2002.

Dikötter, Frank. *The Discourse of Race in Modern China*. London: Hurst, 1992.

Ding Yun 丁芸 (1859–94). *Minchuan guixiu shihua xubian* 閩川閨秀詩話續編 (Sequel to *Remarks on Women's Poetry from the Min River*). Beijing: Houguan Dingshi Jiyunxuan, 1914.

Dobson, Austin (1840–1921). *Four Frenchwomen*. New York: Dodd, Mead, 1895.

Du Deffand, Marie de Vichy Chamrond (1697–1780). *Letters of the Marquise du Deffand to the Hon. Horace Walpole, afterwards Earl of Orford, from the Year 1766 to the Year 1780, to Which are Added Letters of Madame du Deffand to Voltaire, from the Year 1759 to the Year 1775*. London: Longman, Hurst, Rees, and Orme, 1810.

Du Fu 杜甫 (712–70). *Dushi [xiangzhu]* 杜詩[詳注] ([Detailed annotation of] *Du Fu's Poems*). Annot. Qiu Zhao'ao 仇兆鰲 (1638–1717). 5 vols. Beijing: Zhonghua shuju, 1979.

Du Jikun 杜繼琨. "Zai tan *Nü xuebao*" 再談女學報 (More about the *Nü xuebao*). *Tushuguan* 圖書館 (Journal of library science) 4 (Beijing, 1963): 55–56.

Duara, Prasenjit. "The Regime of Authenticity: Timelessness, Gender, and National History in Modern China." *History and Theory* 37.3 (Oct. 1998): 287–308.

———. *Rescuing History from the Nation: Questioning Narratives of Modern China*. Chicago: University of Chicago Press, 1995.

Egan, Ronald. *The Burden of Female Talent: The Poet Li Qingzhao and Her History in China*. Cambridge, MA: Harvard University Asia Center, 2013.

Elman, Benjamin A. *A Cultural History of Civil Examinations in Late Imperial China*. Berkeley: University of California Press, 2000.

———. *A Cultural History of Modern Science in China*. Cambridge, MA: Harvard University Press, 2006.

———. "Naval Warfare and the Refraction of China's Self-strengthening Reforms into Scientific and Technological Failure, 1865–1895." *Modern Asian Studies* 38.2 (2004): 283–326.

Elwood, Anne Katharine. *Memoirs of the Literary Ladies of England from the Commencement of the Last Century.* 2 vols. London: Henry Colburn, 1843.

Fan Dangshi 范當世 (1854–1904). *Fan Bozi shiji* 范伯子詩集 (Collected poems of Fan Bozi [Fan Dangshi]). *Xuxiu siku quanshu* edn., late Qing; rprt. 1995. Vol. 1568.

Fan Ye 范曄 (398–445). *Hou-Han shu* 後漢書 (History of the Latter Han). Commentary by Li Xian 李賢 (651–84). 12 vols. Beijing: Zhonghua shuju, 1965.

Fang Xuanling 房玄齡 (578–648) et al. *Jinshu* 晉書 (History of the Jin). 10 vols. Beijing: Zhonghua shuju, 1974.

Feng Yansi 馮延巳 (903–60). *Yangchun ji* 陽春集 (Collection of the spring sun). *Xuxiu Siku quanshu* edn., late Qing; rprt. 2002. Vol. 1722.

Feng Yingjing 馮應京 (1555–1606). *Yueling guangji* 月令廣義 (Enlarged version of the *Proceedings of Government in the Different Months*). Ed. Dai Ren 戴任 (fl. 1601). Moling: Chen Bangtai Shiquge, 1601.

Fong, Grace. *Herself an Author: Gender, Agency, and Writing in Late Imperial China.* Honolulu: University of Hawai'i Press, 2008.

Fong, Grace, Nanxiu Qian, and Harriet Zurndorfer, eds. *Beyond Tradition and Modernity: Gender, Genre, and Cosmopolitanism in Late Qing China.* Leiden: Brill, 2004.

Fong, Grace, and Ellen Widmer, eds. *Inner Quarters and Beyond: Women Writers from Ming through Qing.* Leiden: Brill, 2010.

Fowler, Ellen Thorneycroft. *A Double Thread.* New York: D. Appleton and Company, 1900.

Frankel, Hans H. *The Flowering Plum and the Palace Lady: Interpretations of Chinese Poetry.* New Haven, CT: Yale University Press, 1976.

Furth, Charlotte. "Poetry and Women's Culture in Late Imperial China: Editor's Introduction." *Late Imperial China* 13.1 (June 1992): 1–8.

Gan Bao 干寶 (d. 336). *Soushen ji* 搜神記 (Records of gods). Commentary by Wang Shaoying 汪紹楹. Beijing: Zhonghua shuju, 1979.

Garrett, Valery. *Chinese Dress: From the Qing Dynasty to the Present.* Tokyo: Tuttle Publishing, 2007.

Gasster, Michael. "Reform and Revolution in China's Political Modernization." In Mary Clabaugh Wright, ed., *China in Revolution: The First Phase 1900–1913.* New Haven, CT: Yale University Press, 1968. 67–96.

Ge Hong 葛洪 (ca. 284–ca. 363). *Baopu zi* 抱朴子 (Master embracing *pu*). *Zhuzi jicheng* 諸子集成 (Collection of philosophers' works) edn. Beijing: Zhonghua shuju, 1954, 1986.

Ge Xiaoyin 葛曉音. "Lun Su Shi shiwen zhong de liqu" 論蘇軾詩文中的理趣 (On the philosophical sophistication of Su Shi's poetry and prose). *Xueshu yuekan* 學術月刊 (Academic monthly), 1995.4: 82–88.

Gibbon, Edward. *The History of the Decline and Fall of the Roman Empire.* Ed. J. B. Bury. 7 vols. London: Methuen, 1896–1902.

Giquel, Prosper. *The Foochow Arsenal and Its Results: From the Commencement in*

1867, to the End of the Foreign Directorate on the 16th February, 1874. Trans. from French by H. Lang. Shanghai: Shanghai Evening Courier, 1874.

"Gleaner." "Monthly Notes: Literature." *Once a Month: An Illustrated Australasian Magazine* 3 (15 July 1885): 76–78.

Goodrich, Frank B. *World-Famous Women.* Philadelphia: P. W. Ziegler & Co., 1879.

Goodrich, Samuel G. *A History of All Nations, from the Earliest Periods to the Present Time; or, Universal History.* Rev. edn. 2 vols. Auburn, NY: Auburn Publ. Co., 1860; Chicago, 1886.

———. *Lives of Celebrated Women.* Boston: Bradbury, Soden & Co., 1844.

Graham, A. C. *Disputers of the Tao: Philosophical Argument in Ancient China.* La Salle, IL: Open Court, 1989.

———. trans. *Poems of the Late T'ang.* Harmondsworth: Penguin Books, 1984.

Grattier, Adolphe de. *Commentaire sur les Lois de la presse et des autres moyens de publication.* 2 vols. Paris: Videcoq: Ch. Hingray, 1839.

Great Britain, Hydrographic Department. *The China Sea Directory.* 3rd edn. 5 vols. London: Hydrographic Office, Admiralty, 1894.

Gu Tinglong 顧廷龍 (1904–98), ed. *Qingdai zhujuan jicheng* 清代硃卷集成 (Collection of examination papers from the Qing dynasty). "Lin Daren" 林大任. 420 vols. Taipei: Chengwen chubanshe, 1992. 340:83–96.

Guerville, Amédée Baillot de. *Au Japon: The Memoirs of a Foreign Correspondent in Japan, Korea, and China, 1892–1894.* Trans. and annot. with an introduction by Daniel C. Kane. West Lafayette, IN: Parlor Press, 2009.

Gugong bowuyuan dang'anbu 故宮博物院明清檔案部 (Beijing Palace Museum Ming-Qing Archives). *Qingmo choubei lixian dang'an shiliao* 清末籌備立憲檔案史料 (Historical archive of the late Qing preparations for constitutional construction). 2 vols. Beijing: Zhonghua shuju, 1979.

Guo Maoqian 郭茂倩 (1041–99), ed. *Yuefu shiji* 樂府詩集 (Collected Music Bureau poetry). 4 vols. Beijing: Zhonghua shuju, 1979.

Guo Shaoyu 郭紹虞 (1893–1984). *Zhongguo wenxue piping shi* 中國文學批評史 (History of Chinese literary criticism). Shanghai: Xin wenyi chubanshe, 1957.

Guo Shaoyu and Wang Wensheng 王文生, eds. *Zhongguo lidai wenlun xuan* 中國歷代文論選 (Selected essays on Chinese literary theories through the ages). 4 vols. Shanghai: Shanghai guji chubanshe, 1980.

Guo Tingyi 郭廷以, ed. *Jindai Zhongguo shishi rizhi: Qing ji* 近代中國史事日誌: 清季 (Daily records of modern Chinese history: Late Qing). 2 vols. Taipei: Shangwu yinshuguan, 1963.

Guo Yanli 郭延禮. "Nüxing zai 20 shiji chuqi de wenxue fanyi chengjiu" 女性在 20世紀初期的文學翻譯成就 (Woman's achievements in literary translation in the early twentieth century). *Zhongguo xiandai wenxue yanjiu congkan* 中國現代文學研究叢刊 (Serial publications of the study of modern Chinese literature) 2010. 3:38–50.

———. *Zhongguo jindai fanyi wenxue gailun* 中國近代翻譯文學概論 (A brief study of modern Chinese translational literature). Hankou: Hubei jiaoyu chubanshe, 1998.

Hale, Sarah Josepha Buell (1788–1879). *Woman's Record; or, Sketches of All Distinguished Women, from the Creation to A.D. 1854. Arranged in Four Eras*. New York: Harper, 1860.

Han Fei zi [*jijie*] 韓非子[集解] ([Collected commentaries on the] *Han Fei zi*). Commentary by Wang Xianshen 王先慎 (fl. late Qing). *Zhuzi jicheng* edn. Beijing: Zhonghua shuju, 1954, 1986.

Han Yu 韓愈 (768–824). *Han Changli wenji* [*jiaozhu*] 韓昌黎文集[校注] ([Collated and annotated collection of] *Han Changli's [Han Yu's] Prose*). Collation and annotation by Ma Qichang 馬其昶. Ed. Ma Maoyuan 馬茂元. Shanghai: Shanghai guji chubanshe, 1987.

Hart, Robert. *The I. G. in Peking: Letters of Robert Hart, Chinese Maritime Customs, 1868–1907*. Ed. John King Fairbank et al. Cambridge, MA: Belknap Press of Harvard University Press, 1975.

He Liangjun 何良俊 (1506–1573). *Yulin* 語林 (Forest of accounts). *Siku quanshu* edn. Vol. 1041.

Hemans, Felicia Dorothea (1793–1835). *The Works of Mrs. Hemans with a Memoir by Her Sister, and an Essay on Her Genius by Mrs. Sigourney*. Philadelphia: Lea and Blanchard, 1840.

Henry, Madeleine Mary. *Prisoner of History: Aspasia of Miletus and Her Biographical Tradition*. New York: Oxford University Press, 1995.

Hershatter, Gail. *Women in China's Long Twentieth Century*. Berkeley: University of California Press, 2007. Ebook http://books.google.com.

Homer. *Iliad*. Trans. Richmond Lattimore. Chicago: University of Chicago Press, 1951.

Hou Yijie 侯宜傑. *Ershi shiji chu Zhongguo zhengzhi gaige fengchao: Qingmo lixian yundong shi* 二十世紀初中國政治改革風潮：清末立憲運動史 (Early twentieth-century torrents of political reform: A history of the late Qing constitutional movement). Beijing: Renmin wenxue chubanshe, 1993.

Howe, Gertrude, trans. "The Provisional Prospectus of the Chinese Girls' School." *Missionary Review of the World* (Jan. 1898): 52–55.

Howe, Julia Ward (1819–1910). *Margaret Fuller (Marchesa Ossoli)*. Boston: Roberts Brothers, 1883.

Hu Bingwen 胡炳文 (1250–1333). "*Ganxing shi tong* xu" 感興詩通序 (Preface to the *Interpretation of* [*Zhu Xi's*] *"Thoughts from My Studio Life"*). In idem, *Yunfeng ji* 雲峰集 (Collected works from Cloud Summit). *Siku quanshu* edn. Vol. 1199.

Hu Shi 胡適 (1891–1962). "Sanbai nian zhong de nü zuojia (*Qing guixiu yiwen lüe* xu)" 三百年中的女作家 (《清閨秀藝文略》序) (Three hundred years of women writers [Preface to the *Bibliographic Treatise of Qing Women Writers*]). In Ouyang Zhesheng 歐陽哲生, ed., *Hu Shi wenji* 胡適文集 (Collected works of Hu Shi). 12 vols. Beijing: Beijing daxue chubanshe, 1998. 4:585–91.

Hu, Siao-chen. "The Daughter's Vision of National Crisis: *Tianyuhua* and a Women Writer's Construction of the Late Ming." In Wang and Shang, eds., *Dynastic Crisis and Cultural Innovation*, 200–231.

Hu Wenkai 胡文楷. *Lidai funü zhuzuo kao* 歷代婦女著作考 (Catalogue of women's writings through the ages). Revised edition. Eds. Zhang Hongsheng 張宏生 et al. Shanghai: Shanghai guji chubanshe, 2008.

———. "Xiao Daoguan" 蕭道管. In idem, *Nüzi wenxue shi* 女子文學史 (History of women's literature). Manuscript. 11 vols. (Shanghai Library collection, not paginated). Vol. 11.

Hu, Ying. "Naming the First 'New Woman.'" In Karl and Zarrow, eds., *Rethinking the 1898 Reform Period*, 180–211.

———. *Tales of Translation: Composing the New Woman in China, 1899–1918*. Stanford, CA: Stanford University Press, 2000.

Hu, Ying, and Joan Judge, eds. *Beyond Exemplar Tales: Women's Biography in Chinese History*. Berkeley: Global, Area, and International Archive, University of California, 2011.

Hu Yinglin 胡應麟 (1551–1602). *Shisou* 詩藪 (Poetry marsh). Shanghai: Shanghai guji chubanshe, 1979.

Huan Kuan 桓寬 (fl. first century BCE). *Yantie lun [jiaozhu]* 鹽鐵論[校注] ([Collation and annotation of] *Treatise on salt and iron*). Collation and annotation by Wang Liqi 王利器. Beijing: Zhonghua shuju, 1992.

Huang Ren 黃任 (1683–1768). *Xiangcaojian ouzhu* 香草箋偶註 (Casual commentary on the *Fragrant Grass Draft*). Taipei: Xinwentai chuban gongsi, 1980.

Huang Xiangjin 黃湘金. "Nanguo nüzi jie nengshi: *Qing guixiu yiwen lüe* pingjie" 南國女子皆能詩:《清閨秀藝文略》評介 (Southern women are all capable of writing poetry: Critical introduction to the *Bibliographic Treatise of Qing Women Writers*). *Wenxue yichan* 文學遺產 (Literary heritage) 2008.1: 94–104.

Huang Xingtao 黃興濤. "Yige bugai bei yiwang de wenhua ren—Chen Jitong qiren qishu" 一個不該被忘記的文化人——陳季同其人其書 (An intellectual not to be forgotten: Chen Jitong, the man and his works). Introduction to Chen Jitong, *Zhongguo ren zihua xiang*. Guiyang: Guizhou renmin chubanshe, 1998. i–xi.

Huang Zunxian 黃遵憲 (1848–1905). *Renjinglu shicao [jianzhu]* 人境廬詩草[箋注] ([Commentary on] *Poetic Drafts from Human-realm Hut*). Commentary by Qian Zhonglian. 2 vols. Shanghai: Shanghai guji chubanshe, 1981.

Huters, Theodore. *Bringing the World Home: Appropriating the West in Late Qing and Early Republican China*. Honolulu: University of Hawai'i Press, 2005.

———. "A New Way of Writing: The Possibilities for Literature in Late Qing China, 1895–1908." *Modern China* 14.3 (July 1988): 243–76.

Idema, Wilt. *The Butterfly Lovers: The Legend of Liang Shanbo and Zhu Yingtai; Four Versions, with Related Texts*. Indianapolis, IN: Hackett, 2010.

Idema, Wilt, and Beata Grant. *The Red Brush: Writing Women of Imperial China*. Cambridge, MA: Harvard University Asia Center, 2004.

Ip, Hung-Yok, Tze-Ki Hon, and Chiu-Chun Lee. "The Plurality of Chinese Modernity: A Review of Recent Scholarship on the May Fourth Movement." *Modern China* 29.4 (2003): 490–509.

Jiang Wanfang 蔣畹芳 [Jiang Lan 蔣蘭]. "Kaichuang Nü xuetang lun" 開創女學堂論 (On the establishment of the Girls' School). In Jing Yuanshan, ed., *Nüxue jiyi chubian*, 20a–20b.

Jiang Zhiyou 蔣智由 (1865–1929). "Aiguo nüxuexiao yenshuo" 愛國女學校演説 (Speech at [the opening ceremony of] the Patriotic Girls' School). *Xuchu Nübao* 9 (30 December 1902): 1a–4b.

Jiaoshi Yilin [*jiaolüe*] 焦氏易林 [校略] ([A brief collation of] *Jiao's Forest of Changes*). Attributed to Jiao Yanshou 焦延壽 (aka Jiao Gan 焦贛, ca. 70–10 BCE). Collation by Zhai Yunsheng 翟云升 (*js.* 1822). *Xuxiu siku quanshu* edn., early 19th century; rprt. 2002. Vol. 1055.

Jin Tianyu 金天羽 (1873–1947) [Jin Songcen 金松岑, Jin Tianhe 金天翮]. *Tiianfanglou wenyan (fu shiji)* 天放樓文言 (附詩集) (Collected prose from Heavenly-Contented Tower, Collected poems appended). *Jindai Zhongguo shiliao congkan* edn. 1927; rprt. Taipei xian Yonghe zhen: Wenhai chubanshe, 1974.

Jing Yuanshan 經元善 (1841–1903). *Juyi chuji* 居易初集 (First collection of Juyi's [Jing Yuanshan's] works). Macao: Jing family edition, 1901.

———. ed. *Nüxue jiyi chubian* 女學集議初編 (Collected opinions on education for women, first edition). Shanghai: Jing family edition, 1898.

Judge, Joan. "Chinese Women's History: Global Circuits, Local Meanings." *Journal of Women's History* 25.4 (2013): 224–43.

———. *The Precious Raft of History: The Past, the West, and the Woman Question in China*. Stanford, CA: Stanford University Press, 2008.

———. *Print and Politics: 'Shibao' and the Culture of Reform in Late Qing China*. Stanford, CA: Stanford University Press, 1996.

———. "Reforming the Feminine: Female Literacy and the Legacy of 1898." In Karl and Zarrow, eds., *Rethinking the 1898 Reform Period*, 158–79.

Kahn, Ida [Kang Aide 康愛德], and Mary Stone [Shi Meiyu 石美玉]. "Correspondence to the Report 'The New Chinese Girls' School.'" *North China Herald and Supreme Court and Consular Gazette* 60.1588 (7 Jan. 1898): 16–17.

Kang Tongwei 康同薇 (1879–1974). "Nüxue libi shuo" 女學利弊說 (On the advantages and disadvantages of education for women). *Zhixin bao* 52 (11 May 1898): 1a–3b; *Nü xuebao* 7 (Sept. 1898): 2a–3b.

Karl, Rebecca E. "'Slavery,' Citizenship, and Gender in Late Qing China's Global Context." In Karl and Zarrow, eds., *Rethinking the 1898 Reform Period*, 212–44.

Karl, Rebecca E., and Peter Zarrow, eds. *Rethinking the 1898 Reform Period: Political and Cultural Change in Late Qing China*. Cambridge, MA: Harvard University Asia Center, 2002.

Knoke, David. *Political Networks: The Structural Perspective*. Cambridge: Cambridge University Press, 1990.

Ko, Dorothy. *Cinderella's Sisters: A Revisionist History of Footbinding*. Berkeley: University of California Press, 2005.

———. "Pursuing Talent and Virtue: Education and Women's Culture in Seventeenth- and Eighteenth-Century China." *Late Imperial China* 13.1 (June 1992): 9–39.

———. *Teachers of the Inner Chambers: Women and Culture in Seventeenth-Century China*. Stanford, CA: Stanford University Press, 1994.

Kowallis, Jon. *The Subtle Revolution: Poets of the "Old Schools" during Late Qing and Early Republican China*. Berkeley, CA: Institute of East Asian Studies, 2006.

Kuhn, Raymond. *The Media in France*. London: Routledge, 1995.

Kwong, Luke S. K. *A Mosaic of the Hundred Days: Personalities, Politics, and Ideas of 1898*. Cambridge, MA: Council on East Asian Studies, Harvard University, 1984.

Lackner, Michael, Iwo Amelung, and Joachim Kurtz, eds. *New Terms for New Ideas: Western Knowledge & Lexical Change in Late Imperial China*. Leiden: Brill, 2001.

Lackner, Michael, and Natascha Vittinghoff, eds. *Mapping Meanings: The Field of New Learning in Late Qing China*. Leiden: Brill, 2004.

Lai Maogong 賴茂功. "Shi Bingzhang sheji luhaijun dayuanshuai jiuzhi jinian youpiao kao" 施秉章設計陸海軍大元帥就職紀念郵票考 (Shi Bingzhang's design of the postage stamp commemorating the inauguration of the generalissimo [Zhang Zuolin]). *Hubei youdianbao* 湖北郵電報 13, special issue on stamp collecting (15 July 2007): 3.

Lai Mayi 賴媽懿 [Maria-Adèle Lardanchet] and Shen Heqing 沈和卿 [Shen Ying 沈瑛]. "Zhongguo Nü xuehui shushu zhangcheng" 中國女學會書塾章程 (Regulations of the Girls' School affiliated with the Chinese Women's Study Society). *Xinwen bao* (17, 19, and 20 Mar. 1898); *Xiang bao* 64 (May 19): 254a–55a. Also under the title "Nü xuehui shushu kaiguan zhangcheng" 女學會書塾開館章程 (Regulations of the Girls' School affiliated with the Women's Study Society, upon its opening). *Nü xuebao* 8 (Sept. 1898): 4b; 9 (Oct. 1898): 4b; and later (not seen) issues.

Lamley, Harry J. "The 1895 Taiwan Republic: A Significant Episode in Modern Chinese History." *Journal of Asian Studies* 27.4 (Aug. 1968): 739–62.

Landon, Letitia Elizabeth (1802–38). *Life and Literary Remains of L. E. L.* Ed. Laman Blanchard (1804–45). 2 vols. London: H. Colburn, 1841.

Laozi Dao De jing [zhu] 老子道德經[註] ([Commentary on] *Laozi Dao De jing*). In Wang Bi, *Wang Bi ji [jiaoshi]*. 1:1–193.

Laozi zhu 老子註. Attributed to Heshang gong 河上公 (early Han). *Siku quanshu* edn. Vol. 1055

Lau, D. C., trans. *Confucius: The Analects*. New York: Penguin Books, 1979.

———. trans. *Lao Tzu Tao Te Ching*. New York: Penguin Books, 1963.

———. trans. *Mencius*. New York: Penguin Books, 1970.

Legge, James (1815–97), trans. *The Chinese Classics*. 5 vols. Hong Kong: Hong Kong University Press, 1960.

———. trans. *Li Chi: Book of Rites*. Ed. with introduction and study guide by Ch'u Chai and Winberg Chai. 2 vols. New Hyde Park, NY: University Books, 1967.

Leibovitz, Liel, and Matthew Miller. *Fortunate Sons: The 120 Chinese Boys Who Came to America, Went to School, and Revolutionized an Ancient Civilization*. New York: W.W. Norton, 2011.

Lespinasse, Julie de (1732–76). *Lettres de Mademoiselle de Lespinasse, écrits depuis l'année 1773 jusqu'à l'année 1776*. 2 vols. Paris: Collin, 1809.

Levenson, Joseph R. *Confucian China and Its Modern Fate: A Trilogy*. Berkeley: University of California Press, 1968.

Li Bai 李白 (701–62). *Li Taibai quanji* 李太白全集 (Collected works of Li Taibai [Li Bai]). Commentary by Wang Qi 王琦 (fl. 1758). 3 vols. Beijing: Zhonghua shuju, 1977.

Li E 厲鶚 (1692–1752). *Yutai shushi* 玉臺書史 (History of calligraphy from Jade Terrace). *Xuxiu siku quanshu* edn. 1833; rprt. 2002. Vol. 1084.

Li, Guotong. "Imagining History and the State: Fujian *Guixiu* (Genteel Ladies) at Home and on the Road." In Fong and Widmer, eds., *The Inner Quarters and Beyond*, 315–38.

Li Hongzhang 李鴻章 (1823–1901). *Li Hongzhang quanji* 李鴻章全集 (Complete works of Li Hongzhang). Ed. Wang Pu 王樸. 9 vols. Haikou: Hainan chubanshe, 1997.

Li Huachuan 李華川. "Qingmo Zhongguo ren chuangzuo de Fawen xiaoshuo" 清末中國人創作的法文小説 (A story written in French by a late Qing Chinese). *Dushu* 讀書 (Reading), 2001.6: 72–75.

———. *Wan-Qing yige waijiao guan de wenhua licheng* 晚清一個外交官的文化歷程 (A late Qing diplomat's cultural journey). Beijing: Beijing daxue chubanshe, 2004.

Li Kan 李侃, Li Shiyue 李時岳, Li Dezheng 李德征, Yang Ce 楊策, and Gong Shuduo 龔書鐸. *Zhongguo jindai shi* 中國近代史 (Modern Chinese history). 4th edn. Beijing: Zhonghua shuju, 1994.

Li Qingzhao 李清照 (1084–ca. 1155). *Li Qingzhao ji [jiaozhu]* 李清照集[校注] ([Collated and annotated collection of] *Li Qingzhao's Works*). Collation and annotation by Wang Zhongwen 王仲聞 (1901–69). Beijing: Renmin wenxue chubanshe, 1979.

Li Shangyin 李商隱 (ca. 813–ca. 58). *Li Shangyin shige [jijie]* 李商隱詩歌[集解] ([Collected commentaries on the] *Collected poems of Li Shangyin*). Commentary by Liu Xuekai 劉學鍇 and Yu Shucheng 余恕誠. 5 vols. Beijing: Zhonghua shuju, 1988.

Li Timotai 李提摩太 [Timothy Richard]. "Shengli fenli zhi fa: Yiyan po wanmi shuo" 生利分利之法: 一言破萬迷說 (Productive and non-productive methods: On one word resolving ten thousand confusions). Trans. Zhutiesheng 鑄鐵生. *Wanguo gongbao* 51 (April 1893): 1a–3a.

Li, Wai-yee. "Women Writers and Gender Boundaries during the Ming-Qing Transition." In Fong and Widmer, eds., *The Inner Quarters and Beyond*, 179–213.

Li, Xiaorong. "Gender and Textual Politics during the Qing Dynasty: The Case of the *Zhengshi ji*." *Harvard Journal of Asiatic Studies* 69.1 (2009): 75–107.

———. *Rewriting the Inner Chambers: Tradition and Transformation in Chinese Women's Poetry, 1650–1920*. Seattle: University of Washington Press, 2012.

Li Yan and Du Shiran. *Chinese Mathematics: A Concise History*. Trans. John N. Crossley and Anthony W.-C. Lun. Oxford: Clarendon Press, 1987.

Li Youning 李又寧 and Zhang Yufa 張玉法, eds. *Jindai Zhongguo nüquan yundong shiliao* 近代中國女權運動史料 (Historical materials on the women's movement in modern China). 2 vols. Taipei: Zhuanji wenxue chubanshe, 1975.

Liang Qichao 梁啟超 (1873–1929). "Changshe nü xuetang qi" 倡設女學堂啓

(Announcement of the establishment of the Girls' School). *Shiwu bao* 45 (15 Nov. 1897): 3a–4a. Also in *Xinwen bao* (18 Nov. 1897); *Qiushi bao* 7 (28 Nov. 1897) (titled "Chuangyi sheli nü xuetang qi" 創議設立女學堂啓), "Fulu," 1a–1b; *Wanguo gongbao* 107 (Dec. 1897), 7a–7b. Also in Zhu Youhuan, ed., *Zhongguo jindai xuezhi shiliao, diyi ji*, 2:883–84.

———. "Gao xiaoshuo jia" 告小説家 (To fiction writers). In Guo Shaoyu and Wang Wensheng, eds., *Zhongguo lidai wenlun xuan*, 4:217–18.

———. "Ji Jiangxi Kang nüshi" 記江西康女士 (Biographic record of Ms. Kang from Jiangxi). *Shiwu bao* 21 (23 Mar. 1897): 2b–3a.

———. "Lin Xu zhuan" 林旭傳 (Biography of Lin Xu). In idem, *Yinbingshi heji* 飲冰室合集 (Assembled collections from Drinking-Ice Studio), *Zhuanji* 專集 (Special works) 1, *Wuxu zhengbian ji* 戊戌政變記 (Records of the 1898 coup d'etat). 12 vols. Beijing: Zhonghua shuju, 1989. 6:103–104.

———. "Lun nüxue" 論女學 (On education for women). *Shiwu bao* 23 (12 April 1897): 1a–4a, and 25 (2 May 1897): 1a–2b.

———. "Luolan furen zhuan" 羅蘭夫人傳 (Biography of Madame Roland). Originally published in *Xinmin congbao* 新民叢報 (Journal of the new people) 17 and 18 (Oct. 1902), under Zhongguo zhi xinmin 中國之新民 (A New Chinese Citizen) and the title "Jinshi diyi nüjie Luolan furen zhuan" 近世第一女傑羅蘭夫人傳 (Biography of the most eminent modern heroine, Madame Roland). Collected in Liang, *Yinbingshi heji, Zhuanji* 12. 6:1–14.

———. "Xiaoshuo yu qunzhi zhi guanxi" 小説與群治之關係 (Fiction and society). In Guo Shaoyu and Wang Wensheng, eds., *Zhongguo lidai wenlun xuan*, 4:207–17.

Liang Qichao et al. "Nü xuetang shiban lüezhang" 女學堂試辦略章 (Provisional regulations for the [Chinese] Girls' School). *Xinwen bao* (18 Nov. 1897). Also in *Wanguo gongbao* 107 (Dec. 1897); *Qiushi bao* 7 (28 Nov. 1897), "Fulu" 附錄 (Appendices): 1b–2b; and 8 (8 Dec. 1897), "Fulu": 3a–4b. Also under the title "Shanghai xinshe Zhongguo Nü xuetang zhangcheng" 上海新設中國女學堂章程 (Regulations for the newly established Chinese Girls' School in Shanghai). *Shiwu bao* 47 (4 Dec. 1897): 7–10; and in Zhu Youhuan, ed., *Zhongguo jindai xuezhi shiliao, diyi ji*, 2: 885–88. Also under the title "Nü xuehui shushu chuangban zhangcheng" 女學會書塾創辦章程 (Provisional regulations for the Girls' School affiliated with the Women's Study Society). *Nü xuebao* 1 (24 July 1898): 4b; 2 (3 Aug. 1898): 4b; 3 (15 Aug. 1898): 4b; 5 (27 Aug. 1898): 4b; 8 (Sept. 1898): 4a–4b.

———. "Provisional Regulations for the Chinese Girls' School." Trans. *North China Herald and Supreme Court and Consular Gazette* LIX.1586 (Dec. 24, 1897): 1138–39.

Liang Zhangju 梁章鉅 (1775–1849). *Langji congtan, Xutan, Santan* 浪跡叢談、續談、三談 (Collection, continued collection, and the third collection of a wanderer's talks). Punctuation and collation by Chen Tiemin 陳鐵民. Beijing: Zhonghua shuju, 1981.

———. *Minchuan guixiu shihua* 閩川閨秀詩話 (Remarks on women's poetry from the Min River). *Xuxiu siku quanshu* edn. 1849; rprt. 2002. Vol. 1705.

Liezi zhu 列子注 (Commentary on the *Liezi*). Commentary by Zhang Zhan 張湛 (fl. early 4th century). *Zhuzi jicheng* edn. Beijing: Zhonghua shuju, 1954, 1986.

Liji [*zhengyi*] 禮記[正義] ([Orthodox commentary on the] *Records of Ritual*). *Zhu* commentary by Zheng Xuan 鄭玄 (127–200), and *shu* commentary by Kong Yingda. In Ruan Yuan, ed., *Shisanjing zhushu*, 1:1221–2:1696.

Lin Changyi 林昌彝 (1803–76). *Sheyinglou shihua* 射鷹樓詩話 (Remarks on poetry from Shooting-Eagle Tower). *Xuxiu siku quanshu* edn. 1851; rprt. 2002. Vol. 1706.

Lin Chongyong 林崇墉. *Shen Baozhen yu Fuzhou chuanzheng* 沈葆楨與福州船政 (Shen Baozhen and the Fuzhou Navy Yard management). Taipei: Lianjing chuban shiye gongsi, 1987.

Lin Lezhi 林樂知 [Young J. Allen] (1836–1907). "Zhuxing nüxue lun" 助興女學論 (On promoting education for women). *Wanguo gongbao* 108 (Jan. 1898): 21a–22a. Reprinted in Jing, ed., *Nuxue jiyi chubian*, 50a–52b.

Lin Ning 林寧. "Li Xuangong de jiashi yu shengping" 李宣龔的家世與生平 (Li Xuangong's life and family background). *Fuzhou daxue xuebao* 福州大學學報 (Journal of Fuzhou University) (Philosophy and Social Science) 81 (2007): 11–16.

Lin Xu 林旭 (1875–98). *Wancuixuan shi* 晚翠軒詩 (Poems from Evening-emerald Pavilion). Ed. Li Xuangong 李宣龔 (1876–1952). *Mochao congke* 墨巢叢刻 (Serial publications from [Li's studio] Ink Nest) edn. 1936.

Ling Hongxun 凌鴻勛. *Zhonghua tielu shi* 中華鐵路史 (History of China's railways). Taipei: Shangwu yinshuguan, 1981.

Liu Fu 劉斧 (fl. 1073). *Qingsuo gaoyi* 青瑣高議 (Lofty opinions from Green Chain Link [Gate]). Shanghai: Shanghai guji chubanshe, 1983.

Liu Hsieh [Liu Xie 劉勰]. *The Literary Mind and the Carving of Dragons*. Trans. and annot. Vincent Yu-chung Shih. Hong Kong: Chinese University Press, 1983.

Liu Jianping 劉建萍. "Lin Xu Wancuixuan shiji tanxi" 林旭晚翠軒詩集探析 (A tentative study of Lin Xu's *Poems from Evening-emerald Pavilion*). *Fujian luntan* 福建論壇 (Fujian forum) (Humanities and Social Science) 2004. 2:63–66.

———. "Lun Shen Queying de shici chuangzuo" 論沈鵲應的詩詞創作 (On Shen Queying's poetic creations). *Fujian shifan daxue xuebao* 福建師範大學學報 (Journal of Fujian Normal University) (Philosophy and Social Science) 123 (2003): 84–89.

Liu Kwang-ching 劉廣京 (1921–2006). "Shijiu shiji moye zhishi fenzi de bianfa sixiang" 十九世紀末葉知識分子的變法思想 ([Chinese] intellectuals' reform ideas in the late nineteenth century). In Yu Ying-shih et al., eds., *Zhongguo lishi zhuanxing shiqi de zhishi fenzi* 中國歷史轉型時期的知識分子 (Intellectuals in China's historical transformation). Taipei: Lianjing chuban shiye gongsi, 1992. 43–54.

Liu Linsheng 劉麟生 (1894–1980). *Zhongguo pianwen shi* 中國駢文史 (History of Chinese parallel prose). Shanghai: Shanghai shudian, 1984.

Liu Rongping 劉榮平. "Juhongxie changhe kaolun" 聚紅榭唱和考論 (On the Red Gathering Pavilion society). *Fujian shifan daxue xuebao* 138 (2006): 105–112.

Liu Su 劉餗 (fl. 742–55). *Sui-Tang jiahua* 隋唐嘉話 (Remarkable tales of the Sui and the Tang). Beijing: Zhonghua shuju, 1979.

Liu Xiang 劉向 (77–6 BCE). [*Gu*] *Lienü zhuan* [古]列女傳 ([Ancient] *Biographies of Women*). *Congshu jicheng xinbian* 叢書集成新編 (New edition of the collected serial publications) edn. 120 vols. Taipei: Xinwenfeng chuban gongsi, 1985. Vol. 101.

Liu Xie 劉勰 (ca. 465–ca. 522). *Wenxin diaolong* [*zhu*] 文心雕龍[註] ([Commentary on the] *Literary Mind and the Carving of Dragons*). Commentary by Fan Wenlan 范文瀾. 2 vols. Beijing: Renmin wenxue chubanshe, 1978.

Liu Xu 劉昫 (887–946) et al. *Jiu Tangshu* 舊唐書 (Old history of the Tang). 16 vols. Beijing: Zhonghua shuju, 1975.

Liu Yiqing 劉義慶 (403–44). *Shishuo xinyu* [*jianshu*] 世說新語[箋疏] ([Commentary on the] *Shishuo xinyu*). Commentary by Yu Jiaxi 余嘉錫 (1884–1955). 2 vols. Shanghai: Shanghai guji chubanshe, 1993.

Liu Yongcong 劉詠聰 [Clara Wing-chung Ho]. *De, cai, se, quan: Lun Zhongguo gudai nuxing* 德、才、色、權: 論中國古代女性 (Virtue, talent, beauty, and power: women in ancient China). Taipei: Maitian chubanshe, 1998.

Liu Zhiji 劉知幾 (661–721). *Shitong* [*tongshi*] 史通[通釋] ([Commentary on the] *Compendium of History*). Commentary by Pu Qilong 浦起龍 (1679–1762). 2 vols. Shanghai: Shanghai guji chubanshe, 1978.

Liu Zuozhong 劉作忠. "Zhongguo jindai guoqi xiaoshi" 中國近代國旗小史 (A brief history of the modern Chinese national flag). *Xungen* 尋根 (Searching roots) 2008.6: 77–78.

Long Yusheng 龍榆生 (1902–66). *Tang-Song ci gelü* 唐宋詞格律 (Tang and Song song-lyric styles). Shanghai: Shanghai guji chubanshe, 1978.

Lu Cui 盧翠. "Nüzi aiguo shuo" 女子愛國說 (On women's patriotism). *Nü xuebao* 5 (27 Aug. 1898): 2b–3a.

Lu Shude [fan] 陸樹德[藩]. "Gengzi quanbian hou Jing-Jin jian zhi canzhuang" 庚子拳變後京津間之慘狀 (Horrible scenes in the vicinity of Beijing and Tianjin after the 1900 Boxer incident). Originally titled "Jiuji riji" 救濟日記 (Relief journal). In Zuo Shunsheng 左舜生 (1893–1969), ed., *Zhongguo jin bainian shi ziliao xubian* 中國近百年史資料續編 (Continued collection of the references to Chinese history of the past one hundred years). *Minguo congshu* 民國叢書 (Serial publications on the Republic China) edn. Shanghai: Shanghai shudian, 1996. 5th collection. Vol. 66, 439–62.

"Lun Zhongguo nüxue" 論中國女學 (On [establishing] schools for women in China). *Yixin xibao* 益新西報, 8 Dec. 1897. In Jing Yuanshan, ed., *Nüxue jiyi chubian*, 49a–49b.

Lunyu [*yizhu*] 論語[譯註] ([Annotated translation of the] *Analects of Confucius*). Annotation and translation from classical into modern Chinese by Yang Bojun 楊伯峻 (1909–92). Beijing: Zhonghua shuju, 1980.

Lunyu [*zhushu*] 論語[註疏] ([Commentary on the] *Analects of Confucius*). *Jijie* 集解 commentary by He Yan 何晏 (195–249), and *shu* commentary by Xing Bing 邢昺 (932–1010). In Ruan Yuan, ed., *Shisanjing zhushu*, 2:2453–2536.

Luo Guanzhong 羅貫中 (fl. 1330–1400). *Sanguo yanyi* 三國演義 (Romance of the three kingdoms). 2 vols. Beijing: Renmin wenxue chubanshe, 1973.

Luo Lie 羅列. "Nü fanyi jia Xue Shaohui yu *Bashi ri huanyou ji* zhong nüxing xingxiang de chonggou" 女翻譯家薛紹徽與《八十日環遊記》中女性形象的重構 (The woman translator Xue Shaohui and her reconstruction of a female image in the *Around the World in Eighty Days*). *Waiguo yuyan wenxue* 外國語言文學 (Foreign languages and literatures) 98 (2008): 262–70.

Luo Suwen 羅蘇文. *Nüxing yu jindai Zhongguo shehui* 女性與近代中國社會 (Women and modern Chinese society). Shanghai: Shanghai renmin chubanshe, 1996.

Luo Zhitian 羅志田. *Quanshi zhuanyi: Jindai Zhongguo de sixiang, shehui yu xueshu* 權勢轉移: 近代中國的思想、社會與學術 (Transferring power: Thought, society, and scholarship in modern China). Wuhan: Hubei renmin chubanshe, 1999.

Lüshi chunqiu 呂氏春秋 (Lü's *Spring and Autumn*). Commentary by Gao You 高誘. *Zhuzi jicheng* edn. Beijing: Zhonghua shuju, 1954, 1986.

Lynn, Richard John, trans. *The Classic of Changes: A New Translation of the I Ching as Interpreted by Wang Bi*. New York: Columbia University Press, 1994.

———. trans. *The Classic of the Way and Virtue: A New Translation of the Tao-te ching of Laozi as Interpreted by Wang Bi*. New York: Columbia University Press, 1999.

Ma Gengcun 馬庚存. *Zhongguo jindai funü shi* 中國近代婦女史 (Modern Chinese women's history). Qingdao: Qingdao chubanshe, 1995.

Ma, Yuxin. *Women Journalists and Feminism in China, 1898–1937*. Amherst, NY: Cambria Press, 2010.

Mann, Susan. "The Lady and the State." In Fong and Widmer, eds., *The Inner Quarters and Beyond*, 283–313.

———. *Precious Records: Women in China's Long Eighteenth Century*. Stanford, CA: Stanford University Press, 1997.

———. Review of Lackner and Vittinghoff, eds., *Mapping Meanings*. *China Review International* 12.1 (Spring 2005): 147–51.

———. *The Talented Women of the Zhang Family*. Berkeley: University of California Press, 2007.

Mao Shi [*zhengyi*] 毛詩[正義] ([Orthodox commentary on the] *Mao Commentary on the Book of Songs*). *Zhuan* 傳 commentary by Mao Heng 毛亨 (2nd century BCE), *jian* 箋 commentary by Zheng Xuan, and *shu* commentary by Kong Yingda. In Ruan Yuan, ed., *Shisanjing zhushu*, 1:259–629.

Martineau, Harriet (1802–76). *Harriet Martineau's Autobiography, with Memorials by Maria Weston Chapman*. London: Smith, Elder & Co., 1877.

Mather, Richard B., trans. *A New Account of Tales of the World*. Trans. and annot. with an introduction by Richard B. Mather. Minneapolis: University of Minnesota Press, 1976. [A translation of Liu Yiqing, *Shishuo xinyu*.]

Meng Hua 孟華. "Qianyan" 前言 (Foreword). To Li Huachuan, *Wan-Qing yige waijiao guan de wenhua licheng*, 1–7.

Mengzi [*yizhu*] 孟子[譯註] ([An annotated translation of] *Mencius*). Annotation and translation from classical Chinese into modern Chinese by Yang Bojun 楊伯峻. 2 vols. Beijing: Zhonghua shuju, 1960, 1981.

Mengzi [*zhushu*] 孟子[註疏] ([Commentary on] *Mencius*). *Zhu* commentary by Zhao Qi 趙歧 (d. 201) and *shu* commentary by Sun Shi 孫奭 (962–1033). In Ruan Yuan, ed., *Shisanjing zhushu*, 2:2659–2782.

Metzger, Thomas A. *Escape from Predicament: Neo-Confucianism and China's Evolving Political Culture*. New York: Columbia University Press, 1977.

Meyer-Fong, Tobie. *What Remains: Coming to Terms with Civil War in 19th Century China*. Stanford, CA: Stanford University Press, 2013.

Miller, Jason M. "Subjectivity in Hegel's Aesthetics." PhD dissertation. University of Notre Dame. 2011.

Montagu, Mary Wortley (1689–1762). *The Letters and Works of Lady Mary Wortley Montagu*. Ed. James Wharncliffe (1776–1845). 3rd edn. 2 vols. London: Bickers, 1861.

Morse, Hosea Ballou (1855–1934). *International Relations of the Chinese Empire*. 3 vols. London, New York [etc.]: Longmans, Green, and Co., 1910–18.

Nylan, Michael. *The Five "Confucian" Classics*. New Haven, CT: Yale University Press, 2001.

O'Hara, Albert R., trans. *The Position of Woman in Early China: According to the Lieh Nü Chuan "The Biographies of Eminent Chinese Women."* 1945; Westport, CT: Hyperion Press, 1981.

Ōmi no Mifune 淡海三船 (722–85) (under Zhenren Yuankai 真人元開). *Tang Da heshang dongzheng zhuan* 唐大和上東征傳 (Record of the Eastward expedition of the Great Tang Monk). Commentary and collation by Wang Xiangrong 汪向榮. Beijing: Zhonghua shuju, 1979.

Osen, Lynn M. *Women in Mathematics*. Cambridge, MA: MIT Press, 1974.

Ouyang Xiu 歐陽修 (1007–72) and Song Qi 宋祁 (998–1061). *Xin Tangshu* 新唐書 (New history of the Tang). 20 vols. Beijing: Zhonghua shuju, 1975.

Paine, S. C. M. *The Sino-Japanese War of 1894–1895: Perceptions, Power, and Primacy*. Cambridge: Cambridge University Press, 2003.

Pan Tianzhen 潘天禎. "Tan Zhongguo jindai diyifen nübao—*Nü xuebao*" 談中國近代第一份女報——女學報 (About the first women's journal in modern China—*Nü xuebao*). *Tushuguan* 3 (Beijing, 1963): 57–58.

Pan Xuan 潘璇. "Lun *Nü xuebao* nanchu he Zhongwai nüzi xiangzhu de lifa" 論女學報難處和中外女子相助的理法 (On the difficulties of compiling the *Nü xuebao* and the way of mutual help between Chinese and foreign women). *Nü xuebao* 3 (15 Aug. 1898): 2a–3a.

———. "Shanghai *Nü xuebao* yuanqi" 上海女學報緣起 (Foreword to the Shanghai *Nü xuebao*). *Nü xuebao* 1 (24 July 1898): 2a–2b and 2 (3 Aug. 1898): 2a–3a.

Parton, James et al. *Eminent Women of the Age*. Hartford, CT: S.M. Betts & Company, 1869.

Ping Shan Leng Yan 平山冷燕. Collation and punctuation by Feng Weimin 馮偉民. Beijing: Renmin wenxue chubanshe, 1983.

Pingzhanlingyan; les deux jeunes filles lettrées, romans Chinois. Trans. Stanislas Julien. Paris: Didier et cie., 1860.

Plauchut, Edmund. *China and the Chinese.* Trans. and ed. Mrs. Arthur Bell (N. D'anvers). London: Hurst and Blackett, 1899.

Plutarch. *Lives.* Trans. from Greek by John Langhorne and William Langhorne. Philadelphia: James Crissy, 1833.

Pong, David. *Shen Pao-chen and China's Modernization in the Nineteenth Century.* Cambridge: Cambridge University Press, 1994.

Preminger, Alex, Frank J. Warnke, and O. B. Hardison, Jr. *Princeton Encyclopedia of Poetry and Poetics.* Princeton, NJ: Princeton University Press, 1974.

Qian, Nanxiu. "'Borrowing Foreign Mirrors and Candles to Illuminate Chinese Civilization': Xue Shaohui's (1866–1911) Moral Vision in the *Biographies of Foreign Women.*" Special issue of *Nan Nü: Men, Women and Gender in Early and Imperial China* 6.1 (Mar. 2004): 60–101.

———. "Li Qingzhao de jiaguo qinghuai ji qi xiqu xingxiang chengxian" 李清照 (1084–ca. 1155) 的家國文化情懷及其戲曲形象呈現 (Li Qingzhao's [1084–ca. 1155] version of patriotism and its visualization in drama). *Nüxue xuezhi* 女學學誌 (Journal of women and gender studies) (Taiwan National University) 16 (Nov. 2003): 213–25.

———. "*Lienü* versus *Xianyuan*: The Two Biographical Traditions in Chinese Women's History." In Hu and Judge, eds., *Beyond Exemplar Tales*, 70–87.

———. "The Mother *Nü Xuebao* Versus the Daughter *Nü Xuebao*: Generational Differences between 1898 and 1902 Women Reformers." In Qian, Fong, and Smith, eds., *Different Worlds of Discourse*, 257–91.

———. "Revitalizing the *Xianyuan* (Worthy Ladies) Tradition: Women in the 1898 Reforms." *Modern China* 29.4 (Oct. 2003): 399–454.

———. *Spirit and Self in Medieval China: The Shih-shuo hsin-yü and Its Legacy.* Honolulu: University of Hawai'i Press, 2001.

———. "Women's Roles in Wei-Chin Character Appraisal as Reflected in the *Shih-shuo hsin-yü.*" In Paul W. Kroll and David R. Knechtges, eds., *Studies in Early Medieval Chinese Literature and Cultural History: In Honor of Richard B. Mather and Donald Holzman.* Provo, UT: T'ang Studies Society, 2003. 259–302.

———. "Xue Shaohui and Her Poetic Chronicle of Late Qing Reforms." In Fong and Widmer, eds., *Inner Quarters and Beyond*, 339–72.

Qian, Nanxiu, Grace S. Fong, and Richard J. Smith, eds. *Different Worlds of Discourse: Transformations of Gender and Genre in Late Qing and Early Republican China.* Leiden: Brill, 2008.

Qian Qianyi 錢謙益 (1582–1664). *Liechao shiji xiaozhuan* 列朝詩集小傳 (Biographic sketches of poets from the former [Ming] dynasty). 2 vols. Shanghai: Shanghai guji chubanshe, 1983.

———. ed. *Liechao shiji* 列朝詩集 (Collection of poetry from the former [Ming] dynasty). *Xuxiu siku quanshu* edn. 1652; rprt. 2002. Vols. 1622–24.

Qian Zhonglian 錢仲聯. "Lun Tong-Guang ti" 論同光體 (On the Tong-Guang school). In idem, *Mengshao'an Qingdai wenxue lunji* 夢苕庵清代文學論集

(Collected essays on Qing literature from Dreaming of Shao Cottage). Ji'nan: Qilu shushe, 1983. 111–34.

———. ed. *Qingshi jishi* 清詩紀事 (Biographic collection of Qing poetry). 22 vols. Nanjing: Jiangsu guji chubanshe, 1987–89.

Qin Hui 秦暉. "Qin Hui tan xinhai" 秦暉谈辛亥 (Qin Hui on 1911). *Nanfang zhoumo* 南方周末 (Southern weekly). 2 Aug. 2011.

Quan Tang shi 全唐詩 (The complete collection of Tang poetry). 25 vols. Beijing: Zhonghua shuju, 1960.

Raphals, Lisa. *Sharing the Light: Representations of Women and Virtue in Early China.* Albany: State University of New York Press, 1998.

Records of the Third Triennial Meeting of the Educational Association of China. Held at Shanghai, May 17–20, 1899. Shanghai: American Presbyterian Mission Press, 1900.

Ren, Ke. "Fin-de-Siècle Diplomat: Chen Jitong (1852–1907) and Cosmopolitan Possibilities in the Late Qing World." PhD dissertation. Johns Hopkins University, 2014.

———. "Painting China with a French Brush: Chen Jitong and the Dual Authenticity of a Late Qing Cultural Mediator." Unpublished paper.

Rhoads, Edward. *Stepping Forth into the World: The Chinese Educational Mission to the United States, 1872–81.* Hong Kong: Hong Kong University Press, 2011.

Richard, Timothy. *Forty-five Years in China.* London: T. Fisher Unwin Ltd., 1916.

Robertson, Maureen. "Changing the Subject." In Widmer and Chang, *Writing Women in Late Qing China,* 171–217.

———. "The Meaning of Literary Authorship for 17th and 18th Century Governing-Class Women." Paper presented at the conference "Traditional Chinese Women through a Modern Lens." Harvard University, 16–18 June 2006.

Rolland, Romain (1866–1944). *Le cloître de la rue d'Ulm, journal de Romain Rolland à l'École normale (1886–1889) suivi de Quelques lettres à sa mère et de Credo quia verum.* Paris: A. Michel, 1952.

Ruan Yuan 阮元 (1764–1849), ed. *Shisanjing zhushu* 十三經註疏 (Commentaries on the thirteen Chinese classics). 2 vols. 1826; rprt. Beijing: Zhonghua shuju, 1980.

Sanfu huangtu [*jiaoshi*] 三輔黃圖[校釋] ([Collation and annotation of the] *Sanfu huangtu*). Collation and annotation by He Qinggu 何清谷. Beijing: Zhonghua shuju, 2005.

Sang Bing 桑兵. "Chen Jitong shulun" 陳季同述論 (On Chen Jitong). *Jindai shi yanjiu* 近代史研究 (Study of modern history) 1999.4: 109–23.

———. *Guoxue yu Hanxue: Jindai Zhongwai xuezhe jiaowang lu* 國學與漢學：近代中外學者交往錄 (National learning and Chinese learning: Records of the communications between Chinese and foreign scholars in modern times). Hangzhou: Zhejiang renmin chubanshe, 1999.

Savarese, Nicola. "The Experience of the Difference: Eurasian Theatre, An Ancient Tradition of Performance and Theory." Trans. Mathew Maxwell. In Erika Fischer-Lichte, Josephine Riley, and Michael Gissenwehrer, eds., *The Dramatic Touch of*

Difference: Theatre, Own and Foreign. Württemberg: Gunter Narr Verlag Tübingen, 1990. 43–48.

Schwartz, Benjamin. *In Search of Wealth and Power: Yen Fu and the West.* Cambridge, MA: Belknap Press of Harvard University Press, 1964.

Scott, Walter, Sir. *The Miscellaneous Prose Works of Sir Walter Scott, Bart.* 30 vols. Edinburgh: Robert Cadell; London: Whittaker, 1834–36.

Shang Xiaoming 尚小明. "Liu Ri xuesheng yu Qingmo xianzheng gaige" 留日學生與清末憲政改革 (Chinese students in Japan and late Qing constitutional reform). In Wang Xiaoqiu and Shang Xiaoming, eds., *Wuxu weixin yu Qingmo xinzheng: wan-Qing gaige shi yanjiu* 戊戌维新与清末新政: 晚清改革史研究 (The 1898 reform movement and late Qing New-Governing Movement: A study of the history of the late Qing reforms). Beijing: Beijing daxue chubanshe, 1998. 143–68.

"Shanghai chuangshe Zhongguo Nü xuetang ji" 上海創設中國女學堂記 (Report on establishing the first Chinese girls' school in Shanghai). By the secretary of the Guangxue hui 廣學會 (Society for the Diffusion of Christian and General Knowledge among the Chinese). *Wanguo gongbao* 125 (June 1899): 1b–2a.

Shangshu [*zhengyi*] 尚書[正義] ([Orthodox commentary on the] *Book of Documents*). *Shu* commentary by Kong Yingda. In Ruan Yuan, ed., *Shisanjing zhushu*, 1:109–258.

Shen Chenghu 沈成鵠 et al. "Shen Jingyu gong nianpu" 沈敬裕公年譜 (Biographic chronology of Shen [Yuqing], the Lord Jingyu). Appended to Shen Yuqing, *Taoyuan ji* 濤園集 (Collection from Roaring-Wave Garden). *Jindai Zhongguo shiliao congkan* edn. 1920; rprt. Taipei xian Yonghe zhen: Wenhai chubanshe, 1967. 167–358.

Shen Queying 沈鵲應 (1877–1900). *Yanlou yigao* 崦樓遺稿 (Posthumously collected drafts from Sunset-Mountain Tower), including *Yanlou ci* 崦樓詞 (Song-lyrics from Sunset-Mountain Tower) and *Yanlou shi* 崦樓詩 (Poems from Sunset-Mountain Tower). Appended to Lin Xu, *Wancuixuan shi.*

Shen Ying et al. "Zhongguo Nü xuehui zhi Houguan Xue nüshi Shaohui shu" 中國女學會致侯官薛女史紹徽書 (To Woman Historian Xue Shaohui of Houguan from the Women's Study Society). *Zhixin bao* 59 (19 July 1898): 8b–9a.

———. "Zhongguo Nüxue ni zengshe baoguan gaobai" 中國女學擬增設報館告白 (Announcement of the establishment of a journal affiliated with the Chinese Girls' School). *Xinwen bao* (17 May 1898); *Zhixin bao* 55 (9 June 1898): 26b; *Xiang bao* 87 (15 June 1898).

Shen Yue 沈約 (441–513). *Songshu* 宋書 (History of the [Liu-]Song). 8 vols. Beijing: Zhonghua shuju, 1974.

Shen Yuqing 沈瑜慶 (1858–1918). "Chen Jitong shilüe" 陳季同事略 (Biographical sketch of Chen Jitong). In Sheng Yuqing and Chen Yan, *Fujian tongzhi*, "Liezhuang" 列傳 (Biographies), *juan* 39, 70b–72b.

Shen Yuqing and Chen Yan. *Fujian tongzhi* 福建通志 (General gazetteer of Fujian). Fuzhou: Fujian tongzhi ju, 1922–28.

Shen Zongqi 沈宗畸 (1857–1926), ed. *Lian'an pianti wenxuan* 鍊菴駢體文選

(Selected parallel-prose from the Wrought-Iron Studio). Panyu: Shenshi Chenfengge, 1910?

Shenxian zhuan 神仙傳 (Biographies of immortals). Attributed to Ge Hong. *Siku qunashu* edn. Vol. 1059.

Sherard, Robert Harborough. *Twenty Years in Paris: Being Some Recollections of a Literary Life.* 2nd edn. London: Hutchinson & Co., 1906.

Shi He 史和, Yao Fushen 姚福申, and Ye Cuidi 葉翠娣, eds. *Zhongguo jindai baokan minglu* 中國近代報刊名錄 (Record of the titles of modern Chinese periodicals). Fuzhou: Fujian renmin chubanshe, 1991.

Shi Zhentao 史甄陶. "Cong *Ganxing shi tong* lun Hu Bingwen dui Zhuxue de jicheng yu fazhan" 從感興詩通論胡炳文對朱學的繼承與發展 (On Hu Bingwen's continuation and development of Zhu Xi's learning via the *Ganxing shi tong*). *Hanxue yanjiu* 漢學研究 (Studies in sinology) 26.3 (2008): 93–122.

Shuyi ji 述異記 (Records of strange accounts). Attributed to Ren Fang 任昉 (460–508). *Siku quanshu* edn. Vol. 1047.

Siku quanshu 四庫全書 (Complete collection of the Four Treasuries). 1501 vols. 1784; rprt. Shanghai: Shanghai guji chubanshe, 1987.

Sima Qian 司馬遷 (ca. 145–ca. 86 BCE). *Shiji* 史記 (Records of the grand historian). 10 vols. Beijing: Zhonghua shuju, 1959.

Smith, Kidder, Jr. et al. *Sung Dynasty Uses of the I Ching.* Princeton, NJ: Princeton University Press, 1990.

Smith, Richard J. *China's Cultural Heritage: The Qing Dynasty, 1644–1912.* 2nd edn. Boulder, CO: Westview Press, 1994.

———. *Fathoming the Cosmos and Ordering the World: The Yijing (I-ching, or Classic of Changes), and Its Evolution in China.* Charlottesville, VA: University of Virginia Press, 2008.

———. *Fortune-Tellers & Philosophers: Divination in Traditional Society.* Boulder, CO: Westview Press, 1991.

———. *The I Ching: A Biography.* Princeton, NJ: Princeton University Press, 2012.

———. *Mapping China and Managing the World: Cosmology, Cartography and Culture in Late Imperial Times.* London: Routledge, 2012.

Smith, William, Sir. *Dictionary of Greek and Roman Biography and Mythology.* 3 vols. Boston: Little, Brown, 1859.

So, Billy K. L. (So Kee-long 蘇基朗) "You fa wu tian? Yan Fu yi *Tianyan lun* dui ershi shiji chu Zhongguo falü de yingxiang" 有法無天? 嚴復譯《天演論》對二十世紀初中國法律的影響 (A law without heaven? The influence of the *Evolution and Ethics* translated by Yan Fu on early twentieth-century Chinese law). *Qinghua faxue* 清華法學 (Tsinghua Law Journal) 33 (2012): 1–24.

Somerville, Mary (1780–1872). *Personal Recollections from Early Life to Old Age, of Mary Somerville.* With selections from her correspondence. Ed. Martha Somerville. Boston: Roberts Brothers, 1874.

Song Lian 宋濂 (1310–81) et al. *Yuanshi* 元史 (History of the Yuan). 15 vols. Beijing: Zhonghua shuju, 1976.

Soushen houji 搜神後記 (Later records in search of the supernatural). Attributed to Tao Qian 陶潛 (365–427). Collation and commentary by Wang Shaoying. Beijing: Zhonghua shuju, 1981.

Spencer, Herbert. *The Principles of Biology*. Vol. 1. London and Edinburgh: Williams and Norgate, 1864.

Staël-Holstein, Anne-Louise-Germaine (1766–1817). *Œuvres Complètes de Mme. La Baronne de Staël, publiées par son fils*. Paris: Treuttel et Würtz, 1820.

Strickland, Agnes. *Lives of the Queens of England, from the Norman Conquest*. 12 vols. London: Henry Colburn, 1840–48.

Su Shi 蘇軾 (1037–1101). *Dongpo yuefu [jian]* 東坡樂府[箋] ([Commentary on] *Dongpo's [Su Shi's] Song-lyrics*). Commentary by Long Yusheng. Taipei: Huazheng shuju, 1990.

———. *Su Shi shiji* 蘇軾詩集 (Collected poems of Su Shi). 8 vols. Beijing: Zhonghua shuju, 1982.

———. *Su Shi wenji* 蘇軾文集 (Collected essays of Su Shi). 6 vols. Beijing: Zhonghua shuju, 1986.

Swann, Nancy Lee, trans. "Lessons for Women: Instructions in Seven Chapters for a Woman's Ordinary Way of Life in the First Century CE." In Victor Mair, ed., *The Columbia Anthology of Traditional Chinese Literature*. New York: Columbia University Press, 1994. 534–41.

Tang Caichang 唐才常 (1867–1900). *Tang Caichang ji* 唐才常集 (Collected works of Tang Caichang). Beijing: Zhonghua shuju, 1980.

Tang Guizhang 唐圭璋 (1901–90), ed. *Quan Song ci* 全宋詞 (Complete collection of Song song-lyrics). 5 vols. Beijing: Zhonghua shuju, 1965.

Tang Zhijun 湯志鈞. *Kang Youwei yu Wuxu bianfa* 康有爲與戊戌變法 (Kang Youwei and the 1898 reforms). Beijing: Zhonghua shuju, 1984.

———. *Wuxu bianfa shi* 戊戌變法史 (History of the 1898 reforms). Beijing: Renmin chubanshe, 1984.

Tao Qian 陶潛 (365–427). *Tao Yuanming ji* 陶淵明集 (Collected works of Tao Yuanming [Qian]). Collation and commentary by Lu Qinli 逯欽立. Beijing: Zhonghua shuju, 1979.

Tcheng-Ki-Tong [Chen Jitong]. *Bits of China*. An authorized translation of *Les plaisirs en Chine* by R. H. Sherard. London: Trischler and Company, 1890. Retitled *Chin-chin, or The Chinaman at Home*. London: A. P. Marsden, 1895.

———. *The Chinese Painted by Themselves*. Trans. James Millington. London: Field and Tuer, 1885. [A translation of *Les Chinois peints par eux-mêmes*, also translated into German and Portuguese.]

———. "L'amour héroïque, vaudeville-Chinois en un acte" (Heroic love: A Chinese light comedy in one act). *Figaro illustré* 9 (Paris 1891): 1–6.

———. *Le roman de l'homme jaune* (The tale of the man in yellow). Paris: Charf pentier, 1890.

———. *Le théâtre des Chinois: étude de moeurs comparées* (Chinese theater: a study of comparative morals). Paris: Calmann Lévy, 1886.

———. *Les Chinois peints par eux-mêmes*. Paris: Calmann Lévy, 1884.

———. *Les contes Chinois* (Chinese tales). 3rd edn. Paris: Calmann Lévy, 1889.

———. *Les Parisiens peints par un Chinois* (The Parisians painted by a Chinese). Paris: Charpentier, 1891.

———. *Les plaisirs en Chine* (Pleasures in China). Paris: Charpentier, 1890.

———. *Mon pays, la Chine d'aujourd'hui* (My country: China today). Paris: Charpentier, 1892.

Tcheng-Ki-Tong and John Henry Gray. *The Chinese Empire, Past and Present*. Chicago: Rand, McNally, 1900.

Thucydides. *The History of the Peloponnesian War*. Ed. and trans. Henry Dale. New York: Harper, 1888.

Toland, John (1670–1722). *Hypatia*. London: M. Cooper, W. Reeve, and C. Simpson, 1753.

Tsu, Jing. *Sound and Script in Chinese Diaspora*. Cambridge, MA: Harvard University Press, 2010.

Tuotuo 脫脫 (1313–55) et al. *Songshi* 宋史 (History of the Song). 40 vols. Beijing: Zhonghua shuju, 1985.

Verne, Jules. *Around the World in Eighty Days*. Trans. Geo. M. Towle and N. d'Anvers. London: Sampson Low, 1873. [A translation of *Le tour du monde en quatre-vingts jours*.]

———. *Around the World in Eighty Days*. Trans. Geo. M. Towle. London: Sampson Low, 1874. [A translation of *Le tour du monde en quatre-vingts jours*.]

———. *The Extraordinary Journeys: Around the World in Eighty Days*. Trans. with an introduction and notes by William Butcher. Oxford: Oxford University Press, 1995. [A translation of *Le tour du monde en quatre-vingts jours*.]

———. *Le tour du monde en quatre-vingts jours*. Paris: Bibliothèque d'éducation et de récréation, 1873.

Wakeman, Frederic Jr. Review of John L. Rawlinson, *China's Struggle for Naval Development, 1839–1895*. *Journal of the American Oriental Society* 87.4 (1967): 603–5.

Wang Bi 王弼 (226–49). *Wang Bi ji [jiaoshi]* 王弼集[校釋] ([Collation and commentary on the] *Collected Works of Wang Bi*). Collation and commentary by Lou Yulie 樓宇烈. 2 vols. 1:1–193, *Laozi Dao De jing zhu* 老子道德經註 (Commentary on *Laozi Dao De jing*). 1:211–2:590, *Zhouyi zhu* 周易註 (Commentary on *Zhouyi*). Beijing: Zhonghua shuju, 1980.

Wang Chunlin 王春林. "Nannü pingdeng lun" 男女平等論 (On Equal Rights between Men and Women). *Nü xuebao* 5 (27 Aug. 1898): 2a–2b.

Wang, David Der-wei. *Fin-de-siècle Splendor: Repressed Modernities of Late Qing Fiction, 1849–1911*. Stanford, CA: Stanford University Press, 1997.

Wang, David Der-wei, and Shang Wei, eds. *Dynastic Crisis and Cultural Innovation: From the Late Ming to the Late Qing and Beyond*. Cambridge, MA: Harvard University Asia Center, 2005.

Wang Hongzhi 王宏志 [Lawrence Wong]. *Fanyi yu wenxue zhijian* 翻譯與文學之間 (Between translation and literature). Nanjing: Nanjing daxue chubanshe, 2011.

Wang Hui. "The Fate of 'Mr. Science' in China: The Concept of Science and Its Application in Modern Chinese Thought." *Positions* 3.1 (Spring 1995): 1–68.

Wang Junwei 王軍偉. *Chuantong yu jindai zhijian: Liang Zhangju xueshu yu wenxue sixiang yanjiu* 傳統與近代之間: 梁章鉅學術與文學思想研究 (Between tradition and modernity: A study of Liang Zhangju's scholarship and literary ideas). Ji'nan: Qilu shushe, 2004.

Wang Mingqing 王明清 (1127–ca. 1215). *Yuzhao xinzhi* 玉照新志 (New records from Jade Moon Studio). *Siku quanshu* edn. Vol. 1038.

Wang Pijiang 汪辟疆 (1887–1966), ed. *Tangren xiaoshuo* 唐人小說 (Tang tales). Shanghai: Shanghai guji chubanshe, 1978.

Wang Qizhou 王齊洲. "Zhongguo xiaoshuo qiyuan tanji" 中國小說起源探跡 (Tracing the origin of Chinese *xiaoshuo*). *Wenxue yichan* 1 (1985): 12–23.

Wang Shuhuai 王樹槐. *Wairen yu Wuxu bianfa* 外人與戊戌變法 (Foreigners and the 1898 reforms). Shanghai: Shanghai shudian, 1998.

Wang Wei 王維 (699–759). *Wang Wei ji [jiaozhu]* 王維集[校注] ([Collation and commentary on the] *Collected works of Wang Wei*). Collation and commentary by Chen Tiemin 陳鐵民, 4 vols. Beijing: Zhonghua shuju, 1997.

Wang Xiaoqiu 王曉秋, ed. *Wuxu weixin yu jindai Zhongguo de gaige* 戊戌維新與近代中國的改革 (The 1898 reforms and the reform of modern China). Beijing: Shehui kexue wenxian chubanshe, 2000.

Wang Yi 王毅. "Wuxu weixin yu wan-Qing shehui biange—Jinian Wuxu bianfa 110 zhounian xueshu yantaohui zongshu" 戊戌維新與晚清社會變革——紀念戊戌變法110周年學術研討會綜述 (The 1898 reform and late Qing social reforms: A summary of the conference commemorating the 110th anniversary of 1898). *Qingshi yanjiu* 清史研究 (Studies in Qing history) 2009. 2:134–38.

Wang, Zheng. *Women in the Chinese Enlightenment*. Berkeley: University of California Press, 1999.

Wanyan Yun Zhu 完顏惲珠, comp. *Guochao guixiu zhengshi ji* 國朝閨秀正始集 (Correct beginnings: Women's poetry of our august dynasty). Hongxiangguan 紅香館 edn., 1831–36.

Wasserman, Stanley, and Katherine Faust. *Social Network Analysis: Methods and Applications*. Cambridge: Cambridge University Press, 1994.

Watson, Burton, comp. *The Columbia Book of Chinese Poetry: From Early Times to the Thirteenth Century*. New York: Columbia University Press, 1984.

———. trans. *The Complete Works of Chuang Tzu*. New York: Columbia University Press, 1968.

Wechsler, Howard J. *Mirror to the Son of Heaven: Wei Cheng at the Court of T'ang T'ai-tsung*. New Haven, CT: Yale University Press, 1974.

Wei Gongren 魏恭人. "Wei gongren shu" 魏恭人書 (Letter from Lady Wei). In Jing Yuanshan, ed., *Nüxue jiyi chubian*, front pages, 1a–2b.

Wei Shou 魏收 (506–72). *Weishu* 魏書 (History of the [Northern] Wei). 8 vols. Beijing: Zhonghua shuju, 1974.

Wei Xiuren 魏秀仁 (1818–73). *Huayue hen* 花月痕 (Traces of flowers and the moon). "Jiaodian houji" 校點後記 (Postscript of collation and punctuation) by Du Weimo 杜維沫. Beijing: Renmin wenxue chubanshe, 1999.

Wei Zheng 魏徵 (580–643) et al. *Suishu* 隋書 (History of the Sui). 6 vols. Beijing: Zhonghua shuju, 1973.

Weidner, Marsha Smith et al. *Views from Jade Terrace: Chinese Women Artists, 1300–1912*. Indianapolis, IN: Indianapolis Museum of Art; New York: Rizzoli, 1988.

Widmer, Ellen, and Kang-i Sun Chang, eds. *Writing Women in Late Qing China*. Stanford, CA: Stanford University Press, 1997.

Wilhelm, Richard, trans. *The I-ching, or Book of Changes*. Translated from Chinese into German by Wilhelm; rendered into English by Cary F. Baynes. Princeton, NJ: Princeton University Press, 1977.

Wu, Laura Hua. "From *Xiaoshuo* to Fiction: Hu Yinglin's Genre Study of *Xiaoshuo*." *Harvard Journal of Asiatic Studies* 55.2 (Dec. 1995): 339–71.

Wu, Shengqing. *Modern Archaics: Continuity and Innovation in the Chinese Lyric Tradition, 1900–1937*. Cambridge, MA: Harvard University Asia Center, 2013

Wu Weiye 吳偉業 (1609–72). *Wu Meicun quanji* 吳梅村全集 (Complete works of Wu Meicun [Weiye]). Ed. Li Xueying 李學穎. 3 vols. Shanghai: Shanghai guji chubanshe, 1990.

Wu Zeng 吳曾 (1127–60). *Nenggaizhai manlu* 能改齋漫錄 (Random records from Willing Change Studio). Shanghai: Shanghai guji chubanshe, 1979.

Xia Xiaohong 夏曉虹. "Wan-Qing liangfen *Nü xuebao* de qianshi jinsheng" 晚清兩份《女學報》的前世今生 (The previous and the present lives of the two late Qing *Nü xuebao*). *Xiandai zhongwen xuekan* 現代中文學刊 (Journal of modern Chinese studies) 16 (2012): 25–33.

———. "Wan-Qing nüxing de xingbie guanzhao" 晚清女性的性別觀照 (Viewing late Qing women from gender perspectives). Introduction to idem, ed., *Nüzi shijie wenxuan* 女子世界文選 (Selected works from the *Women's World*). Guiyang: Guizhou jiaoyu chubanshe, 2003. 1–52.

———. *Wan-Qing nüxing yu jindai Zhongguo* 晚清女性与近代中國 (Late Qing women and modern China). Beijing: Beijing daxue chubanshe, 2004.

———. *Wan-Qing wenren funü guan* 晚清文人婦女觀 (Late Qing literati views on women). Beijing: Zuojia chubanshe. 1995.

———. "Yingci nüjie qin chuaimo: Wan-Qing nüxing de ren'ge lixiang" 英雌女傑勤揣摩: 晚清女性的人格理想 (Conceptualizing heroic women: The late Qing ideal of womanhood). *Wenyi yanjiu* 文藝研究 (Literary and artistic studies) 6 (1995): 87–95.

———. "Zhong Xi hebi de Shanghai 'Zhongguo Nü xuetang'" 中西合璧的上海中國女學堂 (Combination of the Chinese and the West: The Shanghai Chinese Girls' School). *Xueren* 學人 (Scholars) 14 (1998): 57–92.

Xianzheng bianchaguan 憲政編查館. *Qingmo Minchu xianzheng shiliao jikan* 清末民初憲政史料輯刊 (Collected historical materials on the late Qing constitutional movement). 11 vols. Beijing: Beijing tushuguan chubanshe, 2006.

Xiao Daoguan 蕭道管 (1855–1907). *Lienü zhuan jizhu* 列女傳集注 (Collected commentaries on the *Biographies of Women*). 10 *juan*. *Shiyi shi congshu* edn.

———. *Xiao Daoguan ji* 蕭道管集 (Collected works of Xiao Daoguan). Including: *Dao'anshi zawen* 道安室雜文 (Miscellaneous essays from Dao'an Studio), 1 *juan*; *Xiaoxiantang yishi* 蕭閒堂遺詩 (Posthumously collected poems from the Hall of Leisure), 1 *juan*; *Daihua ping'anshi ci* 戴花平安室詞 (Song-lyrics from the Studio of Wearing Flowers in Peace), 1 *juan*; *Ping'anshi zaji* 平安室雜記 (Miscellaneous records from Studio of Peace), 1 *juan*. Ed. Chen Yan. *Shiyishi congshu* 石遺室叢書 (Collected publications from Remnant Stone Studio) edn. Fuzhou: Shiyishi, 1908.

Xie Zirong 謝子榮 [M. E. Sheffield]. "Taixi zhi xue youyi yu Zhonghua lun" 泰西之學有益於中華論 (Western learning benefits China). *Wanguo gongbao* 93 (Oct. 1896): 4a–7a.

Xiong Yuezhi 熊月之. "Wan-Qing jige zhengzhi cihui de fanyi yu shiyong" 晚清幾個政治辭彙的翻譯與使用 (Late Qing translation and usage of some political concepts). *Shilin* 史林 (Historical review) 53 (1999): 57–62.

———. *Xixue dongjian yu wan-Qing shehui* 西學東漸與晚清社會 (Western learning going eastward and late Qing society). Shanghai: Shanghai renmin chubanshe, 1994.

Xu Chuying 徐楚影 and Jiao Lizhi 焦立枝. "Zhongguo jindai funü qikan jianjie" 中國近代婦女期刊簡介 (A brief introduction to modern Chinese women's journals). In Ding Shouhe 丁守和, ed., *Xinhai geming shiqi qikan jieshao* 辛亥革命時期期刊介紹 (Introduction to journals of the 1911 republican revolutionary period). 5 vols. Beijing: Renmin chubanshe, 1986. 3:680–93.

Xu Huiqi 徐輝琪, Liu Jucai 劉巨才, and Xu Yuzhen 徐玉珍, eds. *Zhongguo jindai funü yundong lishi ziliao 1840–1918* 中國近代婦女運動歷史資料 1840–1918 (Historical sources of modern Chinese women movements, 1840–1918). Beijing: Zhongguo funü chubanshe, 1991.

Xu Ling 徐陵 (507–83). *Yutai xinyong [jianzhu]* 玉臺新詠[箋注] ([Commentary on the] *New Songs from the Jade Terrace*). Commentary by Wu Zhaoyi 吳兆宜 (fl. 1672) and Cheng Yan 程琰 (*js.* 1780). Punctuation and collation by Mu Kehong 穆克宏. 2 vols. Beijing: Zhonghua shuju, 1985.

Xu Songrong 徐松榮. *Weixin pai yu jindai baokan* 維新派與近代報刊 (Reformists and modern news media). Taiyuan: Shanxi guji chubanshe, 1998.

Xue Shaohui 薛紹徽 (1866–1911). "Chuangshe Nü xuetang tiaoyi bing xu" 創設女學堂條議並敍 (Suggestions for establishing the Girls' School, with a preface). *Qiushi bao* 9 (18 Dec. 1897): 6a–7b, and 10 (28 Dec. 1897): 8a–8b. Abridged version in Jing Yuanshan, ed., *Nüxue jiyi chubian*, 33a–35a.

———. *Daiyunlou yiji* 黛韻樓遺集 (Posthumously collected writings from Black-Jade Rhythm Tower), including *Shiji* 詩集 (Collected poetry), 4 *juan*; *Ciji* 詞集 (Collected song-lyrics), 2 *juan*; *Wenji* 文集 (Collected prose), 2 *juan*. Ed. Chen Shoupeng with a "Xu" 序 (Preface). Fuzhou: Chen family edition, 1914.

———. "Nanyang riri guanbao xuli" 南洋日日官報敍例 (Editorial introduction to the *Official Daily of the Southern Ports*). *Nanyang riri guanbao* (2 Aug. 1905): front page. Also in Xue, *Daiyunlou yiji*, Wenji, juan B, 6a–8a, under "Daini (on behalf of the editorial board) *Nanyang riri guanbao* xuli" 代擬南洋日日官報敍例.

———. "Nü xuebao xu" 女學報序 (Preface to the *Nü xuebao*). *Nü xuebao* 1 (24 July 1898): 2b–3a.

———. "Nüjiao yu zhidao xiangguan shuo" 女教與治道相關說 (On the pertinence of women's education to the principles of governance). *Nü xuebao* 3 (15 Aug. 1898): 2a, and *Nü xuebao* 4 (20 Aug. 1898): 2a–2b.

———. *Xue Shaohui ji* 薛紹徽集 (Collected works of Xue Shaohui). Punctuated by Lin Yi 林怡. Beijing: Fangzhi chubanshe, 2003.

———. "Yu Hu Jin'an Xue nüshi shang Nüxue tangdong tiaoyi bing xu" 寓滬晉安薛女士上女學堂董提要並序 (Suggestions by Lady Xue of Jin'an in residence at Shanghai, presented to the Board of Trustees of the Girls' School, with a preface). A revised version of "Chuangshe Nü xuetang tiaoyi bing xu," with five more suggestions. *Xinwen bao* (14–17 Jan. 1898).

Xue Shaohui and Chen Shoupeng, trans. *Bashi ri huanyou ji* 八十日環游記. Shanghai: Jingshi wenshe, 1900. [A translation of Jules Verne, *Around the World in Eighty Days*.]

———. trans. *Shuangxian ji* 雙綫記. Shanghai: Zhongwai ribaoguan, 1903. [A translation of Ellen Thorneycroft Fowler, *A Double Thread*.]

———. trans. and eds. *Waiguo lienü zhuan* 外國列女傳 (Biographies of foreign women). Nanjing: Jiangchu bianyi guanshu zongju, 1906.

Xunzi [*jijie*] 荀子[集解] ([Collected commentaries on the] *Xunzi*). Commentary by Wang Xianqian 王先謙 (1842–1917). *Zhuzi jicheng* edn., 1954, 1986.

Xuxiu siku quanshu 續修四庫全書 (Continued compilation of the *Complete Collection of the Four Treasuries*). 1800 vols. Shanghai: Shanghai guji chubanshe, 1995–2002.

Yamazaki Jun'ichi 山崎純一. *Kyōiku kara mita Chūgoku joseishi shiryō no kenkyū: "Onna shisho" to "Shinpufu" sanbusho* 教育からみた中国女性史資料の研究:「女四書」と「新婦譜」三部書 (A study of materials of Chinese women's history from an educational perspective: On the *Four Books for Women* and the three books of *The Manuals for a Bride*). Tokyo: Meiji shoin, 1986.

———. "Shinmatsu hempōron dankai no joshi dōtokuron to kyōikuron" 清末變法論段階の女子道德論と教育論 (On women's morality and education in late Qing discussions on reform). *Chūgoku koten kenkyū* 中國古典研究 (Study of the Chinese classics) 17 (1970): 1–26.

Yan Dichang 嚴迪昌. *Qingshi shi* 清诗史 (History of Qing poetry). 2 vols. Hangzhou: Zhejiang guji chubanshe, 2002.

Yan Yu 嚴羽 (fl. mid-13th century). *Canglang shihua* [*jiaoshi*] 滄浪詩話[校釋] ([Commentary on a collated edition of the] *Remarks on Poetry from Azure Waters*). Collation and commentary by Guo Shaoyu. Beijing: Renmin wenxue chubanshe, 1983.

Yang Nianqun 楊念群. "Lun Wuxu weixin shidai guanyu 'xixing' gaizao de gouxiang jiqi yiyi" 論戊戌維新時代關於'習性'改造的構想及其意義 (On the significance of the 1898 idea of reforming social customs). In Wang Xiaoqiu, ed., *Wuxu weixin yu jindai Zhongguo de gaige*, 209–22.

Yao Silian 姚思廉 (557–637) et al. *Chenshu* 陳書 (History of the Chen). 2 vols. Beijing: Zhonghua shuju, 1972.

Yao Yuanzhi 姚元之 (1776–1852). *Zhuyeting zaji* 竹葉亭雜記 (Jotted notes from Bamboo-Leaf Pavilion). Beijing: Zhonghua shuju, 1982.

Yeh, Catherine Vance. "The Life Style of Four *Wenren* in Late Qing Shanghai." *Harvard Journal of Asiatic Studies* 57.2 (1997): 419–70.

Yin Zhanhua 尹占華. "Liang-Zhu gushi qiyuan yu liuchuan de zai kaocha" 梁祝故事起源與流傳的再考察 (Restudy of the origin and circulation of the Liang-Zhu story). *Qinzhou xueyuan xuebao* 欽州學院學報 (English title: *Journal of Qinzhou University*) 23.2 (April 2008): 54–58.

Ying Shao 應劭 (fl. late Han). *Fengsu tongyi [jiaozhu]* 風俗通義[校註] ([Collation and commentary on the] *Compendium of Customs*). Collation and commentary by Wang Liqi. Beijing: Zhonghua shuju, 1981.

Yongrong 永瑢 (1744–90), Ji Yun 紀昀 (1724–1805) et al., eds. *Siku quanshu zongmu tiyao* 四庫全書總目提要 (Annotated catalogue of the *Complete Collection of the Four Treasuries*). 2 vols. 1822; rprt. Beijing: Zhonghua shuju, 1965.

Yu Fuyuan 余福媛. "Guanyu *Nü xuebao* de kanqi he kanxingqi" 關於女學報的刊期和刊行期 (About the publication dates of the *Nü xuebao*). *Tushuguan* 2 (Shanghai, 1986): 52–53.

Yu Ying-shih 余英時. *Zhongguo zhishi jieceng shilun* 中國知識階層史論 (Historical study of the Chinese intellectual class). Taipei: Lianjing chuban shiye gongsi, 1980.

Yun Yuding 惲毓鼎 (1862–1917). "Chongling chuanxin lu" 崇陵傳信錄 (Records from Chongling). In Jian Bozan 翦伯贊 (1898–1968) et al., eds., *Yihe tuan* 義和團 (The Boxer uprising). 4 vols. Shanghai: Shanghai renmin chubanshe, 2000. 1:47–55.

Zarrow, Peter, ed. *Creating Chinese Modernity: Knowledge and Everyday Life, 1900–1940*. New York: Peter Lang, 2006.

Zeng Caihua 曾彩華. "Xie Daoyun shengzu nian buzheng" 謝道韞生卒年補正 (Supplementary corrections of the dates of Xie Daoyun's birth and death). *Liuzhou Shizhuan xuebao* 柳州師專學報 (English title: *Journal of Liuzhou Teachers College*) 25.1 (Feb. 2010): 43–46.

Zeng Keduan 曾克耑 (1900–76). "Lun Tong-Guang ti shi" 論同光體詩 (On poetry of the Tong-Guang style). In idem, *Songjulu conggao* 頌橘廬叢稿 (Collected drafts from Eulogizing-orange Hut). 6 vols. Hong Kong: Xinhua yinshua gufen gongsi, 1961. 4:423–509.

Zeng Pu 曾樸 (1872–1935). *Niehai hua* 孽海花 (Flowers in a sea of retribution). Shanghai: Shanghai guji chubanshe, 1979.

———. "Zeng xiansheng dashu" 曾先生答書 (Reply from Mr. Zeng). Appended to Hu Shi, "Lun fanyi" 論翻譯 (On translation). In *Hu Shi wencun sanji* 胡適文存三集 (Collected works of Hu Shi, III). 3 vols. 1930; rprt. Shanghai: Shanghai shudian, 1989. *Juan* 8, 3:1125–39.

Zhang Peitian 張培田 and Chen Jinquan 陳金全. "Qingmo yubei lixian de shishi kaolun" 清末預備立憲的史實考論 (Study of the historical facts of late Qing preparations for constitutional construction). *Xiangtan daxue xuebao* 湘潭大學學報 (English title: *Journal of Xiangtan University—Philosophy and Social Science*) 28.6 (Nov. 2004): 81–88.

Zhang Tingyu 張廷玉 (1672–1755) et al. *Mingshi* 明史 (History of the Ming). 28 vols. Beijing: Zhonghua shuju, 1974.

Zhang Xia 張俠 et al., eds. *Qingmo haijun shiliao* 清末海軍史料 (Historical materials of the late Qing navy). Beijing: Haiyang chubanshe, 1982.

Zhang Xuecheng 章學誠 (1738–1801). *Wenshi tongyi [jiaozhu]* 文史通義[校注] ([Collation and annotation of] *Comprehensive Analysis of Literature and History*). Collat. and annot. by Ye Ying 葉瑛. 2 vols. Beijing: Zhonghua shuju, 1994.

Zhao Erxun 趙爾巽 (1844–1927) et al. *Qingshi gao* 清史稿 (Draft history of the Qing). 48 vols. Beijing: Zhonghua shuju, 1977.

Zhao Xin 趙新 (1802–76). *Xu Liuqiu guo zhilüe* 續琉球國志略 (Continuation to the *Brief Historical Record of the Ryukyus*). Fuzhou: Huanglou, 1882.

Zhao Ye 趙曄 (fl. 25–56). *Wu-Yue chunqiu* 吳越春秋 (Spring and autumn annals of Wu and Yue). Punctuated and collated by Wu Qingfeng 吳慶峰 et al. Ji'nan: Qilu shushe, 2000.

Zheng Fangkun 鄭方坤 (*js*. 1723). *Quan Min shihua* 全閩詩話 (Remarks on Min poetry). *Xuxiu siku quanshu* edn. 1754; rprt. Shanghai: Shanghai guji chubanshe, 2002. Vol. 1702.

Zheng Guanying 鄭觀應 (1842–1922). *Shengshi weiyan* 盛世危言 (Warnings for a prosperous age). Its chapter "Nüjiao" 女教 (Education for women) reprinted in Jing Yuanshan, ed., *Nüxue jiyi chubian*, 54a–55b.

Zheng Jie 鄭杰 (18th century), ed. *Minshi lu* 閩詩錄 (Records of Min poetry). Complemented by Chen Yan. *Xuxiu siku quanshu* edn. 1911; rprt. 2002. Vol. 1687.

Zheng Shiqu 鄭師渠. "Liang Qichao de aiguo lun" 梁啟超的愛國論 (Liang Qichao on *aiguo*). *Hebei xuekan* 河北學刊 (English title: *Hebei Academic Journal*) 25.4 (July 2005): 174–83.

Zheng Zhenlin 鄭振麟. "Fuzhou nannü liang shikan" 福州男女兩詩龕 (Two poetic shrines in Fuzhou, respectively for men and women). In Chen Hong 陳虹 and Wu Xiubing 吳修秉, eds., *Minhai guofan* 閩海過帆 (Passing sails in the Min Sea). Shanghai: Shanghai shudian, 1992. 79–80.

Zhi Daolin 支道林 [Zhi Dun 支遁] (314–66). "Da Xiao ping duibi yaochao xu" 大小品對比要抄序 (Preface to a Synoptic Extract of the Larger and Smaller Versions [of the *Prajñāpāramitā*]). In Seng You 僧祐 (445–518), ed., *Chu Sanzang ji ji* 出三藏記集 (Collected bibliographic records of Buddhist scripts and treatises). Beijing: Zhonghua shuju, 1995. 298–303.

Zhong Rong 鍾嶸 (468–518). *Shipin [zhu]* 詩品[注] ([Commentary on the] *Poetry Grading*). Commentary by Chen Yanjie 陳延傑. Beijing: Renmin wenxue chubanshe, 1961.

Zhong Xing 鍾惺 (1574–1624), ed. *Mingyuan shigui* 名媛詩歸 (Poetic archive of famous ladies). 36 *juan*. Published between 1621 and 1644.

Zhongguo jindai qikan bianmu huilu 中國近代期刊編目彙錄 (Collected catalogues of modern Chinese periodicals). Ed. Shanghai Library. Shanghai: Shanghai renmin chubanshe, 1965, 1980.

Zhouli [zhushu] 周禮[註疏] ([Commentary on the] *Book of Zhou Rituals*). *Zhu* commentary by Zheng Xuan, *shu* commentary by Jia Gongyan 賈公彥 (mid-7th century) et al., and *shiwen* 釋文 commentary by Lu Deming 陸德明 (556–627). In Ruan Yuan, ed., *Shisanjing zhushu*, 1:631–939.

Zhouyi [zhengyi] 周易[正義] ([Orthodox commentary on the] *Book of Changes*). *Zhu* commentary by Wang Bi and Han Kanbo 韓康伯 (4th century), and *shu* commentary by Kong Yingda. In Ruan Yuan, ed., *Shisanjing zhushu*, 1:5–108.

Zhu Changwen 朱長文 (1039–98). *Qinshi* 琴史 (History of the *qin*). *Siku quanshu* edn. Vol. 839.

Zhu Youhuan 朱友瓛, ed. *Zhongguo jindai xuezhi shiliao, diyi ji* 中國近代學制史料第一輯 (Historical materials on the educational system of the late Qing and early republican China, first collection). 2 vols. Shanghai: Huadong shifan daxue chubanshe, 1986.

Zhu Xi 朱熹 (1130–1200). *Zhuzi wenji* 朱子文集 (Collected literary works of Master Zhu [Xi]). Collation by Chen Junmin 陳俊民. 10 vols. Taipei: Defu Cultural Foundation, 2000.

Zhuangzi [jishi] 莊子[集釋] ([Collected commentary on the] *Zhuangzi*). Commentary by Guo Qingfan 郭慶藩 (1844–96). 4 vols. Beijing: Zhonghua shuju, 1961.

Zürcher, E. *The Buddhist Conquest of China*. 2 vols. Leiden: Brill, 1959.

Newspapers and Periodicals

Dianshi zhai huabao 點石齋畫報 (Pictorial from Touchstone Studio). Eds. Wu Youru 吳友如 (?–1894) et al. Shanghai, 8 May 1884–1908; rprt. 44 vols. in 5 cases. Guangzhou: Guangdong renmin chubanshe, 1983.

Nanyang riri guanbao 南洋日日官報 (Official daily of the Southern Ports). Ed. Chen Jitong, Chen Shoupeng et al. 1 Aug. 1905 to 28 June 1906. Nanjing.

Nü xuebao 女學報 (Journal of women's learning) (English title: *Chinese Girl's Progress*). Ed. Xue Shaohui et al. 12 issues. 24 July to 29 Oct. 1898. Shanghai.

Nü xuebao. Ed. Chen Xiefen 陳擷芬 (1883–1923). 4 issues. 3 Mar. to Nov. 1903. Shanghai and Tokyo.

Nübao 女報 (Women's journal). Shanghai. Ed. Chen Yiyi. 3 issues. 22 Jan. to 20 April 1909. Plus two special issues: *Nülun* 女論 (On women) and *Yuehen* 越恨 (Anguish of Yue). 28 Sept. 1909. Shanghai.

Qiushi bao 求是報 (English title: *The International Review*). Ed. Chen Jitong, Chen Shoupeng, and Chen Yan. 12 issues. 30 Sept. 1897 to 7 Mar. 1898. Shanghai.

Shenzhou nübao 神州女報 (Women's journal of the Divine Continent). Ed. Chen Yiyi. 3 issues. Dec. 1907 to Feb. 1908. Shanghai.

Shiwu bao 時務報 (English title: *The Chinese Progress*). Ed. Wang Kangnian 汪康年 (1860–1911) and Liang Qichao. 9 Aug. 1896 to 8 Aug. 1898. Shanghai.

Wanguo gongbao 萬國公報 (English title: *Review of the Times*), monthly. Ed. Young J. Allen. Feb. 1889 to 1907. Shanghai.

Xiang bao 湘報 (Xiang daily). Ed. Tan Sitong, Tang Caichang, Xiong Xiling 熊希齡 (1870–1937) et al. 7 Mar. 1898 to 15 Oct. 1898. Changsha.

Xinwen bao 新聞報 (News daily) (English title: *Sin wen pao*). Shanghai.

Xuchu Nübao 續出女報 (Continuation of *Woman's Journal*). Ed. Chen Xiefen. 9 issues. 8 May to 30 Dec. 1902. Shanghai.

Zhixin bao 知新報 (Review of new knowledge). By Kang Guangjen et al. 22 Feb. 1897 to 20 Jan. 1901. Macao.

Index

Note: page numbers in italics refer to figures or tables.